The Emotional Toolbox

To Michael,
I hope you
enjoy the
book.

Dan Buckman

sound recommendations—all in a format full of information, as well as nuance and feeling. It is as if he is there with you, giving comfort, as he guides you with his narrative voice offering you the tools and the blueprints to understand yourself and those around you.

—Robert C. Rollings, M.D., Cardiologist, Savannah, Georgia.

Dr. Dan Bochner brings a uniquely practical view to the human psyche and now he is offering that singular vision in his new book, *The Emotional Toolbox: A Manual for Mental Health*. For the last decade I've watched Dr. Bochner work with my patients, struggling with all manner of anger, depression, anxiety and inattention. Dr. Bochner helps even the most resistant find insight into themselves, and helps their parents see how their child is attempting to cope with the stresses of life. Few can inspire insight like Dr. Bochner, and now that he has created a compendium of methods to find that understanding, I would highly recommend that anyone interested in comprehending their own or their childrens' behavior read Dr. Bochner's *Emotional Toolbox*.

—Keith M. Seibert, M.D., MBA, FAAP, Chairman, Department of Pediatrics, SouthCoast Medical Group, Savannah, Georgia

Endorsements for Dr. Bochner's Previous Book, *The Therapist's Use of Self in Family Therapy*

Although ostensibly a book for the family therapist, the relational systems model that Dr. Daniel Bochner has developed effects a relatively seamless integration of the interpersonal with the intrapsychic and makes this dazzlingly brilliant book a must-read for family and individual therapists alike . . . . This is truly an extraordinary book that is at once inspired and inspiring. Bravo!

> —Martha Stark, M.D. Faculty, Boston Psychoanalytic Institute and Massachusetts Institute for Psychoanalysis. Author, "Modes of Therapeutic Action: Enhancement of Knowledge, Provision of Experience, and Engagement in Relationship."

This book is a much-needed addition to the literature on the use of self in family therapy. It is an inventive, scholarly, clear, and beautifully constructed invitation to therapists to thoughtfully use the whole of their experience in the therapeutic encounter.

> —David E. Scharff, M.D. Co-Director of the International Institute of Object Relations Therapy and co-author of "Object Relations Family Therapy."

Dr. Bochner explains how [a] broader view of the therapist's countertransference reactions informs the family therapist's use of self and contributes to a new, systemic understanding of both intrapsychic and interpersonal functioning . . . Family therapists have much to learn from concepts such as splitting, projective identification, and the paranoid and depressive positions, which have deepened clinical practice over the past several decades. And psychoanalytic thinkers can benefit from Dr. Bochner's original application of these ideas in creating his systemic relational model.

> —Stephen Schultz, Ph.D. Author, "Family Systems Therapy: An Integration."

This is a comprehensive and creative treatment of countertransference, an important but neglected topic in family therapy. It is also a significant advance in the movement to integrate psychoanalytic thinking into family therapy.

—Richard C. Schwartz, Ph.D. Faculty, Family Institute at Northwestern University. Co-author, "Family Therapy: Concepts and Methods; author of Internal Family Systems Therapy.

The Emotional Toolbox

A Manual for Mental Health

Daniel A. Bochner, Ph.D.

To order additional copies of this book, contact:
Xlibris Corporation
1-888-795-4274
www.Xlibris.com
Orders@Xlibris.com
94118

Contents

PART I
INDIVIDUALS IN RELATIONSHIPS

Section 1
Change: Getting *You* Working Well

The one core factor in healthy self-esteem is the knowledge that you're great. Armed with that knowledge, a person becomes more resilient within relationships and recovers more quickly from disaster. If you know you're great, you are less self-centered since focusing too exclusively on oneself is only necessary when you don't know you're great. Knowing you're great is, unfortunately, not an easy knowledge to develop, but to the extent that you do accomplish that achievement, you, and all those with whom you choose to relate flourish and thrive.

The personality with which we grow up is an adaptation to our childhood. Now that we're adults, however, we need to adapt to a world of endless possibilities.

Horrible experiences in one's past unfortunately lead to poor chances for a good future. This article discusses that process and points to ways it can be undone.

Balance is everything in life. It's only when we get too far out of balance, however, that we're motivated enough to make a change.

If there is one common and most important meaning of life, it is that everything is growing . . . or at least trying to.

Section 2
Development: Troubleshooting For Wear and Tear

Observed carefully, the reason for low self-esteem can be traced to holding onto the past as if it predicts our future.

We frequently notice that people with identical circumstances develop opposite personalities. This article shows how those opposite tendencies can be understood as exaggerated methods for distancing the self from what were, initially, similar traumas.

Our greatest accomplishments and our greatest strengths are, strangely enough, always directly related to our most devastating inadequacies.

Loss has its worst impact for mourning and grieving where *who* (or *what*) has been lost is crucial to one's ability to feel whole. Acceptance of loss, however, is rich in potential for carrying on into the future with renewed hope.

Section 3
Living: Your Everyday Maintenance in Interaction

An analysis of what drives our criticism toward others leads to an understanding of our discomfort with ourselves.

This article discusses the connection between our animal and spiritual natures.

People sometimes need power and control over others to help them compensate for weakness and inadequacy in themselves. Nevertheless, power and control tactics often lead to great achievements. Achieving lasting relationships with others who really care, however, is not possible while dominating and controlling. Thus, as compelling as power and control might be, recovery from this addiction is necessary in forging the greatest achievement of all—love.

It's a common term that is not well-understood. This article explains the concept and how it affects our daily lives.

We often fail to be empathic when a situation makes us vulnerable, or when our self-esteem is challenged, but maintaining our empathy is necessary in maintaining our connection with the world around us.

Worry not only hurts the worrier but also has a significant impact on others in the worrier's life.

Section 4
Tools: Caring for You and Your Communication with Others

Notice how you often don't breathe deeply enough—start to breathe better and change your life.

An appeal to all those who feel isolated and alone, suggesting they take care of themselves in the same way they would take care of their very best friend.

When you're really stressed, remember, if you lost everything you have, you'd still have what matters most—those you love.

Writing helps people in many ways. In this article, specific procedures are presented to help people deal with insomnia and traumatic experiences.

Learn to be assertive and you will get what you want and remain in a healthy balance with the world around you.

PART II
UNDERSTANDING COUPLES AND
COUPLES COMMUNICATION

Section 5
Can Two Parts Beat as One?

Although mostly all human beings are more the same than different, understanding the differences between the sexes can be truly instructive and healthy for relationships.

When a relationship moves from chemistry to everyday life, individuals in couples need to accept and accommodate each other's needs and preferences, and assert their own way, if the relationship is to last.

Men and women are made with two very different primary motivations, connection and independence.

Personality Development and Its Patterns in Couples.

Section 6
New Cars, Fast Cars, Backfires, and Crashes

Falling in love is great, but at least in the beginning we're in love with what we want, not who we're with.

There are many reasons sex is so important to human beings, but it is not, as Freud argued, a "drive."

Affairs often seem to occur for the express purpose of causing a divorce. This article examines that process and makes a plea for working out problems and/or divorcing without creating an explosion by having an affair.

Section 7
Communication: Tools for Making Yourself Fully Understood

We have to communicate with emotional expressiveness to be truly understood.

It can be the key to jump-starting change. Sometimes just a word or a signal can help people move past the escalation of negativity that so often bogs down relationships.

Communicate difficult emotions more usefully by stripping blame and defensiveness from what you say.

PART III
FAMILY DYNAMICS AND PARENTING

Section 8
Family Relations

Our most powerful animal instincts influence our entire experience. How we balance and regulate those instincts defines our character and our relationships with others.

There's only so much room for emotions within a relationship—whether you are with your children or your spouse, you deserve to have your share.

Section 9
Parenting

Finding a Balance between Kindness/Affection and Consistency/Firmness.

Authoritarian or Child-Centered or a balance between the two—only you know what's really right for you.

Kids wonder why us parents have so many rules—what they really need to understand is just how much we love them.

Section 10
Building Good Kids

Discussion of the primary attributes of mental health that must be instilled within our children in order to combat the effects of materialism and unbridled selfishness.

When kids don't understand why you won't let them do things, simply point to how freedom is always balanced by responsibility.

The issue of bullying is very complicated, but exploring the reasons it exists and why it's more prominent at particular ages can help in leading to better solutions.

Discusses the insult and the reality.

Girls and women are held to a complex standard of expectations in the world of today. They must compete with men yet stay true to their special feminine know-how. The choices they need to make in life often lead them to a life of doing it all. Unless they do try to do it all, most women will face some lack of fulfillment. If they spread themselves too thin, however, there's also a good chance they'll feel very little appreciation.

Section 11
Using Discipline

There are only two reasons parents have trouble with discipline: consistency and undermining.

It can be difficult to use a reward system when your kids are acting out, but this easy-to-use approach is enough to do the trick in many regular families.

When you think about it, having bad behavior just makes everything worse for a kid. Really, when all is done and told, it's a lot easier to be good than bad.

General guidelines for disciplining your children.

An intricate plan for forging good behavior.

PART IV
DIAGNOSIS AND ITS INTERPERSONAL COMPONENTS

Section 12
Major Diagnoses

It's the most common of all mental health problems and it hits almost everyone at one time or another.

Everyone knows that life can be stressful. We all feel anxiety sometimes.

Being too intense basically describes the bipolar condition. When extreme intensity is part of any disorder, bipolar disorder is likely to be diagnosed at least as a secondary part of the problem. Getting clients to understand their intensity can be a transformative first step in helping them overcome it.

Experiencing psychotic symptoms, hallucinations, delusions, and/or confusion, is perhaps the worst possible psychological experience. These symptoms arise from a combination of extreme emotional intensity and a deeply held feeling that such emotional intensity is too dangerous to express.

PTSD is a devastating psychological disorder that is not well understood. Essentially its cause is the conflict between remembering and avoiding pain. Traumatic experience is simultaneously impossible to remember or integrate and impossible to forget or avoid.

Helps differentiate behavioral and emotional problems from ADHD.

Section 13
Personality Diagnoses

Histrionic personality grows from an inability to feel special combined with an inability to take responsibility and is typically identified in dramatic or flamboyant behavior that satisfies the desire for attention but ultimately leaves the histrionic feeling unloved and empty.

Passive-aggressive personality develops from a need to distance oneself from conflict, which is accomplished by pleasing others while, unfortunately, ignoring one's own needs.

Narcissistic personality is not what it seems. Narcissists act selfish because they have no connection with their true self. They live primarily for the impression they make on others but never achieve what they really need—love and recognition of their true selves.

Borderline personality involves the thwarted striving for independence within a context of abandonment, thus causing clinging with hope of becoming united, withdrawing to avoid being controlled, and rage to maintain control. But only a consistent relationship with a loving other who cannot be manipulated has any chance of helping the borderline recover.

Trying to be perfect has some advantages over the long haul, but it also causes interpersonal problems and leaves the obsessive compulsive especially vulnerable to the disasters they believe they can avoid by attempting to be perfect.

Although the borderline, narcissistic, histrionic, passive-aggressive and obsessive compulsive personality disorders are the most likely to seek psychotherapy, there are several others that do not generally volunteer for psychotherapy in normal circumstances. Nevertheless, these other personality types are equally common and thus are encountered equally frequently within our daily lives.

Section 14
Addictions

The relationship of the addict to a drug is much like a torrid love affair that creates great havoc and that all too often, unfortunately, never ends.

This concept, which basically means being addicted to addicts, is explained and defined. There is only one solution. Be willing to leave.

Dedication

I dedicate this book to my wife, Mary Jo, the most exuberant, spirited, and inspiring muse a man could ever hope for. In living with her, I have learned so much about life, about myself, about her, about couples, and about family, that this book would never have been possible without her love and companionship. She challenges me to be my best and helps me find the best within myself. I love her with all my heart and forever.

Acknowledgments

I would like to acknowledge the love and support of many people in my life: my wife, Mary Jo, for everything; my mother, Sandra, for making me confident; my dad, Shelly, for being the best example of a man a son could ever have; my sons, Henry and Owen, for making it so obvious what love is all about; and my brothers, Ben, Mike, Ron, and Cork—unbeknownst to them, they have driven me to succeed. I would also like to acknowledge some friends and colleagues who have provided invaluable feedback and sometimes more. Erica Rollings was extremely gracious to provide feedback and editing. Robert Rollings provided the kind of feedback only Robert could. Arthur Colman provided inspiration. Daniel Nagelberg, John Adler, Woods Miller, Keith Seibert, John Adler, Julie Hinson, Helene and Dan Suh, and many others have been very encouraging. I thank you all from the bottom of my heart.

USING THIS MANUAL

CஐB

An Introduction to the
"Great Life Machine"

This book is organized like a manual for a great old machine, perhaps a classic automobile, or perhaps, as is more fitting to this context, a "great life machine." Unlike other manuals that focus on all brand-new systems functioning perfectly, however, this manual recognizes the various types of likely breakdown that occur over time and focuses intently on helping the owner bring the old beauty (that is, you and your life) up to full potential. This manual assumes that the owner has developed a good sense of the workings of the machine and is now looking to improve it, perhaps due to some specific kind of fault or defect in its systems, or maybe to recover from a wreck, or maybe just to smooth out some expected kinks. In understanding the manual, it's helpful to understand that the machine is not you. Rather, it is you and how you fit into your life. In a way, in fact, the machine is the whole world around us, but this manual primarily views you as a part of the larger apparatus that is your family and your network of friends and acquaintances. Of course, as a cog in this "great life machine," you have only so much influence on the whole. Nevertheless, the influence you do have can have enormous impact for you and for any part of the machine with which you come into direct contact. This manual points to the ways that you do have influence, encourages you to have more influence, and also helps you understand the workings of the whole system that is this "great life machine."

"The Emotional Toolbox" manual is broken down into four parts, each of which focuses on a different aspect of the "great life machine." Part 1 focuses on individuals, how individuals are shaped by the larger machine, healthy maintenance of the self, and how individuals can have more and healthier influence with others and their families. Part 2 brings couples to the fore, with an understanding of the immense importance of couples in this particular kind of apparatus, where couples are often acting as co-governor to the lower machine parts—that is, the children. Part 2 leads therefore quite naturally to part 3, where the family is discussed, with interpersonal family issues seen in relation to individual "drive" and control mechanisms (motivations and emotions, the control of emotions, and the interpersonal influence of emotions). Part 4 is diagnostic. Much like a classic automobile might have particular kinds of problems that typically arise during its use, human problems fall into definite types, and understanding exactly what kinds of problems arise often helps in discovery of the exact cause, which then leads to a better understanding of how to repair the damage.

Each of the first three parts also contains a "tools" area, where specific ways to handle specific issues or difficulties are offered. The tools in part 1 will help with tuning up and caring for oneself; in part 2, the tools help in communication between partners or pairs of individuals; and in part 3, tools are offered for working with discipline and family rules. Each of the articles in the diagnostic section, part 4, indicates specifically how understanding a particular diagnosis leads to pathways toward change or growth past the complications of that diagnosis.

The organization of this manual, much like one would expect from any manual, was developed so that the owner/operator can find immediate answers to whatever problem he or she might encounter. When people first come to psychotherapy, they are typically either experiencing a problem that indicates a need for change, or they are specifically looking to change because life has not been going well for some time. Thus, the book begins where the typical seeker of self-knowledge might also begin, with articles about change. However, it is not intended for most readers to start at the beginning and read through to the end. Rather, a full index was developed to facilitate the reader's ability to find articles of interest, regardless of what problems they are currently experiencing or what one's specific interests might be. The description of each article under its title in the table of contents will also be helpful in choosing where to start, but those descriptions are not intended to be complete, and many of the articles contain information on related topics that could not be stated in brief synopses.

Although this manual can be read in any order, there might be certain patterns that would best suit particular readers. I have written these articles from a perspective at the crossroads of two different theoretical views known as "Systems Theory" and "Psychodynamic Theory." Most of the articles are informed by my own integrative theory (Bochner, 2000) which connects individual motivations and needs (intrapsychic dynamics) to how people influence one another (interpersonal dynamics). Thus, *The Emotional Toolbox* discusses issues of psychology and mental health at a much deeper level than most self-help books. Because the articles are instructive from the perspective of learning about psychotherapy, students of psychology and psychotherapy, or other professionals, may have an interest in reading the book to better understand how theory is applied to treatment. The perfect springboard for understanding how theory connects to practice is the article "From Id to Family System," which describes my psychological theory at a layman's level, moving from individual motivations and needs to influences in the interpersonal world (the original theory was published in my first book, *The Therapist's Use of Self in Family Therapy*, Bochner, 2000). Students of psychology interested in achieving a rudimentary, yet very clear, understanding of psychopathology may well want to begin with part 4 on "Diagnostics" in order to improve at identifying and knowing where to start with particular diagnostic patterns in practice. These diagnostic articles are also, typically, popular with clients who are either suffering with, or are intimate with someone who is suffering with, those diagnoses. Another way to approach this manual, an approach that might appeal to personal coaches, would be to focus on the various "tools" sections, because many clients frequently seek immediate mechanisms for proceeding with particular problems.

Finally, by way of introduction, I would like to express my wishes for my reader. In using this book, regardless of how one does so, it is my sincere hope that the reader will achieve a better understanding of themselves and their relationships. Because I use these articles as an adjunct to my work with regular everyday people, it should be noticed that they were written to help regular everyday people, yet at a level that informs well beyond the obvious or easy. So many people now face the difficulties of everyday life and barely have the time or the resources to consult a professional. While there is no way any book can replace psychotherapy, this manual, *The Emotional Toolbox*, addresses the most commonly encountered issues of life, explains emotional difficulties and interpersonal communication at a level where the reader can feel personally understood, and offers solutions or redemption where people struggle most. I view the reader of this book as someone searching for answers and hoping to grow beyond their current travails. For that reason, this *Manual for Mental Health* is designed to move the reader, the owner/operator of a life, from an understanding of the connection between inner conflicts and interpersonal difficulties toward an awareness and development of inner beauty and balance. Its aim is to provide a road map for confidence in oneself, interpersonal spontaneity, utility of expression, and family growth. In the end, a meaningful and fulfilling life is derived from a life well-lived. Ultimately, therefore, by offering its wide variety of topics, insights, and tools, and by shedding light on ways to live a healthier, well-lived, emotional life, it is my sincerest hope that *The Emotional Toolbox* will help lead its reader to triumph, triumph in an interpersonally connected world, where the reader is owner/operator or architect of their own constructive, creative, effective, enthralling and, if they are to spread their emotional health to others, perhaps even radiant existence.

PART I

INDIVIDUALS IN RELATIONSHIPS

Articles for Individuals Living
in the Great Life Machine

You are a cog in the Great Life Machine! The machine has a multitude of working parts, all of which fit together in an extensive and magnificent way. Whether you know it or not, you are part of this comprehensive and ubiquitous system of life. As you do what you do, others react in particular ways, and then you react in your way. Your strengths and weaknesses are expressed and become part of your every interaction. As a part of the Great Life Machine, it's important that you are functioning well, for your sake and for others. If you're working well, you'll feel well, while you'll also help to keep all the other parts of the machine functioning properly.

Because it is so essential that you function well within this Great Life Machine, the first subsection of "Individuals in Relationships" will begin with a focus on making changes in your life. That is, "Getting *You* Working Well." As the title of this subsection suggests, people often feel like they need to change, and getting people functioning and feeling well is, of course, a primary focus of this book.

Often in getting better or making changes, it becomes important to understand how things have fallen apart or how they have developed. The second subsection here will thus be "Troubleshooting for Wear and Tear." Getting to the bottom of who we are and why we are that way, including an understanding of what makes us really good at things, leads to a better understanding of the choices we make in moving forward.

There are so many common concerns related to living in general, and living well among other people, that the third subsection was designed to cover "Your Everyday Maintenance in Interactions" with others.

This subsection focuses on many of the common issues we all encounter throughout life.

Finally, because there are so many effective ways of maintaining a healthy life as an individual, the fourth area of focus is "Tools for Maintenance and Lubrication: Caring for You and Your Communication with Others." Several tools for self-care are discussed in this subsection primarily aiming at making the individual more successful among others.

Clearly it is essential that everyone take good care of themselves if they are going to feel good and work well within the Great Life Machine. Although as an individual, everyone is merely a small part of the greater system, for each individual person, it is only in their own life that they have full responsibility and where they have any real control. If it can be assumed that it is healthy to care for others and to have a general desire for fairness in life, then responsibly seeking that which is best for oneself, mental health, leads to being the best possible component part in the Great Life Machine.

Section 1

Change: Getting *You* Working Well

The one common denominator for those first seeking psychotherapy is the desire for change. They are not satisfied with something in their life, whether it be others treating them badly, a lack of general success, feelings of depression or anxiety, or a particular relationship. People seek some kind of change because they're not feeling like things are good enough the way they are. In this short subsection, five articles related to change are offered. The primary focus is on changing yourself, since you are the only person over whom you have direct influence. Change is difficult, however, and these articles are quite focused on that reality. The first article in this section "You Need to Know You're Great," discusses the core goal in developing mental health: self-esteem. The next three articles discuss the efforts necessary for change and exactly how arduous those efforts can be. In "Adaptation vs. Adaptation," the usefulness of personality development for dealing with childhood is contrasted with our need to change our personalities in order to deal with our current life situations. "Balance and the Motivation to Change" is a look at what it means to be balanced and just how out of balance a person must be before they typically commit to making a change. The problems faced in overcoming a truly horrible past are highlighted in "Undoing the Troubled-Past/Troubled-Future Dilemma." Finally, in "The Importance of Growth," the absolute necessity for change and moving forward with life is discussed in recognition that such growth must occur for one to remain healthy, even when there's really nothing wrong.

CHAPTER 1

❧

You Need to Know You're Great

"A man cannot be comfortable without his own approval."

—Mark Twain

You need to know you're great! People often don't understand what it means to have good self-esteem, but it really all comes down to that. You should feel like you are a great person. Yes, I mean really, really great. You may feel that sounds silly or simplistic, and you'd be right if you said feeling that you're great is not the easiest goal to accomplish, but people with healthy self-esteem really do feel that they are great.

And I do mean "healthy" self-esteem. So now you're probably concerned that I'm telling people to become self-centered jerks or that they should think of themselves as better than everyone else. In response, I need to make one thing perfectly clear. I do not think you should think you're greater than others. You just need to think you're great.

In fact, the way you prevent yourself from becoming some selfish maniac is by knowing that you're not greater than anyone else (please see article "From Materialism to Integrity: The Building Blocks of the Healthy Human Structure"). You should know you're better at some things and not as good at others. You should know you can learn a lot, no matter how studied you might be . . . and so can everyone else. You need to know you're a work in progress and that you need to keep working on yourself, but you also need to know you're great. You are great because of who you are and because there is only one you.

This might sound funny, but you are not greater than anyone else just because you're beautiful. You are not greater than anyone else just because you have a bunch of money. You are not greater than anyone else because you have attained more education or because people think you're great or even if you have spent your life doing "good works." You are not greater than anyone else. Everyone is equal! And everyone should know they're great.

As a matter of fact, everyone is equally important too. You are every bit as important as anyone else. Now, I am not saying that a completely unproductive person is equally important to society as the president of the United States. But I can tell you this—on a daily basis this seemingly unproductive person is more important to himself than is the president. The same is true for you. On a daily basis, you have far more impact on your life than does the president. Isn't that right? Then certainly, from your perspective, you are more important to you than is the president. And if you know you're great and you know you're important, then that tends to be enough to make you a productive member of society too.

Okay, Okay . . . I can practically hear you thinking, "Surely he can't be saying that rapists, criminals, mean people, haters, backstabbers, and egotists are great, can he?" My answer to that is, if they truly knew they were great, it would not be possible for them to be any of those things. The primary attributes of each of these "types" at the time that they are engaged in the behavior that gives them that name requires that they ignore the needs of others, which does not happen much if you know you're great. If you know you're great, you have no need to ignore the needs of others because you have no need to make yourself greater by exploiting or "downing" others. If you know you're great, you know you'll manage to get what you need in a legitimate way. That is, because you know you're great, you won't have a problem asking for what you need or for legitimate recognition of your accomplishments. More often than not, you'll feel like you get plenty, so why would you need to hurt anyone else?

Knowing that your needs are legitimate is, in actuality, one of the most important aspects of knowing you're great. When you know you're great, you also know that you deserve to be treated like you're great (please see article "Assertiveness: The 30% Solution"). Of course, that doesn't mean you'll always be treated like you're great, but it does mean that you're not going to spend much time with those who treat you badly. It wouldn't make sense to continuously experience treatment from others that is clearly inconsistent with your view of yourself. People who know they're great don't stay in relationships in which they're not treated accordingly.

If you know you're great, then you know you count. That is, if you know you're great, then you know that what you want and desire and what you think are legitimate desires and thoughts. You may not always get what you want, and you might not always be right in what you think, but if you want it or think it, it should *not* be ignored. At the very least, you should know you deserve your desires and thoughts to be considered. At least that's what you'd think if you knew that you were great.

So you might be wondering if knowing you're great means you don't get depressed or anxious or moody. As a matter of fact, knowing you're great is a way to stay somewhat protected from mental illness, but it does not prevent bad things from happening. Knowing you're great will not prevent a whole slew of hardships that have nothing to do with what you think of yourself. It also doesn't change your genetics or the circumstances in which you're born. However, if you know you're great, you are certainly less likely to be in bad relationships because you treat others with respect and expect the same from them. You're less likely to take ill-advised risks because you have no need to bolster a weak ego. So you're also less likely to have emotional problems brought on by bad relationships and it's less likely that bad things will happen to you. If you know you're great, you are, indeed, less likely to get depressed or anxious or moody for a large variety of reasons.

Perhaps the most important reason that knowing you're great does make you less likely to develop emotional problems is that when things are tough, you feel things will likely get better, and when others are not treating you well, you can see your part in the problem without taking all the blame or taking other's views too personally. You see, if you know you're great, you can consider the opinions of others without thinking you stink and without your pride boiling over and thinking you need to prove others wrong. Because you know you're great, where some would get mad as though insults are too much to bear, you can maintain your knowledge of your greatness without fear that you've been truly damaged by someone's opinion. Knowing you're great works as sort of a balancing mechanism that helps you right the boat when the seas get stormy regardless of what kind of storm is brewing.

Of course, that might make one think that knowing you're great always has a positive effect on every relationship. Unfortunately, the effect of knowing you're great on relationships can be mixed. Knowing you're great does not make you get along with everyone, even if they too know they're great. There are still going to be those who are more like you and less like you and some you like more than others. Knowing you're great might make you more likely to get along with others, but it doesn't make you like them and it doesn't make them like you. Actually, even when you really know you're great, and yet you have perfectly healthy humility, some will dislike you just because you clearly know you're great. Mostly that will come from those who don't know they're great because they'll resent that someone could feel so good and confident. You see, knowing you're great is not the most common phenomenon and is actually a phenomenal accomplishment.

Unfortunately, developing the knowledge that you're great is not exactly natural for many people. Often, life does not treat people like they're great, and it would be very hard to imagine that developing such confidence could occur in some circumstances (please see article "Self-esteem and Its Connection to Cognitive Dissonance"). Even in the best of circumstances, the knowledge that you're great does not always develop because it is not possible to clearly show children that they are loved unconditionally. Even though most parents do love their children unconditionally, the love they offer must always be balanced by the discipline that is required in teaching children to be responsible (please see articles, "Knowing What's 'Right' in Parenting," "The Essentials of Parenting," "Freedom and Responsibility," and "Obsessive-Compulsive Personality Disorder"). So successfully developing really good self-esteem, or the knowledge that you're great, is actually quite rare even in the best of circumstances. It is so rare that, in a way, it is the ultimate focus in any psychotherapy.

Knowing that you're great is, in fact, a great way to simplify what therapy is all about. Even where someone has been traumatized, even in those cases where someone used to know they were great but seems to have lost that knowledge, even when working with a couple and each of them needs to see the greatness in the other, or in families where if only everyone could see the greatness in one another everyone would prosper, knowing you're great helps to solve every problem. If there could be one human idea that could change everything for everyone simultaneously, one truly humanitarian ideal, it would be that everyone would know that they all are great. It would be shared and it would spread. And it starts in each individual (please see article "From Id to Family System"). It doesn't come easy, but if it came, it would make the whole world a much easier place to live, grow, and be healthy.

If you don't know you're great, you do not have healthy self-esteem. That's a problem. I wish I could say it's an easy problem to fix, but that would be a lie. As simplistic as this might sound, if you don't know you're great, then learning that you're great, and believing it, is going to be the most important goal you will need to set in feeling better about your life. In order to accomplish that goal, you will need to accept and know that you are not alone in your greatness. Each in their own way, every person is great, and all are equally important. You are not any greater than anyone else. If you know you're great, you will have no real problem treating others as your equals because you will have no need to demean or exploit them in making yourself feel greater than others. If you know you're great, you'll have little difficulty knowing that your thoughts and feelings are legitimate and should be considered. If you know you're great, of course you'll be less likely to get depressed, anxious, or moody. Of course, you won't get along with everyone, but you'll get along better than most. Unfortunately, you might just find some who dislike you because you've accomplished something unusual. Unfortunately, it's not so easy to develop the knowledge that you're great. But developing that knowledge and sharing that knowledge could be the beginning of a great revolution in your thinking and could be the seed in making the idea grow. If you haven't yet developed it, developing the knowledge that you're great would undoubtedly change everything about your life. If everyone developed the knowledge that they're great, the feeling would spread. If everyone knew they were great, in fact, there is no doubt that the world itself would be a far greater world, a world in which we all could truly live and love freely, and perhaps, just maybe, we could all fully and freely flourish and thrive.

CHAPTER 2

☙

Adaptation vs. Adaptation

"There is a time for departure even when there's no certain place to go."

—Tennessee Williams

Who we are right now—our current behavior and attitudes, our perception of the world—is an adaptation to our past experiences. We grew up in a certain way and made particular interpretations of what was needed from us. Now, we continue to act like we had thought we needed to act in the past based on how we were taught and based on how we had always managed the expectations and pressures that had surrounded us. To the extent that our environment is now different, the way we now act based on our past experiences may be holding us back. So how do we move into the future without our pasts holding us back? The primary purpose of in-depth psychotherapy is to discover how our perspectives on what is happening in our world, that is the particular adaptation we have forged within our personalities, is limiting our ability to adapt to the world as it really is in the present. We see the world as we do because our experiences have shaped how we see the world. But now our world has changed and we're stuck with a personality that was specifically designed to handle those old experiences.

The funny thing is, we all think we see the world accurately. If that were true, however, there would be no explanation for the repetitive nature of our interpersonal troubles. We could think that our circumstances are just really bad or, when a relationship is involved, that it's truly the other person's fault. If the problem is recurring, however, it seems extremely unlikely that the problem is caused by circumstances, right? Why would we be getting ourselves into the same circumstances repeatedly, or why would we repeatedly entangle ourselves with the same kind of people over and over if we can't handle those circumstances or if we can't get along with those people? The fact is, each of us sees the world in the way that most makes sense to us given what we have experienced. We have adapted our views of the world to what has happened in the past. But the world is not really as we see it. The trick to success in psychotherapy, or the trick to getting past our pasts, is to recognize how our adaptations have worked for us but are now working against us. When we recognize what the usefulness of our view was, we can then see how it's no longer useful and how it's getting us into trouble. We can also recognize that, in contrast to the limited view we had previously held, the world is actually filled with endless possibilities. When we recognize that truth, we can begin our journey into a whole new and much healthier adaptation to the world as it is for us now.

Before going any further in this discussion, it is important to note that circumstances do cause significant difficulty in people's lives. Post-traumatic stress disorder, for example, occurs after a specific and harrowing trauma (please see article "Post-traumatic Stress Disorder"). Likewise, significant anxiety (please see article "Anxiety") can grow out of less specific traumas that occur over time and depression (please see article "Depression") can occur because of either significant losses over time or a specific significant loss (please see article "Loss and Hope"). Present-day circumstances are clearly a significant cause of psychological problems. It's also important to note that genetics plays a big part in many disorders such as bipolar disorder (please see article "Bipolar Disorder"), schizophrenia (please see article "Psychotic Disorders"), obsessive-compulsive disorder, or other diagnoses. Interestingly, however, one's past experiences, especially those from childhood, do play a part in each of these psychological maladies as well. Stable experiences in one's past and childhood help one overcome current stresses and can even mitigate a significant genetic predisposition for a particular psychological problem. It is important to note that one's childhood experiences have an impact on current psychological suffering regardless of what kind of suffering that is. For the sake of simplification, however, the remainder of this article will preclude genetics and major traumatic experiences or losses as causal factors in current problems.

So what is the first stage in understanding our childhood adaptation? Once one recognizes that their view of the world is an adaptation, it's essential to recognize that it was really the most sensible way for them to be or to act or to respond, given their circumstances at that time. That's right—the way we have adapted is actually, most often, an excellent adaptation. As strange as it might sound, when we look at the circumstances in our childhoods, including the economic situation, stresses on the family, the various personalities within our families, plus our own genetic temperament as well as many other factors, the particular way we fit into those circumstances can be understood as a great way of fitting in. Our natural tendency as children is to fit into whatever grouping of circumstances we're dealt in such a way as to maximize the amount of love, attention, food, and safety that are available to us. If we have a sibling that takes up a certain role, or who has a particular kind of relationship with one of our parents, we can either compete for that same area and win, or we must choose a different path. We are likely to look to the other parent for our love and affection and, perhaps, develop a different role within the family (please see article "From Id to Family System"). The world at large, however, is not our family.

The world, as suggested earlier, has endless possibilities. In order to observe and make use of those endless possibilities, however, we have to get past our pasts. How we do that is indeed very complicated. At first a person must recognize how their past influenced them, and then they must allow themselves to see things anew. Because people tend to believe their current view to be correct, even this first stage can be extremely problematic. A person believes their incorrect view is true even in relation to their therapist, not to mention every person with whom they work and all their friends. They are likely correct about their view in perceiving their own families, since that is where they developed the view in the first place. It is extremely unlikely, however, that all the people in their life have developed the same kinds of impatience, assumptions, anger, or any other psychological attributes that existed within their own family. With the many nonfamily others in their lives, especially their therapist, they must now see that what they perceive about others because of their family is wrong. Then they must generalize how they have been wrong to how they get along in many other potential relationships. Once a person does realize, however, that maybe their experiences within their families and in the past have had an influence that leads them to incorrect and very problematic views about the world and in relationships, new problems then arise.

If a person realizes they're seeing things wrong, often the first thing they feel is guilt or shame about how they have acted or how they have felt in their relationships up till now. That feeling of guilt or shame can be a good sign in that it means a person is a feeling and caring human being. But guilt and shame have a way of making us want to hide in one way or another. Sometimes we deny the problem and latch onto our old ways of thinking as if there's never been anything to be ashamed about. Sometimes, we continue to blame others in order to reinforce our old way of seeing things. Sometimes we try to deny how we've been seeing the world and how we've been acting, while we attempt to change ourselves in a wholesale, but false, way so that no one will identify us as being the way we were. That is, some people become quite good at acting differently even though they continue to feel about the world in the same way they always have (which really means they are seeing the world the same way as always but are simply controlling their behavior so that it won't seem like they're still the same). It is absolutely essential to true change that moves one into the future, however, that we come to understand why we were the way we were in the past.

Once people understand that they have been seeing things in a distorted fashion, they generally have a need to forgive themselves for that distortion. It can be so difficult to give up old ways of thinking that we often cling to the idea that we must be right, especially about our most personal thoughts and feelings. Admitting that we had seen things in a distorted fashion often feels so embarrassing or shameful, that forgiving ourselves for having been so much the way we were—stupid, mean, annoying, judgmental, controlling, desperate, clinging, petty, cheap, etc., is difficult. Forgiving ourselves requires us to admit that we were that way in the first place. If we don't realize how we've been and forgive ourselves, however, it's very common to continue thinking it was right.

Nevertheless, if understanding and forgiveness for ourselves are denied or forgotten, then new behavior, even if it is learned well and is very effective, feels false and is bereft of true satisfaction. Such new behavior can be used because it seems to work, but it does not truly become a part of who we are. It becomes clear that it's the right thing to do, but we still feel ashamed of how we had been and we secretly feel like we're "bad," "tainted," or "damaged." Dealing with the difficulties of self-forgiveness requires a certain attitude. In order to forgive and understand oneself, people must come to recognize that all human beings do develop their personalities at young ages as an adaptation to their particular environments. It is not really our fault that we have developed as we have. It just happened. In a way, even our parents cannot be blamed (unless they were abusive in some way) since parents are typically doing their best when they screw up (I hope my children understand this when they get older—we all screw up some when it comes to parenting).

It *is* our fault, however, if we continually fall into the same problematic patterns and do nothing to change those patterns. Once we recognize, understand, and truly forgive ourselves for how we've been, there is good news. At this point we must, of necessity, develop a new adaptation to the world of endless possibilities. Our new understanding of what has happened to us in the past and our ability to forgive ourselves actually precludes the old type of thinking. We cannot even think, for example, of picking a mate who is always angry like our father had been and then try to please him. We immediately recognize the anger as unhealthy for us and it is ugly to us. Trying to please someone else in spite of ourselves can also feel alien as we become much more comfortable with pleasing ourselves appropriately. Mates that seem to have true potential are those who we can envision loving us as they expect to be loved. A good potential mate seems to be a person who can be pleased, for example, at the same time that we are pleased.

In the world of endless possibilities, our forgiveness and understanding for ourselves actually makes it possible to see the world as it is rather than as our projection of what our family had been. We have no desire to be with those who do not treat us as we know we deserve to be treated, and we do notice that they're not treating us well. We also have no desire to be with people who would allow us to treat them in any way that is worse than they deserve, and we do notice that they're allowing themselves to be treated badly. At the same time, even though we understand that there are people who fit us well, we also recognize that there are people who are unhealthy, and we don't expect of ourselves that we get along with everyone. On the other hand, although we might not get along with everyone, we also do not need to reject others too hastily.

Forgiveness and understanding of ourselves makes us more forgiving of others. The process of adapting to the world of endless possibilities brings us a new emotional confidence within ourselves as we observe the reality of who we are and how we stand in relation to others. It is that confidence which makes forgiveness of others and letting go of our pain or resentments much easier. If we are confident that we can stand on our own in this world as it is, and we trust ourselves to trust only others who truly can be trusted to avoid hurting us as much as they can, it's not so difficult to let go of bitterness and anger. With the development of emotional confidence, we know the others with whom we choose to spend our life and whom we trust do not intentionally harm us, and those who are less close to us do not have the power to really harm us at a deep emotional level. Thus, bitterness and anger, our pain and resentments, really make no sense because bitterness and anger, as well as our resentments, are based in the belief that others have indeed intentionally harmed us or that things are, in fact, set up in unfair and inequitable ways that we cannot overcome.

With the development of emotional confidence, we feel we can know ourselves well enough to make sure that those with whom we choose to spend our time will not intentionally harm us, and we feel we can overcome the inequities in life. Thus, forgiveness of others is actually quite a bit easier than forgiving ourselves. After understanding and forgiving ourselves for what we feel have been our worst traits, we know ourselves and have confidence. We know when we can trust the world and we know we'll take care of ourselves adequately when the world does fail us. We also forgive easily because we are never really hurt that badly, and because we know we will not allow anyone who hurts us repeatedly and intentionally to remain close to us. Amazingly enough, this new feeling of comfort and confidence and the ability to forgive also makes others comfortable around us and, simultaneously, more respectful of us. With this emotional confidence, we become able to react in an authentic and spontaneous fashion in many more circumstances than ever before, as that confidence allows us to know that, most of the time, everything will be okay as long as we do our best.

This is the path to mental health. We start with a perspective that is incorrect and gets us into trouble. We recognize how that particular adaptation developed and how it made sense given our childhood circumstances. We recognize that, as human beings, we are imperfect, and we forgive ourselves for being less than perfect. As we get more and more familiar with how we viewed things and why we viewed things that way, and we continue to understand and forgive ourselves for how we incorrectly perceive, the old ways of thinking become less and less possible. Those old feelings become increasingly alien to us. And finally, we become who we were truly meant to be. We are confident in our integrity, we have the humility to see that we can be wrong, we can accept that others can be wrong without meaning us harm, and our confidence gives us the ability to be authentic and spontaneous. As we simultaneously treat ourselves well and find ourselves acting unselfishly, we begin to recognize how well our world seems to fit together. We begin to recognize that our own mental health can potentially fit within a world of simultaneous health for everyone. Although that world does not exist at present, when we become mentally healthy and confident, we see that the world is, indeed, a world of endless possibilities.

CHAPTER 3

ⓒ❧

Undoing the Troubled Past—
Troubled Future Dilemma

"Progress is a nice word. But change is its motivator. And change has its enemies."

—Robert F. Kennedy

One ugly truth about the human condition is that bad experiences lead to more bad experiences. It's so unfair, but when you observe the world, this simple truth cannot be denied. Although some people born into poverty, neglect, or abuse (we can call them "Troubled Past" individuals for short) turn things around and find their way into mental health and success-filled lives (we can call these rare people "Good Future" individuals), the odds are certainly stacked against them. The lives of Troubled Past individuals have trained them well to be untrusting, hyper-vigilant, and emotionally reactionary in order to protect themselves. But trust, freedom of thought, and freedom within interaction, all traits that run counter to the exaggerated self-protectiveness that develops in Troubled Past individuals, are necessary in forging successful relationships with others. Without successful relationships, it is impossible for Troubled Past individuals to create happy, fulfilling lives. There are ways around this dilemma.

The key to stopping this cycle is in becoming a person who views the world and relationships through the lens of endless possibilities, like a Good Future individual. The question then becomes, how can a Troubled Past individual become a Good Future individual?

Let us start by examining the traits of Good Future and Troubled Past types. A person with a good past (we can call them "Good Past" individuals) typically becomes a person with a good future (although this is not always the case). Such a person has seen and experienced love without too much strife. They have felt what it's like to have someone care for them and about them. Because of how they've been treated in the past, they expect similar treatment in the future. They have typically had some bad treatment and conflict as well, but not in great abundance. The ill-treatment they have experienced has been ameliorated by positive treatment. Many of the conflicts within which they have been embroiled have resolved. Thus, while they remain open to possibilities within relationships, they are watchful early on, and they develop trust slowly because they know they deserve good treatment. When they trust fully but become dissatisfied or get hurt, they fall back on their own resources of positive self-esteem (a confidence in their own worth that has been proven to them through past experience) to find help in either working out the issues of disappointment or knowing when to move on. They are able to trust others, as well as themselves, and they understand that there is good and bad in the world that requires management, mediation, and constant adjustment. Overall, and most importantly, they have developed faith that things will work out, at least most of the time.

In contrast, when we examine the Troubled Past individual, we typically see someone who expects things to go badly. Why would the Troubled Past person think things are going to go well? That would be foolish, wouldn't it? Such an individual has seen people get angry easily and often. Sometimes the Troubled Past individual has been ill-treated or abused. When they've been nice to others, others have taken advantage of them. When they've behaved in irritable and angry ways, they've often avoided getting hurt. These experiences lead to two basic types of Troubled Past people. The first type is a person who never trusts anyone and must always be dominant (a "Dominant Troubled Past" individual). The second type is a person who continues to believe the goodness within them will eventually lead to someone truly loving them even though they have rarely experienced that love (a "Troubled Past Believer").

Troubled Past individuals of the Dominant type have learned they should not trust anyone. When they meet people, they look for the angle. They need to make sure they remain in control of their situation and, typically, that means they will either control the other person or they will make sure they don't care about the other person (please see article "The Power and Control Addiction"). Underlying their prickly and distant behavior is a feeling of being unloved and unlovable in a cold, harsh world. This feeling of being unlovable in a lonely, frigid world can never resolve because their behavior precludes the possibility of someone becoming close and showing them love or warmth. To the Dominant Troubled Past individual, it seems every interpersonal eventuality includes people competing for limited resources and cheating each other to get what is needed. There is no freedom of thought. There are only winners and losers, dominants and submissives, those in control and those who are weak. The self-esteem of the Dominant Troubled Past individual is typically based on being on top of all situations, with the alternative being a complete crash into depression, anxiety, desolation, and desperation. Without dominance to make them feel adequate, they drown in fear and their own contempt for themselves. Unless somehow someone is able to get close to them, an event that is nearly impossible due to their aggressiveness and coldness in interaction, there is no way for the Dominant Troubled Past Individual to realize they can be loved and that the world is not a desolate landscape devoid of love.

Troubled Past Believers, on the other hand, often have even worse outcomes than those who are dominant. Because they believe in possibilities for life, despite repeated bad experiences, they must deny their bad experiences in wholesale fashion, as though all the harm they have endured has no effect on them. Unfortunately, in the process of denying their experience, the Troubled Past Believers remain blind to negativity in others and yet are attracted, most of the time, to only the most negative types, that is, Troubled Past Dominants. They are most familiar with angry, irritable, dominant people, and those are the people with whom they feel most comfortable. In order to be around such people and continue to believe love is possible, they often find themselves understanding the anger and irritability the dominant types show and use their understanding as a way to mitigate the abusiveness these dominant types spew. They tend to minimize their own legitimacy as human beings so that their own emotions need not lead them to outrage or despondency at the treatment they receive. As a result of the denial of their experience, the Troubled Past Believer's new experiences are limited to bad treatment. They do not believe they should experience anything different. They have very little self-esteem, and there is no way for any self-esteem to grow within them. Although the Troubled Past Believer often has the very worst experiences, their one saving grace is that they allow people to be close to them, making the possibility of their problems resolving much more likely. Although it is actually quite unlikely, the Troubled Past Believer need only let themselves be close to someone who does not fit their familiar experience to have a chance of overcoming their past.

The only way to resolve the dearth of emotional sustenance the Troubled Past individual experiences is for them to let someone in, who then becomes trusted. Someone who loves them clearly, but who is worthy of respect and who has good boundaries, must break the Troubled Past cycle. But such a Good Future person generally cannot even be perceived. All too often, such a person is thought to be nonexistent. Any person who seems to be trustworthy, thoughtful, or kind is thought to be playing a game or is thought to be a fool. The Troubled Past Dominant simply views Good Future people with contempt. The Troubled Past Believer deems themselves unworthy of a Good Future person. Yet the need for love within Troubled Past individuals lives on and constantly seeks out the possibility of recognition and comfort. Thus, occasional forays into relationships with Good Future people seem to occur, yet the awful behaviors of Troubled Past individuals typically lead to assured rejection. When these relationships go badly, that failure is used as proof by the Troubled Past individual that trustworthy, caring people truly don't exist.

In fact, the biggest problem in overcoming a Troubled Past is that Good Past individuals won't spend enough time with a Troubled Past individual to have any curative effect. The Good Past individual generally will not put up with being treated badly by Troubled Past Dominants nor are they attracted to people who have no self-respect, like Troubled Past Believers. The Troubled Past individual is constantly treating those they meet in negative ways or, alternately, act like they are unworthy of love. The irritability, anger, and need to be dominant among the Troubled Past Dominants leave no room for good feelings within the Good Past individual, who typically gets very tired of angry, manipulative, and/or impatient behavior. The enslaved attitude of the Troubled Past Believer makes the Good Past individual feel lonely or burdened as they find little of interest in a person who has no self-interest or self-development. The Good Past person can also tire from the constant need to bolster the Troubled Past Believer's confidence. People who stay with Troubled Past Dominants are generally Troubled Past Believers. They stay and allow themselves to be abused, thus reinforcing their view that the world is bad. The Troubled Past Dominant dominates people who have no self-respect and thus whose love is worthless, while the Troubled Past Believer is dominated by those who believe they are the only ones who count.

The undoing of these processes is rare but is possible. While it is sad and frustrating that troubled pasts lead to troubled futures, there are a few ways that troubled pasts can be transformed into good futures. The very best resolution comes from amazing coincidences. Sometimes a Troubled Past individual does meet exactly the right kind of other to help them past their never-ending cycle of negative relationships. Such a phenomenon is most likely for Troubled Past Believers and is extremely rare for Troubled Past Dominants. The Believer, by believing, leaves open the possibility that a good person is out there. Sometimes Believers are unable to convince a Good Past individual of their worthlessness and, simultaneously, the Good Past individual is able to prove to the Believer that the Believer is a special and worthwhile person. Although it is, indeed, extremely rare, it is also possible for a Good Past individual to be so positive that they are able to create good boundaries with a Troubled Past Dominant who is then able to forge a trusting and positive relationship. When healthy boundaries are set with a Troubled Past Dominant the soil is readied for growth into a good future.

The only other way for Troubled Past individuals (both Dominants and Believers) to overcome their Troubled Future perspective is through psychotherapy. The psychotherapeutic relationship is carved from the combination of therapeutic distance (appointments that occur only in the office at regular appropriate intervals) that makes the therapist adequately safe, and intimacy derived from the ability to express one's true impressions, whether they be shameful, vulnerable, or hostile. If the Troubled Past individual can trust and respect the therapist, then interaction between therapist and patient can be utilized to demonstrate and share the feelings engendered by the Troubled Past individual's attitudes and actions. Over time, the Troubled Past individual can see the way to a Good Future with the archetypal example of positive possibilities developing from within the therapy. The relationship that develops essentially proves that a Good Future is, at least, possible. This possibility leads to less reactionary views in interaction with others, more trust in others, the ability to stay in a relationship where there is no clearly dominant member, and a desire to have vulnerable needs met by others even while others are not seen as essential to one's well-being.

While the Troubled Past/Troubled Future dilemma may be difficult to overcome, it is not an impossibility. When the frustration experienced by the Troubled Past individual becomes overwhelming, the vulnerability experienced does sometimes lead one to rely on others. Although these are typically the most painful times in a Troubled Past person's life, these times also present a rare opportunity for vulnerability to be met with appropriate boundaries and the strength within Good Future individuals who are willing to help. It is absolutely necessary that a Troubled Past individual come into true, fully related, contact with a Good Future individual if there is to be any change at all. Without such contact, faith in a Good Future is stymied forever, and the cycle of Troubled Past/Troubled Future lives on in a perpetual give-and-take within a Troubled Future world where every negative reaction leads to more proof positive that we live in a negative world. Within a lasting relationship with a Good Future individual, however, proof of a positive world can be cultivated into a new and different cycle where perpetual growth and the nutrients of love bring light where darkness once loomed.

CHAPTER 4

 C08

Balance and the Motivation to Change

"Men can be stimulated by hope or driven by fear, but the hope and the fear must be vivid and immediate if they are to be effective without producing weariness."

—Bertrund Russell

Why do some people make necessary changes in their lives while others seem unable? That question may not be quite as complicated as it first seems. Of course, everyone who decides to make a change does so for different reasons, so it is complicated; but there is also one commonality among efforts at change. Generally speaking, people make the changes they make when their lives get significantly out of balance.

So what is balance, and what is change? First of all, it must be said, not just any balance is necessarily healthy balance. In fact, everyone's life is in some kind of balance, but sometimes that balance includes extreme behavior that is needed to counterbalance or compensate for other feelings or for relationships that throw one off balance. A person might work obsessively because he feels the need to amass wealth which, in turn, makes him feel adequate where once he felt inferior. Another person might work obsessively because she cannot stand to be at home where her relationships are extremely stressful and her time seems not her own. While one person might use drugs to help her forget how badly she has treated her children, another might use drugs to make her feel glamorous or confident. Clearly, although balance is a part of all these examples, balance is not necessarily healthy.

Perhaps an easy definition of psychological balance would be: any set of circumstances and attitudes that make it possible to continue on in life without making a psychological change. When an unhealthy balance reaches a precarious state then, or when it causes some kind of extreme emotional discomfort, either a person changes intentionally or circumstances lead to changes independent of choice. In that way, psychological "change" is defined, to a certain extent, by balance. Psychological change occurs when things get out of psychological balance because balance of some kind must always be restored, healthy or not.

Real psychological change can involve leaving a particular situation or doing things in a notably novel manner. For example, in a marriage both partners get into certain patterns of their own to which the other person responds in his or her own unique way. Sometimes one person feels she has done all the accommodating while the other has always had his way. Often, relationships work very well when they appear to be one-sided. The trick to understanding a relationship that works well in such circumstances is in understanding that the accommodating person actually balances herself through her accommodating behavior. That sounds kind of strange, doesn't it? But it happens. The wife in this couple might, for example, feel a need to be charitable to all others due to guilt that she experiences when others give to her. It is possible that she was taught as a child to refrain from asking for anything, or she could have been given so much that she feels overly spoiled.

Unfortunately, there can be a problem when such complementary behavior also leads to some kind of resentment that has no outlet. Our hypothetical woman from the example above gives and gives, just as she has always been taught to give, but something is amiss. Whereas in her childhood there was possibly relief for not being ridiculed or blamed or perhaps praise for being so selfless, now, as an adult, this altruistic trait has little utility within a relationship of equals. Perhaps it even results in ridicule or blame, and praise or appreciation is rarely offered. Thus, resentment builds. It builds and it builds, and the resentment has no outlet, and **BLAM**, a sudden change is necessary to alleviate long-lasting and long-developing difficulties. That change could be therapy, either for the couple or for either of the individuals involved, or alternately, typical sudden changes include leaving, divorcing, disappearing, etc . . . Any kind of change, even far less drastic changes than these, leads to a new kind of balance for everyone involved.

In such tough situations, it is unfortunately very common that things come to a boiling point where the only solution appears to be extricating oneself from the cauldronlike relationship. Changing patterns in relating, however, is far more possible than people often think and can lead to changes in balance and allow for continuation of healthier states of being. What has often not been tried is the heartfelt expression of the feelings that led to current patterns (please see articles "Communication from the Heart" and "'I' Statements"). A man who tends to hold back resentments while trying to accommodate to the wishes of others might start to tell those close to him what is going on in his head. He might say, "You know I have a tendency to just do what you want, but I wonder sometimes why we don't do what I want." If he has had a tendency to leave out his wishes, he will have to add, "I know I rarely tell you what I want to do, but today I'd like to . . ." Such statements have to include some way of taking responsibility for one's own patterns or they will be perceived to be blaming, and that will lead to defensiveness in the partner. As difficult as it might seem to handle such personal communications adequately, doing so with commitment can lead to an entirely new kind of balance between people. In this way, an unbalanced situation is balanced in a new way and can become more comfortable. Although such a change requires great effort, it is typically well worth the trouble, especially in situations where it is far preferable, or perhaps inescapable (such as when children are the ones with whom communication is necessary), to remain within the relationship.

There are many ways that people notice that they are out of balance. In the situation discussed above, the resentment has most likely built into depression or anxiety. However, in other situations, people might notice that their life is out of balance because they lose, or upset, those they love. They might notice they are out of balance because it seems they run into conflict wherever they go. When long-lasting interpersonal conflict is the primary problem, the person who causes such conflict rarely sees what it is they do that causes the problem. They typically feel that others don't do things the "right way" or that others are "too sensitive." They typically think their anger or bossiness is necessary. They often also think that people in this world are either at the top or at the bottom, dominant or submissive, exploiters or exploited. A person develops these traits from feeling dominated or abused at some point in their lives, usually in childhood. They reach a balance for feelings of vulnerability and hurt within themselves by being dominant and in control. But when these dominant types run into serious dissatisfaction in life—when they lose some kind of emotional balance because they find an unmet need for intimate involvement with those to whom they are supposed to be close—they are sometimes ready to start getting close to those they love by expressing their hurts and vulnerability without trying to dominate. When they want to lash out, they might find the strength to see how lashing out is related to having been hurt in the past or to their current sensitivities. At that point, they become ready to make statements that draw their intimates closer rather than chasing them away, and they also become more receptive to such statements from those close to them. Such statements involve admitting and accepting vulnerability and hurt and hoping that more hurt won't follow as it has previously in their lives.

Balance is also involved in other kinds of motivation where change can be even more difficult. Depression, anxiety, and other mental illnesses often indicate that things are not in a healthy balance, but they also make motivation to change very difficult because the illness itself is a way of balancing the afflicted person's inability to handle life's circumstances as they are. That is, individuals with mental illness are often striking a balance by remaining ill. When life seems overwhelming, many kinds of mental illness help a person withdraw or avoid what overwhelms them. The often intractable nature of these illnesses is caused by a desire for things to be different, but an inability to make them so because of the comfort found in the behaviors engendered within the illness. Invariably, however, the change away from such mental illness occurs when, for some reason, the pain and suffering caused by the illness outweigh its benefits. At that point, whether it is because family members become more concerned or because the afflicted person makes themselves overcome some of their symptoms and do what is necessary for recovery, a different balance is accomplished through hard work, treatment, or simply because a change becomes absolutely unavoidable.

The motivation we expect from our children also hinges upon balance. People often wonder how they might be able to motivate their children to perform better in academics, sports, or behavior. The fact of the matter is that whatever your child is currently doing, including whatever attitudes toward school, extracurricular activities, or behavior they might currently express or exhibit is an expression of their unique way of balancing. They might not feel much need to accomplish goals because things are made too easy for them or, alternately, because they resent the pressure they perceive on them. Either way, it's likely that unmotivated children see the goals we adults perceive as so ultimately important as though they are parental goals, which hold little value for themselves. It can be very tricky to help children see how our ultimate goal is for their future happiness (please see article "You Don't Know How Much They Love You"). If we push too hard, their behavior becomes a balance against our pressure, and goals for their future happiness are rendered moot. If we give them too much, including excessive praise not tied to adequate striving, their lack of industry may well indicate little concern for the future since there appears to be little doubt that the future will work out just fine regardless of effort (please see article "Who's to Know What's 'Right' in Parenting?"). Motivation in children is often very difficult to cultivate because we are, in fact, so interested in their success and do so desperately desire to care for their self-esteem. Although clearly there are many important parameters within which to guide our kids' activities and attitudes, helping them find their own balance, one not too explicitly derived to fit with our expectations, is typically key in making that balance one that includes adequate motivation. Children are often interested in pleasing us, or demonstrating their skills to others. They often want to succeed for the sake of success itself. There is no bad reason for being motivated. However, those who will strike the healthiest balance in their struggle to achieve will typically be those who truly follow their own fascination and desire and accomplish goals based on their very own singular and individualistic thirst and hunger for personal growth.

Balance is truly at the center of change and motivation. It is important to notice that people are always in some kind of balance, either healthy or not. When you are feeling like you're unhappy, and you keep wondering why you can't seem to make the kind of change that seems necessary to give yourself a more satisfying life, try to become more conscious of the things you're telling yourself. The way you talk to yourself reveals the way you are accomplishing your current level of balance. "I can't do that because it will hurt the kids"; "what will people think?"; "I'm just not strong enough to do it"; or "my kids are just so lazy." These are some of the many examples of why people don't make changes. Everything you say to yourself is a kind of balancing statement that aims to make staying the same a viable option. If, as in the statement above, you have a desire not to hurt the kids, maybe it is well-founded in your knowledge of how much they need you around, or maybe you're really thinking about how much you need to be around them. If, as in the statement above, you need others to "think" certain things about you, maybe that's another way that you balance your self-esteem. As in the statement above pertaining to "strength," it is possible that you really aren't "strong enough," which would have to mean that you are getting something from the situation in its current state that makes you feel more safe or secure than what would happen if you changed things. If you're concerned about your kids' motivation, as the "laziness" statement above would suggest, maybe you're giving them too much or pushing them too hard, or maybe you haven't been focusing adequately on their unique sets of talent. These thoughts that help you not change are not necessarily incorrect, but if you become more conscious of the balancing aspect of these thoughts, it's also possible that you will become more content with your current situation.

    You could easily change these statements to bolster your happiness and accept your current balance. You could think "my life is good with my kids just the way it is"; "people can think what they like, it doesn't have to affect me"; "I like how things are taken care of this way; I'm better off not rocking the boat"; or "I love to take care of my kids—I know this way they'll always need me." The fact is, in most cases, if you don't change how you do things, you are making a choice not to change. Satisfactory to you or not, if you're not willing to make a change, then your balance is most likely, at least for the time being, good enough for you. Not making a change usually means your current balance is not quite uncomfortable enough to warrant the effort a change will require.

However, if things are not to your liking and are truly out of balance, if you're feeling a lot of pain, and everyday you feel yourself miserable with regret as one more day passes in inaction, please accept your power to change. If you're truly out of balance, you'll be truly motivated. With the proper motivation, there are few changes you can't make. Often, the effort is smaller than you think and involves merely a change in the way you communicate with those you love. With enough motivation, even big changes are often much more possible than you could have ever imagined. If you or your family are truly out of balance, you can make a change. If you do make a change because you're out of balance, perhaps lacking balance can sometimes be a good thing. It is in the lack of balance that we find the motivation to accomplish all things. It is when we're thoroughly uncomfortable in our lack of balance that we truly find the power and motivation to change.

CHAPTER 5

✿

The Importance of Growth

"Growth itself contains the germ of happiness."

—Pearl S. Buck

Growth is the meaning of life! Why are we here? **Growth**! If you ask why growth, well then, we get into a whole different realm of philosophy or spirituality. Nevertheless, no matter how you look at it, it must be accepted that the lowest common denominator of all things, beyond dispute or moral philosophy, is growth. This is an important concept for analysis because it leads us directly to an understanding of motivation itself as well as how motivation fits within the biological necessity of connection to our world and to each other (and that sounds kind of spiritual, doesn't it?).

First of all, let me point out that the universe is expanding (growth), that everything in the biological world starts out small and gets larger (growth), and that, even in metaphysics, all ideas tend toward attempts at inclusion or expansion (growth). It is not a surprise, then, that from a psychological perspective, unless we are growing in some sense, we become depressed, stagnant, feel stifled, and maybe we even fall apart. What I am saying here is, when people are having emotional problems, it is frequently the result of stunted growth.

Now that is a pretty strange thing to say, I suppose, so I'd better try to explain what I mean. Human emotional growth follows human physical growth. In relationships with others, we find emotional sustenance in interaction, just as we find physical sustenance of growth by consuming food and drink. In relationships with others, we protect our feelings in interaction by expressing anger or trying to avoid; just as with physical protection, we defend ourselves through aggression or escape. Through the intake of food and by physically protecting ourselves, we are able to live. By sustaining and protecting ourselves at the interpersonal level, we allow for emotional growth. And when we develop some confidence that we are, and will be, both protected and sustained at the interpersonal level, we begin to expand our realm of emotional growth into the sphere of interpersonal relationships.

We protect and sustain the physical well-being and emotional aspects of our family members (especially children, but also other adults). Caring for others is a more mature type of growth that occurs between feeling responsible for others and feeling a need to care adequately for oneself. When we care for others, we grow beyond our own independent selves. We care for our children to make sure that they grow physically, but we also attempt to feed them emotionally and protect them from an overabundance of pain and suffering. The development of a balance between responsibility and self-care begins when we are receiving emotional sustenance and protection from our own care-givers as children. If it is sufficiently demonstrated to us that we are important but must care about others (especially those who have cared for us), we develop a confidence about the fact that sustenance and protection will be generally, most of the time, adequate. When we gain such confidence, we internalize confidence to such an extent that we know we are important enough to be treated well by others. We also develop the ability to feel responsible for how our actions affect others because we truly care about them, and we develop the ability to take care of others not only because we care about them but also because they are an extension of ourselves, like branches to a tree (growth).

These essential individual and family connections are the building blocks necessary for the growth of a community and for a society, where rules for conduct (laws) are balanced with individual knowledge of right and wrong in interpersonal and inter-group communications. The whole concept comes full circle when you think about the fact that both physical and emotional sustenance and self-protection are more likely in larger groups. From the beginning of man, and in the interactions of herds or schools of fish, we see that there is safety and efficiency in numbers, as well as a better chance of being protected. We are all intimately connected in every way by the existence of emotional and physical needs and desires. Our own growth is a central factor in remaining a part of our families and communities.

Growth is thus at the center of every kind of motivation. That is, everything we strive for, everything we attempt to achieve, everything we want or desire, that is . . . everything we do, is based on a need for growth. We might want a bigger car, we might want more education, we might want to get to know more people, or learn how to love, and all of it is based on a need for growth. In psychotherapy, people strive for better communication so that they can grow within themselves and through connections with others. Part of that communication involves getting to know the inner self, to integrate parts of oneself about which one is not quite aware. Growth involves all kinds of incorporation, integration, and communication.

Since growth is so central to our existence, without it we begin to have serious emotional (and sometimes physical) problems. Obviously, these problems can begin in a lack of connection with others, but we can also start having problems because we do not care for or protect ourselves well enough, because we do not care for or protect anyone else enough (these last two are often intimately related), or because we have not been, or fear that we will not be, cared for or protected well enough. When there is no problem in these areas, we continue to grow and we maintain our mental health. We continue to strive. But when we are not growing, we often become depressed and feel we cannot grow. We can become anxious with the idea that we might damage another person's growth or with fear that we cannot meet the demands necessary to grow. When we are cut off from others, we can feel a lack of growth from the lack of connection (which is, as I have explained, a kind of growth in itself).

As indicated above, there are many ways of feeding and protecting ourselves and others. Intellectual growth or financial growth helps sustain emotional growth, just as learning more about ourselves does. When we insist upon our right to pursue these goals or others, we are protecting ourselves so that we can continue to grow. Similarly, we like to see these kinds of growth in those that we love, and we tend to be willing to protect that growth in them since they are extensions of ourselves, which in turn helps us with our own sense of family and community growth.

The meaning of life? Well . . . I don't know if we will ever know what that is. But if you want to think about the lowest common denominator, the one concept that comes close to explaining why things are the way they are, the one concept that stands at the center of everything from biology to the connection between people, inanimate objects, and the cosmos . . . that one concept is **growth**.

Section 2

Development: Troubleshooting
For Wear and Tear

Where do people's problems come from? This section discusses how people develop difficulties in an interpersonal context. Sometimes a past of traumatic experiences leads us to believe we're unworthy of good treatment or success. "Low Self-Esteem and its Connection to Cognitive Dissonance" explores this complicated phenomenon and implores the reader to reach past this nonsensical but practically inevitable way of thinking. In spite of how negative experiences often lead to problems in one's life, it's amazing how often people manage not to knuckle under and develop aggressiveness, defensiveness, and a need to avoid intimacy. "How Identical Circumstances Lead to Opposite Personalities" uncovers the odd tendency for different individuals to respond very differently to the same experiences. Although emotional problems often do arise from bad things happening, it is absolutely amazing how often significant accomplishments come from a negative past. "Creating Strength from Weakness" discusses how our greatest skills and accomplishments are almost always directly related to our greatest weaknesses. Finally, in "Loss and Hope," the ways in which loss creates very specific kinds of problems for particular kinds of people is discussed, with special emphasis on the way in which loss can also lead to significant realizations and progress in one's life.

CHAPTER 6

❧

Low Self-Esteem and Its Connection to Cognitive Dissonance

"Trouble has no necessary connection with discouragement—discouragement has a germ of its own, as different from trouble as arthritis is different from a stiff joint."

—F. Scott Fitzgerald

Everyone knows what is meant by low self-esteem, but why is it so hard to overcome? We know of people who just cannot seem to get beyond the bad things that have happened to them. They come to believe that the world will continue to frown upon them—that things will not work out. They feel people have hurt them and will hurt them again and again. Some people with low self-esteem will need to be the boss as often as possible. Some will never think themselves worthy of decent treatment. Some will lack any motivation to move ahead in life because they just cannot see the possibility of things going well. Low self-esteem does indeed have many faces, but the one thing that all sorts of low self-esteem have in common is the belief that one's general circumstances will continue on as they have always been.

With low self-esteem, there appears to be an inability to separate what has happened in the past from what could happen in the future.

The question is, how does that happen? The belief that things are the way they will always be, in its essence, is a belief about where a person fits within the world community. It is also a belief about how the world community works. A person can grow up in a relatively harsh and critical environment and thus the pain of the past is transferred into a need to be top-dog within the dog-eat-dog world where there is little room for kindness lest it be taken as weakness. Another example: if a person does not think highly enough of themselves to work toward achievements, it is often because they've been broken down by disparaging comments and have come to believe that they are not good enough to achieve within a world where everyone else is better than they are. Yet another example: if life experience leads one to believe that nothing in life will ever work out, then that person likely will come to believe that making an effort, no matter how diligent, is meaningless within a world that only rewards the lucky few.

The important connection to understand here is that the relatively permanent-feeling state a person experiences within one's mind seeks a permanent explanation about whom he or she is in the world and how the world works. This seeking for explanation within one's mind and psyche is an automatic process that occurs due to cognitive dissonance, a concept that has been well-studied within the field of psychology. Cognitive dissonance is the discomfort we develop when we hold two conflicting ideas or beliefs. When we do hold two conflicting ideas or beliefs, a change in our thinking becomes necessary to reestablish consistency in our thoughts or integration within our minds. The stronger the dissonance, the bigger the necessary change in thinking.

Of course, it's obvious that we tend to look for explanations of our ongoing experience almost constantly. We tell ourselves someone reacted in a certain way because of something either we did or because of something they feel. We look for circumstances within our experience that help explain the ongoing behaviors of others and outcomes we perceive. Interestingly, however, it is when things just don't seem to make sense that we change our thinking or beliefs the most. The most common examples for how this change works are in everyday occurrences. People trying to be vegans (people who will not eat meat or dairy products) who sometimes eat fish somehow try to think of fish as lesser animals. When charitable people act in greedy ways, they typically chalk it up to taking care of their own or even survival of the fittest.

Cognitive dissonance plays an especially important role, however, when accidents happen or, more importantly, when we try to understand why we have experienced some kind of trauma. That is, cognitive dissonance plays its largest role when the world seems to have gone mad or out of control in some particularly hurtful way. When accidents happen, we often look for ways the accident would have been prevented if only we would have done something differently. Often we blame ourselves for the accident even if it seems to have little to do with us. In the mind, making sense of the accident seems to require some understanding of how our actions are part of the cause. Perhaps the most prominent example typically given is Stockholm syndrome. A victim of Stockholm syndrome is a person who starts to believe and espouse the very different values of their captors after being held and tortured. In these cases, only the possibility that the captors' beliefs are correct and momentously important can allow the victim to make sense of how badly traumatized they have been. It becomes more important in the psyche to feel there is a good reason for the chaotic abuse that has occurred than it is to maintain the belief that the captors are criminal or hateful. The need to turn traumatizing chaos into something seemingly logical is the paramount factor in the development of low self-esteem. When we have been traumatized, the explanation we give ourselves to make sense of the torture we have endured almost always makes it our own fault or responsibility. If the trauma was our own fault, then it would seem to be within our control. If things are within our control, on their surface they seem to be less threatening.

Although most childhood experiences are nowhere near as traumatizing as torture, the fact that we are with our families for so many years, and the fact that those years are the most formative within our experience, make cognitive dissonance crucial to our development. To put it simply, we become convinced that there are very good reasons for how we were treated as kids. When we are treated consistently well, with only the typical hurdles to jump and only the typical social storms to navigate, we develop good self-esteem. We believe the world is a mostly good place where we will usually be treated fairly. The better our experience was as children, the more we see the world as a place with endless possibilities that can be enjoyed as long as we do what is necessary to make those possibilities available to us. If the world is mostly good, and things will mostly work out, it makes sense to try your best. It feels good to achieve, and there appears to be a good chance that one can achieve with the right kind of effort. To the extent that our childhood is hurtful, however, we develop much less healthy patterns of behavior.

When we have been hurt in childhood, we attempt to solve a particular kind of cognitive dissonance. A conflict arises between, on one hand, thinking of oneself as valid and worthy of positive treatment and, on another, acknowledging that we are being treated badly or that things are not working out. Our cognitive solution generally leads us to believe either that we are not worthy or that the world is unfair or that we are unworthy and the world is unfair. Only these explanations can make sense of what appears to be senseless pain and failure. We need there to be order in the world to such an extent that we find it helpful to believe the worst. We believe it is because of who we are in this world that things are so bad. Strangely, because it is our fault (we are inferior, unlucky, not strong or mean enough), we can feel that we have some sense of order or control. Although having such beliefs leads to self-defeat, these negative beliefs are preferable to the real truth.

The truth is that there is extreme chaos in the world but also that the world has endless possibilities. Just because a person has the bad luck of being born into a family or country or epoch in which trauma occurs does not mean that trauma will always occur and that the world is mostly traumatizing. In most psychotherapies (excluding, of course, those where ongoing trauma is occurring), the client's situation is such where they really can avail themselves of endless possibilities. It is the belief about who they are and how the world works that seems to limit them most. They are shy because others haven't liked them. But now, people don't like them because they're shy. They are angry because they have been cheated. Well, now they're avoided and miss opportunities because people don't want to deal with someone who is angry. If they have to be in control because others won't handle things to their standards, now others won't even listen to their good advice and won't develop their own skills because they want to be independent or because they're afraid to do things wrong.

Low self-esteem is largely maintained because it's easier to make sense of the traumas we've endured with explanations that fit us, legitimizing reasons for those traumas. It seems the world is less chaotic and, thus, more manageable if we understand our bad treatment as occurring because of who we are and how the world works. But the world really does hold endless possibilities, and we limit ourselves and our achievements by limiting our definition of ourselves and the world. Whether it makes sense or not, it is true that the world has a lot of chaos in it. Most of the bad things that happen, happen due to circumstances and chance. Mostly, bad things that happen are out of our control, and we only make more bad things happen by believing that they happen because of who we are in the world.

The antidote to low self-esteem, although it's difficult to accomplish, is to unshackle oneself from the past, and to see the future as one that can be fashioned as we wish. Our future is only limited by our capabilities and our willingness to work. To view it any other way is merely to limit oneself into low self-esteem. Do you want to overcome low self-esteem? Then you must recognize that your past is over, and you must look to a future comprised of limitless potential and endless possibilities.

CHAPTER 7

❧

The Fork in the Road: How Identical Circumstances Lead to Opposite Personalities

"Every man is an infinitely repelling orb, and holds his individual being on that condition."

—Ralph Waldo Emerson

It's heart-rending when a child loses a parent, isn't it? And it's infuriating when a kid's been abused. The general feelings these circumstances evoke are quite obvious (even if there are more subtle reactions as well). So why is it so hard to predict the personality attributes that will likely develop based on these experiences? It is common for therapists to meet clients who have endured extraordinary loss or abandonment and have developed profound dependency and sadness. But it's equally common for these clients to become angry and controlling. We've also all met victims of significant abuse (both episodic and serial types) who become seriously angry and aggressive people. But it's equally frequent for these victims to become passive and fearful.

When disparate lines of personality development occur, in spite of similar experiential circumstances, it seems like perhaps there is no reliable way to understand the effects of experience on personality.

Notice, however, that development does seem to have a relationship to experience. That relationship is an aversion to the vulnerability caused by trauma. That is, when people have been traumatized, they avoid the feelings of vulnerability associated with the trauma.

For example, when a child experiences profound loss, life in this world is proven unpredictable and out of control. Thus the child looks for ways to prevent loss and to maintain some semblance of control. It may seem strange, but this child actually makes a choice. The choice is an unconscious choice, of course. That is, the child has no idea that they are making a choice. But nevertheless, there is a choice. The child can become a person who tends to take control within relationships and will brook no efforts at control by others. Or the child can become someone who is endlessly pleasing others within relationships with hope that no one will want to leave. Both relational tactics work to prevent loss. If the loss is of a severely abandoning type, it is also relatively common to become a person who alternates between a need for total control and a clinging dependency. That style too, which tends to be much more severe and less stable, also prevents the experience of vulnerability associated with the initial trauma, since the violent swings from clinging to controlling never allow one to experience those vulnerable feelings that occur in between.

For the sake of increasing clarity, an example of the abused child can also be instructive. For the abused child, the world is dangerous and unsafe. As they develop, these children also make an unconscious choice. They must maintain safety for themselves and there are two primary ways to do so. They can become a person most others fear, or they can become a person who avoids real contact with others. That is, they can become aggressive in their general style or they can become avoidant or distancing in their general style. Unlike the last example, there are very few people who alternate back and forth between these two styles since acting fearful does not fit with acting aggressive. It can be said, however, that both aggressive and fearful types avoid real relationships with others, since even the aggressive style makes emotional intimacy impossible.

These are two oversimplified explanations of a complicated psychological process. Nevertheless, they do demonstrate a point. Personality develops in relation to trauma. The more traumatic an experience is, and the more protracted that trauma is, the more likely that the personality will develop in exaggerated and/or unstable ways.

The direction of exaggerated choice seems to depend on a variety of factors, including genetics and family roles. Some people, it seems, simply do not have a genetic temperament that fits with being aggressive. On the other hand, some people simply do not have a genetic temperament that fits with being passive. One's natural temperament is likely the biggest influence in determining which of two particular roads will be chosen in response to harsh and protracted trauma.

Family roles too have an extraordinary influence on the particular adaptation a person chooses in dealing with life's circumstances. If two siblings have very similar temperaments but the elder has already chosen the most natural style for that temperament, the younger will have to choose a different way. Thus, it is very common to have an older child deal with an aggressive parent by being aggressive with everyone except, of course, the aggressive parent, while the younger sibling develops a very passive and avoidant role.

However, even in healthy personalities, the same strains can be observed. That is, people pick one way or another of avoiding whatever their trauma might be, even if that trauma is as small as being teased in school or being ignored by a favored sibling. The level at which a person defends against that trauma consists of the beliefs they have developed to counteract and defend against the trauma. The strangest thing about these defensive beliefs is that they include healthy thoughts. Those healthy thoughts, however, are themselves hypertrophied because they have developed for the purpose of making life livable and have not allowed for the original trauma to metabolize, integrate, and be forgotten. The very same healthy thoughts can become true beliefs about oneself, but only after they are not being used in a defensive fashion.

Imagine a man, for example, whose father had been a wealthy, respected, successful perfectionist. As children, the younger man's older sister struggled intellectually and was thus the focus of their father's disappointment. As a result of the father's treatment, the older sister developed poor self-esteem and became rebellious. She was marked as the "black sheep." The man who had been the younger brother had always been quite bright and quickly learned that the way to get his father's praise was to do well in school and to outshine his older sister. Unfortunately, as a result of his favored treatment, this man has developed within his adult personality an exaggerated sense of responsibility and an exaggerated sense of guilt. He feels he must always do what he has learned is "right" for others, and whenever he desires to have anything his own way, he experiences treacherous guilt and shame.

This man is clearly uncomfortable much of the time, but he succeeds by almost all typical measures, just as his father had. The question is, what is keeping this man in a constant state of guilt and shame when he seems to be doing so well, and what choice did he have as a child? This man has developed a relatively healthy way of dealing with being squeezed within his family between doing what his father expected but trying not to hurt his sister. Of course, as a child, he wanted his father's love and would do anything to get it. However, he also had to deal with tremendous guilt for doing what he could to get his father's love while his sister was being ridiculed. In fact, it's even likely that he secretly rallied against his sister because every time she was ridiculed, he felt like he was especially loved. He has likely thought to himself, "Of course I did what I could to get my father's love—that is only natural." But this leaves the fact of his feeling so guilty completely unexplained and unresolved.

The fact of the matter is, there is a significant part of this gentleman that continues to believe something really bad about himself. There is a part of him that feels like, "Wow, what a selfish traitor I truly am to seek my father's love for exactly what my sister lacked." The extreme responsibility taking he has developed is a relatively successful attempt at defending against feeling like a traitor since taking responsibility seems to constantly prove to him that he is not selfish. Nevertheless, he continues to feel guilty because any attention or praise he experiences or accomplishes in any part of his life reminds him of his survivor guilt vis-a-vis his sister.

Strangely enough, just as was discussed with respect to the abandoned child or the abused child, this gentleman could have just as easily developed in another direction. He could have tried to become even more rebellious than his sister. He would have lost his father's affection, perhaps, but he would have been able to live without guilt. He would have been much less successful and he would have had negative thoughts about himself like, "I was never good enough to get my father's love." That line would have led to a different person and perhaps the defensive thought, "I have always been independent." Either way, the original trauma would not be worked through or overcome.

If a trauma is metabolized or worked through completely, its influence is merely a memory, and no extreme feelings related to that memory are experienced. Thus no defensive positive thoughts are necessary for the purpose of compensating for negative beliefs about oneself. Rather than exaggerated personality attributes related to that memory, the man who has worked through the issue of his position between his sister and his father rarely thinks about what happened. Although he takes responsibility well, he does so because it feels good to maintain good relations with others and to take care of his loved ones. The way in which he takes responsibility feels good to others because it is truly integrated within his personality.

So it can be seen that even in relatively healthy personalities, the avoidance of pain related to trauma will lead to opposing styles within a person's character depending upon that person's circumstances and temperament. While it is thus very difficult to predict how a person's personality will develop given any specific situation, patterns are quite clear in opposing the experience of any particular kind of vulnerability caused by a trauma. It can truly be a wonder when a person we assume should be extremely angry due to some trauma seems, instead, to be relatively placid. That person, however, is generally avoiding any sense of aggression. To them, aggression is so wicked that they cannot tolerate it within themselves. Unfortunately, that is exactly the problem they will have to confront. They will have to find enough aggressiveness within themselves to at least take good care of themselves—to treat themselves with respect and command respect from others. Likewise, the aggressive person needs to learn to tolerate fear or they will never connect with others. The controller will need to learn to feel in control of themselves even when others are independent of them. The person who never takes control at all and lets everyone else have their way will have to feel adequate regardless of whether or not others are pleased. Even within relatively healthy people, it is important to recognize the other side of one's tendencies. Chances are, if a person is almost always one way or another (even if that way appears to be a positive attribute) with respect to any particular issue or kind of experience, that person is that way because to be any other way threatens to reconnect them to some level of traumatic experience that continues to be emotionally intolerable.

While it is certainly not easy to predict how someone will turn out based on what trauma they might experience, one thing we know is that a person tends to do whatever they can to avoid the vulnerability and pain that was most intolerable to them when they were first traumatized. Some people are genetically predisposed to respond more passively or more aggressively. Roles within families also play a significant part in this process. Healthy or unhealthy, people distance themselves as much as possible from pain. The healthier a person is, perhaps, the more indirect or complicated will be their personality-based opposition to whatever makes them most vulnerable. Nevertheless, opposition to, or avoidance of, pain and vulnerability clearly delineates how personalities develop. How do identical circumstances lead to opposite personalities? In effect, very different personalities are truly not opposite at all if identical circumstances brought them to be. What appear to be opposites are merely two diametrically opposed personality styles both designed to avoid the same pain.

CHAPTER 8

❧

Creating Strength from Weakness

"That which does not kill me makes me stronger."

—Nietzsche

To find out what your greatest strength might be, maybe you need only look at your greatest weakness. I know that sounds weird, but it's generally true. Those people you admire most are typically driven by what bothers them most. Doctors and lawyers, CEOs and presidents, priests and rabbis, animal rights activists and veterinarians—all find their strength in the things that bother them most about themselves and/or about the world. So when you're thinking most about your suffering, or when your self-esteem is at its lowest, try to think about how your accomplishments are inextricably connected to the way you're feeling now.

How could this strange phenomenon possibly be true? It's really a very simple process. Successful people are often attempting to overcome the feeling that represents the opposite of their success. Wealthy people are often trying to overcome the feelings engendered within them as impoverished children. People in charge often have felt others trying to control them. Individuals with great intellectual accomplishments are often proving their intelligence. Sports stars, actors and actresses, and musical artists are often looking for special attention to counter a feeling that they are far too ordinary. In addition to being spiritually minded, clergy members are all too often beset by tremendous guilt and have a need to take responsibility in order to appease that guilt.

Although our successes and weaknesses are invariably connected, that connection should in no way diminish our accomplishments. If you were to start talking to your physician and he told you about how he felt foolish when his father challenged him as a boy, would you feel he was any less intelligent? If a member of clergy discussed with her congregation the oppressive guilt she felt having observed her younger sister being maimed in some terrible way, would she be any less moral or giving? Likewise, if you are proud of something you have accomplished, even if there is a reason for the accomplishment in your past, it should in no way diminish your efforts or the accomplishment itself.

The fact of the matter is, when we fight to overcome something due to the pain it has caused us, we work very, very hard. Typically, if you are to observe the great accomplishments of society, you will see that hard work was far more important to those accomplishments than was intelligence, strength, or even luck (although certainly those factors do have a great deal of influence). And if you look for reasons that people work hard, you'll see that hard work is far more related to the process of overcoming than it is to any other factor.

Simply put, people have to have motivation. Motivation typically comes in the form of some kind of unmet need. Need itself typically means that there is something inside us that must be satisfied. When satisfaction merely means you need a drink or something to eat, in our current society, that doesn't require much hard work. Hard work in today's society is typically motivated by the need to become for others, and ourselves, who we want them to see and who we want to be.

The impression we make on other people is a huge motivator, even in those who believe they don't really care. In fact, most people who feel they're sure they don't care what others think are most motivated by a fear of being pawns to the wishes of others. Likewise, thoughtful people are often either afraid of being perceived as selfish or are overcoming how hurt they themselves have been by others being insensitive. Good people are afraid of being bad or have too often been the victims of others being bad. Mean people are afraid of being treated like chumps if they were to act too nice. Hard workers often fear the appearance of being lazy. The list goes on and on.

Of course, that doesn't mean it's really that easy to figure out what makes other people tick. For sure, there's great overlap in the many dominant traits that can be perceived in others and many different reasons those traits exist. We might be able to figure out others over time or with their help. On the other hand, people are really quite good at knowing about themselves what motivates them when they're asked to (or motivated to) explore the things they do. More or less, the only reason people sometimes don't know why they are especially good at a particular thing is because they have no motivation to figure it out.

Primarily, the reason it is important to understand that our weaknesses are directly related to our strengths is that it helps us understand ourselves. We can benefit from appreciating our weaknesses when we're most ashamed of them or when we're feeling really down. We can also benefit from acknowledging our weaknesses when we're at our most overconfident lest we become overconfident and maybe even cocky. As indicated in many of my other articles, balance is really the key. When some problem within ourselves is especially poignant for us, we need to compensate by achieving in a direction that we feel proves the problem moot.

Of course, achievement, or any kind of behavior aimed at compensating for an unresolved psychological issue, doesn't actually resolve the problem. Resolution of the problem requires that it be fully acknowledged and understood and then relieved through maturation and perspective. Compensation for a psychological issue with behavior designed to prove that it's the furthest thing from being a problem actually allows for the problem to be denied. Although people partly use compensating behavior to prove to others that they are not what they fear others might see, they try hardest to prove it to themselves. Typically, people are quite successful in doing so. Most of us believe we have successfully become the opposite of what we fear most within ourselves.

Strangely enough, when we have tried to overcome our inadequacies with achievement, the achievements are truly positive. Hard work leads to success and there is nothing as powerful as the need to overcome psychological problems when it comes to motivating hard work. Great success can be continued when problems are genuinely dealt with as well, because the talents we gain while overcoming our problems continue to be significant. As you might imagine, for example, the person who tries to do things perfectly in order to overcome the fear of things falling apart in their lives will continue to do things exceptionally well even when the fear of things falling apart is adequately diminished.

When looking at our strengths and weaknesses, the truth is society has advanced at least as much because of its psychological problems as it has for any other reason. If we were all raised perfectly in a world where everything was provided, and if our challenges merely led us to become responsible and mentally healthy adults, and if we never felt the pains of inadequacy, loss, embarrassment, and all sorts of fears, it is extremely unlikely that we would accomplish anything very special at all. It must be acknowledged that the psychological problems we face lead us to our greatest accomplishments. Likewise, it must also be acknowledged that our greatest accomplishments are, nevertheless, truly great accomplishments, indeed.

CHAPTER 9

☙

Loss and Hope

"We are never so defenceless against suffering as when we love, never so helplessly unhappy as when we have lost our loved object or its love."

—Sigmund Freud

We need, therefore we attach others. Our attachments run deep within us because they represent our pursuit of love and care at the most elemental levels. When we lose someone, or even some important thing or personal attribute that somehow represents our attachments to others, we feel as though a part of ourselves has been extracted from our very soul. Loss occurs in many different ways and has many different kinds of impact depending on what is lost and how the connection to what was lost originated or was needed. Our connections to others let us know that we're loved and that love truly does exist in the world. We attach the meaning of love to objects as well, whether they be representations of how we show ourselves love or how others have loved us in the past. In truly understanding loss, it is also important to recognize that we develop distinct ideas about what we must be—what we must achieve or what impression we must make—to deserve love.

Of course, loss is directly associated with depression. We become attached to people or ideas or even things, and when they're gone, we feel lost, bereft, deprived, alone, and limited. The loss of a loved one, the loss of one's youth, the loss of one's social status, and even the loss of a car or a house, or maybe even some prized possession that might be meaningless to anyone else, are all losses that can touch off devastating sadness. The very specific way people get attached to others, ideas, things, or even their social standing, however, is very specific to the way they interact with the world and how they have come to understand what goes on around them. People develop this way of being, their personality and character, to a great extent based on a need to compensate for what they feel they have never had. Thus, for most people, in a way, loss is already inside them and they are going about their lives doing their best to overcome that loss. Loss causes the biggest problem for people where the person, idea, or thing that was lost is directly related to how a person manages to compensate where they feel weak. Loss is devastating when what's been lost was imperative in making a person feel healthy and whole.

This is not to say that grief is abnormal, but merely that grief is expressed in a way that is specifically related to how a specific loss makes it difficult to continue on with living. We begin life with only our genetics, but soon we learn how we will be loved and how we are most likely to receive love. We may be told that we are loved unconditionally, and we may fully believe it, but our behaviors will be specifically shaped by the way we're treated when we do or don't do what our caretakers expect, whether we are or aren't who they think we're supposed to be, and whether we have or don't have the things that mean we are doing and are embodying what our caretakers think is right. In essence, the way we attempt to earn love and protect ourselves from pain, makes us who we are. Attachment is certainly related to how we protect ourselves or feel protected, but the way our personality develops for the purpose of earning love is truly the central component in our connections. We become attached to others, ideas, and things primarily based on how we have attached to love. Thus, when we experience loss, the significance of the problem lies in how what we lost makes us feel like we've lost love.

There are many levels of loss that can be differentiated based on how positive a person's experiences in life have been. These levels are also moderated by how significant the specific loss has been.

Understanding how any one person handles any particular loss requires examination of how that one person balances negative feelings with positive attachments and how the particular loss fits into that pattern. Four primary levels can be clearly differentiated and will be discussed here. First, some people have experienced so much chaos in their lives and have become so mixed up about how love can be sought that their attachments to others are extremely tenuous, and they consequently experience repeated losses in life which they perceive as relatively insignificant (even if some members of this group might behave extremely dramatically about those losses). A second group never fully attaches to others due to an inability to take responsibility in relationships and/or a general feeling of unfairness about not being loved enough. A third group of individuals experience full attachment but nevertheless often experience a need to prove themselves largely due to an inability to believe they were loved unconditionally. Finally, a fourth group of individuals represents fully healthy people (really, there is no such thing, and the healthiest people fall somewhere between the third group and this ideal) who have fully attached to others, can fully grieve what the loss has meant to them, and who can continue to fully benefit from how the attachment influenced them as though the attachment will always be with them. The grieving process of each group will be discussed below, with the style of grieving done in the healthiest, last group described as the model for healthy grieving in each of the others.

Grieving among those who have been most damaged within their personal interactions is worst when what's been lost is a rare relationship, idea, or thing that they have managed to attain and keep within their chaotic history. Often these individuals have very little that has lasted within their lives. Family has hurt them more than anyone else. They trust no one. Thus, really they have experienced loss repeatedly within their lives and they have become jaded. Sometimes, however, there have been just one or two people who, regardless of the surrounding chaos, have always been there. Quite often, members of this group have managed to hold on to a few things or have managed to accomplish some level of achievement. If these few people or these very special things or achievements have always been there, in spite of all the troubles, the loss of these things leaves members of this group in complete devastation. Their reaction to most losses is denial and anger, from which they never seem to recover. But a loss of one of these rare people, accomplishments, or meaningful objects leads to depression so deep it may not appear that recovery is possible. Acceptance of the loss is almost impossible since what's been lost is part of the rare evidence that love exists. In fact, quite often, if there are any meaningful attachments for this group, even those did not prove that love exists, but rather merely that there are a few good people whose love is not enough within a cold hard world. Rather than recover and accept the loss, the grieving of individuals from this group typically returns to anger and denial, as the loss of that little bit of love in this world proves just how necessary it is to remain cold and hard. Occasionally, however, if a loss has had enough impact, it can lead to a change in life toward greater involvement and responsibility with others. In just a few instances, a person is lost who was so positive that their death makes those in this group realize they must live the rest of their life, for honor of the dead, in more positive and constructive ways. In that way, in just a few rare instances, a person from this group can be veritably saved by loss.

The second group feels cheated. They doubt if they're special. Taking any responsibility often makes them feel as though others are taking advantage, or even worse, like *everything* is their fault. So their relations with others are marked by halfway attachment. They often love, and they love a lot, but they fear their love's not requited. They try to be special, with special abilities or special attractiveness. Often many people love them and love them all the way, but people from this group can't experience the depth of that love. Their attempt to demonstrate their specialness and their belief that no one really recognizes who they are or their true worth leave them feeling like their hope for becoming fully important is trapped within those whose esteem they covet or the attributes they work to develop so that they might someday be fully recognized. When they lose one of these people, or one of these attributes, they grieve as if they will never become fully human. They bargain for another chance. They feel desperate, and they fear their time is over. Their denial makes them feel as though greater effort might just bring back what or who's been lost. Acceptance requires they get past the feeling that they'll never attain the true full connection they always felt was impossible but nevertheless never gave up on. When they do accept that the attachment is gone, sometimes it becomes possible for those in this group to fully assess themselves in more realistic ways. Often, one must let go of the idea that they might truly earn the recognition of being the most special ever or the nicest or the most accomplished. Often, those in this group must let go of the idea that the one who they have lost might have someday truly acknowledged their worth. Sometimes, with the experience of loss, those in this group are left with only one choice. They must truly accept themselves and give themselves the recognition they have always sought if they are to fully accept their loss. And with the acceptance of themselves becomes the possibility of truly full relationships with others, as these others can now be fully acknowledged instead of being there just to acknowledge the specialness of the individual from this group.

The third group has always understood they are fully loved, but they try to prove themselves worthy of unconditional love after never quite experiencing the love they knew as being truly unconditional. Because the love they've experienced allows them to be fully attached, their effort to prove themselves, however, is not an effort to prove themselves to others but rather is an attempt to prove themselves to themselves. When they experience a loss, their grieving does not represent unfinished business or the need to complete halfway attachments. They do not believe they need to finally attain true love. Instead, they know they are loved, but it's the support and the connection that is missed. The loss represents a part of themselves, and they know where they got that part. It's as if the place they got their confidence, and the place they knew to go to get true recognition of who they are, is now gone. Although they have this feeling of confidence inside themselves, the knowledge that they can go back and have that feeling acknowledged and shared is gone. There is very rarely significant anger or bargaining in this group, but denial does plague them as they attempt to believe that the other is so securely connected within them that they believe the loss will have little effect. Acceptance within this group requires that the true depth of the loss is felt, understood, and grieved. This group sometimes believes themselves to be more resilient than is really healthy, and thus they aim to bypass the necessary grieving or depression that accompanies a real loss. In order to reach full acceptance, this group must fully experience a sense of the world without the earth beneath them, the air they have breathed, or the nutrients that made growth possible. When that acceptance occurs, however, these individuals often feel more securely attached to the one they've lost than ever before, since now they have fully faced just how much their connection to that other made them who they are.

Ideal grieving requires ideal health. If a person were fully healthy, their connections to others and the world around them would fully acknowledge, with everything they do, how everything and everyone is always connected and yet also that we are all completely independent and alone. With such knowledge, loss brings about a full understanding of just how important an attachment has been and how its loss will continue to be felt, but also how what's been lost will continue to exist within oneself. Grieving involves fully honoring what's been lost. Acceptance feels like a weight on one's heart simultaneous to a feeling of awe in remembrance of the wonderful warmth, beauty, glee, and magic that full relations with others implants within one's heart. Full and healthy acceptance of the loss of our greatest attachments holds the reverence and depth of our connection to those we've loved most and fully recognizes how that which we've lost carries on with us and then as well into those who will someday grieve over losing us, throughout our lifetime and throughout eternity. Full acceptance of loss always carries hope that love exists and can be found. Fully healthy acceptance of loss brings recognition that love abounds around us, is within us, and gives us hope that love is there for all. In the end, it is only through embracing the sorrow of what's been lost that it becomes possible to fully engage the poignant beauty of life.

Section 3

Living: Your Everyday
Maintenance in Interaction

So many different issues affect us in our daily lives that we sometimes feel we're being bombarded by new problems every day. The articles in this section represent a smattering of those issues and ways to understand them so that you might be able to function better within your relationships. "Criticism and Us" dissects the issue of judgment, how it affects us, and why it's often so compelling to judge others. In "Balancing the Animal and the Spiritual," the fact that we have animal instincts is contrasted with the fact that we need one another in almost everything we do. The compelling tendency for people to fall into dominant and controlling roles, and the problems or annoyance that causes, is the central topic in "The Power and Control Addiction." The psychobabble concept, "boundaries," is so essential to our interpersonal functioning that "Understanding Boundaries" was an essential article within this collection. "The Failure of Empathy in Everyday Life" points to our need to distance ourselves from the struggles of others even though, really, bad experiences and circumstances afflict good people all the time and the ability to maintain empathy could help us all live much more fulfilling and prosperous lives. This Everyday Maintenance section is rounded out with "The Crippling Effects of Worry," an article that emphasizes the need for faith in our loved ones as an antidote to the self-defeating and undermining (of others) tendency to worry about things we cannot control.

CHAPTER 10

❧

Criticism and Us

"He is a man whom it is impossible to please, because he is never pleased with himself."

—Johann Wolfgang von Goethe

Have you ever found yourself getting really frustrated, and maybe even angry, about something somebody did and then you start mercilessly criticizing them about it? Later you realize that you were blowing it way out of proportion and that you were way too critical. Many of us do that sometimes, don't we? Well, what's that about?

Typically we try to look at ourselves a little to figure it out. We tell ourselves, "I guess I'm just tired," or "Maybe she didn't understand what I was talking about, and I just got frustrated," or "I've been working really hard and he must not have realized that it was a really bad time." Actually, it's good sometimes to give ourselves that kind of break. Some people, after expressing even the smallest irritation, might say to themselves, "I'm just too mean to people," or "I bet they'll really think I'm a jerk." Either way, the irritation within us is clear, and we realize we've become very critical. Yet sometimes there appears to have been little provocation.

When we come to realize that we had blown things out of proportion, we may still believe that we were tired, frustrated, or overburdened, but we feel badly about the feelings we've caused in another. They're feeling downtrodden and undercut. Perhaps their confidence is a bit worse due to our seeming lack of confidence in them. We know we were too hard on them and we want them to know we know it. Apologizing is good. But understanding what happened could help us prevent it from happening in the future.

So I'll tell you something strange. If we've criticized way too harshly, the person we're really being most critical of, but very indirectly so, is ourselves. Excessively harsh criticism might occur when we're tired, overburdened, or frustrated because that's when we are most vulnerable, but the specific thing we became critical about is typically something we fear within ourselves.

I know that might seem odd, but it's true. Imagine yourself helping your child with their homework, let's say it's math, and you start to act like it's unbelievable that they aren't getting it. If that's what's happening, my guess is that you have felt like you were "stupid" sometime in the past (or that others thought you were "stupid"). It doesn't have to be math that was your issue in the past. It's that you have trouble tolerating "stupidity" in yourself, even if you know you've never been "stupid." Now, when you think the person you're helping might have that "stupidity" trait, you have to attack. It's as though you have to prove that the trait is not yours. You distance yourself as much as you possibly can from the trait by acting like it's the other person who is "stupid," thus limiting the possibility that anyone, including yourself, could ever think it was you.

Another example would be the desire to call someone "lazy." Now, I am not saying that there are no lazy people. "Laziness" is a trait that goes along with depression or learned helplessness, and sometimes people have never experienced the benefit of working hard or have no interests to fuel motivation. When your thoughts about someone being "lazy" move into the realm of harsh criticism, however, it's my guess that the issue is really yours. Typically, criticism about "laziness" happens in a context where people have different values about the worth of a particular activity. If you can see that the real issue is that the person who is not doing as much of a certain activity values it less, the issue of "laziness" doesn't come up. If you understand, for example, that a person who keeps a messy home spends all their time working really hard at their job, it's not likely that you'll think they're lazy (even if you don't agree with their priorities). But when the issue is within ourselves, that is perhaps someone used to call us "lazy" or we continue to call ourselves "lazy," our thoughts about differing values gets short-circuited and we come down on others harshly. This leaves the other person feeling deflated and even less able to work hard on that particular activity. They feel misunderstood as well, and it's likely they'll become stubborn and not work at all. Again, when we clearly define the other as the one who is "lazy," we have distanced ourselves. Not only do we successfully feel like we're not "lazy," but when we deflect by leveling the accusation at someone else, it's unlikely others will think we're "lazy" either.

Of course the situation where this criticism is most rife is within families—toward spouses and children. Because we're so close to our family members, seeing our traits in them is especially threatening. When our children do something we recognize as especially reflective of ourselves, we defend ourselves against seeing it's like us. It's almost as if a battle ensues within us, with the ultimate result being that we project that trait into our children and lose all recognition that it's like us at all. Thus, we're primed to become excessively critical when anything our family members do reminds us of our own weaknesses. We also fool ourselves sometimes into thinking it's our job to mold them appropriately, so the likelihood that we'll criticize has great precedent in "normal" parenting. Where we see any behavior in our loved ones that suggests they might be developing the same traits we believe we've overcome, it's as if there's a trail blazed traversing directly to the freedom to criticize.

With our spouses, extreme criticism is most likely to rear its head when we think the family is going in the wrong direction (immoderate criticism also, of course, develops from plain selfishness when one starts to feel cheated by circumstances—that is, one can begin to see their partner as not good enough—but that is beyond the purview of this article). It can be something truly important like a financial worry, but more often it's something small like a parenting issue. We act as though the other parent is too harsh when we feel really irritated ourselves, or we act like the other parent is too lenient when we've just recently been especially indulgent. We can see something we've done or something we do, and then we actually look for it in the other so we can jump on it and prove that it's not us.

Since we've all been excessively criticized before, we know of its effects. It feels terrible and demeaning and rarely has any redeeming effect. It is clear what makes us do it, but what is less clear is how to stop it. You could agree with everything you've read so far and still not see how much this issue affects you personally. You could see that you do this sometimes, but think of it as rare so that it requires no effort to change, or you could try to confront yourself about it and have little impact. The only way to really put a stop to this pattern is to look within yourself every time you become critical and truly explore all your feelings and thoughts about the issue.

It could be "stupidity," "laziness," "fairness," "being afraid," "indulging," "not disciplining," "being a downer," "not being careful," or "being greedy." Whatever it is, if you find yourself being unreasonably harsh about it, you need to go back to your deepest feelings about that thing and really work on accepting you. That is where the problem lies. You may know you're not these things. It's easy to see that a particular trait doesn't fit you. But believe me, if your behavior about that thing is out of bounds or exaggerated, the strength of your feelings indicates it's your problem.

The antidote is to explore the bad feelings and beliefs about yourself related to this area. Let yourself really feel the bad feelings and really try on the bad beliefs. When you've really examined all the negative feelings and beliefs you have about yourself in that area, then you are ready to go back to thinking the positive feelings and beliefs about yourself that you have already developed. You are able to know why you're not "lazy" or "stupid," just like you feel and think you've always known. Only now, if you take the exercise seriously, you will see that you don't see the issues in others as much. Because you understand your own beliefs and feelings about that personality trait, you now find yourself being less judgmental about that trait in others. You'll see that you don't need to criticize people about that issue. Most importantly, when you've really worked on seeing that ugly trait within yourself, you'll find you've freed yourself from the criticism you once heard or felt because you're now free from your own extreme and excessive criticism of yourself.

CHAPTER 11

❦

Balancing the Animal and the Spiritual

"Well-bred instinct meets reason halfway."

—George Santayana

We are animals! Well, I don't believe that's completely true. But it is the fact that we are animals, who are also spiritual beings, that I believe makes psychology an interesting subject. I will not go too far into the spiritual aspect of things from a religious perspective, but instead, let's look at our nature as human beings from a point of view that attempts to understand that we are in balance between self and community. By "community" I mean everyone (our family members, our neighbors, our fellow citizens) who is not you. Although I will not talk about religious matters here, generally speaking, our spiritual nature is expressed most clearly through the way we commune with others. We commune with others more or less adequately or in a fulfilling way based on our ability to balance our animal nature with our spiritual nature.

Human beings have three equally important motivators that are akin to animal needs. We have a need for self-protection that, in its extremes, makes us either aggressive or fearful. We have a need for sustenance that, in its extremes, we experience as either a starved feeling or a voracious, consumptive feeling. And we have a need for relatedness that, in its extremes, we experience as either loneliness or a sort of fragmentation of responsibility (for the needs of others). The more unbalanced these needs of the self, the more uncomfortable they are, and thus the more motivating they are.

When we experience any of these extremes, we are very likely to overcompensate by behaving in the opposite direction. The very frightened often become very violent. The very hungry often become rapaciously voracious and controlling. The overly responsible often avoid others so as to avoid more responsibility. When we are out of balance within ourselves, we make use of our relational environment in a desperate way to bring ourselves back into balance. That desperation results in so much pain and sorrow as we hurt the ones we love, either by hurting ourselves (anything from not treating ourselves well to actual self-injury) or directly violating our relationships with them in some way (being mean or taking advantage, etc.).

As you might have started to notice, the animal needs of self-protection and sustenance have emotional and relational aspects. We experience our emotions in a way that is quite similar to actual animal drives. In fact, long after we can be confident that we are physically safe and have enough food, we continue to fear the judgment or loss of others, and we continue to become angry about the loss or judgment of others. We also continue to pine away for others and make many mistakes in our own judgment based on the experience of extreme hunger for relationship.

In fact, only when we are able to balance the relational and emotional aspects of our animal nature can we start to balance our loneliness and responsibility fragmentation through relatedness. That is, we sometimes try to hold down our unbalanced animal nature by taking too much responsibility for others due to guilt about the harmful nature of those animal tendencies. We also sometimes avoid that unbalanced animal nature by remaining distant from others so they won't know that it exists (due to shame about its harmful nature).

But when we balance our animal needs through relational contacts, when we communicate our needs, weaknesses, and hurts to others, and demonstrate our willingness to help them and accept their needs, weaknesses, and hurts, we then become able to balance our loneliness with responsibility and vice versa. When we are balanced in our relational contacts, with our community, our spiritual nature starts to flow in a give-and-take with our community and the world.

It is also important to understand how we can help to develop these tendencies in ourselves and others. By treating yourself in a kind way, by recognizing your animal tendencies and allowing them to be acceptable, you will start to accept yourself. You do not have to act on your animal tendencies, but denying them makes it more likely that you will act on them in uncontrolled ways that are more shameful to you than mere thoughts. If you accept yourself, then you are more likely to accept others, which helps them become accepting, balanced people themselves. By expressing your own needs, weaknesses, and desires, you also keep those near you in check; since those who love you will take the responsibility they should take when they hurt you or have something you need.

When you stop to think about it, our communal nature is actually part of our animal nature. Once upon a time, and I believe it is still this way, our connection to each other was as important for survival as self-protection or sustenance. In fact, self-protection and sustenance were much more likely in a group setting, which is the Darwinian reason for our developing such heightened awareness of responsibility and a need for others. When we accept and understand our animal tendencies, including our biological need for connectedness, we become one with our communities.

We are always simultaneously alone and in a community, whether we are sequestered, and thus defined as separate from others, or incessantly surrounded by throngs, and thus defined as though we're in a crowd. Although within ourselves we remain alone, our development and our thoughts more often than not involve our relations with others. Thus, within ourselves, although we might be alone, we are also forever in a crowd. With others actually present, by expressing our true nature through communication of our emotions, we take our place in our community. That is, we connect our isolated self to the world all around. To the extent that we are able to spontaneously and genuinely express our animal nature without our developing fear of reprisal from others or developing fear of damaging others, an ability that can only come from having our most powerful needs calmed and accepted well enough within the social/emotional context, we express our true self. Our animal and spiritual natures, thus, coalesce in a healthy, animal/spiritual balance, resulting in a healthy influence in the direction of animal/spiritual balance on all who surround us. In effect, balancing our animal and spiritual nature amounts to living authentically and spontaneously with ourselves and within our community. In essence, the eventual result of an animal and spiritual balance in us all would bring about a wholistic, wholesome, healthy, and wholeheartedly synergistic society. Now *that would be* a spiritual world!

CHAPTER 12

❧

The Power and Control Addiction

"An honest private man often grows cruel and abandoned when converted into an absolute prince. Give a man power of doing what he pleases with impunity, you extinguish his fear, and consequently overturn in him one of the great pillars of morality."

—Joseph Addison

Of course we know why people seek power and why they need to control others. Seeking power indicates the need to overcome an inner feeling of powerlessness. Needing to control expresses a feeling that things in general, and especially other people, are out of one's control. These traits seem to run rampant in the world around us and there is barely anyone who isn't upset by them. In fact, those who want power and control are even more upset by others who want power and control than the rest of us due to their competitive nature and their view that there can be only one dominant person. For someone not afflicted with these desires, the powerful and controlling are irritating because they step on everyone's toes with rarely any awareness or, even more rarely, any regret. It's also infuriating that those seeking power and control often achieve power and control and often seem to garner more respect than anyone else. It is clear as well that those seeking power and control are not mentally healthy. However, their success is intoxicating to them, thus making the possibility of change extremely limited.

Power and control are so intoxicating, in fact, that they can be considered to be addictive, and there are many power and control addicts. There are problems for the person who seeks power and control (that is, the power and control addict) that might make them think twice about their ways, if only they could become aware of those problems. But the prevailing feelings of power and control prevent awareness of the problem. Essentially, power and control are defenses against feelings of inadequacy, weakness, fear, being unlovable or unloved, and being worthless. Obviously, if a person feels such wretched feelings, there is huge motivation to keep those feelings under wraps. Power and control specifically help in keeping those feelings under wraps. Of course, if someone is feeling powerful and in control, it is unlikely that they will feel inadequate, unloved, or worthless.

So where do these needs come from? There are three primary patterns that lead to the development of a need for power and control, and there is tremendous overlap between the three. The first is the experience of being dominated as a child and the observation that becoming dominant is the only solution for overcoming a feeling of extreme submission. The second is the child who tries desperately to please a difficult-to-please parent with perfection in all they do but who never feels they have actually succeeded in pleasing that parent, so in their perfectionism and efforts to please when they become adults, they require that everyone around them be perfect too. The third is a type that is born with so much intensity that they naturally become aggressive when displeased and then never get their intensity under control because it feels so good when others give in. These three types overlap quite naturally since dominating parents are often perfectionists and/or intense. Nevertheless, all three can be separate as well, and, thus, will be briefly discussed below in uncovering the motivations behind each characteristic path.

Dominating parents are of many assorted types. There are those who need things perfect, those who lack self-control and those who lack the ability to love. The need to dominate, however, always indicates a problem with a mixture of feelings involving vulnerability and insignificance. Those feelings are very easily transmitted over generations since the interpersonal solution that balances one's inner feelings of vulnerability and insignificance is dominance, which then leads those who are dominated to feel vulnerable and insignificant. As a child who needs the care that a parent can provide, there is no choice but to submit. However, that same child will often dominate friends and acquaintances and, as an adult, will dominate co-workers and their own spouses and children. Because their dominance helps them feel strong and significant, it is extremely difficult for a dominant type to change. The dominant parent rarely sees that they cause any problems or that they have any problems because their dominance so perfectly compensates for their inner feelings which are the polar opposite of how they behave.

A second type of power and control comes from being as perfect as possible. Those who are trying to be perfect attempt to please themselves in a way that they have learned would be the right thing to do, but which also camouflages and conceals the unconscious desire to finally attain unconditional positive regard (please see article "The Obsessive-Compulsive Personality"). Many such individuals love, and have known love, but also had always thought the love they received was conditional and that they had to be truly good, moral, giving, meticulous, and forthright to finally attain the kind of love they really wanted. Because these individuals often were truly loved, they now see their behavior as the consequence of challenging themselves, as opposed to a reflection of a need to please others. In fact, quite often, they see themselves as exemplifying the pinnacle of correctness or as paragons of virtue. That is where their dominance and control gets involved. These "perfect" people often expect others to live to their standards. They use many different kinds of influence to make sure others do things "right" such as setting the standard, worrying, or disdain at anything they feel is not worthy of their attention. Of course, these traits, just like those in the dominating parent, are also often transmitted over generations as children feel they must comply or fail to achieve approval, which then leads to perfectionism and control of friends, acquaintances, and family members.

The third type of power and control comes specifically from individuals who behave in very intense ways and learn that such intense behavior leads to getting what they want. Some children are born with this intensity, but it can also come from behavior that initially occurred during childhood illness when the child was not disciplined for fear that it would further harm the child or from families where children are spoiled and treated as though they are more important than the parents. The one commonality is that the child learns that intensely aggressive or angry behavior leads to others backing off and giving in. Once that connection is established, the child has a hard time containing the behavior that is so successful at getting the child what is wanted. This third type has their biggest difficulty when someone does attempt to curb their behavior with discipline, or sometimes with even relatively minor suggestions. Because they develop such a strong sense that their intense emotions are legitimate and uncontrollable, they perceive anyone saying no to them as an affront. They respond to very subtle cues of disagreement or of discipline with extreme outrage, and in that way, they achieve their goal of getting what they want.

In fact, this is the commonality that must be overcome to some extent in all three types of power and control. The feeling that others back off or give in when a person acts dominant or controlling creates an indelible association for the power and control addict. Their aggressive behaviors are permanently associated with success at pursuing immediate gratification. If others do not make it clear that aggressive, dominating, or controlling behavior rarely results in a positive outcome, then those who behave in dominant and controlling ways will feel so powerful that they will never want to relinquish their dominant behavior. The thinking pattern goes like this:

"Although in many ways this world seems like complete chaos, and I often feel weak and insignificant or unworthy of love, the world *does* give me anything I want as soon as I become aggressive, unruly, or angry. That means I decide what I get or don't get. I need only become angry or bossy or seemingly lose control of myself and, abracadabra, what I wanted appears before me like magic. I do not need to delay gratification. I get immediate gratification anytime."

This perspective is not actually conscious in most cases. If you observe enough individuals with this problem, however, you will see that their behavior does truly manifest this belief, whether it is conscious or not.

The biggest problem in childhood is when the behavior is initially caused by inborn intensity (when extreme enough, this intensity is considered "bipolar disorder"). When the behavior has developed primarily due to parenting style, changes in parenting style usually succeed in changing the behavior. Parents need to work together and be consistent, and where there has been a problem with giving in, they must inform the child there will be no more giving in and then proceed to never (yes, I mean **never**) give in even if it means the child must be physically restrained, hospitalized, or sent to jail. Inborn intensity, however, truly complicates matters. Intense reactions that start in the womb can create havoc as a child actually perceives their desire for what they want as though it is truly uncontrollable. Many of these types of children grow up being told they have no control of themselves, which worsens matters. They then believe there is little reason to try to change since it presumably would not work. However, when these children grow a little older and they start to see how their behavior causes them very negative consequences, sometimes they start to get motivated to change. Quite commonly, those whose problem is primarily intensity, but who feel very close to their family members, feel horrible when their aggressive behavior becomes hurtful and damages those they love. Nevertheless, the power they have experienced in the past, combined with the intensity of their emotions, makes it seem to them almost impossible to control themselves when the aggressive urge arises.

The power one experiences, regardless of which type, is very much an addiction. In fact, it is the fact that the behavior continues for long periods in spite of negative consequences that makes it so clear that there is an addiction to power and control. In the worst cases, the consequences are very obvious as the aggressiveness gets some individuals in serious trouble with law enforcement or in school. At a more subtle level, however, individuals who crave power and control, and who behave in dominant or controlling ways, rarely maintain good relationships with others. Their family members often avoid them and their friendships rarely last very long. When they have children, the children rarely stay in frequent contact after they've grown. Sometimes it seems remarkable that such individuals even have families. However, their success in life often makes them extremely attractive at a certain level and they do tend to attract mates and have children.

In fact, many power and control addicts do have incredibly successful careers. However, they are always ultimately alone. No one feels close to a person who bullies them. No one feels close to someone who controls them. If others have to do what the power and control addict wants, they will be scared of disappointing that person, but they won't love them. Not only will loved ones leave, but they won't even miss the power and control addict. Instead, they'll feel they've finally gotten free. Bullies lose those they think love them as soon as there is any sign of their vulnerability. Many people will be there for them only because they have had to be, or because they have feared what would happen if they didn't do what the power and control addict expected. To the extent that these relationships were built on the usefulness of the power and control addict, as opposed to love, when the power and control addict is no longer useful, there remains no reason to stay in contact.

Strangely, having power and control over others makes it impossible to even know those others or their motivations, so even those who seem to love the power and control addict are often merely pleasing them. If we believe someone loves us, then we can assume the reason they do things for us or stay true to us or work their hardest to do the things we like is because they want to do it themselves. Unfortunately, people who need someone for any reason can be very good at seeming to be in agreement. The problem is, if they do not feel free to be who they want to be, if they do things thinking they have to and not because they are following their own feelings, then nothing they do can be trusted by the power and control addict. Because they have been forced to do things in their relationship with the power and control addict, even the loving things they do are being done because they feel they must. Many times, people are so controlled by a power and control addict that they don't even know how they feel. When they finally feel free, they often behave in ways that are contrary to the power and control addict's wishes. Even that behavior does not express who they really are, since it merely expresses their desire to be opposed to what is expected from them.

People are only free to love when they are not intimidated and controlled. Only by receiving unconditional love does a person truly blossom into what they really want to be. Only the sense that one is unconditionally loved can lead to a true sense of freedom or a feeling within one that one has true value. This feeling, that one's way of being is valuable and loved in and of itself and not for its utility to someone else, is the cornerstone of self-esteem. Sometimes the lack of self-esteem that comes from being dominated will lead to people staying with, or continuing to please, the power and control addict, since it makes the controlled person continue to believe that the only way to gain positive regard is to successfully please the power and control addict. However, only if a person knows they are worthy of love, only if they have self-esteem, are they able to actually love others. If a person is controlled, their love is meaningless. They are not free to decide who or what they love. They act loving because they must. If they are free, however, they are free to decide who and what they love. Power and control addicts end up lonely and bereft of love. Those around them are not free and thus can't love, and as soon as they have any self-esteem, they leave. The character of the power and control addict makes it impossible to love others because they only approve of others to the extent that others please them. So just as they cannot love, it is also impossible for the power and control addict to be loved by others.

Unfortunately, it is very difficult to show those addicted to power and control the error of their ways. Some, as indicated above, will see that they hurt others and then feel badly. Those are the ones that are genetically intense, however, and once they realize that they seem to hurt others due to their extreme reactions, they often agree to seek treatment. Those who are not genetically intense, but nevertheless dominate and control others with their high standards and dominant attitudes, can also sometimes see how their behavior hurts those they love. Children or spouses of power and control addicts can often be instrumental in getting the power and control addict to recognize how they affect others. They have a huge impact, especially when they want to forge a relationship, but find themselves also wanting to get away and be free. Intervening in a way that has some efficacy, however, requires a very specific kind of communicating. Generally speaking, although it is exactly the opposite of what will come naturally, being vulnerable with the power and control addict is the only way to get through to the power and control addict.

The power and control addict's behavior, one must remember, is directly connected to feelings of vulnerability and inadequacy. They have felt that way and overcome those feelings with their dominant and controlling behavior. Their behavior currently covers up those feelings and they remain capable of identifying with those feelings within those whom they deem important. Therefore, when someone they care about says they are hurt, the power and control addict often can't stand the idea that they are responsible for creating within someone they care for the very same feelings that they themselves can't stand within themselves. In fact, it is within the context of getting in touch with their own vulnerable and inadequate feelings, even if it is within someone else, that the power and control addict is finally able to behave in a loving manner. If the pain they are causing is similar enough to the pain they have experienced, and it is typically almost identical, the power and control addict is actually capable of connecting in a way that causes guilt and responsibility for the feelings of others. This experience of guilt and responsibility makes the power and control addict capable of changing their behavior.

The way to communicate with the power and control addict is actually quite specific. Unfortunately, the power and control addict is extremely sensitive to blame, and can point the finger back at anyone who points the finger at them. The only way to avoid the blame game with the power and control addict is to specifically state how something that has happened has left you "hurt." Sometimes it is even necessary to state, in the most vulnerable way a person can imagine, that much of the fault lies with you. Taking responsibility yourself will help the power and control addict take responsibility as well, and also takes the blame out of the "hurt" statement. It must also be remembered that there are extremely few words for "hurt" in the English language. Most other words one thinks of as indicating "hurt" actually are blame words or words about what the other person has done. For example, "embarrassed" means the other person did something odd, and "disappointed" means the other person is considered to be inferior. Words indicating "hurt" are the word "hurt" and many physiological descriptions of the body. For example, the hurt individual can say, "when X [a certain behavior] occurs," "it ties my stomach into knots," or "I feel a tightening in my throat," or "I feel tension and pressure in my head or chest."

Clearly such "hurt" statements require a mixture of strength and confidence because they engender so much vulnerability. It is also clear that the relationship with the power and control addict must be very important in order to make the controlled individual motivated enough to make such a statement. Getting the power and control addict to see how their behavior is hurtful is, however, the only way to get them to change. Because such statements also put the power and control addict in touch with their own feelings of vulnerability and inadequacy, such statements are exactly what is needed to put them back on the road to recovery from their addiction.

Once the power and control addict identifies with vulnerability and inadequacy in others, they become aware enough of it within themselves to see others in more humanistic and tolerant ways. Their view of others as inferior, weak, or inadequate slowly diminishes as they see a connection between their behavior and the behavior of others who once hurt them. The power and control addict may not see this all-important change at first, but assuming that they have cared about their family members and want them to remain in contact, assuming that they might actually want to learn to give and receive love from their closest family members and not lose them because they stay away as the only way to achieve freedom, it is clear that this change becomes the most important accomplishment of their lives. By relinquishing the need to dominate, the power and control addict makes it possible to finally live life for what is truly most important in life, the connection with others and the development of interpersonal growth that can only occur through bequeathing love from generation to generation.

CHAPTER 13

❧

Understanding Boundaries

"Think twice before you speak, because your words and influence will plant the seed of either success or failure in the mind of another."

—Napolean Hill

What in the world is meant by this psycho-babble word "boundaries"? Even as a student of psychology, it took me a long time to understand it. But it's such an essential concept in comprehending interpersonal relationships and communication that it sure would be nice if someone could give a simple explanation of "boundaries" that would facilitate better interpersonal relationships and communication. I will attempt to provide such an explanation in this article.

The definition of "boundaries" is this: "boundaries" consist of those actions we take or things we say that protect us from being hurt by or keep us from hurting others or ourselves. That sounds a little complicated or maybe too emotionally mushy for some of you, so let's break it down into reasonable terms.

The "boundaries" that are being described when the word "boundaries" is used refers to our emotions and how they are expressed, controlled, and communicated. When we have an emotion, no one is privy to that emotion until we communicate it in some way, either verbally or behaviorally. That is, we control our emotions to varying extents at different times. Sometimes we feel angry and we hold it in. Sometimes we feel angry and other people know it. Sometimes we are hurt and we turn it into an angry response before we allow ourselves to experience the hurt, and sometimes we're hurt and we hide it from others. To complicate matters, we actually have two boundaries. One boundary that specifically regulates whether or not emotions are experienced by ourselves and another that regulates whether or not emotions are communicated or shown to others. These separate boundaries can be referred to as the "inner" boundary and the "outer" boundary.

The inner boundary protects us from acknowledging that we are basically animals with animal needs, desires, and aggressive impulses. This boundary is necessary, just as in the case of the outer boundary, for the purpose of protecting us from hurting or being hurt by others or ourselves. But in this case, the problem is that many of our true emotions are viewed by us as potentially damaging to others about whom we care a great deal or, on the other hand, potentially damaging to ourselves by way of making us think of ourselves in a way that is too uncomfortable. This boundary operates without our awareness and simply allows us to go about our business without too much craziness. It is not likely that someone could go to the bank, pay the bills, write a letter, cook dinner, or do the millions of things we do each day while thinking about tearing meat off the bones of a freshly ensnared carcass or running to escape a voracious saber tooth or engaging in some other equally animalistic but natural animal practice. This tendency to push down emotions that are threatening to us is commonly known as "repression."

The outer boundary refers to the ways in which we protect ourselves from the behavior of others as well as the ways in which we protect others from the emotions we are experiencing. When other people act in certain ways, we allow their behavior to affect us. If we care a great deal about another person, their behavior is more likely to have an effect. But if we hardly know a person, or have a limited relationship with them (like those we see at work but with whom we do not socialize), then our emotions need not be as affected by their behavior, nor should their emotions be too affected by us. An example of a common concern related to this boundary is thinking that other people are upset with you when they're simply feeling tired or upset about something not related to you. In such a case, you're experiencing the effect of a loose boundary that is caused by some form of insecurity. Another example of a concern related to this boundary is common "road rage." When you get upset about how other people are driving and start becoming irate, you're letting your emotions affect others too much (most incidents of "road rage" involve misunderstandings or driving mistakes and, at worst, obnoxious drivers who have little interest in or specific reason to be targeting you).

One of the great problems with boundaries is that we are often not aware of who is close to us and who is not, and we learn to react to the world in a particular way to make us feel more or less protected and safe most of the time. When we allow too many people to affect us, our need for their approval or love and affection costs us dearly since we get hurt all the time. When too many people are affected by our emotions, we make them pay too high a price for our own inability to handle feelings. Generally, the healthy functioning of boundaries occurs through a process of development in relationships.

We learn to trust people over time. When we learn that someone is careful with us (most of the time), we start to feel safe. When we start to feel safe, we can let people be more aware of our feelings, and we can allow them to have more of an effect on our emotions. Very often, people do not protect themselves sufficiently or start to feel free to burden others with their emotions too quickly. For example, the process of falling in love involves a fantasy period when, in our minds, the other person is more what we want them to be than who he or she really is (see article "The Dating Fantasy"). During this period, it is likely that we will think this other is a person with whom we can really open up or, on the other hand, we might think they are a person who loves us enough to take our crap. Sometimes our fantasy of this other person is so strong that we overlook how badly he or she makes us feel or how we have been taking so many liberties with his or her feelings. But people with relatively healthy boundaries balance their fantasy with the reality that they really don't know this person very well yet. With healthy boundaries, when the relationship starts to make someone feel badly, or when one can acknowledge that something he or she did might have been hurtful, there is a natural tendency to back off and protect oneself in a healthy "good boundaries" way.

Quite often, however, the problem with boundaries, even for relatively healthy people, occurs after they have developed through the initial fantasy period and have become quite intimate. A couple might have learned to trust each other slowly, but when they finally do trust each other, their behavior starts getting more hurtful or too dependent and needy. In these situations, it is important to know how to express oneself so that boundaries can be better. There are two basic ways of creating boundaries: responding with anger or responding with hurt.

Angry behavior pushes others away. Hurt behavior can draw others closer. If the relationship is truly caring, that is, if both partners feel a sense of responsibility for the other's welfare, then acting hurt when you truly are (as opposed to allowing the hurt feeling to be automatically transformed into an angry response), will allow the other person to experience your hurt and take some responsibility for what they've done to contribute to it. When the hurt feeling is expressed with someone who cares very deeply, the hurtful behavior abates soon after. On the other hand, when someone is unlikely to feel responsible (and I believe most people truly do care, so they should be given several chances with the hurt response), the angry response is much more appropriate. It is normal to need distance from someone who will hurt you. The angry response also engenders respect from those who act angry on a regular basis.

In healthy relationships, over time, some healthy mixture of boundary setting through anger (sometimes simply acting irritated) and hurt (sometimes just wearing a sad expression) develops so that the relationship can sustain itself in a healthy way. That is, there is no perfect person or relationship that makes it possible for there to be no hurt or anger. What makes our relationships feel alive is that we do have a deep impact on one another. That emotional impact is the very stuff of life whether its derived from joy, frustration, irritation, or hurt. It makes us feel connected. Emotional impact is to relationships what air is to breathing. A good balance means we are neither suffocated nor bloated with that air; that we are sustained by and interested in our relationship but not living in chaos because of it.

If we can understand boundaries, why they're there and how they help us, it can be possible to use them in a new way that really helps us express who we are in a way that is better for us. It is not being manipulative to let yourself act how you really feel, whether you feel happy, angry, or hurt. But doing so does help you create boundaries with others. It helps you communicate your intentions more clearly. It helps you let people know you mean business when you do. And it helps you let people know that you have feelings that they need to respect and care about. In short, learning how to have good boundaries will make your relationships healthier, your life more spontaneous and free, and it will make your endeavors more fruitful as you start to feel more comfortable taking a path that is really right for you.

CHAPTER 14

০৪

The Failure of Empathy in Everyday Life

"The great gift of human beings is that we have the power of empathy."

—Meryl Streep

The world is our emotional mirror. On a daily basis, we interact with others and their collective reaction is reflected back to us. This collective reaction tells us, in a very general sense, how we're being perceived. Of course, the reaction of others is often not the most accurate mirror. It's often influenced by our very personal perception of it as well as by the general views others take about the world itself and about us. But nonetheless, the reactions of others are the most influential mirror we see. For those of you who would say that you really don't care what others think, I would say you are either benefiting from having a pretty attractive reflection or you have given up caring. If you've given up caring, then the ugly view you've seen in the emotional mirror has already had a drastic impact on you. On the other hand, if you know you care, but your reflection in this mirror is not capable of reducing you into a heap of goo, congratulations! You have developed a healthy level of confidence. No matter how you see it, however, the reflection we perceive in the mirror of our interactions is really quite important. Many people only feel good to the extent that the world smiles upon them. Unfortunately, the world often doesn't smile. The reasons for that are very complicated. But at its most elementary level, the problem is a failure of empathy in everyday life.

When we empathize accurately, others really appreciate the effort. Empathy with others involves perceiving the world as though you are the others with whom you want to empathize. Oh, if only everyone could continually put themselves in the shoes of others. But they can't, and they won't. People, without even realizing it, generally develop a perspective about life and about any situation that makes their own feelings okay. It may be unfortunate, but for most of us, it's far more important to maintain our own self-esteem or our own sense of invulnerability than it is to understand others. When our own self worth or need for invulnerability even mildly conflicts with understanding others, a failure of empathy will undoubtedly ensue.

Thus, if someone is downtrodden, they are thought of as, at best, unlucky, and, at worst, failures or undeserving. It's not difficult to understand why we might feel that way. Who wants to think it's possible that terrible things can happen to us as easily as we see them happen to others? Of course, we want to be invulnerable. It's also true that putting effort into prevention, being careful, having forethought, and working hard all help to keep trouble at bay. Nevertheless, we tend to immoderately underestimate the frequency with which bad things can happen to good people.

How many times do you see a family devastated by an accident or an illness or some other mishap that clearly was not in the province of preventable? The fact is, many of us see such things and then immediately grasp for the reasons it could never happen to us. We want to believe that bad things won't happen to us because we're so careful or because it's clear we're "good." Sometimes we even attempt to comfort ourselves by judging those to whom fate has not been kind. It is not unusual to wonder what others have done to deserve their bad luck. It's as if the most natural knee-jerk reaction to the bad luck of others is to say to oneself, "Not me!" This "not me" thought is then quickly followed by the best possible explanation to oneself as to why the disaster did occur to "them."

Nowhere is this more true than in cases where people are truly down on their luck. The worst scenario is when those who "have" harshly judge those who don't. While on the surface, there appears to be many differences between these two groups, by far the most essential difference is opportunity. Most people who have worked out a pretty good life for themselves also come from relatively decent backgrounds. That is not to say the "haves" have not experienced any trauma. But most of the time, they have seen economic success and have felt like attaining such success was an attainable possibility for them. In contrast, when people are born into poverty, opportunity seems completely off limits. Often, being born into poverty means you'll have an inferior education, your neighborhood will be filled with blight, your friends and neighbors will likely discourage hard work due to their own inability to see opportunity, and your parents will likely be somewhat depressed and thus invest little faith in the possibilities in your future. Nevertheless, if you are not making it, or if you seem upset, the "haves" will see only a lack of work ethic or a bad attitude.

How often do you think to yourself or hear someone say, "I know I wouldn't make it if I were in that situation"? That kind of thinking is rarely thought and much less frequently spoken. It is far easier to point out "laziness," "immorality," and "attitude" than it is to see that the development of such traits is virtually unavoidable in some circumstances. While it's very clear that one's circumstances cannot be accepted as an excuse for lack of success (or worse), judging the personality characteristics of those who have been brought up in poverty, without considering the magnitude of poverty's influence, is a clear failure of empathy designed specifically to help the "haves" avoid complicity. After all, the solutions necessary for combating poverty are very expensive and would likely make the "haves" a lot less comfortable.

Quite dissimilar from the need to avoid feeling too vulnerable, as in the examples above, is the failure of empathy that occurs when there is a possible conflict between empathy and our self-esteem. The best example of this is when we negatively judge the intentions of others prior to really knowing their motivations. When accurately understanding the actions of others threatens our own sense of self, we will tend to be very inaccurate in our understanding of a situation. When this happens, whether we are being simply untrusting, or maybe even paranoid, we fail to empathize primarily because we know our own desires and propensities and we project them onto the ones we judge.

It is quite common, for example, that a jealous wife feels strong attractions to other men and that jealous husbands feel strong attractions to other women. In those cases, what one fears most from themselves becomes what they fear in their loved ones. Likewise, when we fear that someone we think is close to us doesn't adequately care for us, it's quite often the case that it is us that is caring less for them. Similarly, accusations of dishonesty often occur merely due to evidence of opportunity because many people feel, given the same opportunity, they would be dishonest. Believing there has been some kind of malfeasance simply because we can see someone's success is also common because we can't stand to look at our own comparative failure. In all these cases, we fear how we would feel if the projected motivation was attributed to us.

But we don't all think the same, do we? Often, people really are more moral than we are. Sometimes they're more motivated than we are or work harder than we do. Other people have been through different experiences, they have developed different skills, they were born with natural abilities we will never possess, and yes, often they have been given far less opportunity. The failure in empathy occurs because we can't stand the idea that bad things could happen to us. It happens because the inequities of the world are so far beyond our ability to fix them and because of the extreme guilt we would have to feel if we were to recognize that the "have nots" differ only in their relative lack of opportunity. The failure of empathy also occurs because we refuse to believe that others might have better intentions than we would ever have, or because we fear our own propensities. We don't want to admit to our own feelings, so we see the reflection of our own motivations in the behavior of others, and then frown upon those others with judgment since we fail to maintain empathy with who they really might be.

When we realize that the failure of empathy occurs only to save us from our own shame, that all human beings are indeed created equal yet we rarely see it that way, and that others are often better than we are in many different ways, hopefully it makes possible a renewed effort at maintaining proper empathy. The problems of the world are truly daunting. Heck, it's overwhelming just to handle the problems in our own lives. But if we all made every effort to maintain empathy in this cold hard world, regardless of our own desire to deny our own tendencies or to admit to our obvious good fortune, perhaps that empathy in itself could be a part of a whole world solution.

If our interactions with the world are like an emotional mirror in which we hope to see an attractive image of ourselves, then maintaining empathy with others as much as possible would clearly lead to better-looking reflections. Better-looking reflections would then lead to better self-esteem, more confidence, greater success in interaction with the world, easier and more spontaneous smiling, and a better reflection in the great big emotional mirror for everyone. If only everyone would make a stronger effort at empathy, we would have better partners, parents, families, neighborhoods, cities, and so on.

Like light amplified by mirrors surrounding a single flame, an effort at world empathy could set this world ablaze with enthusiasm for us all. Our petty fears, like a black hole swallowing the brightness and battling against empathy, must give way to an emanation of radiance from our hearts. Look into the mirror! Wish for the empathy you need to see there! Let the smiling glow begin with you. Let the mirror shine luminous for you and everyone! The failure of empathy need not drag us down disconsolate. Look all around you! You are the mirror! Be diligent in your empathy. It's *your* responsibility! Challenge yourself to stay in tune and empathic with your community and, please . . . let there be light!

CHAPTER 15

❧

The Crippling Effects of Worry

"God grant me the serenity to accept the things I cannot change; courage to change the things I can; and wisdom to know the difference."

—*The Serenity Prayer*, Reinhold Niebuhr

We love our kids. We love our lives. Sometimes we are so grateful for what we have, however, that we fear losing it more than we allow ourselves to enjoy it. This fear of losing those things for which we are grateful is called "worrying." Although sometimes worry can be helpful to us—for example, when it allows us to act proactively in preventing potential disasters—more often than not, it gets in our way by preoccupying us with possible loss when we could enjoy what we have gained. When we worry about others, we cause an even bigger problem since such worrying sends the message that we do not have faith in those others to handle their lives responsibly and efficaciously.

Healthy "worry" is not really "worry" at all, but rather should be called "concern." Concern activates us toward taking sensible precautions to ensure our future well-being. It is healthy to plan for the future or to work toward goals. Some people are so good at managing concern (taking precautions and working on goals) that things usually do go their way. When we worry, however, we are more than concerned. We are scared or sometimes even terrified. We are thinking in drastic terms. Who of us has not, at times, thought things had to go our way, or by some very specific plan, or everything would be ruined.

Excessive worry is typically related to past experiences of things going really badly in situations for which we have taken an irrational level of responsibility. If, for example, when we were young, someone close to us treated us badly or constantly criticized us, one typical reaction would be to think we deserved what happened. If we deserved what happened because we did something "wrong," all we would need to do to prevent future trauma would be to stop ourselves from doing "wrong" things. From this perspective, it feels better to think we are responsible for the bad things that happened than it does to realize how often bad things happen for no particular reason or because someone else had problems. That is, it feels better to think we had some control over things than it does to feel like bad things happen to us in a completely random fashion.

To the extent that these early experiences were traumatic, we overemphasize the possibility of disaster in our current lives. We become desperate to avoid disaster when really we only need to be vigilant. If we think of ourselves as having done something wrong when others treated us badly, then we need only do things "right" to avoid such traumatic pain in the future. We must now work like crazy to make everything work out "right." The need to do things "right" gets exaggerated and develops into a need to do things "perfectly." If we can be "perfect," we will not be wrong, we will prevent every possible problem, we will not be traumatized by others seeing us be wrong, and we can prove ourselves worthy of love. If we are worthy of love, we will not lose love or the affection of the ones we love.

Unfortunately, making everything work out "right" requires us to maintain control over everything in our lives. Maintaining control means working hard. Within reason, there is nothing wrong with that. But it also often means trying to make others do things our way. When others clearly will not do things our way, or when we clearly have no control over a particular situation in our lives, it seems there is nothing left within our control but to worry. We worry about things not working out because we think everything will go to pot, that we will prove ourselves unworthy of love, lose those we do love, and perhaps find ourselves to be worthless.

One of the worst outcomes in all of this is that we often **will** lose those we love if we try to control them. Sometimes we worry about the one's we love so much that they feel we do not have faith in their independence and ability to take care of themselves. Very few people (not healthy ones, anyway) want to have someone else constantly telling them how to do things. We don't want someone thinking they always know the right way, which implies that our ways are wrong. When someone treats us like we do not know anything or cannot do anything right, we tend to shrink from contact with them because they make us feel like we shrink in importance when we are around them.

Thus, when someone is trying to be "perfect" so that they will prove themselves worthy and not lose love, they make themselves into people who are very likely to lose love. In the attempt to prevent the disaster that might befall our loved ones, it is all too easy to lose their love because we do not communicate faith in their ability to succeed or their ability to recover from failures. While it is healthy to try to teach others from our experience, it is necessary to have compassion and understanding for their points of view and what they already know. Sometimes it is also necessary to let them do things their own way because they cannot possibly learn without trying and failing.

Often, when someone worries and tells someone else how to do things, it's as though they have taken that other person's ability away. It is difficult to compete with someone else's way of doing something at the same time we are trying to find our own way. Worrying can create a vicious circle in which those we love stop trying their own ways of doing things and thus never learn from experience and never gain the confidence necessary to do things on their own. If their way of doing things has to be better than ours lest they have to fear our criticism, then they can never feel like their own way of doing things will result in acceptable outcomes. Clearly, we can never hold someone's hand all the time, so it is essential that they have confidence that doing things their own way will result in positive outcomes.

Worrying is unhealthy for us and it is unhealthy for those around us. The antidote to worry is faith. We must have faith that things will work out most of the time if we work toward our goals with a healthy amount of concern. Equally important, we must try to have faith that our loved one's have the strength, tenacity and foresight to succeed most of the time, in their own way, and pick themselves up after their failures. In fact, having faith in our loved one's actually infuses them with the confidence they need to succeed. If we learn to balance our love and concern with faith that things will work out, we maximize our chances for living full, successful, and fulfilling lives, and for maintaining our connections with loved ones who are thus free to live independent, fruitful, and fulfilling lives of their own.

Section 4

Caring for You and Your Communication with Others: Tools for Maintenance and Lubrication of Individuals Living in the Great Life Machine

Sometimes we need only go in for an oil change. Yet other times we need a tune-up or a few small repairs, maybe a new timing belt, or, much deeper, perhaps a new transmission or an engine overhaul. The articles in this section range through various ways of taking care of yourself on a daily basis, when things get rough, or even when you need to address issues long past. Perhaps one of the easiest, yet most valuable, tools a person can learn to use is found in "Breathe!" an article that describes a method for staying relaxed throughout life. In "Be Your Own Best Friend" an odd, but obvious, notion is offered: if you're not feeling good, why not treat yourself like you would treat someone you really love? The ultimate question is asked in "Stress Management for Tough Times": how bad would things really be if you're worst fears came true? For all you do-it-yourself types, "The Writing Cure" gives you an opportunity to be your own therapist and highlights a method for curing insomnia as well as a method for healing the open wounds from a troubling past. "Assertiveness: The 30% Solution" serves as a segue to the interpersonal articles to come, with a formula for taking care of oneself when with others.

CHAPTER 16

౮

Breathe!

"All things share the same breath—the beast, the tree, the man . . . the air shares its spirit with all the life it supports."

—Chief Seattle

The simplicity of this statement may be hard for you to believe, but there is no better advice I could give anyone than, simply put, breathe! There are so many activities in which we engage for which, strangely, we stop breathing. You see, a cessation of breathing, or rather very shallow breathing, is part of the body's sympathetic nervous system reaction, or stress response, which is triggered whenever we fear something. The sympathetic nervous system reaction is also known as the fight, flight or freeze syndrome, or the "three Fs," and includes blood flow to the major muscle groups (upper arms, thighs, and back) and away from the extremities (feet and hands), tension or readiness in the major muscle groups, blood flow away from the other body organs including the stomach, and increased cardiac reaction. If a ferocious lion were to walk into the room where you are now, I hope you would have some kind of reaction. You might need to run (flight). If the lion catches you, you better be ready to battle (fight). Perhaps if there is some chance that you might not be seen by the lion, you would do well to keep perfectly still (freeze).

It is this last reaction, freezing, that is by far the most common in us humans. Unfortunately, we react this way when there is practically nothing to fear at all. Even when you consider those activities that almost everyone considers scary, like public speaking or a meeting with your regional director, there is no chance of being ripped limb from limb, or that your home will burn to the ground. Thus there's little reason the three Fs should be activated. Right? Well, of course we do become somewhat tense in these situations, even if no one can even tell. It's this last part, the part about no one being able to tell, that most involves the stop in breathing. When we stop breathing, we are freezing. With us humans we stop breathing or freeze so no one will notice how we are reacting. We don't want people to see that we're tense when we first meet them or when we're expected to give a rousing speech. Thus we react in the same way an animal reacts when afraid of a predator.

Of course there is no predator in these examples, just the importance of a situation. And perhaps we're not quite as frightened as that animal that is afraid of a real lion or bear. If we were that afraid, we probably wouldn't hide it very well. Sometimes, however, we stop our breathing even when there is really nothing about which to be afraid at all. You see, there is a problem for us humans in having such a huge brain (compared to other animals) in that we significantly overgeneralize danger. Sometimes we stop breathing just because we are trying to explain something to someone or because we are listening intently. Certainly we often don't breathe the way we should when we're having a stressful day at work. When we stay in this tense state, a state characterized by shallow breathing as well as tightening muscles and poor blood flow, for any prolonged period of time, we often develop head, stomach, back, neck, or shoulder aches. Recognizing your tense state, and preventing it from becoming prolonged, can be the key to keeping yourself in a comfortable zone for better performance and a general sense of well-being. The way to keep yourself in that zone is to breathe.

Fortunately, even though our brains are maladaptively efficient to the point that we overgeneralize many experiences as dangerous, the size of our brain can also help us in that, unlike other animals, we have the force of will to overcome our overgeneralizations. That is, unlike other animals, we can tell ourselves to do things that trigger the opposite of the three Fs. The opposite of the three Fs is known as the parasympathetic nervous system reaction, or the relaxation response. When the parasympathetic nervous system is activated we can digest our food, rest, or go to sleep. Part of the relaxation response is breathing calmly and deeply.

Being human as we are, we can activate the relaxation response by forcing ourselves to breathe deeply. The body is a system that gives itself feedback to determine what to do next. The brain reads a certain amount of oxygen in the lungs, and rhythmic body and chest motion, as a sign that it's time to relax. If you breathe deeply, you won't even be able to help but get more calm. Even better than that, when we do breathe deeply, we calm down not only our bodies, but also our minds. The mind looks for consistency between the way we're feeling and the way we're thinking. Just like the tension in your body makes your thoughts more stressful (your heart starts beating hard so you start to worry that you are having heart problems), calm in your body makes you have more calm thoughts ("I'm starting to breathe easy, so everything must be safe"). As you will find out from using it to your advantage, breathing is the best, most obvious, and easiest way to make yourself calm down as quickly as possible.

So let's talk about a way to improve your breathing. While there are many ways to breathe that are helpful, I will describe just one method that has been extremely helpful to me. The one thing that all breathing methods have in common is that such breathing must be "diaphragmatic" breathing. That means that you are not really taking a deep breath unless your diaphragm descends and thus forces your belly to rise (the stuff in your abdomen has to go somewhere when your diaphragm moves downward). To understand what I mean, I suggest you put your hand on your belly and breathe as deeply as you can. If your belly rises naturally from the force of your lungs filling with air and pushing down your diaphragm, then you are taking a diaphragmatic breath.

Many people have difficulty with diaphragmatic breathing at first. Some people force their belly outward even though they have not taken a large breath. Some people simply feel like they can't breathe any more deeply because when a person is in a stressed state it does not feel natural to take large, deep breaths. For some people there is a feeling of self-consciousness because we tend to be very weight conscious in our culture and certainly do not want our bellies to protrude any more than necessary. Other people start to take short quick breaths and can even start to hyperventilate because they are not taking deep breaths. So it is very important to make sure that you are taking as much air as possible into your lungs. Let the air in your lungs push out your stomach. You may even find it easier to push out your stomach first to make sure your diaphragm has moved. When you become comfortable, you will see how it is natural to simply pull down your diaphragm to suck air deeply into your lungs.

Once you get the feeling for a diaphragmatic breath, I want you to try taking such a breath by inhaling through your nose and then exhaling through your mouth (if you're congested, just use your mouth—remember, it's the diaphragmatic nature of the breathing that's most important, not the exact way you breathe). Keep your hand on your belly so you will continue to monitor the depth of your breathing. Now as you breathe in through your nose and out through your mouth, I want you to try to get into an easy, slow, and natural rhythm. Within your rhythm, notice a sensation of floating when you inhale and then a feeling of sinking as you exhale. In and floating . . . out and sinking. In and floating . . . out and sinking, all in a nice, slow, comfortable rhythm. Try floating like a helium balloon and sinking like a lead weight. Or if it suits you better, float on top of a wave as it gently carries you, and let yourself sink as the wave gently passes. As you get yourself into a comfortable pattern, you will see that you are now much more relaxed than you were when you started.

What I will now ask you to do will really sound like overkill, but it generally proves to be helpful. The primary goal in learning to breathe better is that you start noticing your shallow breathing naturally, and then do something about it so that you keep yourself calm and relaxed. The feeling of shallow breathing needs to become a trigger for making you breathe. So what I want you to do is take at least six deep, diaphragmatic, breaths every half hour on the half hour for the next three days. That's right, every half hour on the half hour for three days. Please do not hold yourself to this pattern in an obsessive fashion. If you are a typical person, you are going to forget many times over the next three days. When that happens, just pick it up again and try to stay on track. The purpose, remember, is simply to make you as aware as possible of your shallow breathing. If you monitor your breathing frequently over the next three days, you will start to notice shallow breathing whenever it occurs. When you notice it, you will become accustomed to fixing it.

Noticing shallow breathing is the absolute best you can do. You will never be able to prevent shallow breathing all of the time. If you do become a master of your breathing at all times, you are probably not human. To be alive is to react to your environment. Breathing can simply help you stay as relaxed as possible when you do notice that your breathing has become shallow. If you use this tool frequently and well, however, you will soon find that you are preventing debilitating tension in your life. If you get aches in your body, including headaches and stomach aches, you will notice that they occur much less frequently. You will even notice that sometimes you are able to rid yourself of these aches, especially headaches, after they already exist (although that is much more difficult).

After reading this article, I hope you will make good use of breathing as a tool. If you do, you will notice that you will use it for the rest of your life. It will likely become a cornerstone of your effort at wellness and well-being. Breathing, of course, is absolutely necessary in staying alive. So why not breathe in life itself? Breathe it in deeply and serenely. And while you fill your lungs with oxygen, you may find yourself freer from the tension that had once limited you in so many ways. You may have noticed in your life that people tend to react to you in a calmer fashion when you are calm. Becoming more relaxed can have advantages you never knew were possible. With freedom from excessive tension, you might just find yourself fulfilling your potential as you have always wanted and had hardly ever imagined. With more freedom from tension, you might just find life opening itself up to you in ways for which you'd always merely dreamed.

CHAPTER 17

❧

Be Your Own Best Friend

"One must learn to love oneself . . . with a wholesome and healthy love, so that one can bear to be with oneself and need not roam."

—Nietzshe

What would you do if your very best friend, your BFF, was in real trouble? You know how it can go sometimes. A lover breaks up with you and you think maybe you're an ugly loser. Or maybe you're struggling to find a job, and no one seems to want you. Maybe it's just one of those periods when it seems like everything is difficult, and you think it's because of who you are. You start to doubt everything you once thought you knew. Have you had some times like that? Well, imagine that's your best friend now. Maybe it's even worse. Maybe your friend has always felt uncomfortable. It could be nervousness or depression, and your friend reveals that they've always felt that way. Let's say your friend has problems in the family and/or financial trouble. Maybe your friend has been victimized, or is being victimized in some intolerable way.

What would you do for your friend? You would listen and show you care. Right? You'd likely buy them some comforting things that would make them happy; or you'd likely cook them a wholesome, hearty meal. I'll bet you would give them a warm hug and hold them tight—try to radiate your warmth and love right into their very bones. You'd try to make them feel like their ex-lover was the loser or that the potential employers who'd passed them over had made a truly stupid mistake. You'd certainly reinforce their self worth in every way possible. You'd let them know how valuable they are to you and to others. You'd try to build them up and get them moving. You'd want them to exercise. You'd want them to feel strong. You'd want them to make sure they know they can do what may become necessary if they need to change their lives.

Of course all that is true. You know you would do all that for your best friend. So here is my question, and you have to take this question very seriously. Why the heck don't you do all that for you? It might sound strange, but you should be your own best friend. For sure you're going to be there for the rest of your life. So be your own BFF. You have to. It's the only thing you could do that really makes sense.

Now I know treating yourself like you're your own best friend sounds like it could be selfish. Or maybe it just seems like you can't do for yourself like you can do for a friend. But why not? How can anyone be more important to you than you? You feel your own pain, but if you're like most other caring people, you pay more attention to the pain you empathize with in others than you do to your own. Most people will get angry to protect themselves or retreat when they're sad, but they never think about caring for themselves in a deeply nurturing way. That depth of aid and tenderness most people reserve for others. They don't even dream of doing it for themselves. Many of these truly loving people feel isolated and especially alone, which makes it especially difficult to overcome their sadness, fear, and shame. If you are thinking that being your own best friend sounds crazy, I can tell you something that is much more disturbed. It's far, far more disturbed to refuse to be your own best friend.

Not only should you, but you really need to be your own best friend. Even if you think you should care for your own children before you care for yourself, that does not make sense. If you've ever flown on a commercial airplane you've heard what the flight attendants say as they speak their mandatory safety spiel. They emphasize very clearly that, if the oxygen masks descend, parents must put the masks on themselves before putting the masks on their children. That's right; you are of no use to your own children unless you care for yourself first. You are also not of much use to anyone else unless you care for yourself first. You have to nurture and care for you if you want to care for and nurture others.

But that is not the only reason you should take good care of yourself. It just simply makes sense that you should care for yourself a lot. Unless you care for yourself adequately, you won't stand up for yourself when you're with others, either friends, family members, or co-workers. If you don't have the proper respect for yourself, why should anyone else? You need to keep in mind why you're great, and if you're having trouble figuring that out, you need to look a little more thoroughly. You need to be very serious about the impact the world has on you because you deserve to be treated in a way that is consistent with how truly great you are. One of the funny things about greatness in a person is that it's usually the greatest people who have a hard time recognizing how great they are. One of the reasons they are so great is that they don't think they are (But don't worry about getting completely full of yourself. Those who don't treat themselves with great care typically don't have it in themselves to ever become self-centered, selfish, and grandiose).

So if you can think of what you'd do for your very best friend, or perhaps even your dear children, certainly you can figure out what to do for you. That's right! When you're having a hard time, you need to do the things you know would make a person like you feel better. If you like tea and a bath, you have to have some tea and pour a bath. Maybe you need to make yourself a good, hearty, meal, or a delicious bowl of chicken soup. Maybe you need to tell yourself to get going and get things done because you know you feel better when you're active. Sure you're going to show yourself the ways in which you know you're a winner. You could list out the great experiences in your life. You could also remember those times when others seemed to love you most and let yourself feel, and soak up, that love. Perhaps, with just a little effort, you'll be able to conjure up those emotions you experience when you imagine what others must have been thinking about you when they were loving you up so much. If you've done some things about which you're not proud, maybe you need to decide to change those kinds of actions. But please, please, please give yourself a break about what you've done, especially if, and this is usually the case, the person who was most damaged by what you did was you.

In short, you need to be your own best friend. You need to be for yourself the nurturing parent you have in your heart. You need to hug yourself and give yourself that warmth we all so badly need. You need to be able to rely upon yourself to always be there for you. You can be your own best friend and feel resilient and loved. You will be able to get over any kind of trouble with knowledge that everything is going to be okay. You'll know that you'll be able to take care of yourself and your loved ones and you'll be able to get along without things, or certain others, when times get tough. You'll see that what others think about you doesn't matter much compared to what you think about yourself. If you can be there for you, you will never feel alone. If you can truly, deeply, be there for you, you will accomplish perhaps the greatest possible psychological achievement of all: you will have become your very own best friend.

CHAPTER 18

❧

The "Big What If . . ." Stress Management for Tough Times

"All you need is love . . ."

—John Lennon

When all we've worked hard to build seems threatened by the times, how do we keep going? How do we deal with all the stress of losing everything? A lot of folks have been asking those kinds of questions lately. We tend to like nice things and comfort. We want to know that everything is going to be okay. But sometimes it seems there just might be a chance that things won't be okay, like we're holding on by a thread or that the thin cracks we've been diligently patching might open into gaping fissures. Sometimes, it seems like the bottom might literally fall out and we'll be left groundless, plunging into a nosedive, wildly out of control.

Perhaps in merely reading those many metaphors for these commonly felt emotions, a slight panic began to well up inside of you. In writing them, I know such feelings were not completely alien to my experience. In fact, maybe the most important thing to say in this article, before imparting any particular advice, is that no one is immune to these feelings. We work hard to have things a certain way because we want some kind of security against these feelings. But when that security is threatened, of course we get scared. It would not be normal not to be scared. Nevertheless, when things are truly out of our control there has to be something we can do. Maybe, at the very least, we can establish a particular attitude toward our circumstances that will help us get through.

Since you have likely already been inundated with ways to deal with stress, I will leave that part of this article simple. It is absolutely true that dealing with stress requires that you take good care of yourself. You need to use relaxation techniques, eat right, exercise, and balance your commitments wisely. But when things get really rough and seemingly way out of control, there is something you must do for yourself that goes well beyond balancing things in your life. You have to ask yourself the question that I call the "Big What If . . ."

The "Big What If . . ." is the question that helps you sort out things, people, and values that are really important in your life. It helps you understand what it is that you really need and what's just fluff. It helps you understand who is truly important to you and who it is you're trying to impress. In a way, it helps you figure out who you are and what it is about life that makes life valuable to you.

The "Big What If . . ." you ask to yourself. In this case, the question is, what if I lost all my worldly possessions? The "Big What If . . ." can also be used to help you deal with other horrifying eventualities like the possibility of becoming ill or injured or a loved one becoming ill or injured. It can even be used for worries like, "what if my spouse stops loving me?" or "what if my children stop calling?" When we're thinking about tough economic times, however, it's important to limit our discussion to those things that we have accomplished or built up specifically for the purpose of protecting ourselves or making our lives secure. Those other noneconomic categories can be especially scary because they're hardly in our control at all, but when we're threatened with losing the things over which we did think we had control, a whole different kind of thinking is necessary.

So what if you did lose everything you've worked so hard for? Imagine yourself as poor as you could possibly be. You'll have to think about where you'll stay and what you'll eat. Will you even find warmth at night? How often will you be comfortable? You'll have to think about what kind of clothes you'd wear. Will they keep you warm? Will other people like how you look? How are your kids going to take it? Will your spouse still love you?

What are some possible answers to those questions? Maybe you'll live with family members or friends. Maybe none of them would have you. Maybe you'll work at McDonalds. Maybe you'll need to work two jobs. You might even have to have your kids working. Your clothes might be more comfortable but less flattering. You might find yourself burning some of your possessions for warmth. Is it possible that your spouse won't be able to stay with you? Could your kids go live with someone else while you seek some kind of itinerant work? Maybe your kids will blame you.

The final question to be asked in all this is the most important, and it's the one that will determine whether or not the "Big What If . . ." works for you. The question is, if all those terrible things happen, will you be all right? Is the essential you someone who would be okay if you lost all your worldly possessions? This is a question about values. When I ask myself these questions, I don't exactly feel comfortable. I'm not saying that it would be just great if I had nothing. I like a decent house and car. I look forward to my cup of coffee every morning. I want to have comfortable clothing. I love to give my children gifts and bring home flowers for my wife. But when I ask myself the "Big What If . . ." I need to recognize those things that I really prize. If I do recognize those things, maybe it's possible to see that I do have some control over their quality, especially if I can look to the future knowing these are the things that I will really need if I do in fact lose everything.

Even if I have to live with friends, which would be embarrassing and uncomfortable, at least I can know that I'll have friends. I know that no matter what I have to do, my wife and children will eat and be comfortable before I will allow such comforts for myself. I guess my personal value there suggests I'll keep them around me no matter what. I've got a lot of cheap, washable clothes that don't look so good, but they don't have to go to the dry cleaner either, so maybe I'll figure out a way to make them last. I could walk anywhere I really need to go. Right?

The answer to the "Big What If . . .," regardless of who you are, will always come back to the people you love. If you lose everything, what you're really going to need is your connection to others. You're going to need to give it, and you're going to hope to receive it. You may look upon yourself as a "good for nothing loser," but you'll need loved one's to see that you're as great as you've ever been. Your spouse and children might get ground down in thinking about how hard life has become. They will need you to provide the comfort you have in your heart much more than any comfort you could have provided from your pocket book. Will you be all right? The answer is a resounding yes, if you are spending the proper time taking care of those you love and who love you.

Now I'm just guessing, but I think most likely you didn't think it could get quite as bad as some of what was evoked above. That's the great thing about the "Big What If . . . ." If you take the process seriously, you will almost always surface from it saying to yourself "there's no way it's going to get that bad." If it's not going to get that bad, and you figure out that you'd be okay even if it did get that bad, then your worst fears are no longer a nightmare. The truth is, you can handle a lot. You probably already have, and whether or not you lose everything, you'll handle a lot while progressing into the future. Losing all your material possessions is not a life-or-death situation. Life can get much harder and you'll still have your life. In fact, if you're taking proper care to foster and nurture your current relationships, maybe if you lose everything, you'll find out you've really got something special. Maybe, just maybe, you'll find you have more with nothing than you've ever thought you had before.

CHAPTER 19

❧

The Writing Cure

"There is nothing to writing. All you do is sit down at a typewriter and bleed."

—Ernest Hemingway

Writing is an amazing psychological tool. Many people write on a daily basis to help them keep abreast of some semblance of continuity within their lives. It helps them put together and make sense of things that sometimes seem nonsensical, and it helps them get in touch with feelings from deep within. Writing is a natural way to unleash one's creative flow. Although words were developed for communication, when we write, it often seems we communicate first and foremost with ourselves. As such, writing is a marvelous way to make sense of ourselves and our lives. Writing is also invaluable in some much more specific ways. For getting to sleep, and for working through upsetting or traumatic experiences, writing works wonders. Although writing is a powerfully versatile tool for maintaining mental health in so many ways, the focal point of this article will be these more specific uses of writing for insomnia and for trauma.

Writing for Insomnia

So many people these days use sleep aids for insomnia, but many really wish they didn't have to. Maybe you really don't have to! It's amazing how easy it is to get words out of your mind and onto paper. In a way, it's really just a simple trick of the mind. Our minds work to integrate experience. So when we're overfocusing on something at night, apparently our mind is afraid we won't be able to integrate what we're thinking into our overall experience. On the other hand, as long as we ensure that we won't forget what we're thinking about, our mind will often trust that we will take care of integrating later. That's the trick. You may not know it, but your mind just wants to make sure you won't forget. So for insomnia, in most circumstances you need only write out what's on your mind to free your mind for sleep.

Insomnia can seize us because we're excited about something almost as much as because we're worried. We might be planning all sorts of details or we might be challenging ourselves with the most indecipherable problems. We might be fantasizing with anticipation about some fantastic upcoming event or an accomplishment we see emerging upon our horizon. We might also be dreading a necessary or feared confrontation. Or perhaps our financial situation has us dreading every bill and searching for ways to overcome our debts. Whatever it is that's on our mind, a pen and pad can help us get it off, because our mind is often willing to let it go, as long as we are willing to write it down.

So here is the method for writing yourself to sleep: approximately fifteen minutes prior to bedtime, start to write everything that's on your mind. Write your list of things to do, perhaps, but also write down everything else you can think of related to that list. Write down why it's important. Write down how you feel about it. Anything you think you might need to think about that list, or anything else that might be on your mind, write it all down. This might require pages and pages of writing. Keep writing until you have nothing left to write. Now, go to bed.

If you're still awake in thirty minutes, make yourself get up and write again. You will not want to get up. You will most likely decide that this writing thing is an exercise in futility. Maybe you'll even convince yourself that you're almost asleep. Nevertheless, if you're still awake in thirty minutes, and you want this method to work, make yourself get up. Get up and write.

Anything that was on your mind while you were still trying to sleep, write it now. Often you will need to write down more about the emotions related to what you are thinking. Write down the reason you think you are still thinking. What is so upsetting or exciting about what you're thinking? Write it down. If there is unfinished business related to what you're thinking about, write down how you'll handle it. Why is the unfinished business so important to you and what will be others' reactions to how you'll handle it? If it's going to be hard to handle, why will it be so difficult? Write it down. Keep writing. It might require pages and pages. Keep writing until you have nothing left to write. Now, go back to bed.

Repeat this process until you go to sleep, no matter how many times you must get up. It might seem like this method is burdensome, but it's certainly not as irksome as a night full of insomnia. Many people go whole nights without sleeping. Sometimes what little sleep is accomplished is needlessly restless and brings absolutely no refreshment. Writing everything you think, regardless of the number of times you need to get up and write again, will assure that you get restful and refreshing sleep. Not only will you gain salutary repose, but you will undoubtedly also gain some clarity in your thinking, develop wonderful plans, and maybe even, through your writing experience, discover novel insights.

Keep It and Keep It to Yourself

Before moving on to using writing for painful experiences and trauma, it is important to mention a couple of things. The first is simple. You should not ever throw away what you write until you're 100% sure that those thoughts will not keep you awake. As soon as you throw them out, of course, your mind is quite likely to begin thinking those same thoughts again.

The second thing I need to mention makes holding on to what you write much more difficult. That is, you might find the things you write would be shameful if others saw them. The nature of our strongest emotions is often not very pretty. We generally don't like people to even see us fretting or incensed. We desperately don't want them to see what we're actually thinking when we're overwhelmed by worry or anger. An added caution to writing for insomnia, or for any other mental health reason, thus, is that you'd be best off if no one ever sees what you write. So feel free to keep it personal. Even your closest confidante need not see what you write when you're writing for your psyche. But also, please don't be ashamed. While there might be certain thoughts that suggest you need to go speak with someone (like thoughts of hurting yourself or others), your thoughts and feelings are yours. I do not know of one single person who, for any reason, should share with others every emotion experienced.

The Writing Cure

For dealing with trauma, or painful memories, or for any issue in your life that might be upsetting you, writing can be used more specifically to relieve long held fears and self doubts as well as to make sense of emotionally baffling ordeals. Before moving on, however, there is one serious caveat about dealing with traumatic experience alone and on one's own. When post-traumatic stress disorder (PTSD) develops, one's psyche often hangs in a precarious balance. One's emotions are in utter turmoil as a struggle ensues between warding off, and integrating, painful experience. Anything that evokes feelings about, or similar to, an initial trauma, can send one spiraling free-fall through the trauma once again, as though it's occurring right now! If you believe you might have PTSD (please see article "Post-traumatic Stress Disorder), or anything similar to PTSD, please consult a therapist prior to using the following writing method. This method is designed to help you get straight to the problem, but it does not ensure that you will do so slowly and safely. Only an experienced professional can adequately guide those with PTSD at the proper rate and depth to ensure that the treatment of the trauma is not traumatic in itself.

To deal with traumatic experiences or memories we generally need to face our fears about them, reprocess them, and form new insights and beliefs about ourselves in relation to the trauma. Painful experience, including embarrassment and shameful events, accidents involving danger to ourselves or our loved ones, memories of others treating us in ways that were uncomfortable or insulting, and experiences that resulted in a loss of confidence, as well as any other kind of emotionally wrenching circumstance, results in a conflict between one's need to avoid pain and one's need to integrate experience. We naturally avoid things that hurt us, much like we would avoid sticking our hand into a garbage disposal. On the other hand, we need to integrate all the things that happen to us so that we can maintain an ongoing sense of who we are (for a fuller discussion, see the "Post-traumatic Stress Disorder" article). These two biological imperatives, *avoiding pain* and *integrating experience*, come into conflict when painful events make it difficult to move on.

In working with traumatic experiences while writing, much can be learned from a large variety of therapies that encourage integration of memories and emotions by connecting logical thought and verbal knowledge with impressionistic thought, including body sensations and our emotions. After traumatic experiences, a person typically separates the thoughts about the trauma from the emotions, images and body sensations experienced when the trauma occurred. By separating thoughts, emotions, images and body sensations related to a trauma, the effects of the trauma can be delayed, and the pain of the trauma can be denied. Unfortunately, as indicated above, traumatic experiences have a way of pushing to be recognized and integrated because integration is so important in understanding ourselves. The effects of a traumatic experience become far more damaging because they have not been fully integrated and processed, and they push their way back into experience against the will of the victim. By using the techniques in these integration therapies while writing, thoughts, feelings, and images from the past can be integrated, and then given new, healthier, meanings that actually help a person move forward in life.

The entire process presented here should be performed over a three day period. Each day should be given time to sink in. Specific writing duration will vary, but serious consideration will require a minimum of forty-five minutes per day, and each day will likely require much more time than that. If any part of the exercise seems to cause significant discomfort, do not complete the exercise. The experience of significant discomfort suggests you are working on something much more important than simply a problem from your past, and that the trauma you are attempting to address is so significant that a therapist should be involved. If you need to ask, "What is 'significant' discomfort?" you are probably experiencing "significant" discomfort.

Day One

Writing with this technique begins with "resourcing," which is discovering resources within yourself to counteract those feelings that are bringing you down. In order to deal with traumatic experiences, a person must first develop a place to turn within their mind where they know they will be safe. To find your safety, you must begin developing an image of a person with whom you have felt nurtured, safe and truly cared for. Finding such a person might take some doing. You might need to write a list of people with whom you have felt that way, and then number them from most comforting and nurturing to least (the inability to confidently identify a powerfully nurturing resource person is another sign that you need to seek a psychotherapist). Once you have confidently identified your "resource," imagine yourself with that person. Notice everything about what it's like to be with that person.

(The next three paragraphs will be revisited within each day of the exercise and thus are numbered 1, 2, and 3.)

1. Notice everything you see—everything far and near, in front of you and behind you, to your left and right, above and below you. Notice every shading of light, every contour, every texture, every movement, every color. Take your time and write it all down. Now, notice everything you hear—every sound both far and near, in front of and behind you, to your left and right, above and below you. Notice loudness and softness, rough sounds and soft sounds, high pitched and low pitched sounds, the contour of sound, everything you hear. Take your time and write it all down. Now, notice everything you smell—sweet smells and salty smells, the smell of clean or the smell of dirt, green smells and brown smells, earthy smells and smells of objects, pungent smells and musty smells, everything you smell. Take your time and write it all down. Now, notice everything you taste, clean tastes, metallic tastes, tastes of food or candy or drink, the taste of air, the taste of water, everything you taste. Write it all down. Now, notice everything you feel—notice the feeling of your skin and your clothing or other fabrics/objects touching your skin,

notice warmth and coolness, texture and weight. Notice how your head feels, your hands, your feet, your legs, your belly. Notice how your back feels, and notice the feeling in your throat, neck, and chest. Notice the feeling in your face. Write down anything and everything you observe about how you feel.

2. Now, ask yourself, what does this experience mean about me? The fact that it has occurred means something about who you are. It means something about who you are in the context of it happening. It seems to mean something about who you are right now. Mold the meaning of the experience into a definitive statement. What you write must be a statement of fact. Do not attempt to consider how true you think it is. This person you imagine with you, the way they're treating you, the fact that you two are having this experience together, the fact that it is possible for you to experience this feeling—it means something about who you are. Write it down. Write several various meanings down and then pick the one that seems most important.

    Examples of common definitive statements that emerge while *resourcing* are:

    -   I am a wonderful, well-loved person.
    -   I am truly important.
    -   I make people feel good.
    -   I am funny.
    -   I am brave.
    -   I have good ideas.
    -   The world is mostly safe.
    -   I can keep myself and/or my family safe.
    -   I am important.
    -   I'm special.
    -   I am great at _____.

3. Now, focus on that thought. Focus on that thought while putting yourself back in the original image with the feeling and that thought. It is of utmost importance that you combine, to the best of your ability, these three elements. Focus on *the*

thought, in the *experience*, while *feeling the body sensations* you imagine or imagined occurring at that time. Keep imagining for several minutes, or until something important occurs to you, and then write that down. Whatever is foremost on your mind, write that down. If your mind wanders to something else related to the thought, the image or the feeling, let yourself focus on that for several minutes, or until something important occurs to you, and then write that down. If your mind wanders to something unrelated to the thought, image or the feeling, go back to focusing on the original image, thought and feeling that you are now attempting to focus upon. Write down whatever you are focusing on related to the image, thought and feeling. Keep writing until you feel you have written as much as you can about that experience with that particular thought.

Adequate resourcing can require several sessions or days of writing. Before delving deeper into your problems, it's extremely important that you know where in your mind to turn when things get rough. Quite often, the process of resourcing is in itself significantly transformative. Take your time with this part of the writing cure. You will enjoy it and will glean endless therapeutic advantages.

Day 2

On Day 2 you will write about something that upsets you. Focus on a troubling event. Begin with an event or experience that was somewhat, but not extremely, upsetting. You will want to become familiar with this process prior to tackling the more traumatic memories (once you have mastered the process, you will be able to work on more difficult experiences). Contemplate the event. Think about what that experience meant to you. Why was it so upsetting? Be very careful. If you are properly resourced, you will notice that extremely difficult experiencing during this process will sometimes result in movement to your resource. When you are not too upset, challenge yourself to stay with the upsetting memory, and try to remember all the details and write them down. Now start to work on the first paragraph in "Day 1."

When you feel you have fully remembered the incident using paragraph 1, move on to paragraph 2, but now focusing on a negative statement about yourself related to this upsetting experience. Examples of typical negative statements about oneself which originate in upsetting experiences are as follows:

- No one likes me.
- I'm not good at anything.
- No one has ever loved me.
- No one will ever understand me.
- I'm just a fearful, weak person.
- I hurt those I love.
- I must take care of everyone before myself.
- I might as well not get close to anyone because I will get hurt.
- I am completely ordinary.
- The world is uncontrolled chaos.
- Life is unfair.
- There's no way to keep myself and/or my family safe.
- I am a constant disappointment.
- I can't do anything right.
- I am completely alone.

Once you have chosen a negative statement that seems to represent a strong feeling you have about yourself, move on to paragraph 3 from "Day 1" above. Be careful during this step. When you match this negative thought with the image and the feelings in your body, you will likely begin to experience the most difficult aspects of the original incident. You must be able to handle that level of distress in order to achieve some benefit. If you start to wonder if you can tolerate this experience, that likely means you should cease the exercise and not try to tolerate it. However, if you are able to handle the emotions evoked, feeling upset is an essential element of this process. Again, it is important to realize that extreme trauma must be handled with the help of a trained therapist.

After you feel you have written as much as you can about the bad experience, and associated it with the negative thought, return to your resourcing image of a kind and nurturing person. Complete the writing exercise from paragraph 1 again with your resource, again writing down all the new thoughts and associations that come to mind.

Day 3

On day 3 you will replace the negative thought from day 2 with a positive, preferable thought. The positive thought is typically related to the negative thought, although not always directly. Pick the positive thought as what you would have liked to think about yourself within that traumatic context. That thought will mean something positive about you. It will mean something positive about who you are right now. Mold this new meaning of the experience into a definitive statement. What you write must be a statement of fact. Do not attempt to consider how true you think it is. It must be a possibility and it must be how you'd like to think of yourself related to that situation. Write it down. Write several various meanings down and then pick the one that seems most essential to who you know you could be. When you find the right positive thought, begin with paragraph 1 from "Day 1" above, imagining the bad experience, but now with the positive and preferable thought, and allowing yourself to experience whatever feelings arise. Then move on to paragraph 3 above (skipping paragraph 2), using the positive thought throughout the process, writing down every new thought that emerges.

Examples of positive, preferred thoughts that might coincide with the negative thoughts above are as follows:

- I am well-liked by many in spite of what some think vs. No one likes me
- I do have many skills vs. I'm not good at anything
- I know I am loved vs. No one has ever loved me
- Many people really want to know me vs. No one will ever understand me
- Many things I do are very brave vs. I'm just a fearful, weak person
- I always try my best for others vs. I hurt those I love
- It's okay to be good to myself vs. I must take care of everyone before myself
- Even if people sometimes hurt me, I'm strong enough to handle it vs. I might as well not get close to anyone because everyone will hurt me
- I need to let people see the real me vs. I am completely ordinary

- Although there's no way to control everything, I can keep most things together vs. The world is uncontrolled chaos
- If I work hard and treat others fairly, things will mostly be fair in life vs. Life is unfair
- I can take precautions for myself and/or my family that will keep me/us safe vs. There's no way to keep myself and/or my family safe
- I like what I do vs. I am a constant disappointment
- I am a valuable person vs. I can't do anything right
- There are many people who care about me vs. I am completely alone

Day 3 again ends with returning to your resource image and paragraph 1 from "Day 1," the positive thought from the resource experience, and the feeling from that image. All written once again to reify the strength of that image.

The Day 3 process is the final step in reprocessing and integrating a hurtful or traumatic event. Your resource, now installed securely within you, helps modulate the hurtful feelings from experiences that cannot be seen as positive. With the pain of the original experience far less overwhelming than it had been, since it has now been confronted, more moderate thinking is clearly sensible. The reprocessing of the event can also now be generalized so that future experiences are seen more realistically, benignly and constructively. The pain of the event that had previously caused us to be overly sensitive, and which had caused reactionary impulses in us, can now be fully integrated to help inform our understanding of the world and our lives, but not in such a way as to overwhelm. Where once our guarded thinking influenced by that negative event was an obstacle to growth, stunted our perspective on life and relationship, etched blind spots into our psyche preventing us from perceiving situations for what they were, and kept us focused only on the meaning of those situations as our pain permitted, the writing cure frees one to think more flexibly, and with each trouble confronted, brings writing cure adherent one step closer to the ultimate goals of authenticity and self-actualization.

CHAPTER 20

ℭℬ

Assertiveness: The 30% Solution

"Real firmness is good for anything; strut is good for nothing."

—Alexander Hamilton

The concept of assertiveness is not well understood. Most people know what it is by knowing what it's not. That is, to most people it means not being aggressive and not being passive. Of course, everyone also knows it is supposed to be a good thing. But what really constitutes an assertive response and why is it so important?

To be assertive is to be aware of, and communicate, your true wishes, desires, disappointments, and frustrations, while weighing the impact of those feelings on the others around you. There are two main ways that people fail to be assertive. First, some people simply do not let others know what they want or what upsets them because they are afraid of what others might think. Such a person is known as "passive." Second, some people just seem to take whatever they want, and get mad whenever they don't get what they want, while giving no thought to the effect their actions have on others. This person is known as "aggressive." Both of these styles lead to significant unhappiness. The passive person feels others take advantage of them, and generally experiences life to be unfair. The aggressive person, on the other hand, never develops any genuine closeness with others, and experiences life as good only to the extent that they are able to take from life what they want.

Life seems like an uphill battle, a constant struggle, to the passive person. He is constantly doing favors, trying his hardest, hiding his anger or sadness, and attempting to be the "best" person he can be. But when most people around him don't understand how he feels, or when they think his feelings can wait based on how he's acting, then these others assume that their feelings can take priority. If he says what he thinks and feels, on the other hand, others around the passive person will learn that certain things upset him or make him happy, and that he will take care of himself in making sure he gets what he needs.

To the aggressive person, the current moment seems pretty darned good. To most of us she looks like she's getting everything. And in fact, she will likely lead a very "successful" life to the extent that she's able to get what she wants. Unfortunately, she will rarely feel much better about her life than the passive person. That's because life is about loving and being loved, not power and acquisitions. Power and acquisitions are only very inadequate replacements for love that people learn to acquire when their efforts at love have been thwarted. So the more aggressive and irritable person, who seems to get what she wants, typically has very poor relations with her spouse, siblings, and children. In fact, in the end, the aggressive person often seems much worse off than the passive person. When the material things are gone, no one really wants to stick around.

The solution to either being too passive or too aggressive is assertiveness. In fact, I call assertiveness the "30% solution." I often notice that my clients, many of whom are suffering from depression or anxiety, only get what they truly want about 5% of the time. THAT IS UPSETTING! As discussed above, the passive person rarely gets what he wants because no one even knows that he needs anything. Why would they put off their own needs to accommodate the passive person if they don't even know he wants something? Alternately, the aggressive person seems to get everything she wants in the moment, but her constant chase for winning what she wants occurs because her life seems empty—she is trying to fill herself up before she might experience even an infinitesimal amount of that looming emptiness. Either way, when people make a point of stating their needs, wants, desires, and frustrations in a way that takes the needs of others into account, they can expect to actually get what they need or want about 30% of the time.

It may not seem like it, but getting what you need and want about 30% of the time will make you extremely happy and content. Since each of us is merely an individual amongst millions of others, it should be no surprise that we don't get what we want approximately 70% of the time even when we're assertive. But compare 30% to the 5% level attained by the passive person. The generally happy and content person gets what he wants six times more than the passive person. It is very important to understand that the goal of 30% also helps a person even if she thinks she gets what she wants almost 100% of the time. The aggressive person may think that she is getting what she wants, but the very fact that she is getting what she wants so much of the time actually precludes the possibility of achieving closeness with others. If those around you never get what they want, they certainly are not going to develop a positive relationship with you. Besides, it's not possible to have loving relationships with others who are not our equals, at least as far as respect and equality as human beings is concerned. We can only love someone if we know who they are, and we can only know who they are if they reveal their preferences and desires.

If you are a person who seems to fit in one of the two major categories above, even if only a little bit, start being more assertive today! Half the trick is knowing what you want. The other half is knowing what is influencing others. It just so happens that passive individuals are very good at gauging the emotions and pressures on other people, while aggressive people are generally pretty good at knowing what they, themselves want (at least in the immediate moment). The trick is merely becoming more aware of the half you have not developed, and then making sure that that awareness is clearly shown when you communicate with others. That is, if you don't express your needs, you will not get what you want. If you don't take others feelings and the context of a situation into account, you may get what you want, but your inability to recognize the needs of others will undoubtedly result in loneliness.

Really, it all comes down to realizing that we live in a world of choices and responsibility. If you look at life accurately you will start to see that absolutely everything you do is a choice. You must also recognize, however, that everyone else has a choice as well. Perhaps sometimes we make one choice based on the perceived consequence of making a different choice, and perhaps that makes us feel like we don't have choices, as if the consequence of choosing what we really want is so bad that we have no choice at all. However, you are the one who decides what you do, and the others around you decide what they do too. Everyone should make decisions based on the possible consequences as well as the possible rewards. Knowing you and everyone else are making choices really just makes you a responsible person. If it is your choice to do what you do, you cannot blame someone else for what you do. If you clearly communicate to others that you understand that they can make choices too, then when you express your desires you are simultaneously taking responsibility for your part in the relationship between you.

Assertiveness is merely a way to clearly communicate our awareness of the fact that we live in a world of choices and responsibility. Assertiveness includes making a statement of our own desire or wish (what we would like to do), coupled with a recognition of the other person's likely desire in the same situation (the other person's likely choice) along with a recognition of the context of the situation (the existing possibilities). When we successfully communicate in an assertive way, we often get what we want while also demonstrating how much we care. Most of the time, in fact, assertive communication is appreciated by those around you who want to know your wishes so they can make choices for what they want without feeling like you weren't taken into account. In many circumstances there is tremendous overlap between what people want, which means assertive communication can lead to several people getting what they want at the same time. Maybe then, assertiveness helps mix an even higher octane solution for mutual satisfaction, maybe even a 40% or 50% solution.

So if you're ready for better, more responsible communication, with a much better chance of getting what you want, while simultaneously maintaining positive, caring relationships, then think of assertiveness as a simple equation. It works like this: Assertiveness (A) = (Y) knowing and confidently stating what **You** need and Want + (O) knowing and saying what **Others** need and want + (U) knowing and stating your **Understanding** of the context of the issue over time.

That is, $A = Y+O+U$. With that equation you can put yourself on the road to happiness in relationships and get what you want out of life. So use the equation well and consistently . . . and, good luck in your pursuit of the 30% solution.

PART II

UNDERSTANDING COUPLES AND COUPLES COMMUNICATION

Coupling is at the center of the Great Life Machine. Everyone wants to couple! And the machine won't run without an adequate fit between the two essential and complementary parts at the core. But it's not always so easy to get these parts functioning in unison. Communication breakdown is all too common, and, often, it seems these two cogs run at odds. While two cogs must be complementary in a multitude of ways for there to be any fit at all, complementarity also leads to differences that cause conflicting cross purposes of function. Of course, the vicissitudes of couple life are often trapped within gender differences. More often than not, however, the simple truth is that intimacy is difficult. Coupling challenges us to be vulnerable, caring, loving, and connected but, simultaneously, genuine, striving, strong, and independent. A couple is a team, and as a couple, two people have an unparalleled opportunity to really be there for each other like no one else will. Yet as equals, two people in a couple can each lead down disparate paths, thus pulling apart and often against one another. Coupling is truly complicated. In this part, I hope to shed light within the depths of the Great Life Machine to see how the coupling mechanism at its core can function most smoothly.

The first subsection asks the question, "Can Two Parts Beat as One?" and answers with articles highlighting gender similarities and differences, focusing on acceptance, accommodation, and assertiveness, and understanding how particular ways of relating fit together within the couple unit.

The second subsection peers into the thinking involved in dating and sex and the relation between those experiences and getting serious or committed to another. This subsection, "New Cars, Fast Cars, Backfires, and Crashes" warns against driving too fast, questions what it means to drive, and cautions against driving your comfortable, safe, slow-riding town car as if it's a rough and ready roadster.

In the "tools" section here, the wrench, screwdriver, and hammer are found in various kinds of communication tools. The articles in "Tools for Making Yourself Fully Understood" range from relating that one's viscosity is breaking down or signaling the anticipation of engine failure to a method for simply requesting minor adjustments in the current workings of the machine.

Couples are at the very center of the Great Life Machine. Reproduction occurs in couples as does child-rearing, and thus, obviously, the Great Life Machine is not sustainable without couples. Getting couples working at their best creates happiness in each individual, but also gets the rest of the machine working well, as the smooth functioning of the couple is passed down into healthy functioning within children and, in the greater scheme, within the community.

Section 5

Can Two Parts Beat as One?

Relationships are arduous work! It may not always seem that way at first, but if a couple remains intact for any significant length of time, the work part of love either becomes quite evident or there's not enough differentiation between the partners. The articles in this subsection deconstruct patterns within couple relationships and get to the meat of the question involving why relationships are difficult. In "Women and Men" gender similarities and differences are explained as part and parcel to human evolution with hope of creating better understanding and communication in couples. Healthy functioning within any relationship between equals is examined in "The Three As of Relationship," with an emphasis on the balance between flexibility and staying true to oneself. The issue of togetherness vs. self-motivation is discussed in "Connection and Independence" since it is such a common area of dispute within couples. In the last article of this subsection, "Understanding Personality Styles in Couples," the patterns of relating between various individuals who have developed very specific personality styles is outlined. The "Can Two Parts Beat as One?" subsection focuses primarily on how various cogs have been machined to fit together in very specific ways, but also how that machining (human development) leads to problematic patterns and requires understanding and acceptance.

CHAPTER 21

⊗

Women and Men

"The basic discovery about any people is the discovery of the relationship between men and women."

—Pearl S. Buck

Women and men are clearly very different, but I don't think we're from other planets. In fact, people of all kinds, regardless of gender or race, are a lot more alike than different. Our emotions are derived from the need for love, for companionship and desire, for safety and independence. We're all motivated by success, no matter how differently defined. Loss makes us depressed, whether it be loss of love, loss of hope, or loss of trust. We all like to win. No one likes to lose. Whether or not we're in control, feeling things are within our grasp is generally desirable. We all can feel overburdened with the responsibility of caring, but we all need relationships (to a higher power even when not with others). One thing is absolutely definite on this matter. First and foremost, men and women are earthlings. Nevertheless, it also can't be denied that the roles we've played through time, and by design, make us different too.

We need only extrapolate from the obvious physical differences between the sexes to understand what the psychological differences might be. That is, women bear children and are more naturally soft to the touch while men develop strength and are more naturally rough and coarse. The roles the sexes have played throughout time have clearly been delineated along these lines. Because women bear children and because men are more likely to be bigger, stronger, and faster, each has been more likely to develop psychological characteristics suitable to the roles their biological differences determined for them. No one can know for sure whether these differences in psychological characteristics were innate from the very beginning. But there can be little doubt that gendered personality characteristics exist and that they are either innate or have apparently become biological over time simply due to the force of nature's influence. Human beings develop tendencies over time that make them adapt to the necessities of their environment. Since women have spent more of their time watching over and nurturing their offspring, they developed psychological abilities and tendencies that helped them take care of the home-fire and nurture others. Since men have spent more of their time hunting for meat and protecting the family unit, they developed those psychological abilities and tendencies that helped them hunt for food and guard the family. These appear to be the greatest differences between the sexes.

That is, women are like nurture/nesters and men are like hunter/guardians. Although women are often fantastic at accomplishing tasks, and many women are much better at it than many men, there is a general tendency for most women to be best at those tasks that make use of nesting skills. For example, many times, but not all the time, women are especially skilled at accomplishing tasks because they include, as part of their approach to those tasks, the ability to nurture. Women are much more likely to make good use of encouragement and connection with others within a group setting than are men. Quite often, it is also noticed that women will bring a superior multitasking ability to their work. That too likely derives from the necessity to do many things at once in the process of nesting, which includes child-rearing, making a suitable home, feeding, and preparing for the future. Nesting skills involve nurturing, connection, communication, and making people feel good and understood. Although women do often like independent activities, most activities in which they engage involve direct care for others, and most of their pleasurable activities involve others as well.

Men, on the other hand (and as stated above), are like hunters or guardians. They can be great at child-rearing and nurturing, and many men are much better at it than many women, but there is a general tendency for most men to be better at defining and completing clearly circumscribed tasks as would be necessary in hunting or guarding. Many times, but not all the time, men are especially good at accomplishing group tasks if it is important to specifically manage the role each participant must take. That is, men are more likely to be good at telling people what to do without mincing words or having second thoughts. In a group hunt, or when a group is to protect a community, the ability to see each person's role in an instrumental way would be essential. It can also often be noticed that men are less likely to be distracted in their tasks by the aspects of those tasks that are outside their role. It seems quite likely that designing specific plans, and careful follow through on those plans, are skills that were developed in the process of hunting and guarding, which include protecting the family, providing a home and food, and providing for the future. Hunting skills include "bringing home the bacon," getting things done, meeting goals, and getting people motivated to move forward. Although men do get involved in group activities, it is generally the independence they express, either in groups or while alone, that defines their character, and many of the pleasurable activities in which most men engage do not necessitate the involvement of other people.

Even with all that said (and I hate to repeat myself, but due to the sensitivity of the issue it is likely necessary), it is so important to remember that we are much more alike than different. It is also extremely important to remember that in many individual men and/ or individual women these gendered differences seem to be either completely or almost completely untrue. But these differences do hold true so often that defining them, and developing and understanding them, is essential in helping many couples. People, in general, believe too much that others are just like we are, which actually leads to misunderstandings. If we believe others know they should see something just as we do, and then they do something different, we are far too likely to believe they have purposely done something hurtful even if they truly had the best intentions. With that in mind, what follows are the primary ways that gendered differences are so commonly exhibited within relationships. Understanding these differences can lead to increased understanding where previously certain actions have been thought to be evidence of bad intentions. As will be seen, understanding these differences is often very helpful in developing communication between men and women in relationships.

The most salient difference between the sexes involves their disparate approaches to problem solving. The typical scenario involves the woman seeking acknowledgment and understanding for a problem she's experiencing, as befits her desire for connection. Of course the man, instead of providing the sought after intimate connection that would help his mate feel nourished in her time of need, starts to offer solutions, as befits his desire to get the job done. That is, the man tries to fix the problem instead of understanding his mate's needs. Strangely enough, the man cannot even fathom what could be wrong with offering his solutions. Really and truly, he has the best of intentions. Unfortunately, he just does not see the possibility that listening, connecting, and reassuring are the actual goal. In his mind the goal must be to fix the problem. The woman, on the other hand, may be very upset by the problem she is experiencing, but she either doesn't need a solution because she already assumes it will work itself out, or she simply believes it's part of life and must be tolerated. She may even want to find a solution, but that is not the primary reason for her communication. Mostly, the woman often wants to be able to express how she is feeling so she will be understood by her mate who can offer the connection she seeks, which then soothes her and makes it possible for her to either tolerate the problem or find her own solution. When the man does offer solutions, because the woman does not feel the connection she seeks, his efforts often lead to a breakdown in understanding, the problem is left unsolved, and the woman feels no benefit from her effort at communication.

When a man has a problem, on the other hand, he typically expresses it only because he is announcing his solution to handling the problem. He doesn't want solutions offered any more than the woman does. Unlike women, who at least look to communicate about problems, men will mostly seek alone time when they have a problem. During that alone time, men will often try not to think about the problem, but rather will wait for a solution to come to them spontaneously. When a man does express some kind of problem, and is announcing his solution, women cannot fathom that men are not looking for connection and understanding. Rather, men are more likely looking for recognition and respect, since they are announcing a solution to a very difficult problem they believe they have solved. That the woman tries to offer support is viewed as insulting by the man, similarly to how a woman can often view the man's problem-solving tactics as insulting when she brings up a problem. By offering connection and understanding through her assistance, the woman is experienced by the man as providing the opposite of respect and recognition because the man sees that assistance as a rejection of the solution he has presented. This feeling of rejection within the man often leads to a total breakdown in communication, and thus the woman's bid for connection leads to its opposite, and the man feels his solution is not supported by the woman.

The breakdown in communication men and women experience can often turn to arguing as well. The hunting and nesting view of men and women in relationships is quite instructive in understanding the general patterns of argument between the sexes. How often do men complain, or joke in support of one another, about their mates' amazing ability to remember every hurtful thing their man has ever done? This amazing ability women possess undoubtedly comes from the great import they assign to taking care of their loved one's feelings. Women need to perceive emotions in order to care for them, which thus elevates the importance of emotion. The great understanding of emotions women exhibit may also develop from the need to perceive the relative safety or trustworthiness of those allowed close to offspring or the home. Because emotions are so important in taking care of others and in judging the safety of others and situations, women remember quite well being wronged or hurt. Interestingly, women often do not even believe they have done hurtful things themselves because they believe they try to be so sensitive to others. It's hard for women to believe they could actually hurt others with their opinions and criticisms because their intention in expressing them is to make sure others are cared for, or to teach their man how to be more sensitive to them. For women, the back-drop issue in arguing often involves whether or not they can trust their man to be close to them. Thus their emotions are an essential sensor and tool, and their memory is often directly related to the emotional impact of an event.

When men argue, they typically believe the argument is about the current situation and figuring out what to do about it. The fact that women bring up what the man has done so many times before seems almost immaterial to the man, who looks at this situation as different from all the others. The woman's point about the past is that intimacy in the relationship is being damaged by the repeated bombardment on her ability to trust. She is actually fighting about who the man is or about his character. The man doesn't see that trust is the issue. The man assumes an instrumental view of the circumscribed problem at hand and separates the past from the current situation in order to see things as clearly as he possibly can. In fact, the man's not especially concerned about trust in the moment, and his trust for his mate is much less often brought into question. Although men are certainly concerned about trust, their view of themselves as independent makes them mostly believe they can go it alone, thus making trust a far smaller issue for them. Because the historical view brought out by the woman is, in fact, a challenge to the man's trustworthiness or character, the man does not perceive it as a bid to make him more sensitive, but rather as an attack on his character. Quite often arguments between men and women are not about the topic at hand at all, but rather for the woman it's about not trusting and needing more intimacy which requires trust, and for the man it's about proving the integrity of his character or about not being allowed independence.

The hunters versus nesters dichotomy is also helpful in understanding what makes most men and most women feel good within interactions. As stated above, because men are like hunters or guardians, they look for respect and recognition from their mate as the mainstay of their self-esteem. Nothing makes a man feel better than his mate expressing her feeling that he is a good provider or protector. Expressing the opposite, that a man fails to provide or that he might leave his family vulnerable, sinks a man to the lowest depths.

As a subset to recognition, men view the material things they acquire as prizes for their achievements. In a way, they view gifts as prizes that acknowledge their achievements, and to whatever level they do achieve, they like to give themselves prizes as well. The bigger the prize, the more the man feels he is being recognized as a good hunter or guardian. The prize is often something expensive, but sometimes the biggest prize a man could want is the wife's recognition of his desires and her willingness to satisfy those desires. When men give their mate something that is expensive, they view it as the greatest possible acknowledgment of their mate's worth because big prizes are what they themselves desire. Sometimes a man views as one of his greatest gifts his great attention to detail with respect to satisfying his woman's desires. When women wonder aloud whether their mate truly put any real thought into that fabulously expensive gift just given, or whether their man's desire to satisfy was more for him than them, men cannot understand how their intentions were misunderstood because they truly intended that their gift express the utmost affection, just as a similar gift from the woman would have been interpreted by the man as true appreciation.

Women, on the other hand, look for confirmation of their specialness and want to feel desired and treasured by their mate, thus they aim to reach a deeper intimacy or connection. They want their mate to want to spend time with them, much more than to spend money on them. Nothing makes a woman feel better than when her man extols her singular qualities, her inner beauty and powers of attraction, her special character traits and her unique skills. When a man treats his mate as ordinary or compares her to others who he deems to be similar, when he acts as though she means nothing special to him, a woman's relationship self-esteem withers to nothing.

While men view the big gift as recognition of their achievements, women generally view the thoughtfulness of others as indicating the highest compliment because it demonstrates thinking about their special needs and traits. The more thoughtful a gift or group of gifts given, the more treasured and cherished a woman feels. When a woman gives a man many gifts, each representing a special need or desire she knows he has, she intends him to feel as special as possible. When men wonder if the woman's many gifts suggest avoidance of buying them the one big thing they truly wanted, women cannot understand how their intentions were misunderstood since they truly intended their gifts to express the most perfect understanding of who their mate truly is. Typically, if a woman were to receive a gift similar to the one she gave, she'd feel it was the best gift imaginable. When the man takes each thoughtful part and puts it aside, seeming disappointed that he didn't receive the big gift desired, women are often quick to be hurt for the man's lack of recognition about just how truly special and thoughtful the gift truly was.

The hunting and nesting patterns are often so much a part of male/female relationships, that they actually affect almost every aspect of how men and women view their roles together. It can often be observed that men and women are trying very hard to please one another, but each do it in ways the other can't understand. Men are so goal oriented in their view of relationships that they see pleasing their wife as the primary goal in making their relationship good. But because the man believes pleasing his mate will come from providing and protecting better, moving to a bigger house or a more serene community, he neglects the connection part of the relationship, which includes cherishing and treasuring. Women are so connection oriented in their view of relationships that they see pleasing their husband, not as a goal, but as a way of becoming more connected. The woman offers recognition in the form of wanting to spend time with her man, thinking that her desire to do so expresses the recognition and respect he must want. However, because the woman sees connection as a goal in and of itself, and because while she is connecting she craves true two-way understanding and does not give credence to her mate's need for having light shown on his achievements, she can often neglect the man's need for recognition and respect. Men please women to be good at pleasing, while they fail to connect, and thus fail to please. Women please to connect, but fail to give recognition, and thus fail to please.

The answer to this riddle involves recognizing that men and women truly are different. It is generally the case that we try to communicate with others as though those others feel about things in the same way that we do. But if different people are truly different, and we try to incorporate our understanding of that difference into our communication, we can start to have better relationships. Too often men treat connection or any kind of nesting behavior as unnecessary or relatively unimportant. Too often women treat any kind of independent, goal-directed behavior, or any kind of hunting/guardian behavior as either unnecessary or as de facto parts of life. If men can't see the importance of connection and nesting, they will never understand that their mate's need to be treasured is the number one prize a woman can receive. If women can't see just how hard their mate tries to be that great hunter/guardian and get things done, they will never understand their mate's greatest need, which is to be recognized and respected as a great provider and protector.

On the other hand, if in a relationship members of a couple want to accept that men and women are different, then it becomes possible for them to please one another in just the way that will make each of them get what they truly need from the relationship. If a woman wants to treat her man as the most special person to her, sure she should spend time with him. While she does, however, she should be sure he knows just how much she recognizes his efforts at providing for and protecting the family, and she should do her best to appreciate his independence and his ability to find solutions to difficult problems. Save your time when it comes to gifts. Just get him the big thing you know he really wants or accept and meet his desires as they are without expecting that they always involve connection. If a man wants to give his wife respect and recognition, sure he should spend more time with her. While he does, however, he must be sure she knows just how special she is and how much he treasures her. He must desire a connection with her and make an effort to stay as close with her as possible in seeing the importance of her concerns and valuing her unique way of seeing things.

In short, the correct understanding of the opposite sex leads to a simple solution for healthy relationships. Since men are goal oriented, they must attempt to see their goal as creating a feeling of specialness and intimacy with their mate. Men must attempt to demonstrate how much they treasure their mate, not by bestowing great gifts, but by being as thoughtful as possible. Since women are connection oriented, they must attempt to be as connected as possible with who their mate really is, including his desire for independence and his need for recognition, rather than supposing a good connection with him means he should desire the same kind of closeness as does she. If a man achieves the goal of making his mate feel special, and a woman truly connects with her man as he really is, they might just see together the fact that neither of them is from either Mars or Venus. Nevertheless, although they might not be from Venus or Mars, with the right goal for the man, and the correct kind of connection for the woman, the health of their relationship together might just blossom into other-worldly proportions right here on Earth.

CHAPTER 22

CB

The Three As of Relationship in Couples: Acceptance, Accommodation, and Assertiveness

"When you make the sacrifice in marriage, you're sacrificing not to each other but to unity in a relationship."

—Joseph Campbell

Once you have fallen in love—that is, once you've become infatuated and obsessed with your partner—and once you start slipping into the less tumultuously blissful period of relationship in which you are relating within the pleasant but mundane context of the day to day routines of life, without even knowing it, you start a process of wonder in which you are deciding whether the individual with whom you're spending so much time now is a person with whom you can spend a really long time, or perhaps even the rest of your life. Of course that typically happens without any real thought. In general, people don't like to overthink things, and that's good. Nevertheless, the way this process begins is profoundly important because it will set a pattern that will likely last for the duration of your relationship. If things go well, if you're creating your relationship to last, you'll be either naturally or intentionally making sure your relationship is based in the three As: acceptance, accommodation, and assertiveness.

A good relationship is initially based in "chemical" attraction (perhaps "attraction" should be a fourth "A"). We become infatuated with another and we literally want to be with them all the time. In fact, the process of falling in love follows a prevailing pattern of addiction (please see article "The Dating Fantasy"), except that, within certain bounds, being "addicted" to another person while you're falling in love is doubtlessly the norm. Once the powers of infatuation and desire inevitably simmer down, however, the natural workings of two personalities together begin to solidify into more enduring patterns. Those patterns will either make for lasting relatedness or will dissolve the relationship. Relationships can dissolve due to a pattern of stagnation and entropy (boredom) or a pattern of mutually assured destruction (competition). These patterns of relating most importantly involve the yet to be discovered, but undeniable, differences and similarities between love partners.

A successful relationship is dependent on the presence of two whole people. That means things must be worked out. You know those couples that never argue? Most of the time, those couples are not very healthy. If two people are together constantly, and they never argue, then they are likely in a static pattern in which one of them is typically getting their way and the other is giving in. Although that is a kind of relationship that can last for a long time, it is amazing how often the partner who always gets their way grows bored of the relationship and figures out a way to get out. Of course it's also common for the partner who rarely gets their way to grow dissatisfied and move to dissolve the relationship.

That things must be worked out is actually a good thing. In fact, a truly good relationship exists within the tension that is created between two people who find each other interesting and equal. To remain deeply engaged in a relationship, each person's views must be considered important and valid. Because no two people are the same, those important and valid viewpoints will frequently differ. If two people do not differ enough, they will grow bored. It would be almost as if both people are one person. There can be no relationship if there is only one person. On the other hand, two people need be only sufficiently challenging to one another in their differences. Either too much difference, or more importantly, too little ability to accept the validity and importance of the other's view, will lead to competition and the dissolution of the relationship.

For a love relationship to be healthy, then, partners need to see their differences and accept those that are tolerable. As part of that acceptance, there often must be accommodation. If one partner likes to engage in an activity that does not include the other partner, that must be allowed to the extent that it is feasible. If one partner likes to discuss an area of interest that does not naturally grab the interest of the other, the other certainly can try to find the topic interesting so that ideas can be shared. This process of *a*cceptance and *a*ccommodation accordingly involves each partner negotiating their wants and needs in an *a*ssertive way (the three A's). To be assertive, a person must take their own needs and desires seriously and then weigh them in the context of the entire situation and relationship. That is, one's own needs and desires should be assertively presented with knowledge of what is possible and fair given that one's partner's needs and desires must also be considered.

Each partner, therefore, must weigh their love of the partner against those characteristics in their partner that are more or less difficult to tolerate. If one partner has a need that is not recognized by the other, the need should be stated. If one partner has difficulty tolerating a behavior or attitude of the other, that too can be stated. Whether needs, wants, and preferences are stated has to be considered within the context of understanding the effect such a statement would have on the partner. One's own level of need has to be weighed against the possible negative aspects of making the need known. If the need or preference is powerful enough, it should be stated even if the impact of stating it could cause significant conflict. If that need, desire or preference is strong enough to chance ending the relationship, it should be stated even if it might end the relationship. On the other hand, not everything needs to be stated. If a need, desire, or preference might hurt one's partner so much that it could be devastating to them, and one prefers to tolerate that need or preference without having it solved or even acknowledged because it is not important enough to cause that much pain, then, of course it should be tolerated and not stated. As partners, we decide to accept who our partner is and then accommodate them where necessary. We also expect them to accept us and accommodate us where necessary. If we love each other enough, this process should be easy, right?

So why does it seem to be so difficult? The fact is, people generally believe a few things that make the three A's very difficult. For one, we believe that others should see things the way we do because we are "right." We also expect others to do things the way we do them because we do things "right." Of course, there are relatively few ways of seeing things or doing things that everyone agrees are "right," so part of accepting and accommodating requires a commitment to thinking in more flexible ways. You may have noticed the word "preference" is used or inferred many times throughout this article. "Preference" is used so much within this article because most of what we think we need is merely an indication of what we prefer. Nevertheless, it tends to be very difficult to see what we think are needs as though they are preferences, so it is very difficult to commit ourselves to more flexible thinking. Although there are so many different personality types that it may seem silly to try to outline specific traits that generally give people trouble, there are two primary ways of being that are repeatedly exhibited in couples with communication problems.

Most commonly, when people are thinking they are "right" within their style (to such an extent that they have trouble with the three A's), they are either especially obliging or especially authoritative. Obliging people often expect others to give to them as much as they give others, even though they give without others asking. That is, they don't expect to have to ask for others to do for them since they don't require others to ask of them. These individuals are sure that everyone should have a generous spirit and give willingly even with little suggestion that anything is needed. Obliging individuals try to anticipate the needs of others and meet those needs, sometimes even before the other realizes they may need something. Interestingly, the obliging person would never agree that they want anything from others. Believing that about themselves does not fit with their own idea that they are very generous and giving. But because they believe they are "right" in having such a generous spirit, they assume it would be "right" for others to anticipate their needs. Unfortunately, obliging people also do not argue that their needs should be anticipated because that too would not fit with the ideal of being generous and giving. However, if the obliging person can be shown that they're working this way in relationship, they often can change and start asking for what they want. These individuals are often viewed by others as passive and need to become more assertive. In becoming more assertive, they often need to amplify the legitimacy of their own feelings and preferences so that others will become aware of those feelings and preferences.

The authoritative person generally believes things should be done a certain way and that they know how. Hesitancy in others is not understood as giving thought to how things should be handled, but instead is read as a lack of know-how in the other. Authoritative people tell people what they want and how they want things done. Because they are "right" they often expect things to be done a particular way without ever saying anything only because they believe it is obvious that things should be done the particular way they know. Authoritative people would never think they are infringing on others, or that their way of doing things could lead to disagreement. In fact, because they are "right" they generally see only that they are helping. Actually, authoritative individuals cannot understand why others become upset with them. While the obliging person borders on being passive, the authoritative person borders on being aggressive. Often they are perceived to be controlling. When the authoritative person does see how they are working in a relationship, however, and when others make it clear that their preferences are not being considered, the authoritative person can slow down the quickness with which they act and start to weigh the preferences of others more keenly. Because they are trying to help others with their know-how, the authoritative person generally cannot tolerate that they are hurting others. If others communicate that they're hurt, the authoritative person can become quite motivated to change. The authoritative person generally must recognize that what they believe are needs or "have tos" are actually preferences. Authoritative people need to become more assertive, just like obliging people, but their assertiveness depends upon this ability to differentiate needs from preferences, and upon truly seeing the value of input and preferences within their partner.

The three A's, acceptance, accommodation and assertiveness, are the hallmarks of a good relationship. If partners are to turn the natural chemistry of their initial relationship into an enduring love, they must accept one another's differences, accommodate one another's preferences, and assert their own preferences where important. Relationships are rarely, if ever, completely peaceful from the start. Because a healthy relationship requires two whole people, with totally different ways of looking at things, it is obvious that there will not always be agreement and there will often be some conflict. If two people love each other, however, growth and happiness spring from each individual recognizing the other as a whole human being.

In communicating, each individual must truly weigh the needs and preferences of the other against their own, and a compromise must be met. Only by striking a balance between those needs and preferences, by working on understanding through the three A's, can any relationship nourish itself, sustain growth and mature. If the right chemistry is there, however, and the three A's are utilized in developing sustained growth, a healthy love can last a lifetime and yet never grow old.

CHAPTER 23

☙

Connection and Independence

"I know there is strength in the differences between us. I know there is comfort where we overlap."

—Ani DiFranco

It is not just a matter of fairness. I hear that it is a lot. The man in the couple says, "It really isn't a problem for me when she goes out . . . she should go out just as much as I do." The woman says, "If he loves me and wants to be with me, like I do him, he would not have to go out so much." Both parties are sure they are being completely fair. They both assume they are being completely rational.

In fact, they *are* being fair and rational. Both members of this couple expect only that the other live by his or her fair standards. The man really means it when he says he wouldn't be upset if she went out. She really feels like she loves him to stay home so much that, if he loved her back, then he would want to stay home too. Where they are failing in their "fairness" is in failing to understand the logic of connection and the logic of independence.

Although the genders do not always go in the directions depicted above (and the two sides will be presented here in a much more all or nothing way than is really the case), it is very common for women to emphasize connection while men emphasize independence.

When they are upset, women want to hash it out and work toward understanding. When men are upset, they want to do something active to forget about it. The man wants to show his love by being a good provider and thinking about the physical needs of his loved one's. The woman believes that love involves care for one's emotions as shown by thoughtfulness, coziness, and depth of understanding. While a typical man prides himself on knowing his own thinking, many women pride themselves on intuiting what others are thinking. Plainly stated, men emphasize and cultivate **independence** while demonstrating that they care by taking care of business, and women develop and nurture **connectedness** while demonstrating their care through paying close attention to others' needs and feelings.

One of the best examples of this dichotomy in thinking involves the after-hours pharmacy. The scenario goes like this: a parent discovers that his or her child is out of a medicine without which he will become extremely sick. Unfortunately, all the pharmacies are closed. In picking from possible ways to deal with this sticky situation, men most often allowed their child to become sick while reproaching themselves for lacking forethought and emphasizing responsibility and the need to obey laws. Women, alternately, indicated that they would break the window of the pharmacy after exhausting all other lawful approaches. Clearly the women felt that the well-being of the child was the most important consideration. When men were asked about their thinking, very few had even considered the option that included breaking the pharmacy's window. The women valued caring and connectedness above all other issues, even considering a possibility that meant breaking the law. Men, on the other hand, could not reach beyond their well-honed sense of responsibility and lawful view to consider an option that would require breaking the law.

Interestingly enough, although men value independence and develop their relationships with responsibility, and women value connectedness and develop their relationships through demonstrating thoughtfulness, each often has problems in the opposite area of their strength when they are dealing with those closest to them. Men often become quite dependent upon their female counterparts for the only thoughtfulness and love they know, while women are less likely to be thoughtful toward their partners than they are toward their friends. It turns out that practicing any one way of being in a way that is not thoroughly balanced by the other, leads to opposite reactions with those with whom we are most comfortable. When we are comfortable and let our hair down, those things we value become less important than our needs in the moment. So the woman actually needs independence from her normally very thoughtful and connected ways and the man needs some closeness to counteract the independence he values so highly.

When couples talk about these issues, they rarely recognize how often they behave as though they are really the opposite of how they most often appear to be. But when a man is treated in an inconsiderate way, he is every bit as hurt as a woman would be. And when a woman isn't allowed a certain amount of independence, she is just as likely to feel controlled as any man might complain of his wife. Likewise, women are often so torn by their connectedness to so many people, that they simply cannot do for their husband like they do for others. And men are likely so overwhelmed by taking responsibility at times that they are likely to be the least responsible when with their wife.

It is important to remember that neither view is a more correct view. Both views serve a purpose, and both views are valid. In couples we tend to balance one another. If both partners had the same view, they'd likely make each other sick. Could you imagine two members of a couple so concerned with connectedness that they rarely do anything independently? They might stop functioning productively, with both members spending their day accommodating the other without regard to making a living or having any separate interests. On the other hand, they could spend all their time in independent pursuits and find themselves with no relationship at all.

The solution to this many-sided conundrum is much more simple than it would appear. To be fair in a couple you need to extend beyond your own point of view. Fairness needs to involve becoming more like the other person and seeing things more from their point of view. Each member of a couple has to put themselves in the others' shoes. The man has to say to himself, "If I thought connectedness was the most important thing, then I would think . . ." And the woman has to say to herself, "If I thought independence was the most important thing, then I would think . . ." If both members practice this kind of empathy, many problems soon resolve themselves. The man starts to see the pleasures of staying home. The woman starts to understand the value of going out with her friends. The man thinks of being thoughtful and understanding. The woman starts to see the value in more independence.

Healthy love within any intimate relationship tends to involve wanting what's best for one's partner, without losing sight of what's best for oneself. Every relationship strikes a different balance somewhere between independence and connection, but every relationship absolutely requires them both. If you really think about it, connection and independence actually define one another. And thus, without either one, really there can be no relationship at all.

CHAPTER 24

C3

Understanding Personality Styles in Couples

"Love is union with somebody, or something, outside oneself, under the condition of retaining the separateness and integrity of one's own self."

—Erich Fromm

Most relationship problems involve relatively simple differences in preferences or conflicting styles of communication. Typically, better understanding is the key to making the relationship healthier. But on the other hand, there are some personality styles that just don't mix in a relationship. Really, to put it plainly, these opposing personality styles simply cannot communicate. To make matters worse, much of the time these opposing personality styles are mutually attracted. Initially, disparate styles can lead to incredible excitement. In the long run, however, many people wonder how they could have ever gotten involved. They often become so miffed by their partner's infuriating habits that they can't imagine how it would be possible to overcome their current conflicts. Basically, there are three primary levels of character style that correspond to three levels of personality development, the "*Responsible*," the "*Independent/Passionate*," and the "*Hungry/Controller*" (In this article, I refer to certain types in the male or female form for convenience and clarity, but all types can be either male or female).

The *"Responsible"* individual's main motivation in life is to avoid deeply hurting those they love (through taking care of every possible daily concern and/or through always looking for ways to help—both of these types are often perceived to be a perfectionistic, controlling, and/or patronizing and have great overlap with the Obsessive Compulsive Personality—see article in section IV). The "Responsible" person in a couple is the personality type for whom self-help books are written since at least one partner in any relationship has to be responsible enough to obtain that self-help book. Unfortunately, self-help books sometimes have little utility because "Responsible" type personalities are often paired with one of the other two types (to whom normal "responsible" thinking seems naive and weak). "Responsible" types are typically observed to be hard-working, if not obsessive, about work. They care tremendously about what other people think, even though they hold their own values in higher esteem. Some "Responsible" types can be very out-spoken while others are very ingratiating, but either way, they have enough confidence to think freely about what they're told (even when they don't choose to act on it).

The main personality objective of the *"Independent/Passionate"* personality is to prove that no one controls her. This tendency is either shown by a constant need to do the opposite of what has been proposed, or by initially agreeing to do things but then consistently failing to follow through. Either way, the "Independent/Passionate" person often seems to be filled with resentment or anger, even though he/she may present as very kind and shy or very cute and sociable (or bossy and sociable). One of the hallmarks of the "Independent/Passionate" is the tendency to become very emotional about many things. Those that initially agree to do things and then fail to follow through are often passionate about everything except their relationships. Those that typically oppose what is expected tend to use mock passion (or drama) to avoid intimacy or to avoid real feelings in relationships.

Finally, there is the *"Hungry/Controlling"* personality. The "Hungry/Controlling" personality has less self-control and rarely does anything in moderation. Many of his actions are meant to fill some emptiness or exact some vengeance, and he feels those actions are absolutely necessary to his self-preservation. His actions are typically controlling in the extreme, or unctuously influential, as his needs are experienced to be so overwhelming as to throw him into desperate dominant behavior or obsequiousness. While the "Independent/ Passionate" fears that others seek to control her, the "Hungry/ Controlling" personality experiences so little self-control that he grasps at every bit of control over others that he can extract, impose or exploit. His presentation can be charismatic, bossy, desperate, or needy, but is rarely observed to be calm or relaxed (although feigned calm or complete indifference are often utilized to create an impression or to bolster influence).

Given that there are three levels of personality development, there are, of course, three combinations of these types, as well as the possibility that each type can find someone in her own category. Thus there are six types of couples initially derived from the three levels of personality development. In each of the paragraphs below, I will discuss the areas of difficulty each of the six kinds of couples is likely to experience. I will also give general hints about how to adjust interaction so that these relationships can become healthier. Sometimes, very simple adjustments can help in bringing about great change.

When each of the types stays with its own kind, it is easy to predict the most likely areas of difficulty. Two "Responsible" types will likely fight over the "right" way to do things. If they do not tend to get into conflicts over who is "right," the relationships of "Responsible" couples will, alternately, tend to stagnate with no real passion or even interest because "Responsible" types are so careful not to hurt others with their more intense emotions.

Two "Independent/Passionate" personalities will constantly struggle over control, as each of them constantly perceives the other as trying to control, and neither of them realizes that he or she truly has complete control over him or herself. That is, all of us control ourselves, but we simply make choices, given the likely consequences, about whether or not we will do as others ask or expect (so that it doesn't matter if anyone tries to control us unless the consequences are so dire that we must do what others want). In essence, every individual is ultimately free, but "Independent/Passionate" personalities believe they must control or be controlled.

A relationship with two "Hungry/Controlling" personalities is likely to be extremely exciting and filled with fireworks until, ultimately, it ends in a nuclear meltdown. The continuation of the

"Hungry/Controlling" relationship requires that each partner must have absolute control over the other who is only being used, and often abused, in the mind of the other or in reality, which makes such continuation chaotic in the extreme. If it just so happens that two "Hungry/Controllers" have perfectly complementary interests—that is, if they can each have the other in a position where they are using or abusing the other in a way that suits each of them—then they can have a lasting relationship. Nevertheless, abuse and exploitation are always ugly and messy, and any lasting relationship between two "Hungry/Controlling" individuals is likely to disintegrate at any time.

An interesting and extremely pertinent phenomenon should be mentioned here. It is frequently found that one partner moves into another position when two of the same personality levels come together, thus leading to the appearance that the partners are much more different than they actually are. This occurs because relationships require some complementarity for stability, and such complementarity is often difficult to negotiate when two personalities communicate at the same emotional level. The most frequent example is within the "independent/passionate" couple. Often one partner has, throughout their life, sought attention through seeking special treatment, acting wild, and taking little responsibility, for fear that they were ultimately very ordinary and also crucially responsible for extreme conflict between two parental figures. When this partner meets another who is even more dominant in those traits, and falls in love with their perfect match, it becomes natural to complement those behaviors with accommodation. Accommodation with resentment, amazingly, fits perfectly with an "independent/passionate" personality type, just as flirty, wild behavior does. In fact, when someone behaves flirty and wild and irresponsible, it's quite natural to act accommodating to please, yet resentful due to feeling insulted for lack of recognition. It is also quite natural to behave in a wild and irresponsible way when one's partner acts accommodating and appreciative of wild, irresponsible behavior, which is the typical scenario in spite of the resentment that develops because of it. Similar patterns of style switching between different types who share the same emotional communication level can be observed in the "Responsible" couple (moving from being rigid to ingratiating or vice versa) and the "Hungry/Controller" couple (in a variety of ways, for example moving from condescending and aloof to controlling and dramatically clinging or vice versa).

There are, of course, three other couple combinations derived from each of the emotional communication levels meeting up with either of the other two.

When a "Responsible" person becomes involved with an "Independent/Passionate" type, it is typical for the "Independent/ Passionate" to appear to be in control. He makes demands for fear of being the one controlled, and the "Responsible" person typically makes adjustments since she is not so sensitive to being controlled. Unfortunately, the "Responsible" person starts to feel downtrodden and abused, but continues to feel like complaining is inappropriate and weak. Meanwhile, the "Independent/Passionate" is not satisfied with the lack of control attempted by the "Responsible," since he generally finds meaning in relationships by wresting control from some other. If these patterns continue, most likely someone will become significantly depressed, anxious, angry or otherwise emotionally handicapped to the point that the relationship will end, or some kind of therapy (psychotropic or psychotherapeutic) will become necessary.

If the "Responsible" type wants to change things with the "Independent/Passionate," she needs to express emotions more spontaneously. She can get the "Independent/Passionate" to be more responsible by allowing the "Independent/Passionate" to truly see how his actions affect her very deeply. When the "Independent/ Passionate" sees the "Responsible" feeling truly sad or upset, he will feel responsible (and maybe guilty), which helps build responsibility in the "Independent/Passionate." Since the "Responsible" has so much self-control, however, sometimes it can even be helpful to get angry. While hurt and sad feelings help build closeness and a feeling of responsibility in the relationship, anger helps create a boundary that says "I will not let you treat me in a way that is not consistent with how I see myself."

When the "Responsible" joins a "Hungry/Controlling" person, the relationship becomes very "co-dependent" very quickly. That is, the "Hungry/Controller" sucks up all the willing tendency of the "Responsible" and keeps sucking until the "Responsible" feels "crazy" (again, I'm talking about significant emotional problems necessitating intervention). The "Responsible" will tend to feel like it is his duty to continue because to set up appropriate boundaries would be seen as too cruel or too costly (imagine allowing someone to be abusive to you because she might fall apart if you don't, and that might result in leaving your children without their mother). The "Hungry/Controller" doesn't intentionally deflate others, it's just that she never feels satisfied, and thus her emotional emptiness creates an emotional vacuum. In order to combat starvation (or inadequacy, lack of confidence, or vulnerability), the "Hungry/Controller" feels a need to be dominant, in control, and revered. Since the "Responsible" doesn't feel the need to be so dominant, he doesn't fight over it. He also comes to the relationship thinking others will play fair, and he never gives up hope that others *will* play fair. The "Hungry/Controller," on the other hand, assumes no one will play fair and plays to win at all times, often resorting to manipulation. Eventually, such a relationship is headed for disaster, as the "Responsible" gets warn down after trying to provide or take care of everything, and the "Hungry/Controller" never feels sustained by, or in control of, the "Responsible" because the "Responsible" will not allow access to their inner self. The "Responsible" always appears to be in control of himself, and the "Hungry/Controller" can only experience control by seeing the "Responsible" lose self-control.

To change the relationship, similar to the case of the "Responsible" who is with an "Independent/Passionate," emotions must be more spontaneous, thus giving the Hungry/Controller" what she needs to sustain herself. But because the "Hungry/Controller" can be so toxic in her responses, it can be necessary to emphasize the angry boundary-making response, rather than the intimacy-building hurt and sad response (unfortunately, many "Hungry/Controller" types are too volatile to handle an intimate relation acting angry—that is, if such a person has a history of violence it may be necessary to get out of the relationship rather than fix it).

Finally, there is the "Independent/Passionate"-"Hungry/ Controller" relationship. Such a relationship will often cause fireworks, almost to the same degree as two "Hungry/Controller" personalities getting together. Some stability can be found in these relationships, however, because the "Independent/Passionate" often takes a more responsible role and behaves much like a "Responsible" personality. Nevertheless, such relationships are typically fraught with constant arguing as the "Independent/Passionate" tries to be very controlling with the "Hungry/Controller" who will not be controlled. The most common cases of extreme co-dependency involve an "Independent/ Passionate" who is with a "Hungry/Controller." Such an "Independent/

Passionate" is typically in very bad need of taking care of someone because that is how they experience control, while the "Hungry/ Controller" is always needing more and more care (care that makes them feel like they're controlling the "Independent/Passionate) which results in their behavior spinning out of control (although such a person may become addicted to something, their behavior is typically out of control in many ways in addition to the abuse of substances).

The basic cure for such a relationship is in making boundaries in any way possible. The "tough love" approach was largely founded as a result of the need to move completely in the opposite direction of co-dependency. The ideal in the long run for any relationship is a balance where one can do for the other without worrying about it being taken the wrong way or contributing to other problems. But with tough love, the "Independent/Passionate" must become strict in the extreme in her guidelines as she makes sure that she never contributes to the difficulties of the "Hungry/Controller" by making things seem all right or allowing anything less than responsible behavior (again, dangerousness must be considered).

Although understanding these disparate types of personalities, and the combination of the three in relationship, might be quite confusing at first, identification of the patterns can lead to quick understanding. Personality types may change in relation to one another, but the basic needs of the personality type, which can be found in the emotional communication level ("Responsible," "Independent/Passionate," or "hungry/controller"), must be satisfied if any relationship is to last. Relationships of any kind require that the particular needs of the personality (which is not necessarily what individuals think they want) are satisfied. Some personality types require a partner who opposes them, or who is often difficult, or who will be dominant, or who will be submissive, even if they are unaware of needing those attributes in their partner. As a person identifies the kind of relationship he or she is in, or which type of individual they are with, clarity can be found about how to either adjust within the relationship or, when necessary, how it is necessary to get out of the relationship. If you are in a relationship that is anything other than a "Responsible" relationship, outside help, that is psychotherapy, will most likely be necessary to bring about desired change. Of course, even the "Responsible" couple often requires such outside help to comprehend how basic personality dynamics cause difficulties in relating.

Section 6

New Cars, Fast Cars, Backfires, and Crashes

How do we get together, why are we attracted, and what goes wrong? What revs the engine, keeps it running fast, and what leads to engine breakdown? Those are the questions addressed in "New Cars, Fast Cars, Backfires, and Crashes." In "The Dating Fantasy," the natural falling-in-love phenomenon of being love-addicted or infatuated is discussed in terms of projecting the attributes of our ideal mate onto a new found love. Of course, sexual attraction or chemistry is typically a central factor in new love, and issues related to sex continue throughout life. In "Sex Is Not a Drive: It's Just Real Important," the true reasons why sexual activity is such a driven behavior are uncovered and lead to a better understanding of love and happiness. In "Affairs and Divorce," the all too common circumstances involving the link between affairs and divorce is examined. The articles in this section generally aim at the heart of coupling. Coupling is a part of almost everyone's life and dating usually begins with our needs and desires as well as how we view our future lives. Sexual desire is always a part of coupling, even when actual sexual activity is postponed, restrained, withheld or renounced. Unfortunately, sexual activity is also often involved in the ending of relationships. Coupling always involves getting the engine started, and the engine must be kept warm. But running hot, without a doubt, can lead to definite instability, and often grave danger.

CHAPTER 25

❦

The Dating Fantasy

"Gravitation is not responsible for people falling in love."

—Albert Einstein

What you see is what you get! Right? Well . . . not exactly. It's interesting to think about how people fall in love. Typically, when two people "fall" they really don't know much about each other. When it comes to the first few dates, beauty is truly in the eye of the beholder. I don't just mean that we all have different tastes (although that is certainly true). I mean that *who* we perceive the other person to be is truly a fantasy that comes primarily from within our own minds. In fact, with respect to falling in love, it could be said, what you see is what you want.

When we become infatuated with someone, without really knowing much about that person, we allow our desires or fears to dominate our view of them. If a new person seems kind and we have a need for kindness, then we feel sure that the other person is very kind. When we have that need for kindness we are also likely to assign a thousand other wonderful attributes. On the other hand, if that same person seems kind, and we tend to be distrustful, or if we fear becoming intimate too quickly, or if we find ourselves most attracted to only very "strong" people, then we think they are trying to manipulate, or that they are too naive, or that they are too needy.

The truth of the matter is that we see people for who they really are only with time. The more experience we have with someone, the more we know that their actions truly reflect their general tendencies. When we first meet someone, not only are we likely to see what we want to see, but they are most likely going to show us what we want to see. It's not that people are intentionally duplicitous in hiding their true nature (although that does happen often). Rather, most people simply try to portray themselves in the most positive light when they first meet someone of interest. If you find someone interesting and you want to know them better, it would be really weird if you immediately revealed those attributes you think them most likely to despise. Right?

Sometimes it takes a really long time for people to reveal their true selves. Some people are especially good at managing the impression others have of them. That might even be something that others find attractive. Usually, for example, people who spend a lot of time on their physical appearance, including the material items with which they surround themselves (clothes, cars, restaurants, etc . . .) are pretty good at managing the impression that others develop. Sometimes, however, they have spent so much time perfecting the *image* they project that as soon as they feel comfortable enough to act naturally, they turn out to be very different than what they had presented (sometimes angry, sometimes controlling, sometimes vulnerable or dependent, but generally very different).

Image, however, can be important enough in the eye of the beholder that the real personality underneath, although less than perfect, can be tolerated if the image is powerful enough to meet other needs. In the final analysis, whether or not someone is acceptable in the long term will depend upon a balance of their attributes, both those projected and those hidden. Do they provide security, are they good looking, are they respectful, thoughtful, strong, angry, neglectful, caring, arrogant, etc . . . The problem is, we don't weigh things very evenly when we are in the midst of the dating fantasy. Infatuation is like a drug. Because we see exactly what we need, we simply cannot get enough. Even if something doesn't seem quite right, our love and desire keep us going back for more. We feel compelled and compulsive. We feel like we must. We feel we can't help it.

When people fall in love, in a way they fall in love with themselves. They have an idea in their head that what would cure their ailments or complete their lives is directly before them. They will lie to themselves about what they experience so that the fantasy stays alive. But I do not write this to discourage falling in love. It is perhaps the best feeling in the world and, in fact, it is not induced by drugs. Everyone should enjoy falling in love, and they should make it last as long as possible. The only danger is in making life lasting decisions too fast. Because the dating fantasy is dangerous, because we can tend to be too rash when we're feeling so good, it is essential that we take our time with relationships. Until you have dealt with some difficulties in your mate, until you've had a few arguments, or have had to tell yourself you're okay with some of the things that you don't like so much about your partner, you have not waited long enough.

When you're ready to make long term decisions, I hope you will be sharing moments of fantasy and fun. I hope you will still be infatuated with your partner. But if you have not yet seen some behavior about which you're not quite sure, or if you're looking past disrespect, aggressiveness, or certain behaviors that make you feel horrible just because sometimes you feel great, then you are still too much in the fantasy zone to make the decisions you're making. Meanwhile, enjoy your fantasy, enjoy the one you're with, and allow yourself to experience the dating fantasy with all its amazing emotions and fantastical wonders. If you are in your dating years, and you're just like most everyone else, I don't think you can help it.

CHAPTER 26

❧

Sex Is Not a Drive: It's Just Real Important

"It is impossible to overlook the extent to which civilization is built upon a renunciation of instinct."

—Sigmund Freud

Sigmund Freud, the progenitor of psychotherapy as we know it, said that sex or libido was, along with aggression, a drive. That is, he thought that sex and aggression were the two primary motivators in life. I will grant that many people are driven by sexual goals, but I do not think that sex is actually a drive. The truth is, sex is a great motivator because it involves everything that is a drive. So you might suggest, maybe sex is even more important than a drive. I don't think so, but let's cover a few other areas before we get to that.

A drive (for lack of a better term) is a primary motivator. It is inside us and makes us tick or go, but it connects to something on the outside by which it can be satisfied. In Freud's view the two drives were sex and aggression. Aggression could be satisfied by becoming dominant and then occasionally, as it fits the fancy of the dominant one, someone or something around him could be given a beating to satisfy the aggressive urge. Thus, according to that view, everyone seeks dominance over someone or something. The sexual drive, on the other hand, could be satisfied by obtaining a sexual partner and planting a seed, and thus dissipating the restrained urge. But there is a much better explanation for how drives work than that, since there are so many situations in which a person clearly feels comfortable without being aggressive or dominant, and there are also so many situations in which a person manages to be okay without the pursuit and capture of sexual partners.

This alternate explanation involves the balance of three primary motivators. The first two are sustenance and self-protection. From the moment we are born (and perhaps before that, inside the womb), we attempt to find a balance between intake of food and being sated. On one extreme is starvation and on the other extreme would be eating till you pop (the second is rarely a real danger, but you know what I mean). Likewise, we attempt to find the balance of self-protection or safety and, from the time we're born, we stand ready to shrink or bolt in fear, or on the other hand, attack with aggression. As a parent you can see how your baby gets you to protect him or her and how he or she can occasionally cry with such fury that it nearly knocks you out. These two drives become a part of everything we know so that we can thirst for knowledge or feel crammed with information; likewise, we can cream a baseball or fear the pitch.

The third drive, relatedness, includes sustenance and self-protection as they involve our relationships with other people. From the time we're born (and perhaps before) we thirst for the human comfort of our mother, but can also be overwhelmed by her presence. We feel a need to protect ourselves from the aggression of others and either fear them or become aggressive in return. And when we come to develop an awareness of real safety with others, the knowledge that they will be there and will not overwhelm us or hurt us, or that we are capable of securing safety and sustenance independently through our own negotiations with the world around us, we begin to develop our sense of relatedness into true caring for others. When such confidence develops, we need to balance our desire to do for others with our need to care for ourselves. At the extremes, we need to avoid becoming isolated and alone in selfishness or, alternately, we need to avoid becoming responsibility fragmented with our desire to take care of everyone and be responsible for everything.

So in life, the importance of everything is based on its relation to these three drives. Food is important only to the sustenance drive, even though we have all known people who use food to comfort themselves because it becomes associated with love (the relatedness drive). Shelter is important only to the extent that it protects us from the elements and unknown carnivorous beasts, even though there are many aspects of shelter that are akin to relatedness and even sustenance. Your mother is important because she is related to all of these needs and tensions. The point is that we are constantly trying to balance these needs and tensions with reality. Sometimes we want more, sometimes less. Sometimes we are afraid and sometimes we feel angry. Similarly, sometimes we want to be alone or selfish, and sometimes we want to be with others or give.

Why does sex seem like a drive? Because it is related to all three primary motivators or drives and helps us balance ourselves in these areas when it seems like there is no other way to balance. For example, did you know that most people who are attracted to being sexually dominated are relatively dominant in their daily lives? There can be no argument that sexuality involves aggression, fear, pursuit and capture, desire, emotional consumption, taking responsibility for the pleasure of another, hedonism, and relatedness. Sex feels driven because it involves all of the most basic human functions.

But we do not **need** sex. There are ways to balance all of these areas without sex. And there are ways of being balanced without sex and enjoying sex too. Sex is not a drive because it does not involve driven behavior that can only be satisfied by some target outside of us. It can be controlled, and should be controlled under many circumstances. It can also be sought in fantasy, thus causing the necessary release, without any other person being involved. If sex interferes with too many of the other driven areas, then it is likely being pursued too much. This is an important point because so many people get caught up in the idea that sex is necessary or that it is the only true hallmark of a good relationship, when that is simply not the case. It is true, however, that if your relationship helps you balance in all other driven areas, then you are likely to enjoy sex even more than you do when you use it to balance because you must. Although sex is not a drive, it reaches its full maturity, and heightens intimacy to the fullest, only when all the other true drives (sustenance, self-protection, and relatedness) have been relatively satisfied.

Is sex a drive? I don't think so. Sex definitely involves all the real drives, which is certainly not a biological accident. Because it involves all the other drives, sex is uniquely compelling among all the human motivators. We need to mate to procreate. We also can satisfy the unsatisfactory parts of our lives through sexual fantasy, thus creating emotional balance. Sex is not a drive, no matter how much someone might want to argue the point. I do not know of any person who would choose sex over food while in a starved state. I do not know of any person who would prefer sex over protecting themselves in the presence of a threat to life. No, sex is not a drive. It's just real important.

CHAPTER 27

☙

Affairs and Divorce

"When cheated, wife or husband feels the same."

—Euripides

Why do people have affairs? One of the primary reasons for having an affair is that cheaters actually want to ruin their marriages. Of course that's not the only reason for having an affair. It is possible to fall in love outside one's marriage by accident, especially if one is not getting his or her needs met inside the marriage. But really that goes in the category of unconsciously needing to ruin one's marriage, doesn't it? There are also many people who simply have a hard time controlling their sexual or flirtatious impulses even though they believe they are in love with their spouses. But really that person is not fully engaged within their marriage if their own impulses so easily overwhelm how their behavior will affect their spouse. There are also people, believe it or not, who know darned well that having an affair will not result in a divorce because their spouse will allow it without serious confrontation. Those individuals, it could be argued, don't really have a marriage.

You see, affairs occur in a state of unhappiness. The person who has the affair feels a need for excitement at the least, and typically they are looking for a release from the drudgery they perceive within their marriage or their life circumstances. The problem with that is, we all know the grass appears to be greener on the other side of the fence. We also know that marriage is often extremely difficult. That's a powerful combination. When it's getting difficult to pay the bills or when one of the children is having problems, couples often get bogged down in blaming each other instead of working together. In difficult circumstances it's especially likely that a spouse will seek a way out. Someone outside the marriage, someone who is not associated with the problems impacting the marriage, can be very attractive indeed.

Sometimes things really have gone bad within the marriage. The spouse who seeks an out has grown dissatisfied, or perhaps both partners are miserable. It could be that one spouse has started taking the other for granted. Maybe one spouse feels the other is "lazy," "foolish," "messy," or "mean." That person might seek someone who is "active," "smart," "organized," or "sweet." In the desperation within their minds, the person perceiving awful traits within their spouse just absolutely must escape, and when they find someone who appears to be the antithesis of their spouse, their deep unmet needs and untapped insecurities, all of which have been conjured up within their discontent, create an irresistible urge toward this perceived anti-spouse.

Unfortunately making decisions or letting yourself fall in love when you're feeling lousy makes for lousy outcomes and lousy relationships. People generally don't really know the person with whom they cheat like they do their spouse. Although they clearly see all the attributes they need within their paramour, what they see is merely a projection of the perceived answer to their needs (please see my article "The Dating Fantasy" for a fuller discussion of this process). It is the fulfillment of those unmet needs and untapped insecurities that is sought, and it is that fulfillment that seems to be found. Typically, those very same unmet needs and insecurities led to their marriage that now appears to be defunct, even if things looked much different at the inception of the marriage. The new love is not truly a love at all. The new love is, most typically, merely grass that appears to be very green.

If the real problem is the marriage, there is no good reason that an affair would be the answer. The answer would be to either fix the marriage or seek a divorce in an appropriate fashion. In fact, sometimes an affair is merely an escape hatch for an unhappy spouse who can't confront their partner about the problems in the marriage. An affair is considered unforgivable much of the time and thus, with one big bombshell, the unhappy spouse avoids the whole uncomfortable process of working things out with one huge explosion. They have often already convinced themselves that the marriage is unworkable and they just want it to end without discussion. The discontented spouse believes the affair will make them happy and they don't want to deal with the mess of acting like their trying to save their marriage.

Unfortunately, in the process of avoiding the work it would require to confront the problems in their marriage, the discontented spouse moves so quickly that many important aspects of their situation are ignored. Most importantly, it is extremely rare that the discontented spouse has given any real thought to how their own psychology contributed to the problems they experienced in the marriage. They have assumed that their unmet needs could not be met by their spouse. Most of the time, however, because they have not attempted to work out the problem, they don't really know whether it could be worked out. Even worse, they take no responsibility for what they have done within their marriage, and tend to think their own perspective is 100% clearly correct.

What if the real problem, to oversimplify, is that the unhappy spouse has an extreme need for freedom, but they perceive their partner to be unreasonably controlling. Thus, they find someone who would seemingly give them as much freedom as they'd like? What if one spouse has an exaggerated need for togetherness—so much so that they perceive their partner as abandoning them whenever their partner needs to leave. They then have an affair because they want someone who pays them more attention and seemingly has little need for independence? There are thousands of similar examples. The point is, often the cheater actually perceives themselves as vindicated in their affair or desire for divorce, but they make no attempt to see their own part in the problem.

Another significant factor is the denial that overcomes the cheater while in the throes of their affair. This denial causes the cheater to forget how truly disastrous it can be to have an affair. People forget about the effect the affair and/or divorce might have on their children, as well as on their spouse. Even more amazing is the fact that the spouse who is having the affair fails to think forward to how a divorce might affect themselves. They forget what they once had with their spouse and why they've been together. They forget about how difficult it is to build a relationship over time. Perhaps most of all, they forget how much they love to spend time with their children within the context of an intact family home, and they give no consideration to how fragmented things will be for, and with, their children if there is a divorce.

A byproduct of the cheater's denial is that they start thinking they have nothing in common with their spouse. This is a byproduct of denial since, of course, children are the biggest thing people could possibly have in common. The spouse who cheats does not fully recognize how unimportant their differences with their spouse are when compared with having children together. How could anything be bigger? And for anyone who has enjoyed the company of their children while with their spouse, that is the completeness in the feeling of the cohesive happy family, it is impossible to see the grass greener anywhere else. Children fully thirst for the love of their parents together, and when it's clear that their parents love each other, children drink in the abundance of that love. Clearly, if there is any chance that a spouse could be in love with their partner, that is the very best chance for happiness for all.

Beyond the huge issue of the children's happiness, it's obvious that what could be called "affair denial" also makes the cheater forget other important changes that will be necessary when divorced. Financial well-being after divorce is often shattered. Not many people can afford to maintain life as it once had been with the advent of two households. Divorcing couples also often do not seem to consider what it will be like to either have the children alone for half their time or to have much less contact with them. Most divorcees feel lonely when their children are gone and overwhelmed when their children are with them. That eventuality is typically equally difficult for both spouses, regardless of who might be perceived as responsible for the divorce.

So what is the thing to do if you're unhappy in your marriage? It may sound contradictory, but the *first* thing to do is to be honest with yourself about your unhappiness. If you're trying to fool yourself into being happy, or if you're managing or denying your absence of happiness, you leave yourself especially vulnerable to meeting your needs in inappropriate ways. When someone is unhappy but is using their emotional resources to feign happiness, they are most likely to find something that gives them immediate gratification. One of those things can be an affair.

Second, once you see that you're unhappy, you must express it in some way. The effort you apply to saving your marriage must be equal to the happiness you would feel if you and your spouse were in a happy marriage and your children were able to benefit from your mutual love. If there is any chance that you could be happy, even if working it out will require shameful sharing and embarrassing revelations about your true feelings, you are far better off if things work out.

Third, if your efforts to express your discontent fall on deaf ears, or if you think you need the help of a professional, of course you need to go to counseling. Everyone is uncomfortable with airing their dirty laundry with a stranger. But therapists are trained to be neutral, understanding, and to see problems in communication as well as unconscious unmet needs. Therapists tend to connect even the most bewildering and unattractive human foibles to a person's vulnerability. They generally prefer to see people as human rather than bad. If even your worst traits can be shared and understood within the marital context, and you can improve your communication with your spouse about those traits, maybe things can be good, really good. Maybe things aren't quite as bad—and people tend to think things are really bad—as you think.

Fourth, and finally, make sure you are being honest with yourself about what it would be like to be divorced. It is so easy to see only the virtues of change without seriously considering the ensuing sorrow that such a change would create. Some of the negatives have been laid out above, but more explanation regarding the effects of divorce on children should be detailed. As everyone knows, it is often said about children that they are amazingly resilient. Childhood Resiliency, however, really only means that children manage to keep on going in their lives. The impact of experience in childhood is the regular purview of everyday psychotherapy. We're all impacted by everything that happens to us, and the terrible experiences stay with us forever. You need to know that in most cases, children feel like the divorce of their parents rips them in two. You need to know that the child will likely feel abandoned by whichever parent has initiated the divorce (or by both parents). It is true that when a marriage is so bad that parents spend all their time arguing, or worse, kids can be so damaged by the marriage that a divorce brings relief. But improvement in a marriage can be so curative in demonstrating the importance of the family that it can undo much of the damage that's been previously done. The tear that rips through children of divorce leaves them unable to trust their parents, and thus, unable to trust anyone else. That lack of trust makes it nearly impossible for the children of divorce to become truly close to anyone again.

If divorce is necessary, please don't have an affair. Most of the affairs people have are merely an instrument of divorce and leave the whole family bereft of the family feeling all should enjoy. You owe it to yourself and your family to try hard to save your marriage. People seldom stay in love with the object of an affair. When people are extricated from their marriage, they typically start to see their new partner in a more accurate way, and then become disenchanted with them as well, just as they had with their spouse. It is also important to realize that, even though people rarely start to think they made a mistake in divorcing, if they never really tried to work things out, their thinking about relationships is clearly suspect. They typically fall into the same problematic patterns in their next relationship because they have never worked out the kinds of problems they themselves create within relationships. In those cases where a divorce actually is the best possible outcome, if you have really tried everything you could to save the family before divorcing, that effort to save the marriage itself can make for a healthier divorce in which everyone gets along after the divorce is final. The only possible saving grace of divorce in its aftermath is when the children see their parents work as a team motivated by their common love for their children. Only in that context can they understand that they are important enough to both their parents that their parents will share their love for their children with each other even after divorce and no matter what happens. Although divorce should be avoided when there is any hope for a good relationship, at the very least there can be love that goes into a good divorce that helps the children preserve a sense of love. If children can observe their divorced parents sharing love for them, the good divorce can help children heal and trust, and can help them maintain hope for true everlasting love in their own future families.

Section 7

Communication: Tools for Making Yourself Fully Understood

There is no assemblage within the Great Life Machine where the junction of two parts, and their tightness of fit, is more essential than in the human couple. The articles in this "tools" section involve the oil of relationships, communication. Communication lubricates the joints and ensures proper coalescence of attachments in couples, as in all relationships. And the goal for couples, of course, is the perfect union. While such perfect machining may not be possible, the tools offered here will help the reader calibrate connections as closely as possible. "Communication from the Heart" encourages more passionate responsiveness, especially with reference to being more vulnerable, so that your partner, or even your child, will be more connected with how you really feel. Passionate communication, as discussed here, promotes effective interpersonal boundaries and thus bolsters healthy relationships. Sometimes, however, people have too much passion in their relating, which can lead to selfish, angry and destructive behavior. In the article "Key Signals," the reader will find help for repairing negative behavioral sequences in which both parties involved have become dissatisfied with the way hurtful behavior is damaging their relationship. In the article "'I' Statements," it is the clarity of expression that becomes the focus. This well-known tool for discussing interpersonal differences, while avoiding blame and defensiveness, is outlined and delineated with hope that it will be easy to utilize.

CHAPTER 28

൙

Communication from the Heart

"The eloquent man is he who is no beautiful speaker, but who is inwardly and desperately drunk with a certain belief."

—Ralph Waldo Emerson

Isn't it strange that most people rarely say what is really on their minds or act how they really feel? Even many of those who do practice explaining exactly how they feel often seem to lose the utility of the 95% of communication that is nonverbal because their nonverbal behavior doesn't adequately correspond to the feelings they want to express. Everyone has a constant stream of thought, and a large proportion of that thought is related to possible behavior or things to say, much of which is thwarted, avoided or controlled because it is thought to be inappropriate, unpopular, or too emotional. Only by matching what we say to how we feel, however, with behavior that reveals how we feel at least a little bit, is it possible to have clear communication. Only by expressing ourselves with clear communication that does match our behavior and our words to what we feel, can we possibly hope that others will get the correct impression of our intentions, our seriousness, or our true desires.

Unfortunately, much of the time it doesn't even occur to us to act how we feel, or to behave in a way that reveals what we really want. I call communication that is void of feeling or passion "dead communication." Dead communication is ineffective and cold and leaves its listeners numb. The opposite of dead communication is "passionate communication." Simply put, "passionate communication" is communication from the heart. It is communication that is not only assertive (that is, communication that takes into account our needs, the needs of those with whom we wish to communicate, and the context of the situation—please see article "Assertiveness: The 30% Solution"), but is also expressed with enough of the emotion that's been evoked in us to be understood in the way we really mean it. Because we often do not communicate from the heart, we often do miss out on getting what we want. We also miss out on developing satisfying relationships.

So what does it mean to express oneself passionately and with emotion. There is certainly no benefit in aggressively berating everyone with whom we disagree. And it would be equally unhelpful to have fits of sobbing and wailing every time a thoughtless word is spoken. But when we decide to say we're hurt or angry, we can only be really heard if we say it like we mean it. Just as a parent must use some commitment in their voice when admonishing a child, other kinds of communication require a commitment of emotion. We need to tap into, but not allow a flood of, the emotion we are experiencing, and then attach it to our words when we communicate how we're feeling. We need just a sprinkle, and sometimes a spring, for adequate communication, but typically a deluge or a thunderous waterfall merely leaves us all wet. We have to learn how to draw on some of our emotions, and use them wisely, without losing all control. We must be passionate about what we want and what we deserve, without acting as though failing to get it will be disastrous or lead to untold disaster.

Saying we're hurt by someone's actions is really the most difficult thing to say with passion. Most people don't really ever want to say they're hurt. It sounds too weak or pathetic, right? Perhaps it's something about our culture. Weakness is considered so pathetic that we hardly even have any words that mean "hurt." Most of the words we think might express hurt feelings are much more like insults. If we say we are "embarrassed" by something someone has done, then we're really saying the other person is embarrassing. If we say we are "disappointed" in someone, then we're really saying that they blew it in some way. The comments most people make when they are hurt are comments about what the other person has done. It is very rare that people comment on their hurt experience or their hurt feelings when they're hurt. If someone does want to comment on their feeling of being hurt, they will find very few words in the English language that mean "hurt." In fact, the only word for "hurt" is, well . . . "hurt."

The only other way to express hurt feelings without using the word "hurt" is to describe the physiological response stirred up within us. For example, we can say, "When 'x' happened, I felt like my stomach was tied in knots," or "The pressure in my head made it feel like I might explode," or "It felt like my heart was literally breaking to pieces in my chest." To communicate with passion when we're hurt, we need the other person to understand how their actions have truly impacted us. When we run out of ways to say "hurt," expressing the bodily response related to the hurt, while letting ourselves look how we really feel, often gets the point across.

Although expressing hurt feelings is not easy or simple, doing so effectively is so enormously beneficial in relationships that it is one of the most valuable skills a person can cultivate. In almost any relationship where two people care about one another, it is practically taboo or forbidden to continue on in behaviors that are known to be hurtful to the other. On the other hand, when we see that someone acts angry, we are very unlikely to worry about controlling our anger or hurtful behavior unless they scare us. And that is a big problem in relationships since most people do act angry when they get hurt. Angry behavior causes defensiveness, which is typically also angry. Because anger is a strong emotion, there is no reason to believe that we've hurt someone when they behave in an angry fashion. When we see anger, we don't take responsibility for what we've done because we feel bad about what we've done. The only reason to change our hurtful behavior when someone is angry is because they have demonstrated that they are dominant. That is, anger develops an escalation of negative behaviors in which there must be a victor—a person whose retaliation is strongest and therefore must be respected.

If our connection to another person is the most important aspect of our relationship, however, then being scared of that other person merely damages our connection. If a person acts hurt, on the other hand, and we feel badly about what we've done because we don't want to hurt them, then the connection between us is maintained and acknowledged as the most important aspect of the relationship. The act of expressing hurt develops a sense of responsibility between both members of a relationship, and nurtures the connection between them, as each person then responds by trying not to be hurtful. Angry responses may develop a sense of responsibility in some very indirect ways, but only due to fear of possible repercussions and not because of caring and connection.

With respect to anger or frustration, expressing those emotions with passion is generally extremely easy, at least as far as words are concerned. Our culture is apparently far more comfortable with the strength of anger than the vulnerability of being hurt. There are so many words that mean we're angry, it's almost ridiculous. We can be mad, irritated, riled, aggravated, annoyed, offended, outraged, and the list goes on. But expressing anger too passionately is a problem in and of itself. Several other articles I have written specifically address how problematic the expression of anger can be (for example, see "The Power and Control Addiction"). Too much angry behavior will, of course, turn people off and make them defensive. Angry responding rarely has a positive effect in the long run even if it might get people to back off or give in within the immediate moment. Anger can be extremely destructive when expressed without enough self-control. There are times, nevertheless, when anger needs to be expressed more passionately than it is.

When a person feels extremely uncomfortable with expressing anger, they often do so with very little passion at all. Although it is generally more disturbing for others when someone has trouble controlling their anger than when they have trouble expressing their hurts, there are many individuals who, in spite of the many words that mean we're angry, need to be much better at actually acting angry when that's how they feel. If a person tries too hard to use just the right words to express their anger, without acting angry, their communication will be unclear or "dead" to the extreme. The most significant examples come from those individuals who say they're angry when they feel angry, and they often use just the right words to state how they feel, but they smile and look pleasant when expressing that anger. If someone is angry, but is smiling and pleasant, the person who would take them seriously is a very rare find. For those who have a hard time expressing anger even when it's really necessary, while it might be useful to choose the right words to explain their position, it is absolutely 100% essential that they learn to act how they feel. If anger is to be taken seriously, it must be expressed with conviction.

So why don't people express themselves with passion? There are, of course, many reasons, most of which are related to one's upbringing. When we're growing up we learn how to say what is "appropriate" and how to control our emotions. In essence we learn how to please Mom and/or Dad. When we are children, saying things right or wrong feels like it is directly connected to whether or not we will earn Mom's or Dad's love. This is true even in the most unconditionally loving families. That is to say, learning to hide our emotions to some extent is normal. From our brothers, and sisters, and our peers at school, we also learn what is "cool" and what will make others think we're "losers." To kids, and even to some adults, there is nothing more painful than not fitting in. So clearly, we cover up what we really feel, need, and think, because we want to fit in, and be loved.

Sometimes we don't say what we really think or feel because to do so really would be inappropriate, or maybe even cause problems for which we're not prepared. Telling your boss or your neighbor your most poignant vulnerable experiences, or telling your children about how your spouse damaged your self-esteem, are clearly inappropriate revelations that would lead to rejection on one hand, and increased family strife on the other. How close or intimate we are with others, and what relation they have to us in the bigger scheme of things, clearly limits what would be wise to express. But no matter with whom we are speaking, if people frequently seem to overlook us, there can be more expressiveness, emotion, or passion in what we say.

When we're disappointed or overwhelmed at work, our supervisors and peers are more likely to recognize what we want if our behavior reveals some of what we're feeling. Our children are more likely to understand our expectations when we act hurt, disappointed, or angered by their behavior (but only a little, and, of course, with clear evidence that we are able to handle our feelings). Even in the most mundane aspects of social discourse, it's beneficial to act like we feel. Our neighbors are more likely to keep their dog off our lawn if we act like it bothers us, right?

Communicating with passion, saying what we want and acting like it, allows us to have good "boundaries" and leads to clear understanding between people. "Boundaries," a concept that is rarely understood, basically means allowing others to know what you will or won't put up with, and what you expect and would appreciate (see article "Understanding Boundaries"). Basically, it means letting people know who you really are. When people can feel you through your passionate expression of your desires and upsets, as well as interests and preferences, then they are more likely to respect you. When people treat you with respect (not awe or fear), it is generally because you have made yourself clear through passionate communication. Passionate communication, that is communication from the heart, helps you, and it helps those around you, since we are all together negotiating our social terrain every day. Communicating from the heart is an absolutely essential skill for living life to the fullest. Only by learning to express yourself passionately is it possible to take your rightful and respected place within your family, at work, and in the greater community.

CHAPTER 29

❧

Key Signals—the Key for Jump-Starting Change in Relationships

"Every cloud engenders not a storm."

—Shakespeare

Poised for a much needed change in your communication with someone very important to you? Do you and your partner, or maybe even you and your child, know what you do that makes the other react with anger or sadness? Does it seem like the only barrier between where you are and where you want to be is the inability to prevent or control the behaviors or attitudes that get you started in the wrong direction? If you and the person with whom you want to communicate are unequivocally in agreement about what those behaviors and attitudes are, perhaps you can agree on a Key Signal to clue you in that the behavior has been noticed. When behaviors that cause bad reactions can be checked with a signal upon first notice, the chain reaction of negative communication that is typically initiated can often be avoided.

A Key Signal is a word or hand sign that is used covertly to signal another person that a behavior has been noticed. If two people agree in advance that they each will stop a particular behavior or attitude when given the Key Signal, then the chain reaction of behaviors that are typically triggered by that behavior can be averted. If a word is to be used, it is important that the word be considered neutral by each party. It is especially useful if the word is humorous. Examples of words that have been used by my clients include "bubble," "tiddly winks," "tug boat," and "bananas." When stealth is especially important in the process, that is, when it is important that no one else in the vicinity is aware of the communication, a hand Key Signal is especially useful. People have used signs like pulling their ear lobe or touching the top of their own heads. With stealth in mind, it can be important that the sign be simultaneously noticeable and inconspicuous. An example of a furtive Hand Key Signal that works especially well when privacy is preferred is scratching one's shoulder with the hand from the opposite side of the body (scratching left shoulder with right hand). Of course, it's easy to invent an endless number of hand signals for covert use, or any other kind of Key Signal. It is the agreement on when to use Key Signals that is truly critical. Before we can understand what constitutes a good agreement on when to use a Key Signal, however, it is necessary to discuss our understanding of negative communications.

Most hurtful behavioral chains start with intense feelings and impulsive, thoughtless response. In such circumstances, Key Signals become an essential tool for circumventing an escalation of destructive communications. Key Signals are necessary when automatic responses have become so habitual that we are unable to notice them or stop them from happening without someone else letting us know about them. Reactions that seem negative or intense are largely a response to the perception of being attacked, and then the feeling that we must defend ourselves. We often react before we even know we've reacted when the actions of others seem to have personal impact. We then act like we have an "attitude" or we become angry. Once one person has responded with attitude or anger, the other person moves to defend with either a response meant to repel the other, or a response meant to defend against the attitude or anger. From there, the all too familiar spiral of negative and hurtful communication takes flight as each person attempts to strengthen their position in relation to the other. All too often, unfortunately, this spiraling flight of defensive behaviors escalates into complete chaos.

Even after two people agree on how a particular chain reaction of behaviors is triggered, and even when they want to try their very best to avoid those behaviors, they typically continue to react automatically in the same ways they always have. Thus, even though they really no longer desire to react in the same hurtful ways, they get into the same troubles they always have. The Key Signal helps those who are dedicated to preventing this awful spiral of angry and resentful power struggling, refrain from the behaviors that fuel it.

Of course there are some important potential roadblocks to relational progress when using Key Signals. The most common obstacle is when the two parties, although acting as though they are truly dedicated to change, are not really in agreement about what causes the problem. If one partner tells the other that they become insulting at times when they believe they know the best way to handle situations, the partner being told may actually agree and apologize. They might even state that they will try to be better and that the partner indicating that they've been harmed can use a Key Signal to let them know they have started engaging in that insulting behavior. However, the fact that they have agreed that what they do is hurtful is not really enough. In order to accept use of the Key Signal, such a person has to actually understand and feel that their behavior is wrong and uncalled for. They also need to believe there will be no harm to them if they stop the insulting behavior. Most of the time, however, as indicated above, the reason for the negative behavior is some sense of harm that either has already taken place or that will take place if they don't react with the "insulting" behavior. It is quite likely that the insulting party engages in that behavior for fear of being insulted themselves or because they feel they've already been insulted. Alternately, as in the case of someone who thinks they know the one and only way to do things right, a person can believe there will be an awful crisis if something is done incorrectly.

For Key Signals to be effective, each party who agrees to stop their negative behaviors must recognize that the targeted behavior is unjustified. They could be right in feeling that they have not been treated well in the past. They might be right in assessing that things could go badly if not done their way. Either way, however, they must see that the escalating spiral of negative behaviors does not help and will not help. They must see that the escalation in behavior is actually worse than the level of hurt they feel or the level of problem that will occur due to things being done differently than they want. It helps if both partners also commit to talking things out and really trying to gain an understanding of each other, but it is the willingness to stop the behavior that is of most concern when using Key Signals. If a person feels so upset that they truly believe their attitude or anger is justified enough to create escalating negativity, they will never abide by the Key Signals no matter how much they have agreed to do so. In order to actually respond to a Key Signal a person typically needs to truly understand their motivations. It might be quite difficult, to continue our example, for a person to see that they have a need to be in control which results in insulting or officious remarks. Simply stated, however, if they cannot see their motivations, they will continue to feel a need to be critical and bossy because they will feel their behaviors are justified.

Another significant problem in using Key Signals is that people often start to feel the Key Signal itself has inadvertently become an insult. If a person does not see and understand their own behavior, when they hear or see the signal, they view it as a personal attack. When attacked, of course, most people will respond defensively. A perceived attack is typically the reason the unwanted negative behavior has developed in the first place. The defensive response to the Key Signal then leads to the same spiraling behavior that has always occurred. Overuse of the Key Signal may not only result in the Key Signal being perceived as an inadvertent insult, but also will likely make people believe the Key Signal is intentionally being used as an insult or maybe even as a means of control. Using the Key Signal can be interpreted as "you loser, you're doing it again," or "hah, I've got you now because you've agreed not to act that way and I can act any way I want." Key Signals must be used sparingly or they will quickly lose all utility. Again, there can never be enough talk about when and why, or even how often, the Key Signals are to be used.

In cases where the Key Signal being used will, in itself, be interpreted as an insult, one way to avoid such misinterpretation is to actually give the Key Signal a specific interpretation. Instead of the Key Signal simply meaning "stop that thing you do that makes us/me get upset," a meaning can be given to the Key Signal that ensures it will not be taken as an insult or a criticism. Most of the time, the best meaning for the Key Signal is "I'm hurt, please be careful." If someone tells a loved one that they have done something hurtful, it is rare that they continue to act in a hurtful manner. That is especially true if they have already agreed that the behavior is hurtful. Of course, Key

Signals are not only used for hurtful behaviors, so many meanings can be given. Examples would be, "I'm scared," "I'm uncomfortable," or "I am worried what people think." The one commonality each of these Key Signal meanings has is that none of them indicates blame. Rather, the meaning of the Key Signal must be a statement about the mental state of the person using it, and not a meaning that suggests the one being given the Key Signal is wrong or bad. "That behavior hurts me" is a far better communication for maintaining good relationships than "You have bad, hurtful, behavior," which is truly insulting and clearly suggests blame.

In fact, the meaning given to the Key Signal may just be its most important attribute. Where once a negative behavior was met with an equally defensive response, with Key Signals the new meaning is one that is a healthy response. When a person does something that hurts us, it is so difficult to say that we're hurt or why we're hurt. The Key Signal makes it possible to say that we're bothered without saying the other person is a bother. If the meaning of the Key Signal is one that clearly shows responsibility for stating our pain rather than one that seems to be an aggressive or controlling ploy, then the person receiving the Key Signal can truly start to understand their effect upon others. At the same time, the Key Signal is much easier to communicate than it would be to actually say "I'm hurt," or "I'm uncomfortable," or "I'm worried what people are thinking." When the Key Signal is given an appropriate, responsible, and vulnerable meaning, it simultaneously promotes real communication and prevents negativity.

Finally, it is important for each party to the Key Signal to review how the Key Signal will be used. In reviewing together, it can be very helpful to role-play various scenarios of the behaviors occurring, or at least to examine them as hypothetical situations. If both people are truly in agreement, then everything will be well-understood and prepared for, and defensive responses should not occur. Role-playing scenarios is extremely useful for anyone trying to use Key Signals. When using Key Signals with children, however, role-playing is absolutely essential. Children really do not generally understand why they react the way they do. When their defensive behavior leads to escalating negativity, children not only have less insight than adults, but they also have less self-control. Role-playing with them often leads to better understanding of their motivations so that they can truly agree without feeling as though the adults around them are asking for yet one more thing.

Key Signals are a fabulous tool when two individuals agree that certain actions between them must change. They are by far the most useful when there is clear understanding of the problem and the motivations behind the behaviors which cause escalating behavioral negativity between two people. Key Signals help people get past the intense volatility of extreme emotions by bringing clear communication into the picture before old patterns of poor communication can take hold and a situation morphs into chaos. Key Signals can say with a simple word or sign the things that words fail to say. Instead of insulting meanings being drawn from one's behavior, the behavior's effect on the other is quickly and appropriately understood. So many people are afflicted by negatively chained interactions that are simply caused by a failure of understanding, which makes Key Signals a supremely powerful tool for bringing clarity to communication. When Key Signals are introduced, they can lead to far more loving interactions. When you're in a relationship poised for positive change, but you just can't seem to let go of old adverse patterns, Key Signals might just be the key. If you're ready for a positive change, and so is your partner or your child, act right now and get a jump start on change, making use of this essential tool, Key Signals.

CHAPTER 30

✂

"I" Statements

"Precision of communication is important, more important than ever, in our era of hair-trigger balances, when a false, or misunderstood word may create as much disaster as a sudden thoughtless act."

—James Thurber

"I" statements are perhaps the most commonly endorsed communication tool for relationships in existence. That makes perfect sense. "I" statements are one of the most important communication tools we have for developing effective communication. When there's a problem in communication related to feelings (as opposed to a lack of grammatical clarity, form, style, or enunciation), one culprit is typically found lurking. "I" statements, when used correctly, can completely expose and redress the culprit. That culprit, the buggy little varmint, is blame.

When people are told they've done something wrong, they typically become defensive. Most people don't like to think they're wrong even when it has nothing to do with blame. When we think someone is finding fault with us, however, we simply just can't stand being wrong. In a way, that's a good thing. Thank goodness most people don't want to do wrong or hurt others. When we get defensive, in a way we're just saying we don't want to hurt anyone. Yet the fact is, people do hurt each other. Most of the time, it's really not intentional. When we want to tell someone they've hurt us, we want to do so because we hope they really didn't want to hurt us. If the reason for telling someone they've hurt us is, thus, to resolve some issue, then there should be significant interest in expressing a hurt in a way that can help. Successful communication of feelings requires that blame be minimized so that the communication can be accepted.

That is the main purpose of the "I" Statement. It is designed to express a feeling responsibly and without blame, so that it can be accepted and answered without defensiveness. "I" statements have **three primary elements**, each of which helps to prevent feelings of blame. Although one person starts a communication with an "I" statement, the process works best when two people have agreed in advance to make use of "I" statements. **First**, the feelings experienced by the party who wants to communicate needs to be connected to an objectively described circumstance or behavior. **Second**, the communicator needs to take responsibility for his or her own feelings. These first two elements are very frequently put together in one sentence and can be in any order. In the **third** element (which is only part of the sequence if both parties have agreed to use "I" statements in advance), the party to whom the "I" statement is being made reflects back what has been said as accurately as possible.

While this process seems simple at first, give it a try and you will quickly find that taking responsibility for feelings without assigning blame is much more difficult than one might think. It is also strangely difficult to connect your feelings with an objectively described behavior or circumstance. In fact, it is generally also very difficult to accurately reflect back what has been said. Constructing a really good "I" statement communication is actually fairly difficult at first. Only practice makes useful use of "I" statements possible. In that vein, perhaps some examples would be helpful.

Example 1

Man: When you came into the room, I felt irritated because I perceived you to be stomping and possibly upset with me.

Woman: I understand you to be saying that you felt irritated when I walked in because you perceived me to be stomping and possibly mad at you.

Example 2

Woman: When you said you were going out to do the lawn, I felt so angry because I thought we were finally going to spend some time together.

Man: You're saying you felt really angry when I said I was going out to do the lawn because you badly wanted to spend time together.

Example 3

Man: I heard you ask me to help you hang the pictures and I felt really frustrated and mad because I had already told you I wanted to get to my tennis match and it seemed like you didn't care.

Woman: You're saying you got upset when I asked you to help hang the pictures because it seemed to you like I didn't care about what you wanted to do.

Example 4

Woman: When you were asking me about how I paid the bills, I started getting really ticked off because it seemed to me like you were acting as though I have no idea what I'm doing.

Man: So you're saying you felt insulted by me when I was asking about how you do the bills because it seemed to you like I was acting as though you don't know what you're doing.

* * *

The most important points to make in reviewing these examples is that it is avoiding blame and defensiveness that is paramount, which makes the objective description of behavior a must.

1. With respect to blame, instead of saying (from example 4) "you really ticked me off," you have to say "I started getting really ticked off." Instead of saying (again, from example 4), "you acted like I don't know what I'm doing," you have to say "it seemed like you were acting as though I don't know what I'm doing." Qualifying oneself and softening how things are said may be a poor communication technique for getting business done at the workplace, but within relationships doing so helps the listener feel less blamed.

2. With respect to defensiveness, it is important that the reflection back to the initiator of the communication must not immediately jump to disproving the initial communication. Instead of saying (from example 3), "you know I always let you do what you want," you have to acknowledge what has been communicated by saying "it seemed to you like I didn't care about what you wanted to do." Instead of saying (from example 1), "I wasn't stomping or mad—you're the one who . . .," you have to say "you perceived me to be stomping and possibly mad at you." Although it can be quite difficult to use "I" statements well, if they can be performed without blame or defensiveness, and as objectively as possible, they will be successful.

Quite often, the next step after a successful "I" statement is a new "I" statement. In example 2, after the man has successfully reflected the woman's communication, he might say "I can tell that you want to spend a lot of time together, and I like that too, but sometimes I feel really squeezed by all my time constraints and I feel pressured by you saying you have a need for more of my time." To which the woman would correctly reflect, "You're saying that me saying I need more of your time makes you feel pressured, like you just can't get everything done." As you can see, it is not as if any one "I" statement can be expected to resolve an entire issue. Some issues go truly deep inside people's views of themselves and how they perceive things in relationships. With "I" statements, a positive chain of effective communications can be initiated that actually leads to resolve, without the traumatizing chain of bad communications that prevent accurate understanding.

If a couple has trouble making headway with "I" statements, it is likely that competition within the couple short-circuits the desire to be fair. People are often so caught up in the desire to win, they lose all faith in any give and take. We come to believe that the same patterns that have always occurred mean that the other person just wants their way, and so we become stuck on getting our way as well. We believe we are right, but we do not believe the other person will ever understand. Thus, when we complain, we attack and when we hear a complaint, we defend. Instead of using communication that suggests something like, "please understand me—I know you'll try," we communicate, "I am right and you are wrong, so do what I say or you're a jerk." If two people who are trying to communicate behave as though they need to win, no level of "I" statements will ever lead to resolve.

All interpersonal communication is a bit like playing catch. In couples there is a tacit assumption that each partner is willing to play. When we speak, it's as though we've thrown a ball expecting our partner will catch it. Competitive communication, however, leads to wild pitches and bean balls that are impossible to catch, and thus no communication is accomplished. Sometimes when one partner is defensive, it's as though they block the ball away instead of catching it, or maybe they don't even lift their hands to catch. When we're trying to communicate, though, we can be somewhat insistent, especially if we believe there really should be an agreement that our partner will cooperate. So when the ball is blocked or dropped, we throw the ball again. We think, "Hey, she's right here with me; why won't she catch the ball?" Or when our partner throws especially errant and wild pitches, we might think, "wow, if he wants me to catch the ball, why in heck is he throwing it at me like he's trying to knock me out of the game?" "I" statements simply make it possible to have a satisfactory game of catch in which the ball is always thrown to be caught, and even if the ball is dropped, it's fielded relatively quickly and then tossed back gently with hope that it will be caught the next time.

"I" statements can also be useful even when two people do not agree in advance to use them. Because "I" statements clearly communicate a feeling without blame, even if only one person in a relationship uses them, it is much more likely that healthy communications will follow. Because the "I" statement takes responsibility and attempts objectivity, the listener is far less likely to become defensive. Although the responder might not be able to respond in a reflective manner, if the person using "I" statements continues to respond to each new communication from the responder with a new "I" statement, the responder will be much less likely to escalate any negative feelings they might be experiencing. They might catch the ball clumsily and throw it back a bit too fast, but if an "I" statement is used well, it's almost a reflexive response to catch and toss.

"I" statements are an amazing tool for getting passed everyday blame and defensiveness that exists in almost every relationship. In order to use them well, each member of a couple must have a loving spirit so that they can literally practice stating their upsets without blame and as objectively as possible. In order to listen and respond to "I" statements in a healthy manner, it is necessary to reflect your understanding of what's been said without defensiveness. If couples need to "win" their arguments, rather than attempting to see that a compromise through mutual understanding is possible, they will never become good at using "I" statements. With honor and respect, however, and with an effort to treasure one another as cherished companions, "I" statements might just be one of the most important communication tools you'll ever acquire. Use "I" statements consistently and with care, and though it might be difficult to do so well at first, with the right spirit you'll soon feel practiced in using "I" statements, just as if you're playing an effortless, but very advantageous, game of field and toss.

PART III

FAMILY DYNAMICS
AND PARENTING

The Family Machine and the
Governing Function of Parents

The Great Life Machine is a construction of an infinite number of interconnected and interdependent systems. From a psychological point of view, the family group is the system of preeminent importance. It is from the family that each individual develops his or her style and awareness of others, and from which each individual will learn how to couple, and then create a new family. It's as if each individual within a family, and then each group that can be derived through the combination of any part of the family, is a cog, a gear, a spring, a sponge, or a subcomponent of the whole family system. The family system works together to be one unit even as the various parts can be viewed separately. Because each part is a component of the larger machine, however, it is typically a grave error to view any one part in isolation from the larger machine. In fact, it is also incorrect to view the family in isolation from the community or communities of which it is part. The family bears its imprint upon each individual, much like DNA from parent to child and back through the generations. Likewise, the health of the family bears its imprint on the larger community and on society itself.

The first subsection of "Family Dynamics and Parental Leadership" focuses on the family as a whole, first in describing how the individual is influenced and influences the other parts of the family as well as larger groups, and then in discussing how emotions take up space within the family unit.

In the second subsection, we turn to parenting issues, from the essentials, to dealing with the judgment of others, and then to getting in tune with the importance of the connection between children and parents.

Understanding what goes into making a good kid is the emphasis of the third subsection. Building block issues such as the balance between materialism and integrity or the balance between freedom and responsibility lead into the more protective issues, like dealing with bullies and teaching children how to be true to who they are.

The ubiquitous parenting issue of discipline wraps up Part III, with articles that will bolster the parenting team and appropriate parenting methods. This subsection hones in on how parents can support one another, make expectations more clear for children, and also searches for an explanation of seemingly nonsensical bad behavior.

In Part III, the family will be discussed as a conglomeration of its parts as well as on its own merit. The primary emphasis will be on getting the family to function in the healthiest manner. The health of the family as a whole is our best hope for individuals and for society, as the healthy functioning family churns out each part onto the world, thus freeing them to create new systems of all kinds and everywhere.

Section 8

Family Relations

Families can be truly complicated. Nevertheless, it is essential to understand how the depth of psychology comes directly from family dynamics. When viewed through an understanding of the connection between inner, life sustaining and protecting, motivations, and how those motivations are nurtured, damaged, neglected, or balanced, it becomes clear that the depths of the psyche, at either the individual or the group level, are similar within us all. Our lives, as unique as they might seem, fall into very definite patterns. Because the motivation to live is essentially the same in everyone, the pitfalls in living are readily understood once one has a true grasp of family functioning and interpersonal influence from the depths of each individual and throughout the family unit. Although the topic can be quite complicated, this section provides articles that will shed light and provide clarity. In the article "From Id to Family System," the mechanisms of human life are discussed from the engine outward. Within the engine of the system is our desire to thrive itself, and that desire influences every other part of the machine. When the individual machine loses balance, the balance it seeks within others and from the environment can seem to unbalance everything. On the other hand, that lack of balance is yet just another kind of balance itself within the Great Life Machine, where ultimately some kind of balance is always found or entropy (the disintegration of everything) prevails. "Emotional Space," the other article in this section, discusses how emotion takes up space, and how space too must be balanced within the family.

CHAPTER 31

❧

From Id to Family System or The Id Is the Engine in the Great Life Machine

"In human society, at all its levels, persons confirm one another in a practical way, to some extent or other, in their personal qualities and capacities, and a society may be termed human in the measure to which its members confirm one another."

—Martin Buber

Is there any systematic way of understanding the relationship between our individual psyches and the whole world that surrounds us? There are many simplistic ways to explain how individuals work within their communities. Those who really like things simple might take the Social Darwinist view and say we all just do what we do, and the strongest survive. Another simple, but somewhat more humanistic view, would be to say we all just need to work toward understanding one another and try to recognize that we are in a world community so that we all may prosper together. There are so many disparate ideas about how life works in a general sense, but is there a way to specifically and systematically describe how people function, both within themselves and at the interpersonal level?

Comprehending the complex connection between the animal nature within us all and our interpersonal behavior at every level of society is an issue that requires examination and analysis if we are to develop true understanding and clarity. Any truly useful understanding will span the distance between the need to survive, compete, and prosper, as in the Social Darwinist view, and the desire to embrace the depths of our humanity, which is the focus of any humanistic perspective. A useful understanding of this complicated topic informs psychological intervention at many different levels so that we can help some do better for themselves, others do better within and for their families, and yes, even perhaps so that we can help the world get along just that much better, one individual, one family, one business or one city, state, country or continent at a time.

Although there is really no one legitimate place to start or finish in an explanation of how we all fit together, since all of us have an effect on one another one interaction or impression at a time, the best example of how all interpersonal systems fit together can be found in the family. In the family each individual fits his or her own internal (or intrapsychic) system of emotions within, around and between the interpersonal system that is generally referred to as the family system.

DRIVES AND DRIVENNESS

Starting with the individual then we can simply ask, what is it that really makes us tick? This question in and of itself seems to suggest that we need something or that we are wound up in such a way that we will keep on going. The most salient psychological concept that attempts to describe what makes us "tick" is the concept Freud (arguably the progenitor of all psychotherapies) termed "drives." The "drives" Freud described were sex (or "libido") and aggression. Now, I don't think Freud was exactly correct about what the "drives" are (for information about how I view the sex drive, please see my article "Sex Is Not a Drive, It's Just Real Important") but, like any first that develops (the first car, the first computer, the first cell phone), Freud's theories as a first have evolved into more accurate and complete concepts. Certainly, with respect to "drives," no one would deny that we all experience a feeling of drivenness. That is, we all experience a feeling of being compelled or impelled to act based on definite and powerful needs.

The best examples of this feeling of drivenness include the everyday occurrences of hunger and the need to stay safe or protected. We know that we are frequently and unavoidably in need of food, and of course our desire to stay safe is expressed constantly in the ways we choose to be careful (locking doors, covering ourselves with clothing, managing to drive without crashing into one another). With respect to hunger, we get a sense of needing to fill ourselves and then we eat until we are adequately satisfied. When we are extremely hungry, however, we can almost get a sense that we are starving and we can become so voracious that we become gluttonous with consumption. With respect to safety, we sometimes avoid those things that scare us, but sometimes the possible occurrence of what we fear is such a threat that we become very angry or even aggressive. These aspects of life "drive" our behavior.

The fascinating thing about how hunger and the need for self-protection "drive" us is that most of our experience for what we need or what we fear can be expressed in the exact same terms as the terms used to describe actual need for food or drink and actual fear of, or aggression and anger toward, potential predators. That is we appear to symbolize almost every experience into being like some aspect of hunger or self-protection. We can say we hunger for more money, more freedom, more friends. We can say we are terrified of public speaking or that others judging us makes us furious. Often these two experiences, hunger and fear/anger/aggression, can be intertwined in our pursuits. For example, when someone pursues power, they can be said to hunger for it but, simultaneously, it is clear that power makes a person less vulnerable, thus clearly linking it to fear/anger/aggression. Really, the same thing could be said about money, freedom, or friends, all examples used above to site things for which we have hunger. Each of these pursuits, in its own way, also makes us feel safe, and if someone interferes with anything related to our safety we can become extremely incensed or frightened.

SUSTENANCE AND SELF-PROTECTION

It becomes clear then that the experience of drivenness is primarily about two essential areas of life that all living creatures have in common, the experience of hunger and the experience of fear/anger/aggression. These two aspects of drivenness I will call the need for "sustenance" and the need for "self-protection." With respect to the need for "sustenance," a desire for something is very much like hunger, and when we have had enough of some activity it is as though we have been sated—we then lose interest, or possibly even start overflowing when we've had too much. Thus, there is a "sustenance" continuum between extremes of sustenance (see Figure 1, a representation of all three continua in relation to one another). Although these extremes are rarely experienced in reality, on one end would be the feeling of abject starvation, while on the other end would be a feeling of being stuffed like a snake after it's swallowed a raccoon.

Describing these rarely experienced extremes is necessary because we are driven to act to the extent that we experience the extremes in these feelings. For example, we would be far more motivated by a feeling of abject starvation than by having a mere craving. Feeling stuffed like the raccoon-sated snake would be motivating to the point of overflowing and could lead to purging in some way, which is far more drivenness than that which comes from merely being sated. While it's easy to give examples of feeling motivated by being starved such as clinging to others when starved for affection, or the drive to amass large quantities of material goods due to being raised in poverty, it's somewhat less typical to think about the motivation that arises from being overstuffed. The best examples are actual purging by the bulimic, and starving oneself as seen in cases of anorexia. Those afflicted with such maladies have often, among other experiences, felt controlled within their life experiences to such an extent that it's as though they are stuffed with the concerns and wishes of others. Frequently, experiencing similar control leads to other kinds of "purging," such as the need to perpetually do for others, and thus leave nothing for oneself.

With respect to the need for "self-protection," we can become fraught with anxiety when there is not any real physical danger (public speaking being the most common example), but when we realize that there's little to fear we can calm down and

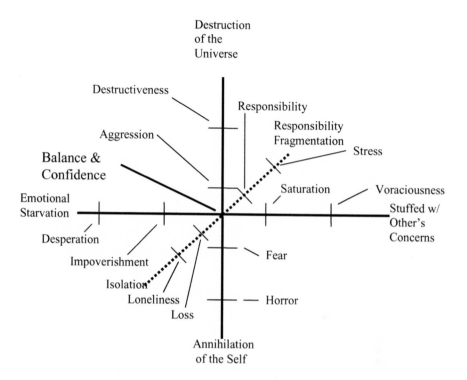

Figure 1: The three "Life Continua" or aspects of "Drivenness" presented in relation to one another in three dimensions. These Life Continua represent issues related to x (sustenance), y (self-protection), and z (relatedness), which are the primary motivators in life. The extent to which x and y are not balanced by interpersonal experience limits the extent to which relatedness can develop in a healthy way. The extent to which all three continua are balanced by and within interpersonal experience determines the level to which a person can be called psychologically "healthy." Balance falls toward the center of the three continua and thus the ends of the three continua represent emotional experience that tends to lead to wild emotional swings which cause exaggerated behavior due to one's difficulty in managing such powerful feelings. The three continua are presented here as each perpendicular to the other in the three dimensions since they are postulated to be orthogonal in nature. That is, each of the three continua is seen as a fully distinct factor.

perhaps be just a little uncomfortable. Likewise, we can feel explosive at times when there is really no physical need to defend ourselves, but when we realize there's little threat, we can calm to being irked. Thus, there is a "self-protection" continuum between extremes of self-protection (see Figure 1). Although these extremes are rarely experienced, on one end would be a fearful withdrawal so strong that it would be almost like an experience of completely vanishing or ceasing to exist, while on the other end would be a feeling of being so destructive one might destroy the entire universe.

We are driven to act by emotions experienced within the self-protection continuum depending upon how extreme they are, just as was the case in considering the sustenance continuum. One would be far more motivated to act by a feeling that their existence was in jeopardy, for example, than they would be by worried anticipation. Likewise one would clearly be much more motivated to act by rage so explosive that it made them want to obliterate everything around them than by trifling aggravation, irritation, or annoyance. Fear at a level akin to feeling one's existence is in jeopardy might occur if one's life was actually being threatened. A feeling of explosiveness so intense that one might desire to annihilate humanity might occur in someone filled with rage due to experiencing a lifetime of being abused and exploited.

RELATEDNESS

It is obvious that something to do with hunger/sustenance on one hand, and fear-aggression/self-protection on the other, is very central to our experience of drivenness. These emotions involve very real biological needs on one hand, but also symbolize our experience of almost all other experiences in one way or another. Yet these most powerful of the emotions, the ones that are actually intrinsic to maintaining life itself, are not the sum of all human experience. Because human beings are social animals, that is because we live in relation to one another at all times, and because we depend upon the fact that we are communal animals to progress, either through reproduction or development or by using teams to accomplish what no one human can accomplish alone, there is a third factor in the experience of drivenness, "relatedness."

"Relatedness" is a drive that develops toward a healthy balance only to the extent that the first two types have become relatively balanced. Balance of the need for sustenance requires that one's environment has been adequately nurturing for his or her particular level of need in that area based upon genetic loading. Balance of the need for self-protection requires that an individual's environment has been adequately safe given his or her particular level of need in that area given his or her genetics. Without adequate balance in sustenance and self-protection, relatedness only develops to rudimentary, very unbalanced levels. When these two aspects of experience do develop toward relative balance, then the third kind of drivenness, the need for "relatedness" can develop more completely. Although it is not nearly as primordial an experience as the need for sustenance or the need for self-protection, the need for relatedness can be seen in all our social behaviors. The currency of relatedness is very different than the other two, however. While being sated is the obvious currency of the need for sustenance, and safety is the obvious currency of the need for self-protection, responsibility is the far less obvious currency of relatedness.

This idea, that responsibility is the way we express ourselves with respect to relatedness, might seem strange at first. Although almost everyone believes responsibility is an important factor in successful living, most people do not think of responsibility as a primary and rudimentary factor of life. But when you think about one factor that allows people to be close or "related" in their feeling to one another, it is how much responsibility they take. In order to develop a feeling of being "related" we must trust the other person to take us seriously, call us back, do what they have said they are going to do, or to, in general, reciprocate the level of relatedness we feel toward them. We must also trust them not to hurt us or, even more importantly, not to damage us. At a more elemental level, for example, the baby must trust the mother to maintain a healthy level of satiation and safety. This is true about food and shelter, but it is also true about the mother's reactions of lovingness. When the child then matures, he or she will have to be trustworthy and responsible with others in life, eventually with his or her own children, in order to engender good relations with them.

In describing the "relatedness" continuum, its relationship to responsibility becomes clear. At one end of the continuum lies "responsibility fragmentation" which is a state of experience in which a person becomes so overwrought with responsibility for everyone else that they start to feel as though they are breaking into pieces.

Complete isolation and alienation lie at the other end of the relatedness continuum, which occurs if a person takes so little responsibility for others, or for their effect on others, that they cease to maintain any relation with others at all. Because responsibility is the currency of the relatedness continuum, the feeling of drivenness involved with the relatedness continuum is generally shame or guilt. A person may attempt to avoid guilt and shame by doing everything they possibly can for others and then become fragmented. Such a person is typically avoiding the possibility of isolation which they fear could develop if they do not behave well enough or do enough for others. They hold themselves to high standards so they will be good enough and so they can avoid guilt, but they wind up being fragmented. On the other hand, a person can attempt to avoid the feeling of fragmentation by perfecting the way they do things. These individuals want to do things so well, so properly, and so morally, in the context of a world of relatedness, that they need not feel guilt or shame. However, such individuals perfect themselves in such an exaggerated way that they become almost completely rigid in their interactions with others and maintain within themselves virtually no vulnerability. This form of perfectionism leads to isolation since there can be no emotional connection to others without at least some level of vulnerability.

Again, it is at the extremes that the relatedness continuum leads to the most driven behavior. When a person fears complete isolation, they are far more motivated to commune with others than if they are merely a tad lonely. Likewise, a person is far more driven to free themselves from obligations when they have become completely fragmented than when they merely feel they've taken on a bit too much. The relatedness continuum does lead to significant drivenness but, as is obvious here, the level of drivenness involving the need to relate to others cannot compare to drivenness related to sustenance and self-protection. While sustenance and self-protection involve emotions, at both real and symbolic levels, comparable directly to survival itself, relatedness is at a whole different level of humanity in which, as indicated above, sustenance and self-protection must already be in balance to some degree if it is to develop at all. If relatedness is to develop beyond complete isolation/alienation or constant fragmentation, some relative balance of the sustenance and self-protection continua is necessary. For that to happen, parents must adequately nurture and protect their children.

THE INTRAPSYCHIC AND INTERPERSONAL BALANCE OF EMOTIONS

Of course, parents cannot always act loving and nurturing without kids becoming screaming brats. In fact it is absolutely essential that parents do not provide everything for their children while expecting nothing in return. When everything is provided with no effort from the child, and the child is completely safe from any kind of concern or worry, the child is not going to become balanced. They would never adequately care for themselves or become independent because there would be no need for self-development. When too much is provided the child feels justified in greed and aggressiveness at every whim and will fail to become responsible for others or how others feel. The human animal develops independence from the tension created between each of the three primary continua of life, with the ideal external influence from parents providing adequate protection, sustenance, and relatedness, but not an overabundance or a paucity of any of the three. Self-development occurs, to a great extent, because a child needs to balance his or her own needs for himself. But in order to do so and develop confidence, an adequate amount of interpersonal sustenance, protection, and relatedness must be available. So how is "enough" love and protection restrained from being "too much?" And how is relatedness balanced so that we are not either too isolated or too fragmented?

The way we balance our feelings of drivenness has a huge impact on everyone else in our environments. Based on how we balance our own drivenness, and expression of that drivenness, others will have to balance their own feelings. When we are balancing ourselves in unhealthy ways, others in our environments are also likely to balance in unhealthy ways, especially if we are necessary for their well-being, as parents are to their children. Similarly, the more well-balanced we are in expressing our feelings, the more likely it is that others, especially our children, will also balance in a healthy manner. In order to have a fuller discussion of balance, we will have to understand what a lack of balance in each of the three types of drivenness looks like. We will also have to understand what factors lead to expression of unbalanced feelings, on the one hand, or the holding in of unbalanced feelings ("repression"), on the other hand.

Let us start with balance of the sustenance aspect of drivenness. When one is balanced in this area, one knows one can easily get enough when one needs it. One would have enough food, enough love, and enough material possessions. When such a person hungers for something, they know they will be able to satisfy that need somehow. This confidence in the ability to satiate oneself makes greedy behavior a rarity. Depression is also a rarity, since such a person knows they will be able to get their needs met and that things will work out. Because these individuals are relatively balanced with respect to the sustenance drive, their expressions of hunger or need for control are also relatively balanced. Their impact on others is one of definite expression and clarity with respect to the sustenance drive, and others understand them and feel free to appropriately express their feelings in the same arena.

However, when the sustenance aspect of drivenness is not in balance, one can behave greedily to the point of needing to devour control over others or material possessions. Others around them thus feel starved for recognition or control or material possessions. When the sustenance continuum is not in balance, and one feels and behaves as though starved, they can act completely hopeless and helpless and may feel their needs will never be met. Others around them will generally feel a need to take control in coming to their aid or to offset their ineptitude. Thus, it becomes clear how the sustenance drive, and the lack of balance in that drive, leads to expression and then intrapsychic and interpersonal balance of a particular type. The interpersonal balance attained when one is unbalanced at the intrapsychic level is, of course, unhealthy to whatever extent that it negatively impacts those from whom sustenance is taken.

With respect to balance of the self-protection aspect of drivenness, when one is balanced, one knows they can adequately protect themselves when they sense tension, judgment, or pressure. This can mean they are able to physically defend themselves, but it also means they can verbally defend themselves and that, inside themselves, they know that the thoughts of others need not affect the way they feel about themselves. They know themselves well enough, through trials and experience, to feel relatively unintimidated by the world and others. They can take feedback without being defensive, but they are equally able to tell others their own opinions and maintain their own opinions when others present a challenge. Because these individuals are relatively balanced with respect to the self-protection drive, their expressions of anger are also relatively balanced and indicate adequate assertiveness. Their impact on others is one of definite expression and clarity with respect to the self-protection drive. Others understand the assertive person and feel free to reciprocate in the assertive expression of their own feelings related to self-protection.

However, when the self-protection aspect of drivenness is not in balance, one can behave very aggressively and dominantly with seemingly little provocation. Alternately, another type of poor balance in this continuum can lead to extremely frightened behavior when there seems to be little to fear. When one does behave aggressively, to the extent that they dominate a situation, others shrink due to fear. Likewise, it is often the case that some people will react to fear in others with dominant and aggressive behavior. Thus, it becomes clear how the self-protection drive, and the lack of balance in that drive, leads to expression and then both intrapsychic and interpersonal balance that is, just as in the case with the unbalanced sustenance continuum, not especially healthy.

Balance of the relatedness aspect of drivenness is quite similar to the other two. When a person is balanced with respect to relatedness, they are able to manage their responsibilities adequately. They take on the right amount of work given the level of support they have and the level of obligation they have within their families and communities. They know they can maintain a healthy level of intimacy with those they love, while also maintaining good relations with friends and a trustworthy reputation among workmates. Because these individuals are relatively balanced with respect to the relatedness drive, their expressions of responsibility are also relatively balanced. Their impact on others is one of willingness to cooperate, but clarity with respect to the responsibility others should take on as well. Others understand the person who is balanced with respect to relatedness and know they can be counted on, but also know that such a balanced person will not allow themselves to be exploited.

When a lack of balance occurs with respect to relatedness, two different kinds of difficulties can arise. When a person takes on too much responsibility, they can become overwhelmed and develop responsibility fragmentation, a feeling that there is nothing left for oneself and that all one's time, energy, and efforts seemingly belong to others. The response of others to a relatively fragmented person, one who is trying to be perfectly responsive to everyone but themselves, is two-fold. Others try to get away from them because the fragmented person appears to be controlling about the morally correct way to do things, and/or they take advantage of them because such a person seems to have little need for themselves. In fact, the acquaintance of the responsibility fragmented person typically perceives them to be completely giving, open, and willing to help in any way possible. However, with their offspring, the moral rectitude the responsibility fragmented person will typically espouse often brings about rigid perfectionism as children attempt to develop a style that is beyond moral criticism and also precludes the possibility of being hurt by moral judgment.

That style of rigid perfectionism derives the other type of unbalance on the relatedness continuum. Some individuals can become so rigid and perfectionistic that they have practically no chance of feeling guilty or being hurt. Without guilt or vulnerability, or the humility of being merely human, such individuals become interpersonally isolated because they never need to take responsibility, or even accept the possibility that they might be responsible, for being wrong. Generally, family members of individuals who isolate themselves with perfectionism respond by trying to please, and often experience themselves as somewhat responsibility fragmented because the rigid, perfectionistic person is critical and can never be pleased. Acquaintances who come into contact with the rigidly perfectionistic person typically find them extremely cold and unable to connect. Thus, we clearly see how the a lack of balance within the relatedness drive leads to certain types of expression and then both intrapsychic and interpersonal balance that is not necessarily healthy.

It must also be said that the influence of relatedness as it pertains to expression and drivenness is not nearly as polarizing as the influence of sustenance or self-protection. While unbalanced expression of emotions related to sustenance and self-protection will almost always pressure others to engage in complementary behaviors (domination bringing about submission and desperation bringing about control), unbalanced expression of emotions related to relatedness can often bring about identification in exaggerated expressions instead of complentarity. Parents who engage in a responsibility fragmented way of life greatly appreciate similar behavior in their children, who often develop similar tendencies instead of developing the opposing, perfectionistic, rigid, and isolated style discussed above.

Likewise, parents who engage in the rigid and perfectionistic style tend to appreciate similar behavior in their children, who thus can develop similar tendencies instead of developing the complementary, responsibility fragmented behavior that is so often observed.

BOUNDARIES AND THE CREATION OF COMBUSTION, COMPRESSION, AND FORCE OF EXPRESSION

In the paragraphs above, it has been shown how feelings become extreme when they are unbalanced, and then lead to specific kinds of behavior and expression. However, this explanation cannot fully demonstrate exactly how or when feelings will be expressed or how much influence they will have when they are expressed. It is certainly true that sometimes very healthy people can experience very powerful emotions without those emotions resulting in extreme behavior. It is also obvious that very extreme emotions can be expressed in very extreme ways by people even though there seems to have been very little stress involved. Balance is clearly one aspect of this expression, but another aspect that is necessary for complete understanding of how the psyche is systematically involved in interpersonal systems is the concept of "boundaries." The unbalanced drives are like the fuel in the intrapsychic system, but in order for combustion of this powerful fuel to give the system force, compression (inward pressure) and directional release (outward pressure) is necessary.

Compression and directional release is provided by boundaries (see figure 2). When a person is said to have poor boundaries, it typically means either of two different things or both. Poor boundaries can refer to behavior that results in more influence or pressure on others than is appropriate given a particular situation, or that the feelings of others have too much influence on a person. The expression of emotions sometimes seems extreme or has too much impact. On the other hand, when a person is particularly sensitive, the behavior and expressions of emotions from others can be quite subtle and yet, nevertheless, cause extreme emotional reactions. When a person does seem to influence others too much, or experience the influence of others too much, it can be said that their boundaries are too porous. But to be more exact, there are actually two boundaries within any person. There is an internal boundary and an external boundary.

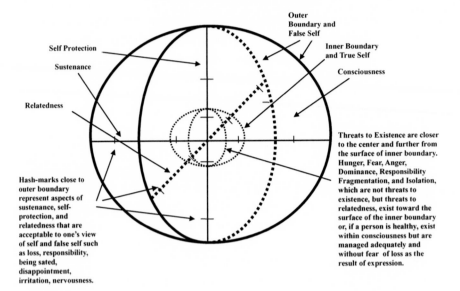

Figure 2: The model turned inside out. The three primary Life Continua are presented here inside out. Extreme emotions that are unbalanced within the "sustenance," self-protection," and "relatedness" spectrums are contained within by the internal boundary, while the outer boundary determines what or who will be allowed to effect an individual and how one's emotions will be allowed to effect others. The emotions contained within the internal boundary are often "repressed" (pushed downward and out of awareness) because of their potential for damaging one's connections with others. To the extent that repression is successful, those emotions do not damage relationships. But with repression comes the development of a true-self/false-self dichotomy. In the hypothetical case of complete balance within the relatedness issue, the extreme emotions or threats at the inner core would be modulated and thus acceptable enough that a person could spontaneously present the self to others without fear of loss or damage due to unbalanced emotions influencing interaction. As the extreme emotions of the inner core become less threatening, the inner boundary approaches the outer boundary, which signifies *"confidence"* within oneself and *authenticity* within one's behavior. This process could be likened to the true self coming up to the surface so that the false self is no longer needed. On the other hand, when emotions within

the inner core are so unbalanced that they require expression and balance from others, repression merely works to prevent direct expression. When emotions within the inner core are too unbalanced, the part that is most threatening to oneself is held within, while often something similar to its opposite emotion is expressed for the purpose of creating a more balanced feeling. This kind of interpersonal balance is necessary when someone is unable to adequately contain themselves in a healthy way which requires the ability to directly ask for needs to be met. This kind of interpersonal balancing is not healthy in that it makes the individual dependent upon others for that balance (either by needing others to submit or by borrowing others strength) and damages one's relationships with excessive influence.

To understand what is inside and what is outside of each of these two boundaries, and how each of the boundaries works, it is necessary to look, once again, at the three primary factors of life. As has been described above, the sustenance, self-protection and relatedness continua can be viewed as being balanced in the middle, with the extremes of each represented at the ends of each continuum. To fully comprehend the workings of the internal and external boundaries, however, requires us to look at these continua slightly differently. Because our most intense feelings are held deep within us, turning the three continua inside out allows us to see how the boundaries function with intense emotions at our unconscious core and less intense emotions available for expression within our conscious minds. With our most intense emotions represented at the core, it becomes much more clear how these intense emotions, in combination, drive our interpersonal behavior. These intense emotions are, so to speak, combustible and must be contained. Their power is harnessed and given direction by the boundaries. The internal boundary contains our most intense emotions and governs our awareness of those extreme emotions. The external boundary determines which emotions are allowed expression and which emotions expressed by others are allowed to have personal impact on us. The three continua presented with their most intense aspects represented at the center, and the internal and external boundaries presented as they work, is illustrated in Figure 2. The external boundary is the one to which most people are referring when they use the term "boundaries," thus it will be discussed first.

The external boundary not only determines whether or not feelings will be expressed, but also if they'll be steadfastly held inside, or absorbed from others. We have all had the experience of deciding whether or not to express something, and we have all wondered why the expressions of others have had unwanted influence on us. That is the external boundary in operation. There often seems to be a lot of pressure on the external boundary. We think about whether the expression of a particular emotion will have too large of an impact on others. We also think about the level of desperation seemingly imposed upon us by the experience of emotions, either from holding on to them or from having them foisted upon us. The final outcome is rarely the result of a measured understanding of all possible outcomes. More often than not, we simply succumb to a natural balance that is different for each of us as individuals, and which depends upon our particular way of experiencing pressures within us and around us.

The external boundary manages our presentation to the world and how much outside influences effect that presentation. It shows others what they perceive about what we feel and think. Some people are especially good at maintaining the particular kind of outward appearance that they wish others to see. In that case, the external boundary represents what is often called in psychology, a "false self." In other words, a false self is a presentation that is maintained for effect or which develops to have a certain effect, but which does not accurately represent one's true feelings. Some people have too little control of what is presented and have extreme impact on others when they should actually be able to contain themselves. Others absorb more from others when they should be able to maintain themselves without allowing such influence. When one's emotions, that is the drivenness experienced from the unbalanced need for sustenance, self-protection, and/or relatedness, overwhelm the external boundary, the balancing emotions that are complementary to what is held within are displayed or absorbed and do actually lead to balance within the person expressing or absorbing the feelings, but not in a healthy way. The emotions displayed in such people misrepresent the emotional state of such a person and thus also are a presentation of false self.

A person's outer presentation of themselves is only an analog of "true self" to the extent that the person has managed to adequately balance the inner emotions so that they can be genuinely and spontaneously expressed without impacting others unnecessarily. Expressing true self does not preclude impacting others, but does require that such impact be reflective of one's true emotional needs and requirements. For example, if a person feels afraid, they act afraid, which could elicit a protective response from others to balance the fear. Such a person does not, however, balance by acting especially angry and fearless to camouflage the fear they experience beneath. Likewise, a person can act angry when angry, which could elicit a fearful response from others. They do not, however, balance themselves by acting annoying to elicit an angry response, thus camouflaging their true anger and resentment.

The external boundary is the most crucial of the two boundaries for this current discussion since it so directly involves interpersonal influence, but the whole topic of boundaries cannot be explained without also mentioning the internal boundary. The internal boundary governs whether or not we are aware of, or impacted by, our own most extreme feelings, or whether the feelings we absorb from others will be allowed to affect us at the deepest level. Like the external boundary, the internal boundary also can be too porous. When the internal boundary is too porous, which typically occurs because drivenness from lack of balance in sustenance and/or self-protection cannot be adequately contained within the inner recesses of our minds, extreme feelings flood our awareness, we are dramatically impacted by those feelings, and the feelings are so intolerable that they cannot be contained. Thus the severity of these needs is so powerful that they seek immediate expression in some form and are not well modulated.

The internal boundary can also be too rigid or impermeable instead of being too porous. Most long-term psychoanalytic or analytic therapy focuses on uncovering aspects of very deeply held extreme feelings that are actually too well governed by the internal boundary because it is not porous enough (at least with respect to certain specific feelings). These extreme feelings are so well repressed (pushed down inside) that the individual experiencing them is not at all aware that the feelings exist. What is so interesting about this phenomenon is that the drivenness from relatedness is quite well-established in these individuals even though some aspect of the drivenness that is held deep within is so extreme that it cannot be tolerated. That is, the thoughts about that feeling actually threaten relatedness to such a degree that the feelings are held deep within, yet outside (actually too far inside if viewed from the perspective shown in Figure 2) of awareness. This threat to relatedness involves the guilt or shame possible if one's inner feelings leak out or must be acknowledged. Although individuals with such difficulty are relatively well-balanced with respect to sustenance and self-protection, problems with repression involve difficulty in balancing relatedness since the potential for harm in one's thoughts involve the possibility of hurting others.

For example, perhaps a person must think of him or herself as extremely generous and helpful, but expresses the selfish need of being in control by taking charge when they help others. That control allows them to be sated by knowing where their nurturance will come from—gratitude from others—while simultaneously keeping them safe and protected because no one will be able to aggressively dominate them and make them feel vulnerable. Such an individual actually has a relatively nonporous inner boundary that is too powerful in repressing specific feelings of vulnerability, aggressiveness, or extreme need for nurturance. Nevertheless, some feeling escapes the inner boundary and seeks expression. Balance comes only from being in control as a boss, but this satisfaction is indirect as the individual allows themselves to feel very giving while denying the taking they simultaneously experience. True health, and thus the reason for psychoanalysis, comes only from uncovering the need for repression, and acceptance of the feelings that are so threatening (a need for nurturance/appreciation and a need to be dominant).

The simple "denial" that is so commonly discussed in everyday conversation is related to this repression. With denial there is a need to keep oneself from knowing something that would be too upsetting. The knowledge that is denied can be related to one's own feelings, but can also involve the feelings that could be stirred up if one were to allow themselves knowledge about something else that is happening in their relationships. Denial works with repression, that is the pushing down of one's feelings to prevent them from becoming overwhelming, so that many kinds of knowledge can be ignored, and so that feelings that could threaten relationships can continue to be held within the internal boundary where they cannot effect one's important relationships. Typical examples include the cuckolded husband who successfully ignores every sign of his wife's infidelity so that he will not have to confront her and jeopardize his relationship with her or perhaps his children. Another typical example is the wife of the addict who never thinks her husband has a problem in spite of numerous addiction related mishaps and difficulties so that her relationship with him can continue on in its current pattern. In these situations, denial is a valuable defense for maintaining the status quo in relationships and works through the repression of one's awareness of facts that would seemingly require disruptive action.

We see in this discussion that the strength of influence from the expression of emotions involves both balance of emotions, and boundaries to contain or not contain emotions. We see that poor balance in general tends to result in poor boundaries and expression of extreme emotions with little provocation, or absorption of emotions in spite of relatively little intensity of expression. We also see that too much emphasis on relatedness, especially without adequate development in the balance of sustenance and self-protection, can lead to a very indirect expression of emotions due to the workings of the boundaries which hold off the worst of one's true emotions. That is, people typically express the opposite of their most uncomfortable feelings in an effort to deny the truth of the emotions while also balancing one's own mind by evoking within others those feelings that are most threatening. If those feelings can be created in others, it becomes possible to balance one's own feelings by proving to oneself that those feelings are much more true of others than oneself. Most importantly, the influence of drivenness and boundaries within people are clearly shown to have significant interpersonal influence. That interpersonal influence is the basis for understanding interpersonal interaction at a systematic level. The psyche is the engine of interpersonal discourse, with drivenness as the fuel and boundaries creating compression and power by variably containing or releasing the combustion of drivenness to particular parameters set by a combination of life experiences and genetics.

BALANCE OF EMOTION AND FAMILIES

Moving from the individual's expression of emotions and it's particular way of creating influence at the interpersonal level, we can now see that seeking balance of internal pressures is *the* specific and singular purpose of expressing emotions (it could even be argued that balancing is the purpose of all communication). The individual experiences feelings and needs and those feelings and needs are then expressed to the extent that the individual requires a balancing reaction from one's environment. Balance is then either accomplished, or the feelings and needs continue to be experienced and uncomfortable or even intolerable.

Whenever balance is not accomplished, it continues to be sought. Sometimes a person accomplishes balance completely internally by talking to themselves differently about a certain subject or realizing that they don't really need what they had thought they needed. Other times, a new way to balance is sought, and a completely different behavior develops to supplant the behavior that is no longer effective in helping the individual balance. For example, a person might develop a buying addiction, but then becomes unable to spend (all credit gone, or put in jail, etc). Such a person may have been expressing a need for nurturance that did not necessitate the vulnerability experienced when more directly asking for closeness or attention from others. When they become unable to spend, they might develop hypochondria in an effort to gain attention and nurturance while maintaining control of their experience with others (i.e., the hypochondriac's symptoms help them achieve nurturance without vulnerability since sickness is not thought of as weakness by the hypochondriac).

But how does the need for balance effect families, or even communities, countries or the world? Essentially, within any kind of group, the person who, or entity which, is perceived as the most powerful is able to balance his feelings first, and everyone else must follow suit, or alternately, challenge the current authority. This hierarchy of balancing authority occurs even when people are mentally healthy. When the interpersonal system is healthy, balancing behaviors promote health within everyone who is involved. For example, a mother works hard, takes responsibility, and along with her husband perhaps, makes sure everyone in the family is nurtured and protected. She then commands and deserves respect from her children. The fact that she commands respect might seem like a weakness, but quite the contrary, it is simply the way it should be since she works hard to make sure the needs of everyone else are met. She deserves respect. The fact that she demands respect does not diminish anyone else. Rather, it teaches the children that hard work is respectable and that they too should try to work hard and be responsible so that they too can have respect. In fact, if they work hard to get respect, they also make less work for their mother, and the entire process remains wholesome. To the degree to which a family is healthy, every member's needs are met simultaneously much of the time because the needs of the parents automatically bring about meeting the needs of the children. For example, the father wants to work hard and succeed which allows him to support his family and which also provides the children a good example of how they too should behave.

In the case of less mentally healthy people, however, strong needs and emotions are expressed and because they are expressed so dominantly, the other less dominant people in the family must absorb those feelings in such a way as to complement or accommodate those feelings. The word complement as I am using it here means *opposite* in such a way as to fit together, but is not a positive attribute when used to describe extreme emotions. That is, dominant behavior necessarily results in submissive behavior. One person in a family has to have his way because that is the only thing that will make him feel adequate. So others in that family specifically cannot have their way. If the dominant person has to be smart, someone else must be foolish. If the dominant person must define himself as sweet, then someone else must be rotten. The more complementary one's responses must be, the less healthy they are in general and the more diminishing they are as well. But because this action requires, and thus results in, a lack of balance within those other family members, that lack of balance seeks balance as well, and an unhealthy dominance hierarchy is created within the family.

BALANCE AND ROLE DIFFERENTIATION

Oftentimes balance can occur in healthier families in relatively healthy ways through role differentiation. In healthy families balance is found when the parents have relatively equal dominance, yet with role differentiation between them. In the traditional family, for example, the father might be in the disciplinarian role and the mother the more nurturing role, but if both parents give each other mutual and equal respect, and neither attempts to be dominant overall, then their example of balance can be passed down through the children. The children in following the lead of the parents are likely to differentiate their roles in relatively healthy ways as well. Perhaps one child becomes the smart one who is "like" Mom and another child becomes the athletic child who is "like" Dad, and both ways of being are considered equally positive.

In the unhealthy family, however, no one really feels balanced. The reason the unhealthy parents need to express so strongly within the family is because of some extreme needs left in them from their own past lives or genetics. The children cannot possibly balance the feelings foisted upon them by their parents, and they either express them in a negative manner within the family, with other children outside the family, or hold the feelings deep within while saving them up for expression at a later time in life (or any combination of the three).

PROBLEMS IN BALANCE AND DIAGNOSTIC CATEGORIES

Whenever you see extreme expression of emotion, there is clearly a problem in balance. This is true even in cases of depression, PTSD, bipolar disorder, or even schizophrenia, when it is clear that there is an extreme experience or some genetic component involved. If the experience (either a loss or a trauma) occurred recently, it can be far too difficult to tolerate for even healthy people. However, the less healthy a person is, the more likely that any trauma or loss will be intolerable. With depression, an otherwise healthy person can suddenly experience a loss of some sort which then leads to an inability to balance within themselves because of what that lost thing or person provided for them. In the case of bipolar disorder, many times a person is born with extreme intensity (it exists at a genetic level) and yet the fact that their parents have trained them to care, love, and take responsibility creates an extreme pressure to be good even while the intensity of their emotions leads them to seek immediate gratification, thus making them "bipolar" (the vast majority of "bipolar" diagnoses these days refer to people who have been brought up poorly rather than those who have been brought up well but have extremely intense emotions). In the case of schizophrenia, there is a sudden inability to maintain an adequate internal boundary and thus the mind is flooded with the most extreme, irrational emotions that then seek balance through the creation of an alternate reality that balances those feelings.

BALANCE AND SOCIETY

Amazingly, all of these phenomena—balance of intensity, balance of relatedness, boundaries, interpersonal balance, balance through role-differentiation—occur at all levels of society. One family affects another family as they try to balance their own standing within the community. One city balances its needs against the other cities in its county. One company seeks hegemony over other companies, just as countries try to rule over one another. It all starts in perceived needs within each family, city, company or country. Boundaries get involved within each level that I have mentioned in a very similar way to how they are involved in every individual. Whole societies have certain ways of being that are simply not tolerated (an internal boundary) as well as certain aspects of experience that simply shouldn't be, or always must be expressed (an external boundary). In everyday discourse between these various companies or cultures, various pressures seek balance through interaction with the others. At all these levels, role differentiation can be seen in the roles taken by families, cities, companies, countries, and even continents.

There are healthier ways of communicating and less healthy ways, with more aggressive and dominant expressions of the family's, city's, company's, or country's needs often winning out until the more oppressed build up so much angst in their lack of balance that their expression takes form against the more dominant. From a psychological perspective, the system will always balance, no matter what any one individual wants. The only way for everyone to seek balance in a healthier way is to do so mindfully and intentionally. Unfortunately, in almost all of us, even within me and most likely within you, it is our own needs that take precedence most of the time. Strangely enough, watching out for our own needs first, but in balance with everyone else and our world, is the healthiest way for any of us to be. That is, every one of us is most healthy when we are able to have enough self-respect to make sure our own needs are met, but simultaneously we have enough confidence that our needs will be met that we can take responsibility for others and try to work toward the greater good. In this way we can see that true mental health, at the individual level, the family level, the city, company, state, country or world level, requires strength in convictions and confidence within the self or the organizational culture, along with balance of needs and healthy boundaries at every level. The world itself must balance if there is to be health for everyone, and the more every individual takes responsibility for himself and his culture, the greater likelihood that the world will become healthier and healthier for us all.

CHAPTER 32

ɔ

Emotional Space

"Between stimulus and response there is a space. In that space is our power to choose our response. In our response lies our growth and our freedom."

—Victor E. Frankl

Did you know that emotions take up space as well as time and energy? Have you ever noticed that emotions can crowd a room, or that when one person is very emotional others tend to tone their emotions down (except in mass hysteria where a competition for emotional prominence ensues). When one person is having great difficulty, others tend to come to their aid. Others get out of the way when another person is being especially aggressive or obnoxious. When the parents in a family tend to fight, the first reaction of young children is to be as good as possible with hope that their parents will fight less. When someone is expressing intense emotion, that expression is generally dealt with immediately. Intense emotion tends to take precedence over everything else that is currently happening.

The concept of "emotional space" is little known, but it helps explain why even some healthy people can find themselves in difficult situations with emotionally unhealthy people. It is important to realize, of course, that there are appropriate times for emotions to be expressed. If a mentally healthy person really gets upset, they typically should express the feeling to someone at some time. Also, the less controlled expression of emotions is expected from children. The younger a child is, the more desperately they perceive their emotions, and thus the more desperately, immediately, and dramatically they will express those emotions. A serious problem often develops, however, when people take up too much "emotional space" even though it is not developmentally appropriate.

This problem is most difficult to understand when the person who is emoting too intensely is engaging with someone who really has no problem handling their own emotions. Believe it or not, there is such a thing as being too emotionally controlled. What I mean by this, however, is not that the emotionally controlled person has reached a perfect balance in life. Quite to the contrary, the problem here is that such a person has not learned to balance the overwhelming amount of love, luck, and good discipline they have experienced in their lives with the idea that others should not be allowed to take advantage of them or treat them badly. It is also often the case that a person develops emotional control because they have been exposed to extremely damaging emotional expression in their childhoods and have vowed to themselves to control their own emotions no matter what. Unfortunately, whether due to good fortune or bad, often the emotionally controlled person will allow others to hurt them, or not take them seriously, because they do have the inner strength to maintain their self-esteem or composure in spite of maltreatment.

It is necessary to make a side point here in differentiating the emotionally controlled person from other persons who have greater difficulties. There are many people who allow others to treat them poorly for reasons that are quite different than having the strength to maintain control. A person can allow others to treat them poorly because they are desperate for approval and love, and will cling to others no matter how badly they are treated. But the emotionally controlled person rarely stays in a bad relationship for too long. Although such a person might not be direct in handling a conflict, behavior aimed at them that is abusive is so inconsistent with how they see themselves that they will often find a way out of relationships that do not fit them. They will rarely stay in a relationship if someone is not treating them in a positive way that is consistent with what they know they deserve.

There is one caveat to that suggestion, however, and this phenomenon is essential to understanding many family situations. What happens when an emotionally controlled person has children? It is a common occurrence for such a person to meet another person, a spouse, with similar strength. That is, of course, the emotionally controlled person feels good when with someone who is used to being treated well, has received good and fair discipline, and thus treats others well as would be expected given their background and experience. When the emotionally controlled couple have children, however, problems can arise because they provide too much "emotional space" for their children. There can be a tendency to allow too much attitude, anger, or neediness without requiring equal amounts of discipline and responsibility since, as a parent, the emotionally controlled person has the mental and emotional strength to absorb quite a bit without it causing too much impact. No matter how their kids act, the emotionally controlled person is quite capable of dealing with that behavior without getting too upset. Unfortunately, when such a parent does absorb all that emotional intensity without getting upset, the child does not benefit from having to take responsibility for his or her effect on the parents. He is given too much "emotional space" and thus has too much room to act out (angry or irrational or spoiled).

The "only child" is often the worst case scenario. Only children (especially when they have two parents within an intact marriage) have parents who are capable of responding to their every protest, distress, or displeasure. If those parents are relatively mentally healthy, and generally emotionally controlled, then the emotional space they provide is often almost endless. It is only natural to love one's children and to do whatever one can for one's children. When we have only one child we are able to do too much, and we often do. Exacerbating the accessibility and willingness of such parents is the fact that the only child does not have to share their parents, or anything else for that matter, with a sibling or siblings. Only children often never learn to control their emotions or needs because there has never in their lives been a need to do so.

The essential element here is that people need to learn how to accommodate their behavior to the needs of others and to take responsibility for the effect of their emotions on others. When others are too accommodating to them, they never learn. Sometimes, when a person has never learned such accommodation, they become very aggressive and they will even tend to get their way. The problem with that is, of course, that if they are always getting their way they will never truly develop any intimacy with others. Consequently, although they might seem to be in almost complete control within the many interpersonal involvements they develop, they will often end up lonely and isolated because no one has ever really grown close to them.

Emotional control is a necessary and important aspect of living, but there is such a thing as controlling yourself too much. You cannot afford to let anyone close to you treat you less than respectfully, even if you are strong enough to handle your emotions in the face of that treatment. If it is someone who is supposed to be your equal, they need to know their behavior is unacceptable and that, if it continues, they will have to deal with the consequences. That is, you will leave.

If the offender is a child, there are consequences for them, as well. For children, the consequence of less than respectful and appreciative behavior, let alone aggressive behavior, should be that they have to deal with your feelings, either hurt or anger (if you get angry too frequently, however, then you yourself will be guilty of taking up too much emotional space). If your children truly care about you, which almost all children do, they will not feel comfortable when you really show your feelings (please see article "Communication from the Heart"). If you bring up your real feelings, you are taking up the emotional space that they will take if you do not. You will be taking up the emotional space that is rightly yours.

In many circumstances, it is also essential that children receive appropriate consequences for their behavior. With the caring child, when the disrespect is minor, it is often enough to simply let them know you're hurt. If such a statement is taken seriously, and is not overwhelming to the child, nothing more will be required. In many cases, however, a consequence helps the situation in two ways. First of all, it is obvious that consequences are typically meted out for the purpose of making the child take things seriously. That is a great benefit in itself. Where the parent is able to express their feelings appropriately about a particular infraction, and the child feels badly, giving a consequence has an added benefit. A child will often actually feel less guilty, but still be serious about what they have done, when they are given the chance to compensate by redeeming themselves. In that vein, the very best consequences are those that will be helpful to the wronged party so it feels to the child as though the consequence has partially repaired the damage.

The concept of emotional space is essential for understanding how we all balance our emotions within families and even in other organizations. In any normal family, while children might be of utmost importance to parents, it is fundamental that parents occupy the greatest amount of emotional space. Parents lead and children follow. Thus, even when parents do everything they can to ensure the health, well-being, and future accomplishments of their children, they also must set the stage and structure for the family, and the children must fit themselves to that structure. When parents take their own feelings and needs seriously, children have to do so as well. Since the number one concern of most parents is that their children lead healthy, successful lives, the leadership and structure (emotional space) set by parents has an excellent chance of leading to a healthy family structure overall.

Likewise, even in nonfamily situations, it is central to your own mental health that you set the structure of your own life. You must set the tone for others to take you seriously about your preferences, desires, irritations, and hurts. (Please see article "Assertiveness: The 30% Solution"). So be good to yourself. Take up the emotional space you deserve, and do not let anyone intrude without some kind of response, even if your reaction need only be minimal. If someone is hurting you to the point that you cannot be with them any longer, or if you need to show that you absolutely will not tolerate their behavior, then anger is likely the most appropriate response. In most circumstances, however, if the person is one with whom you want to be closer, or if that person is a child, it is important to let them know that you are hurt or disappointed and make sure they have to deal with some real consequences. You are the master and architect of your own existence. You need only be confident that you deserve an equal share of the existing emotional space in your life.

Section 9

Parenting

Parenting is potentially both the toughest and the most rewarding part of life. Any parent knows that the minute their first child is born, their life changes forever. All that you thought was important before pales in comparison to the health, well-being, and future success of your children. Thus, the parenting function of the couple in a family is obviously of crucial importance for the efficient, or at least sufficient, functioning of the family machine. In this section, the articles emphasize the basics for good parenting, protecting the parents from disruptive outside influences, and helping kids understand just how much their parents care. In "The Essentials of Parenting," the balance between four primary parenting skills is outlined and discussed. "Who's to Know What's 'Right' in Parenting?" encourages parents to trust their own judgment in picking the basic kind of parenting they want to practice. Finally, in "You Don't Know How Much They Love You," a "talk" is presented that one might want to have with an ungrateful or disrespectful child or adolescent, with hope that any child who is loved can see just how passionate parents are about the welfare of their children. This section, when combined with the next section on *Building Good Kids* and the next on "discipline practices," offers a good basis for quality parenting. Quality parenting leads to building good kids, and there can be no doubt that discipline practices are central to that process.

CHAPTER 33

⚘

The Essentials of Parenting

"Deliberate with caution, but act with decision; and yield
with graciousness, or oppose with firmness."

—Charles Caleb Colton

As every parent knows, there is no occupation as difficult as
parenting. We want the most for our children, but we have many other
concerns and stresses that we attempt to balance simultaneously.
Few parents are completely satisfied with their parenting. The issues
involved are so complicated. In fact, sometimes it seems parenting
is so complicated that we have difficulty remembering the most
essential elements involved. In that regard, it can be helpful to have
the essentials of parenting presented within just a few basic guidelines
which will assure that you are the absolute best parent you can be.

The essentials of parenting are these: parents must make a
constant effort to look upon their children with kindness and affection,
balanced by consistency and firmness. If parents make such an effort,
even if they often falter, their children will feel loved and appreciated,
and will also understand the importance of rules. Equally important,
a consistent effort at good parenting will ensure that children will
maintain a connection with the specific desires, and the all-important
vision for their future, of those who love them most.

Since this sounds way too easy, perhaps I should elaborate on the meaning of these factors. Each of these concepts is complicated by individualistic attitudes and the stresses of everyday life in our fast-paced world. It is not possible to be kind all of the time, and we do not always feel like hugging, even if our children deserve it. Consistency is difficult for many reasons, but mostly because we feel differently about things at different times. Consistency is also difficult when two parents disagree about their approach to parenting. The problem with being firm is typically a lack of adequate energy, but firmness can also be difficult when we are feeling especially loving despite some of the bad behavior we see in our children. When we are not firm we are also, typically, inconsistent. Perhaps it will be helpful to elaborate on what I mean by kindness, affection, consistency, and firmness.

Kindness

In essence, kindness involves putting yourself in the shoes of your child, thinking about your child's motivations or intentions, and realizing that what they're going through, or the way they're acting, is related to their age, and the vulnerability of their situation. When we disapprove of a child's behavior, we are likely to overreact if we see their actions exclusively from the adult perspective. It is common to think children should know better without considering what they are experiencing. When we're tired or stressed it can intensify a less than empathic reaction. Likewise, when children are acting in ways that we like, we have to remember that their actions require effort on their part, and if we do not demonstrate our appreciation, our children might feel little desire to make similar effort in the future.

Affection

One way that we can show our appreciation is through affection. It feels good to be hugged and snuggled as long as it's invited. The desire of most children for affection is so great that they'll often rub up against their parents, or flop into their laps, like hungry kittens. Sometimes children will behave in positive ways just because they want affection. But it is also often the case that a child is in a moment where they want and need independence. It is important for parents to understand the independent spirit of their children and to refrain from being too affectionate when their child desires, or should be developing, independence. As much as a parent must recognize that their child needs affection, they must also realize that holding off on being affectionate might be almost as crucial since a child can perceive overwhelming affection as thwarting independence.

Consistency

Consistency is made difficult by our own changing moods and by our differences with our partners. Children are better able to negotiate the family and watch their behavior when parents' expectations are clear, and the consequences are set for what will occur when expectations are not met. If we are able to remain consistent in spite of stress or unpredictable circumstances, we build stability into the family environment. Nothing can be more important than the ability of parents to support one another in their views and their interventions if consistency is to be maintained. The confidence children develop as a result of parental consistency carries over into other parts of life, and into your child's future.

Firmness

Firmness, of course, goes hand in hand with consistency. When a parent is serious and behaves in accordance with their feelings, children feel it in their bones. This is not a recommendation for angry or mean behavior. Rather, tone of voice, body language and facial expression easily reveal seriousness. Children who are used to a consistent, yet loving and affectionate, home, know when they should not cross the line. Testing of parental limits occurs with almost all children, but if children know with certainty that parents will stand firm when they've had enough, children learn their limits while simultaneously learning the limits they should set in their interactions with others.

Make the Effort

There is one point that is essential to repeat. As a parent it is necessary to *make the effort* to keep these attributes in mind and in balance. But it is not always going to be easy, and sometimes it may not seem possible. Parents need to give themselves a break when they are impatient or snap in frustration. As long as there is an *effort* to be kind, affectionate, consistent, and firm, children will get the message that they are loved, valued, and cared for in a consistent and knowable world. If they internalize that message, they will carry it with them throughout their lives, and they will pass it on to the next generation.

CHAPTER 34

❧

Who's to Know What's "Right" in Parenting?

"A child becomes an adult when he realizes that he has a right not only to be right but also to be wrong."

—Thomas Szasz

Have you ever wondered why you treat your kids so differently when other people are around? It's a common difficulty in parenting to be influenced by the judgment of others, even when you're confident about how you want to handle your kids. Most of the time this difficulty occurs around the issue of discipline. Maybe you tend to be the kind of parent who likes to let your children have a little freedom, and you find that others seem to suggest, through body language or sideways glances, that your children are getting out of hand. Suddenly, and right out of the blue, you become some wicked and maniacal control freak whom your children hardly recognize. Or perhaps your kids know you always follow through, and you're very careful about what they do. Then your friends or family seem to suggest, through some twisted crack or smarmy witticism, that you're way too "anal." "Just let kids be kids, for goodness sake," they say. Suddenly, and right out of the blue, you become some free love flower child that your kids, not surprisingly, are all too eager to meet. While these characterizations might be exaggerations, what is important to know is that consistency of approach, not any one parenting style, is what leads to the best results in raising kids.

The basic problem here is that no one, and I mean no one, really knows for sure what single parenting approach is best for children in the long run. It is much easier to know what is not good than what is good. Extreme beliefs in any direction are definitely not good. What is good boils down to a few basic principles that are necessary to ensure emotional maturation. Each of these differ considerably depending upon the viewpoint of the individual parent. Let's say that loving your children means providing proper guidance through kindness and affection, balanced by firmness and consistency (please see article "The Essentials of Parenting"). If that is so, then how do we know how much kindness and affection to give before becoming firm and making sure we are consistent? Unfortunately, that is a very complicated question. Nevertheless, two basic approaches to parenting can be easily outlined, and the basic strengths and weaknesses of each are easily delineated. One, the authoritarian approach to parenting, balances toward the side of discipline. The other, the child-centered approach to parenting, balances toward the side of kindness and affection.

The authoritarian approach, when properly balanced, will definitely lead to driven children who are quite likely to succeed in very conventional ways. Children from well-balanced authoritarian homes very much want to please their parents as youngsters. Then, as young adults, they typically identify with their parents in becoming extremely moral and responsible, and as full grown adults they are, most of the time, very hardworking. Of course, there are no guarantees, and deciding whether the authoritarian approach is relatively balanced or not often has to do with the particular temperament and personality characteristics of any individual child. When the authoritarian approach is not well-balanced, that is when it is either too harsh and controlling or when it is being employed with a child who naturally tends to look at things in a different way, certain problems are likely to occur. Problems in authoritarian homes often develop from children believing they have to be "perfect" to please their parents when authority is too strict, harsh, or controlling. On the other hand, when a child simply doesn't fit with seeing things as right or wrong, many kinds of depression and anxiety can develop from feeling as though one's specialness is never recognized.

In the more child-centered home, when freedom and discipline are relatively well-balanced, children do feel special and know their worth to their parents. Such children often find the occupations that really suit them and follow their heart in making decisions for their lives. Children from well-balanced child-centered homes work to develop their creative thinking. They tend to see kindness and independent thinking as the most important attributes for any person, and they prize being fair above respect or what others unthinkingly believe to be right or wrong. Of course there are no guarantees in the child-centered approach either. A child's temperament is equally important in deciding goodness of fit within the child-centered home. Many children do want things to be simple and benefit from a clear and concise approach to what will please their parents. Such children don't feel natural in finding their own creative solutions and they can feel alienated in the child-centered home. When the child-centered approach is not well-balanced by proper guidance and discipline, very significant difficulties can arise. Many children from unbalanced child-centered homes feel exceedingly entitled if they receive excessive unearned praise. Often they feel too comfortable in being at their parents' level authority, so they can actually be quite disrespectful. Many children from such homes can also get lost in figuring out who they are or what they are supposed to do. They struggle to find meaningful goals since meaning itself is so important. There is often not enough satisfaction for such children in working hard or a job well done. Children from child-centered homes also often lack adequate ability to compete because kindness is so highly valued. Sometimes they develop a distaste for competition which further strips them of any desire to "get to the top." Depression and anxiety can develop in the child from the child-centered home when work seems too hard or when one finds no really special meaning in life.

The trick to finding a good approach to parenting, generally speaking, whether you are more authoritarian or more child-centered, is to know yourself, your own preferences, and your child. The proper amount of kindness, affection, firmness, and consistency, must come from inside you, the parent, and must fit your particular child. When intervening with your children, if you maintain conscious concern for them, you will always be able to make an adequate choice for what to do in any situation. The only time to worry about your choices is when you are feeling stressed or influenced by others, or when you are unable, for any reason, to be thinking of what is best for your children. If you are handling a situation as you think is right, from your heart but with enough thought to demonstrate concern, you will be relatively consistent. And since you truly believe what you are doing is right, firmness will generally not be a problem. If you are staying connected to your child's feelings in the moment, then the right time to be kind or affectionate will also be obvious.

The most difficult complication of influence arises when you do not agree with your kids' other parent. Disagreements can be handled later, and I strongly suggest that the solution chosen in the moment should simply be safe and cause the least anxiety for the children. With respect to kindness, affection, firmness, and consistency, it should not be a problem for parents who have a good relationship to come to an agreement and then be consistent and firm, as well as kind and affectionate, on agreeable terms. If parents love and/or respect each other, the instinctual commitment to parenting (love) holds plenty of motivation in itself to ensure that your parental decisions come from your true convictions.

Of course, working together to have a consistent approach after a separation can be far more complicated, especially because the same differences that lead to divorce often have specific correlates for the "right" way to parent. In these situations, love for the children must win out. Any disagreement that lasts hurts the children more than any one parenting approach possibly could (unless someone is abusive). Thus, love of the children must lead to compromise on a more or less permanent basis. No matter what each parent thinks is the "right" approach, whether they are parenting in one household or when separated, agreement will lead to consistency, and consistency of approach is the most important attribute for ensuring healthy, balanced children.

Who's to know what the "right" approach to parenting is? No one really knows because different people value different aspects of life or attributes of character. There is not one specific approach that is clearly the best. What comes naturally to you hopefully will help you choose between a more authoritarian or a more child-centered approach, or some other approach in the middle. Whatever choice you make needs to be agreed upon between you and your spouse, or any other individual involved in parenting the children. Even when there has been a separation between parents, hopefully both partners can agree that consistency is best for the children, and thus the approach chosen can be a compromise between the two separated parents. Either way, your approach should be the one you believe will be best for your children. The more natural it is to you, the better. If you understand your own motivations well, and your primary concern is for your children, even when others feel the need to interfere you will have little difficulty following through in your way. Keeping things consistent for your children is of utmost importance and may require you to simply let people know to back off. You need not explain to others why you are doing what you know is right. If you're balanced between kindness, affection, firmness and consistency, your children will know your path and feel good about themselves even as they learn to work hard for what they want and to stand up for what they believe. Who's to know what the "right" approach to parenting is? In a way, there's a simple answer . . . You.

CHAPTER 35

❧

You Don't Know How Much They Love You

"We never know the love of a parent till we become parents ourselves."

—Henry Ward Beecher

So many times in my office I hear a child, often a teenager, upset about the rules their parents make. Sometimes they act like their parents are such a pain to them. I don't always disagree with the specific arguments the child is making, but as I look at the anguish on the parents' faces, as a parent myself, one thought re-occurs to me over and over again. The fact that the child is reacting toward their parents with so much distaste, and the fact that their own view brooks no compassion for their parents' angst, certainly means at least one thing. They have no idea how much their parents love them.

It is the rare parent who is able to keep in mind just how much it's true that love is really a very one-way process between parents and children. But if I want to be honest about it myself, I have to admit that I had no idea how much my parents loved me until I had children of my own. On a daily basis, however, because I love my children so much, it is relatively automatic for me to assume that my children love me in return to that very same level. My love for my own parents, however, grew so tremendously after my children were born

246

that I know it really doesn't work that way at all. If you assume your children love you as much as you love them, you are unfortunately going to be at a significant disadvantage in every argument you have with them.

It is natural for children to get what they can. They do so in the context of loving their family but, if they are normal, they are thinking far more of themselves most of the time than they are of us. In fact, that is their job. They are attempting to grow, with us parents in the roles of earth, nutrients, and sun. Simply stated, they need us. That's not exactly the same as love. So it only makes sense that we love them far more than they love us. We constantly think of sacrifice for them without even thinking of it as sacrifice, while they often don't even notice what we do. In fact, all of this fits very nicely into nature and evolution from a survival perspective. In order to grow, children must experiment with things and branch out. If they are too fearful, they will not gain adequate experience through healthy discovery. In fact, the child-adolescent forebrain is not even sufficiently developed for being truly careful and future oriented. In contrast, parents are supposed to protect their genetic "line" for generations. Thus, they need their children to grow up well, be successful, and become good parents themselves. Within that context, children try to branch out while parents simultaneously attempt to make that branching safe and auspicious, sometimes by way of painful pruning. This relationship between branching and pruning can create extreme tension that all too often morphs into significant conflict.

This is what children really don't understand. It is our protective love, our pruning so to speak, that makes us react to them in ways they do not like. When we make rules, we do so, of course, because we aim to make them safe. Even when we behave in controlling ways, typically we are doing so because we are so scared of what could happen to our precious babies if they were allowed to use, what we believe to be, poor judgment. We are desperate to keep them safe. Seeing them in pain, or failing, brings us so much excruciating pain, it's as if the pain we see in them is our own. We are incessantly and exasperatingly focused on their future. We want an insurance policy for their success and happiness, but our vigilant diligence is the only insurance we can get. They have no idea how much we love them, and it's our gargantuan love that makes them hate us.

In that vein, I will write the rest of this article as though I am talking to the child who doesn't understand why his or her parents are being so "hard," or making so many rules, or why they are limiting behavior they think is dangerous. Feel free to share this article with your children. Meanwhile, keep in mind, there is a natural tension between their need to gain experience and your need to make them safe. They may not understand just how much we love them, or even how we can't help but try to guide them adequately, but maybe we can benefit too from knowing that they have to do what they do too.

To the Child Who Wants to Know Why Parents Make So Many Rules

You really don't understand how much your parents love you. I'm sorry, but you don't. And you can't because you have not yet had children of your own. Now I am not saying that your parents are always right. Please don't think that's what I think. I am a parent, and I am often wrong. But most of the time when I am wrong about what I want from my children or about what I say to my children, it happens because I love them so much and not because of what I need for me.

Have you ever thought about how much time your parents spend doing things so your needs will be met? I am not just talking about how they go to work each day. In fact you could easily argue that they do that for themselves, or to uphold some image, or because that's how they view their roles. No, I'm not just talking about their work. What I am really talking about is how often they cook for you, clean up after you, work on your homework with you, take you where you want to go, think about what you'll need for school, or what you'll need to feel good when with your friends. If you are willing to think about it, in fact, if we take your parents work days completely out of the equation (even though it's true that they do that partially for you too), you can see that they spend at least 1/2 of all their nonwork time doing something for you, or your siblings, or for taking care of the home you share with them.

On the other hand, have you noticed that they don't expect anything like that from you? Yes, they expect you to do your homework. In fact they even make you do it sometimes which, believe it or not, is far harder than just letting you do what you want. Yes, sometimes they make you do some jobs around the house too, which, believe it or not, is mostly harder than just doing it themselves. And yes, sometimes they get mad at you about silly things that you just don't understand. But can you say that they expect you to do anywhere near as much as they do? Do you spend 1/2 of your free time doing something for them or the home? If you do, your parents are probably not complaining about you, and they probably don't think of you as someone who needs a lot of extra rules.

The question then is, why do they do so much for you? And why do they care so much about what you're doing? From your point of view it probably doesn't even make sense. Sometimes it probably seems like they spend almost all their time thinking about you. In fact, they seem to notice everything about you. This is so much true that sometimes it makes you sick. Right? You just wish they wouldn't notice so much. It's weird how your mom always seems to know what you're up to. She knows your mood better than you do sometimes (even though you tell her she's wrong when she says she knows your upset). Without even looking, your dad knows which of you or your siblings enters a room. Right?

The reason they care so much is complicated. It has something to do with how much time they have already put into you. You wouldn't believe what it was like in the early years before you can remember—diapers, constant crying, making sure there was always a warm bottle, all that whining, and all the stuff you got into and messed with all the time—wow, what a pain! It also has something to do with how much their parents put into them. Finally, it seems to have something to do with instinct. Although there are many reasons that your parents care so much, one thing is for sure, it has nothing to do with just wanting to make your life miserable.

For whatever reason, your parents care so much about you, it's almost as though you are a vital organ of their own bodies. It's like you're a second heart, and if something happens to you, your parents feel like they themselves will die. What's even worse than you being like a second heart, though, is that you are not inside their bodies. If you were inside their bodies, they would be able to keep you protected by carrying you everywhere (that's probably what they'd really like to do). As it is, however, your parents view you as though you're that heart, but instead of being safely in their chests, you're lying out in the middle of a highway somewhere with nothing but those stupid orange cones placed around you for protection. Those flimsy cones, haphazardly strewn about you, are how most parents think about the quality of their kids' judgment. Without their guidance, those cones are your parents' only hope for protecting you from the multitudinous variety of cars and trucks whipping by, any one of them at any moment, with just a minor nudge at the wheel or a gust of wind, ready to smash you lifeless into the pavement. Your parents are clinging desperately to the idea that they will be able to guide you unharmed through the dangers of life so you'll survive and prosper, but they perceive you to be so vulnerable that sometimes you think their protective actions are evidence of their desire to completely control you. The fact is that your parents are scared out of their minds about something happening to you, and about your future, because they love you so extremely and intensely.

Although they might seem like a pain sometimes, there are many great benefits of your parents' gargantuan love for you, but I want to tell you two benefits that will likely surprise you. If you start to try to recognize how your parents love for you is their primary motivation, then these two things will happen.

First, when arguing with your parents, you will not be able to be so angry at them because you will see that they are not your enemy. In fact, if you look at it correctly, they are <u>for you</u>, on your side, and thinking only of your safety and proper guidance. If you don't agree with them, you must see that they are not against you. Rather, they are merely misguided and in need of information about how you really do have your own best interests in mind. If you see that your parents are not against you, but are merely misguided, you will not act angry and you will have a much better chance of benefiting from the second benefit.

The second benefit, believe it or not, comes from the fact that you do recognize your parents love for you. That is, if you verbalize your understanding of how your parents' motivation in guiding you is the motivation and/or intention behind their perspective, they are far more likely to listen to your perspective. If you are, in fact, correct in your point of view, if you want your parents to listen to you, the first thing you <u>must</u> do is figure out how their point of view is related to your welfare. Then, simply tell your parents specifically how you know their perspective is related to your welfare, and proceed to tell them how your point of view takes your welfare into account just as much as theirs (if your point of view does not take your welfare into account, you might as well just give it up because they will not give in). Verbalizing your understanding of your parents' perspective is a convincing and promising strategy for you that does not include you being disgusted with them. You see, because your parents love you more than you could ever know, they are also going to give you exactly what you want as long as what you want makes them feel like you're getting what is in your best interests. They can't help it. Their only motivation is to see everything work out beautifully for you. If what you want will make your future bright and will pose no danger, then what you want is what they want too.

So you see, all you have to do, if you really want to get what you want, is truly want what's best for you. If you can do that, and you can explain why it's best for you to your parents, you'll typically get what you want. And maybe you'll get one step closer to understanding something that it also took me a long to recognize. There's nothing you can do about how much your parents love you. I know it's a pain, but you're just going to have to deal with it. But even though your parents will never stop loving you (more than you could ever know), and even though that's really a big pain, at least you can recognize that they're only trying to do their very best for you, and yes, sometimes they'll even control you, just because they truly, deeply love you.

Section 10

Building Good Kids

How do you build a great kid? Well, shoot, they're just born great, aren't they? Of course, even though that's somewhat true, it's really quite a bit more complicated than that. There are certain core values that must be instilled or implanted within our children, and particular ways in which they must develop resiliency, if they are to reach their maximum potential. This section offers articles about installing components of integrity, and helping children remain true to themselves with a powerful, protective personality structure of their own. In "From Materialism to Integrity: the Building Blocks of the Healthy Human Personality," image and authenticity are contrasted, with a path toward growth clearly paved by the core values that make people good working parts of their community. How freedom tends to be balanced by responsibility is the subject examined in *Freedom and Responsibility*, with special emphasis on kids seeing that they must earn rewards, and on parents seeing that their kids should be given the freedom they earn. The demonstration of one's character is brought into focus in the article "Bullying," with an emphasis on indifference to the opinions of those who have no real bearing on one's life. In "Be a Man," the stereotypes regarding how boys are expected to act are challenged, and being true to oneself is encouraged. In "It Must Be Hard To Be a Girl," the complex expectations on girls, based in the fact that they are really asked to do it all, is highlighted in demonstrating just how much girls and women should be appreciated.

CHAPTER 36

☙

From Materialism to Integrity: Building Blocks of the Healthy Human Structure

"Without an acquaintance with the rules of propriety, it is impossible for the character to be established."

—Confucius

Many articles are written about specific issues in child rearing, but rarely do we find a way to discuss the basic building blocks that are necessary for making children grow into great adults. There are a few essential components that must be cultivated in our children if we are to fashion them into healthy, thriving, connected beings. These components, when properly placed and integrated during childhood, work in unison to help people function both as individuals and within the larger community. Before it's possible to jump into the specific problems any one population might have, it is necessary to have a clear understanding of these basic components and how to ensure that they will be installed properly. The question that is of most importance in child rearing, therefore, is not a question about what is wrong with particular children, but rather, how do we make sure to build *integrity* in all children?

In answering this general question, it appears that there is an associated general problem area that seems to be a regular correlate to problems with integrity in our society. That one problem area is materialism. Our society is so fast, and materialism runs so rampant at every economic level, that almost all children get most of the things they want with very little effort. Sometimes it's X-boxes, sometimes it's nice clothing or a new pair of Jordans, but most of the time parents do whatever they can to obtain these things in our current society, regardless of whether or not they're affordable or whether it's ill-advised to give these things to their children. Sometimes, it seems, we run so fast to attain the things we desire that we forget the more important parts of life. Integrity of character involves one's relation to others in the world, and thus materialism, to the extent that we pursue selfish pleasures, image, and ego, becomes the primary symptom of a lack of integrity.

We need to ask how empty materialistic pursuit grabs a hold of us. What happens, for example, when a person is given everything without appropriate effort? On the other hand, what happens if a person sees that others need make little effort and get everything anyway? Are matters made worse when a person's parents feel that their children should be given everything as a reward for the parents' hard work? Are matters made worse when a parent gives their child everything merely due to guilt about what they perceive to be their own failure to succeed? What if, to make matters worse, a child grows up believing that the only worthwhile accomplishments in this world require huge success since that's what they're parents have pursued? On the other hand, what if a child grows up thinking there is no chance they'll be able to earn the things they want for themselves or their families in a legitimate job? All of these pressures lead people to resentment, laziness, and/or unearned entitlement, and away from integrity of character, as parents and children alike pursue many desires, but not their connection with each other. The current state of materialism pulls us away from one another even as we try to buy our way into each others' hearts.

As has now been well-publicized, most notably quite recently in Madeline Levine's book, "The Price of Privilege" (2006), the current state of affluent materialism has left many well-to-do children feeling empty, depressed and angry, as they act out either through wild behavior and substance abuse, or equally damaging self loathing and self abuse. Meanwhile, in far less affluent homes, in spite of material possessions provided through great sacrifice, desperation grows as children see their parents working endlessly, or falling hopelessly into debt, while attempting to give their children those things the media and advertisers seem to suggest that every child deserves. These children also turn to wild behavior due to resentment, feelings of emptiness and depression, which show up behaviorally in substance abuse and other forms of self abuse, but also criminal behavior, which can seem to be a legitimate option for getting ahead in a world where so many others can get things so much easier than the underprivileged can.

The antidote to materialism, and the key to integrity, is thus connection and relatedness within society in general, and especially between parents and their children. But this too is a complicated issue. It can be difficult to find time for connection and relatedness based on how we run our lives. Our society has seemingly made material possessions and wealth paramount over relationships. Many people work to achieve greater and greater success even if it means there's no time for one's family. This is true in spite of the fact that individual or family happiness does not grow once the basic needs have been confidently secured, no matter how much material success is attained. In contrast, many less affluent families, trying to make an honest living, simply don't find time for family togetherness. Often the stresses they face make their time at home nothing more than independently sought salve for the hardships of the day.

To make matters worse, in many affluent families, children must achieve, either academically or in athletics, so that they will accomplish the proper reflection on their parents, who are overly image conscious in their pursuit of an image of success. That is, the pressure on these children exists too much because of how things will look, and not enough because the child is succeeding in pursuit of something he or she truly loves. This pressure leaves children feeling especially disconnected and empty since their external success itself becomes more important than who they truly are or how they really feel. Even worse, however, is the feeling in less affluent families that there is nothing a child can do to distinguish him or herself within the family or within society, since having to struggle, in and of itself, seemingly means that you're no one important. Regardless of that bereft feeling about one's worth, parents in these families are often too stressed to notice the specialness in any child anyway.

With all that said, if connection and relatedness are indeed the antidote to materialism and the key to integrity, the primary question remains, what exactly must happen within the parent/child relationship in order for the child to grow up to be a healthy, independent, confident, related and caring individual? Healthy development requires that one's parents strike a healthy balance between protecting their children and allowing for their children's independent action. As part of that balance, parents are, of course, always trying to impart certain values for children to live by. But balancing protection of one's children with allowing for autonomy, especially while simultaneously trying to make sure your children learn to be good people, is a complicated task.

In the few paragraphs to come, I will delineate the six most important factors in balancing protection of our children with the necessary independence they must develop. These six factors are the most important for all children whether they be affluent or impoverished, but are more or less difficult to accomplish based on a variety of family variables that include economic standing, but also, just as importantly, other variables such as the character in the parents and their ability to work together as a team. These six factors of emotional health, if well-balanced within the parents' approach to child rearing, lead to integrity and confidence within a child, who will then become a responsible and caring individual within his own relationships, and a well-functioning member of society. When these six factors are truly cultivated in a person, the connection to others and confidence within oneself that they imply, makes rampant materialism a virtual impossibility. These six factors are specialness, humility, hard work, responsibility, gratitude, and a desire for growth.

Being Special

Although these six factors coexist, with none greater than another, perhaps because balance is so important in life, it would be best to make our first factor the one that is at the center of everything when it comes to our children developing integrity. Making sure our children know what it is that makes them a special and important individual is at the fulcrum in balancing all the other factors. Our children learn about their own special attributes through seeing and feeling us listen to them with intent concern for how they feel. I am not implying, however, that we should make children feel like everything they do is special and wonderful. Making children truly aware of their own specialness is much more related to them understanding their very special connection with us than it is to pumping them up without reason.

It is almost as if our reactions to our children are a mirror in which they see themselves. Of course, when we are pleased with them, or when we just feel loving toward them because we do, we can look fondly upon them and demonstrate how much we care by responding intently to their concerns or special attributes. It is equally important, though, to respond with our true feelings even when those feelings are negative. Otherwise, children never attain an accurate understanding of their special connection to us. If our children do something that makes us angry, they must see themselves as the cause of that anger. If they have done something to intentionally harm us or someone else, or if they have been acting selfishly in a way about which they're unaware, then our irritation is exactly what they should see. That irritation is a true reflection of the impact their behavior has had.

On the other hand, if our irritation occurs in response to them having a legitimate need when we are tired, or because they have asked a legitimate question that for some reason embarrasses us, then the feeling that develops from that interaction is that they are not worth our time or that their legitimate needs and feelings make us irritated. These interactions based on our own selfish nature are unhealthy and diminish the child's true sense of legitimacy or specialness.

A child learns to know him or herself in a healthy way based on healthy reactions from the environment in which he or she lives. The extent to which the environment accurately reflects back to the child his or her importance, impact, and specialness will determine the level to which the child really feels that he is legitimate and has legitimate needs that are equally important to the needs of everyone else. The attributes that make him or her a true individual, a unique person with his or her own great ways of doing things, as well as personal foibles, must be reflected back to the child through the parents' reactions if the child is to gain a solid understanding of him or herself. When a child's parents are generally successful in responding with spontaneous concern for their child, and yet have adequate concern for themselves in relation to their child as well, the child develops a healthy sense of self, specialness and legitimacy. The child will then, in turn, react within the world with true compassion for others as well as healthy concern for themselves.

Humility

As a second factor, the child understanding that he or she is no better or worse than anyone else, or humility, helps to temper the feeling of specialness as stated in the last paragraph. Every child must know that birth into any particular family, within any particular country, within any particular period in history, is merely a matter of luck. No matter what any particular person might believe about the importance of intelligence, athletic prowess, street smarts, ability in mathematics, artistry, social ability, color of skin, quickness of wit, or the multitude of other possible human attributes, it is absolutely essential that every child be brought up believing that they are equal, no better or worse, to everyone else. They must know they have a right to be treated well, and they should expect to be treated well. They also should never expect to be treated better than others or to be given special treatment over others. They must learn to treat everyone else just as they want to be treated (we all know that one, right?). In fact, it really helps if the child is able to see him or herself, in addition to knowing they have certain rights within this context, as just an infinitesimally small part of a huge universe. That is, although they must see themselves as very special, and must treat themselves like they deserve just as much as anyone else, they must also see themselves, just like all of us, as extremely unimportant within the larger scheme of humanity itself.

Hard Work

Every child must also know, as a third factor, that hard work is the key to all success as a human being. If a child is asked to observe all the people for whom they have great respect, it is very unlikely that any of these respected individuals will have become famous for winning the lottery. You may not appreciate the same people that your children appreciate, but if you ask them, you will soon see that the people they do respect are people who have worked extremely hard to get where they are. Rock musicians, athletes, movie stars, rich guys, or even that kid at school who seems to have it altogether, are generally all people who work really hard. You might worry that they'd use some "screw up" at school that they think is really funny as an example of someone they respect, but they won't be able to name anything the person does that they really think is worthy of respect unless the kid is really working hard at something (even if they're working really hard at being funny). When you think about it, relationships themselves require hard work. So if you're concerned your child won't respect you because you don't have a job outside the house, my guess is that your lack of an outside job makes you a person who works especially hard at relationships. You are likely spending your life making sure that the others in your life are properly supported.

Once your child sees that hard working people are the ones he or she respects, it becomes necessary for them to see that hard work very rarely fails to lead to success. Even in the most impoverished families, if a child knows hard work is the key to success, the fact that he is always working so hard will make him a sought after employee everywhere he works. He will not be able to prevent himself from succeeding, even if he is prevented from succeeding at the same levels possible for those raised by more affluent parents who can afford to give him or her a fine education. Believing in hard work, in fact, is an antidote to the learned helplessness that so often accompanies poverty. It was largely the undeniable belief in hard work that brought so many people out of the Great Depression, and success seemingly materialized then almost as though from nothing but the strength of will in hardworking people.

On the other hand, a child from an affluent family may be pushed through the finest schools and be given every advantage, but if she does not desire to work hard due to a belief that it should not be necessary, she will never achieve anything from her own efforts, and will never experience the esteem that such hard work earns. He or she may be handed a position of authority with adequate pay, but that position, if hard work was never necessary in securing it, will have no meaning. That child, now adult, will get no satisfaction from work. It is only through hard work that a healthy adult achieves a sense of satisfaction. It is only through hard work that anyone develops anything meaningful.

Responsibility

Hard work is really not possible without the fourth factor being simultaneously present (which may be true of all these factors). Being responsible is an absolute necessity for integrity to develop. Responsibility largely grows from the very connectedness that parents have with their children in that, if we care about others, we do our best not to hurt or disappoint them. In a healthy family the children do not want to disappoint or harm the adults and the adults definitely don't want to harm the children, even if they must disappoint them at times.

When things get complicated within daily interactions, however, with children struggling for increasing autonomy as they should, children must know that parents can give them only as much freedom or autonomy as they earn by being responsible (please see article "Freedom and Responsibility"). Of course we seemingly control our children at times due to our desire to protect them. We have no real desire to stop them from doing things except that they might get or be hurt. When we know that they will handle things in a way that will make them safe, we generally don't have a problem with giving them freedom.

Likewise, in relationships we allow people to get closer to us when we know they won't hurt us. On the job we give our workers more authority as it becomes clear that they will handle tasks adequately. When our children take responsibility for their actions in how they treat us and others, they are allowed more leeway in their relationships with us and others. With few exceptions, freedom and responsibility always balance each other in life.

Kids may think us parents get to make all the rules and get to do, within reason, anything we want to do, but what they don't see is how our freedom is limited because our responsibilities in the family make it impossible for us to do many of the things we want to do every single day. We have to work and make money to pay the bills. We have to be punctual in transporting ourselves and them. We need to make sure everything is organized so that the family will keep moving in a healthy direction. We need to get meals to the table. All our many responsibilities make doing what we want to do a relatively low priority for us, and thus we actually often don't have much freedom at all.

Children too will get as much freedom as they deserve based on how much responsibility they take. If they take so little social responsibility that they become criminals, they will end up in jail with no freedom at all. If they don't break laws, but take no responsibility within their relationships to others, they will find they have no real freedom within relationships (at least not relationships that last in any kind of healthy or meaningful way). When they take adequate responsibility for themselves, for their work, and for their relationships with others, kids should be given the freedom they deserve. When they grow up, our children's ability to be responsible will give them the freedom and desire to take on the many responsibilities which will make them fully functional and successful adults.

Gratitude

Gratitude or thankfulness is also a huge factor. It goes without saying that in more affluent families there is much for which to be thankful. Especially if one's parents are recognizing their child's specialness, and attempting to inculcate the mores of equality, hard work, and responsibility, the child certainly should be thankful. On the other hand, when a child has been given everything and nothing has been expected in return, or when a child's true self has been largely ignored while the parents' needs for a grand image is pursued, the child will fail to develop an understanding of gratitude.

With respect to less affluent, or impoverished families, it might be far more difficult to be grateful. Nevertheless, without gratitude integrity cannot develop. Gratitude must be found simply for one's relationships, having enough to eat, or having a roof over one's head, or it is impossible to have enough esteem to work hard, or to see the need for responsibility. Why work hard or take responsibility if you've always been cheated and you have never been blessed in any way. Further, accepting one's smallness in the universe, or humility, is an insult to one's self if you feel like you've been cheated or like you have nothing, unless you can be grateful for something that you do know you have. It's strange but true that it's impossible to feel a sense of humility unless you also feel like you're lucky in some way. Simply put, thankfulness must be found in anyone who aims to be mentally healthy. Without gratitude a person merely thinks selfishly and feels entitled, or on the other hand, responds to the world with anger and entitlement, regardless of the circumstances within which they've been reared.

Growth

Finally, growth must be understood as a constant in the healthy life. Growth is at the center of everything in the universe (Please see article "Growth"). The universe is growing and expanding, life is a process of growth; we are typically always pursuing some kind of growth. Healthy growth involves expanding our abilities, our intellect, or our integrity itself. Every child must embrace the fact that he is trying to grow so that such growth can be healthy.

Many people try to grow by stockpiling material possessions or a more fabulous image. The pursuit of some types of growth is a compensation for areas where people feel inadequate. Sometimes the pursuit of material possessions is an attempt to grow where one feels nothing but emptiness inside and there is really no feeling of growth at all. In such circumstances, it's as if growth must come from soil, and must receive the nutrients from that soil as well as energy from the sun, but there is no soil and there's insufficient nutrition. When materialistic pursuits reign over integrity, even when the sun does shine, darkness always looms, as every new possession brings only ephemeral pleasure. Similarly, people who attempt to grow in their power over others are merely compensating for deep-seated feelings of weakness and vulnerability.

Readily apparent is the upheaval or disintegration (or entropy) that occurs when people are not getting any sense of growth. For example, while people might turn to materialism or a pursuit of power to get a sense of growth, when those pursuits are recognized as futile, desperation in the form of anxiety, depression, or anger often take command.

It is absolutely essential that the healthy person pursue growth. The only sufficient growth involves goals that are meaningful and consistent with the individual's unique personality characteristics. Growth within a person implies the pursuit of goals that expand a person's abilities and stretch a person where they could do their best. We all like to grow in different ways, but growth is certainly at the center of things, right alongside specialness.

The Six Factors and Us

With these six factors, balanced by parenting that aims to protect our children while simultaneously encouraging autonomy in them, integrity is developed and becomes the antidote to the troubles found within our materialistic world. Connection and relatedness with our children helps to develop all six factors. Through positive interaction with us, our children come to understand their special place within our hearts, while they also understand that they are no better than anyone else in this world. They learn to work hard and earn the respect of others as they learn to earn our respect. They take responsibility for their work, as well as their safety, while they pay attention to the affect they have on our emotions and the feelings of others, and they also make sure they themselves are treated as well as they deserve. They learn to appreciate our efforts and what they are given. They also learn to appreciate simple pleasures. In addition to gratitude for food, shelter and safety, they learn to appreciate the world itself in all its wonders. Through their relationships with us, our children learn to appreciate beauty and understand horror. Through their relationship with us, they learn about the love they will know for themselves and the love they will share and spread.

CHAPTER 37

❧

Freedom and Responsibility

"Most people do not really want freedom, because freedom involves responsibility, and most people are frightened of responsibility."

—Sigmund Freud

Responsibility is essential to doing good work, having good relationships, and creating a successful life. That's certainly not news! But if everyone knows that fact, why is it so hard to encourage it in our children; and why is it so hard to understand what that means in our relationships? There is a simple formula that makes the workings of responsibility comprehensible for everyone. This formula facilitates movement toward taking more responsibility in all facets of our lives. It points to ways we can cultivate responsibility in our children, and it clarifies what it means to be responsible within our families. This is the formula: Freedom = Responsibility.

Freedom and responsibility are forever in balance. This simple fact can be seen everywhere. Babies have no freedom (of course, we're talking about freedom of will, not freedom of impunity) and they have no responsibility. As children get older, the more responsibility they take on (chores, caring for a pet, doing a good job on homework), the more you, as a parent, should trust them. The more you trust them, the more you will let them do what they want. As adults, we have all the freedom in the world bounded only by cultural norms and laws (beliefs, of course, are our own, and thus we are free to believe in them). But in the balance between freedom and responsibility, it is important to notice that freedom comes at the price of responsibility. Unless we do take responsibility in a large variety of ways, we will have little freedom.

The Freedom = Responsibility equation is of supreme importance in child rearing because, unfortunately for parents, it is quite common for children to believe they should be allowed to do whatever they want in spite of the fact that they have very little responsibility. Their home, their food, their clothes, their insurance, their telephone, their use of a car, their physical well-being as a whole, is not their responsibility. That is why their freedom is rightly held in their parents' hands. Now look at the freedom that parents have. Sure, we parents can do whatever we want, but if we don't go to work, we can't pay the bills. If we don't communicate with our children, we worry that they will feel unloved. If we don't discipline our children, we worry they will not be ready for the world in which they will have to take responsibility. The fact is, there is a reason we can do whatever we want. It's because we have chosen to take responsibility.

In turn, it goes without saying that us parents tend to want our children to become responsible too. Helping our children develop responsibility is a never-ending, back and forth process between letting go of, and then gathering in, the proverbial reins. In order for children to learn to take responsibility, parents have to lengthen the tether they have on their children till they find out how much responsibility their children can handle. When children demonstrate that they have too much freedom by doing things that are clearly irresponsible, it is our job to gather in the tether for the purpose of taking adequate care of our children. The irresponsible acts of children often cost money that our kids do not have, or really put someone in danger, thus making their importance obvious. But irresponsible acts can also include simply breaking our rules (whatever those rules might be, since we have the freedom to make those rules), or acting disrespectfully. Whatever those acts might be, clearly parents must intervene for the sake of society as well as four our children. It is actually neglectful to give our children freedom when they are obviously not ready for it. For one thing it can be dangerous, but we are also certainly responsible for what our children do if we unleash them upon the world without at least trying to temper their feral impulses.

The balance between freedom and responsibility is not only important with respect to general behavior as discussed so far. There is also a balance between freedom and responsibility within relationships. Although the concept of freedom and responsibility is more abstract in its application to relationships than it is in its application to child care, it is really the same thing. In relationships (even with and among children) trust is given when one's experience is consistent with being treated kindly, lovingly, respectfully, and safely. When a person takes responsibility for their impact on others, emotional and otherwise, those others will trust them and thus allow more emotional freedom. They will give them the benefit of the doubt when things don't go as planned, and they'll allow emotional closeness or intimacy. When a person is mean, uncaring, or untrustworthy, others will not allow that emotional closeness. They will be forever on the defensive, and in that guarded position, they too will be more likely to be aggressive or withdrawn in their responses.

Part of this interpersonal exchange is taking the responsibility to let people know when they have hurt you so that they can have the opportunity to take responsibility for doing so. If someone really cares about you, they will typically try their best not to hurt you. But they have to know what they've done that is hurtful, which means that you have to accept the possibility that you could be even more hurt and communicate to them that you have been hurt (see article "Communication from the Heart). You have to have faith in their love and let yourself be vulnerable. If you let someone who cares about you know that they have hurt you, they will try to change their ways. If you do make yourself vulnerable in this way, and you find that you are being hurt repeatedly in spite of it, then they are likely incapable of taking responsibility. If they cannot take that kind of responsibility, then they are incapable of the kind of love you deserve.

When a person takes responsibility for their actions, the things they do that hurt other people, and the things they need to do to take care of their own life circumstances, then they are allowed every freedom. That Freedom = Responsibility is one principle that applies to children as well as adults, and also applies to family situations, workplace issues, and even our intimate relations. The more this simple principle is accepted, the better people can get along. The more widespread is such acceptance, the greater will be the cohesiveness of any community. If it is applied to relationships as well as behavior, Freedom = Responsibility is the core principle of civility and culture. It is clearly true that we are all completely free. We have a choice in everything we do. But if there can be no denying that we are free, we must also see that the more we choose to take responsibility, the freer we tend to be.

CHAPTER 38

❦

Bullying

"Power is not revealed by striking hard or often, but by striking true."

—Honore de Balzac

Bullying is awful. Just hearing the word twists our stomachs, doesn't it? Certainly there have been significant efforts to put a stop to bullying. Yet it seems to be a stubborn problem stemming from developmental processes in children as well as the nature of society. Bullying is sometimes significantly reduced by school and community administrators who successfully create a culture among our kids that views intimidation as "uncool," but such an accomplishment is relatively rare and requires significant parental involvement. Successfully preventing the desire to bully within the bully himself, presents a more complex issue due to difficulty in truly understanding the bully. The most frustrating part of the puzzle by far, however, is that the suggestions for the victims of bullying are quite often almost useless. So let's look at each of these areas one by one to see if it's possible to get a better handle on the problem (for the remainder of this article, bullies, victims, and administrators will be referred to in the male form for the purpose of clarity).

The first thing to understand about bullying is that it stems from a natural human desire for dominance. Dominance is built into us as animals, as is the need to work with one another because communal efforts lead to cultural development and all sorts of progress. We need leaders and we need workers, and that's just the way it is. In many ways we do our best to level these traits in our children when they're very young. On the one hand, we want our children to get along with other kids and, for example, be good sharers. On the other hand, however, we teach our children to compete and we want them to have a desire to win. Is there really any parent who wouldn't want their child to be a "leader" among his friends? We do know, however, that there are many ways to be a leader, and many of them are not very good. We want our children to lead from the front with good judgment and good influence on their peers, but certainly there are many children who are leading from the rear, trying to get other kids to do things that are unsafe or bad for them. Many bullies intimidate and demean others for the express purpose of leading, and entertaining other kids, in a negative direction. But the desire to bully always comes back to the common and natural human desire to dominate.

The need to dominate in a bullying fashion, that is the need to intimidate others, essentially comes from poorly balanced character or lack of integrity within one's personality (please see article "The Power and Control Addiction"). This absence of balance and integrity can come from a variety of factors, including inborn intensity combined with relatively minor difficulties at home, or very bad problems at home which manifest in poor balance of character regardless of the genetic level of intensity. Sometimes there exists within an individual a significant inborn intensity combined with very bad problems at home. Such a combination leads to the most vicious kind of bullies. The problem is even worse when a child is born with significantly good social ability. We have all known children who seem to understand social situations better than we do and who swim through every social challenge. When these especially socially skilled children are especially intense and/or have certain kinds of problems at home, there can be especially cruel, and sometimes very complex forms of bullying.

From a developmental perspective, it is easy to observe certain stages where bullying is more or less serious. Clearly bullying occurs before fifth grade and even in a very immature fashion within the preschool years, but the bullying seen in the middle school years is typically the very worst. Of course, the high school years can also be quite rough. There are very good developmental reasons for why these years are so bad. At the very same time that children are gaining a better understanding of the world around them, they are simultaneously feeling more vulnerable than they have ever felt before. At this age responsibilities grow and puberty makes sexual attraction a focal point. Between the ages of 11 and 14 the ability to think more abstractly develops extremely quickly right alongside the sexual awakening.

This development of the mind is great in that kids can learn to look for symbolism in literature and can start to figure out algebra, but what is not so great is that they are developing the thinking power of little adults, even though they still feel very much like little children. It is obviously quite common to have young teens acting as though they think they're smarter than their parents. In a way, that makes sense since they roughly double their thinking capacity within one to two years. With their sudden increase in intelligence kids do not think, "Wow, I must have been really stupid before." Instead, they think, "Wow, I'm so smart now I really must be smarter than everyone—certainly I must be smarter than my stupid parents."

This increased intellectual capacity makes kids think they should be able to handle much more than they have ever before. In fact, parents and teachers start heaping on the responsibilities, and increase expectations at the same time. In addition, the sexual awakening of this age makes early teens want to be more like adults as well. Since all of this happens simultaneously, it's actually very scary for kids who don't really feel that much more capable in the maturity arena than they had been just a few years prior. Unfortunately, they aren't able to admit to this feeling of vulnerability, which they would view as making them more childlike at a time when they so desperately want to feel like adults. Thus, they resort to behavior that makes them feel the opposite of vulnerable.

Bullying becomes an alternative to feeling vulnerable and weak in the face of seemingly insurmountable new challenges that are supposed to be "no big deal." In the kids who are already prone to bullying, as outlined above, the need to be dominant becomes overwhelming. These kids need to bully in order to feel any sense of adequacy at all. In the case of those with natural social ability, it simply becomes such an easy way to fend off the vulnerability of the early teen years that bullying is used with immediacy and very little thought to successfully establish dominance as an alternative to being as childish as one really feels.

With individual personality integration and childhood development as they are, it is amazing how successful some schools have been in creating a culture where bullying is simply not "cool." Although the transformation in teens is not complete anywhere, when school administrators truly focus on developing a caring atmosphere within our schools, and when they put serious consequences in place against bullying, most kids tend to fall into line. So far, this has been possible really only in places where there is a homogeneously high level of parental involvement. Only with parental involvement will kids have to care about their parents' opinions enough to care about the opinions of teachers or the consequences their teachers give.

When the culture of the school has not, or is not enough to, overcome bullying, the question remains what to do about the bully and his victim. Starting with the bully, it is important to understand that his efforts to fend off vulnerability or fear are completely unconscious. That is, the bully thinks of himself as dominant and strong—in fact, that is the whole purpose of his behavior. The bully does not know that he feels weak and vulnerable. This is true even in cases where the child is abused by a dominating parent. In those cases the bully simply sees himself as doing what his parent does. He doesn't understand what the behavior accomplishes for him (or for his parent either).

The trick to helping the bully overcome his behavior is very complicated. It requires that he see and feel the pain of his victims so that he can feel some shame and take some responsibility. Shame, believe it or not, is the simple antidote to bullying. It connects the bully to his own feelings of vulnerability and weakness. And thus, it connects him to the feelings engendered by his bullying. In fact, the administrator or teacher dealing with a bully will typically find that the bully seems almost incapable of taking any responsibility or feeling any shame for what he has done. When the bully does say the right thing, it is rarely if ever heartfelt. It is evidence of just how much the bully needs to feel dominant that he seems so incapable of being sorry for what he does.

Further complicating the issue, the victims typically cannot be expected to make the vulnerable statements that are necessary to get through to the bully, get him to see how his behavior has hurt someone, and to help him understand why he should be ashamed. Instead, administrators must do their best to get the bully to put himself in the shoes of the victim. For those bullies that face such treatment at home, this can be an especially painful, but necessary, process, as the bully breaks down into his shame while he comes to terms with exactly how pathetic and weak he really feels.

One final way to get bullies to feel proper shame is for adults to notice when the bully's behavior makes the adult himself, feel vulnerable. At that point, if that adult is capable of staying in their role of authority as parent or administrator, while simultaneously remaining vulnerable and true to their own experience, the authority must communicate to the bully how the bully's behavior has been hurtful to the authority. Once the bully is able to communicate an understanding of how their behavior affected the adult personally, the adult must follow through with appropriate consequences even within the context of being hurt (please see article "Communication from the Heart"). It is absolutely essential that a consequence be given so that the incident will be taken seriously. Merely thinking that the bully seems to truly understand is not the only consideration. When people are truly sorry and ashamed, they actually benefit from the feeling of compensating for their behavior. Thus, if the consequence involves some form of reparation, it is especially useful.

Finally, and most perplexing, figuring out how to help the victim is extremely complex. We have all known the kind of kid who almost seems to be a magnet for bullies (those who seem sullen or different or who get hurt very easily). However, there are also many kids who are bullied just because it is so obvious that they deeply care what other kids think. Some kids are simply shy or sweet and find it almost impossible to be mean, which leaves them totally defenseless when more dominant and spontaneously mean kids challenge them with cruelty. So how do we talk to these kids about getting out of the victim situation?

In an abstract sense, it is easy to see that self-esteem is the culprit. If a kid who has been bullied starts to feel really good about himself, either due to therapy or a change in his life, the bullying invariably vanishes. When a kid feels good about himself, it simply doesn't make sense to him that other kids are treating him like he's something he's not, such as pathetic, useless, or idiotic. Thus, he won't react to bullying in the way the bully wants and needs. That is, the bully expects his victim to act afraid or pathetic, but if the victim is neither afraid nor pathetic and, in contrast, feels confident, his reaction to the bully will not be satisfying to the bully. The bully will then lose interest and choose another victim.

The problem in this easy truth, however, is that we cannot typically get the victim to develop a sudden burst of confidence. We typically deal with our own frustration about the victim's difficulties by suggesting that the victim defend himself with nastiness equal to that of the bully, which the victim is incapable of enacting because he is generally too nice. The worst thing we suggest, or that victims sometimes try to do, is come up with "comebacks" to ugly bully comments. From a child who is not feeling confident, "comebacks" will always fall flat, and will ultimately play into the hands of the bully who invents his next line with the alacrity and enthusiasm of a grand master chess player eyeing checkmate, and with the iniquity of the most venomous snake. Victims are not pathetic, but their ability to be mean, even with the best prefabricated lines, is typically nonexistent. Most victims are automatically nice and only think of the mean things they could have said after the incident is over. Simply put, they don't want to hurt anyone. In contrast, the bully takes pride in being viperous and has become very skilled at it. The victim is simply not going to win by engaging the bully on the bully's terms. The bully will always be better at verbal jousting than your typical victim.

There are, however, some simple tactics the victim can use. Although victims are quite awkward in inventing derisive or contemptuous slams, slights or even snubs, they certainly can act more confident. He can learn to act like he doesn't care and like the bully doesn't matter. He can act, and hopefully become, indifferent. Of course, we all know even that is difficult, but it is far easier than "comebacks." If you watch the kids who are not bullied, but who themselves don't bully, it can be observed that they are simply able to look a bully in the eye, seemingly without fear, and walk away. Sometimes they are particularly effective with a disappointed shake of the head or a one word expression of distaste (Yichhkkkkkk! or Wowww!) and then a turn away. No one ever, however, really achieves success in dealing with a bully when they decide to engage in mutual insults, unless they themselves enjoy bullying.

The bully only bullies if he is capable of making his victim feel the feelings he doesn't want to feel. He wants to be dominant which requires that someone must be weak and/or submissive so he won't feel that way. All the potential victim must do to frustrate bullying is to behave like he is not weak or feeble no matter what the bully does, and the bully will move on to someone else. Behaviors that communicate indifferent strength are the key and include: 1. looking the bully in the eye without fear; 2. thinking to oneself, but in a way that can be read in one's behavior, that the bully is behaving foolishly; and 3. successfully acting like the bully is foolish, but without calling the bully foolish. These behaviors can easily be practiced at home. Because they involve only facial expressions and body language, they do not require a quick wit, a better "comeback," or even real confidence. When they are successful, however, behaviors that show indifference toward bullying will, indeed, help the victim build very real confidence and self-esteem.

While bullying is a complex social phenomenon, it can be understood more fully. Great strides have been made in developing more supportive cultures in middle schools and high schools. There is a lot of room, however, to handle bullies and their victims in more helpful ways. The key to helping bullies is in getting them to feel shame and take responsibility, which puts them in touch with their own vulnerability. The key to helping victims is to keep our advice very simple—the victim must be able to confidently behave as though the bully's behavior is not having the bully's desired effect. To make this problem really disappear we all have to look it in the eye and accept our own vulnerability. Only by seeing and accepting our own vulnerability can we hope to get the bully to see his vulnerability. Only by accepting our own vulnerability, instead of trying to get the victim to act strong like we might think we are, can we get the victim to see that he can look the bully in the eye himself because, truly, all there really is to fear in dealing with the bully is fear itself.

CHAPTER 39

ﾃ

"Be A Man"

"There never was a truly great man that was not at the
same time truly virtuous."

—Benjamin Franklin

"Be a man!" Now that's a phrase that brings up all sorts of feelings. Typically when it's said, "be a man" is said as an insult. But what does it really mean? Is a "real man" someone who is always strong—someone who never wavers in his views or opinions? Is a "real man" a good provider—a person who fiercely protects his family from danger? Is a "real man" tender and forgiving—an emotional support for his family for whom he provides strength and encouragement? What is a "real man?"

Perhaps by exploring the feelings conjured up by the statement, "be a man," some light can be shed upon the importance of understanding why the statement is so much a part of our culture. It has many forms, such as "don't be a girl," "you're gay," "don't be a sissy," "don't get your panties in a knot," and there are many, many more. The statement likely has different meanings, depending on who is making the statement to whom. It means one thing if it is a guy's buddies, challenging him to do something daring or possibly ill-advised. "Be a man" means something quite different if it is said by a father or a mother. Parents who say this sort of thing are often trying to make a boy act more masculine or take more responsibility. However, one commonality seems to exist no matter who is making the statement. Whoever makes the statement, "be a man," is uncomfortable with what the target person is doing, and is attempting to get him to do something, or be a certain way, that is not natural for him.

When it's the buddies saying it, their probably suggesting that the guy is a wimp if he doesn't do the thing they're suggesting. Or maybe they're just sick of hearing their buddy express feelings. It's probably both. Guys like to be entertained by their buddies doing foolish things that they can suggest would make them tough or cool. Then when there's a mishap or a blunder, it's a laugh riot for the rest of the guys. Boys also like to dare their pals to do things that really would be impressive, but most of the time they're expecting failure. No one wants to be shown up as less tough when they dare their friend to take a risk.

Guys can also be tough on each other when it comes to being emotional. Many guys never express any feeling that could be considered even the slightest bit vulnerable. Boys act like they can handle anything and nothing is a big problem. For many boys the only emotion that is acceptable is anger. Any other emotions make them feel vulnerable or soft, and that's an unacceptable way to feel. So if anyone has a sad thought, or a fear, or gets hurt in any way, it is not too unusual for his buddies to act like he's weak. Essentially then, when one's buddies say "be a man," the statement suggests "do what I say and shut up about it, so we can all act tough" or, "I don't want to hear about any feelings because maybe I'm just as vulnerable as you."

When it's the parents saying "be a man," it is likely most damaging. Of course kids look to their parents for guidance. Kids are generally desperate for their parents' love. So when a parent makes any kind of sharp comment, no matter what type, it is heard loud and clear by the child and it's felt in his very bones (even if he doesn't seem to acknowledge it, which is even more likely to happen if the comments are heard regularly). The comment "be a man" actually suggests to the boy that he is acting like a girl or a woman. For some reason, perhaps based on male dominance in our culture, there is really no comment that could express more disgust and disrespect to a boy. Really, for the boy who hears this comment from his parents, "be a man" is about as close to total rejection as his parents could get.

Now why would a parent say such a thing? It is interesting to note that we generally pay most attention to those aspects in others about which we feel most uncomfortable or vulnerable. Within our children this phenomenon is even more stark because we believe everything they do reflects upon us. It is not only true about their masculinity. We also feel our children's intelligence, quickness, respectfulness, and almost any other personal attribute you might think of, are a direct reflection on our character. With respect to manliness, our feelings can be especially sensitive. Many men feel that their manhood is constantly being challenged, so they avoid any behavior within themselves that could be even remotely associated with femininity. When such a man sees his boy act in a way that makes him feel vulnerable, weak, or feminine, he will often immediately criticize the boy to stamp out those feelings within himself. He may act as if making sure that the boy acts "like a man" will make it clear that he, as the father, is plenty manly himself.

Mothers also have feelings of vulnerability that cause this cruel behavior toward their boys. For mothers, however, the problem is more in the arena of the criticism they fear for raising a feminine boy. Many women are desperate to have their mothering be unassailable. Although it hurts any mother to have her maternal instincts too closely examined, some mothers cannot stand for there to be any possibility that they might be doing something incorrect. That factor, combined with our society's deep seated fear of homosexuality, makes any seemingly feminine behavior in a woman's son dreadfully intolerable due to how that behavior would reflect on the mother's mothering. A boy's feminine behavior often makes a mother feel guilty if she feels she has not allowed the boy to be independent. Similar to the cruel behavior seen in the man with his son when he sees feminine behavior that brings question to the man's own manhood, the mother can become cruel and question her boy's manliness when her mothering is brought into question.

Interestingly, in a way, these kinds of comments likely have the opposite effect to what is intended by the friends or parents who say "be a man." If there is any one trait that could most fully be associated with being "a man" it would be independence. In the traditional model for families, grown women are often focused on caring for family, and adult men are focused on making sure the family has what it needs. Making sure the family has what it needs requires "a man" to go out and get what the family needs without allowing for too much interference from the influence of others. But emasculating comments tell a boy to stop being independent and do what the friends or parents seem to need. It may seem strange to think possible, but when the boy actually gives in to "be a man" type comments, he is becoming less of "a man." Boys who give in to the demands of their friends for fear of being "wimpy" typically behave in a way that is irresponsible. But the fact that a consummate "man" is a responsible man is unquestionable. Boys who fear their father's masculine wrath will often submerge that fear, and the weakness associated with that fear, and turn it into criticism of other boys they deem to be "wimpy." On the other hand, when a boy doubts he can ever be masculine enough to please his father, it is not too uncommon for him to reject the very manliness the father is trying to foist upon him. If a boy is unable to identify with his father due to the father's lack of acceptance, he might actually seem to take on more feminine characteristics as he turns to his mother for identification. Boys who find it impossible to differentiate themselves from their mothers due to their mothers' critiques, and a desire to chase her approval, either become more feminine to identify with her and please her, or become angry at women in general as the only way to finally differentiate as males.

No matter how one looks at it, the comment (or others like it) "be a man" is harmful at best, and at worst has the opposite effect from what must be intended by those who say it. Men are independent and responsible, and have both assertive and nurturing tendencies. A balance of these attributes is necessary in making the "real man." Friends often simply want to have some fun teasing or daring someone to do something foolish. They want to accentuate their toughness and often try to do so by diminishing the masculinity of others. Parents often want their boys to be especially masculine for fear of what others will think of their parenting. Strangely, criticizing a boy's masculinity can turn him toward more feminine interests if he feels he can't fit in with the boys, or if he can't be like dad, or if he tries especially hard to please a critical mom and thus tries to become like her. One way or the other, comments like "be a man" clearly have little to do with the person to whom they're said. Almost always, such comments involve the inadequate and vulnerable feelings of the person who makes the statement. Friends who are real friends won't try to diminish each other with humiliating quips. Parents who are capable of staying focused on their love for their child won't express their own insecurities by emasculating a son. What we really want from our boys is that they be themselves and show that they can be counted on. Since independence and responsibility are the real hallmarks of manhood, real friends and good parents will encourage a boy to be who he wants to be, and to be careful, they will not challenge him to "be a man."

CHAPTER 40

❧

It Must Be Hard To Be a Girl

"A woman's work is never done."

—Proverb

It must be really hard to be a girl! We really ask a lot from them. First of all we tell them to be sweet and kind and gentle. And actually, that's pretty natural for the typical girl. But then we tell them to be strong, direct, independent and competitive. Well, that might be indispensable in this cold, hard, world, and a lot of girls don't have any problem demonstrating those qualities, but somehow those qualities don't fit that great with being kind and gentle.

Clearly, the place of the female in our society is extremely complicated. Some of this complexity is merely a result of genetics in that females have always had to multitask as the keepers of the children and the home, dating back to prehistoric times. On the other hand, some of this complexity is clearly foisted upon girls as we expect them to manage things in the simplistic, linear, fashion that men have developed because it has always suited men best.

Males have historically had to work toward very specific and discrete goals like building, hunting, and protecting—activities which lend themselves to linear thinking and less finesse than what is required from females. Unfortunately for girls, however, with so-called equality between the genders taking prominence, it has been far more often the circumstance that girls have had to learn to do things like guys, rather than the other way around.

It's sort of funny, really, that it's far more frequent that boys are the ones complaining. Many men think it's horrible that they should have to care for children, cook dinner, or clean up. Heaven forbid if some men have to change a diaper. Many men think all of that is "women's work." And in a way, all that had been women's work before the late twentieth century. It's also true, really, that many men aren't naturals when it comes to doing much of that.

When you think about it, so called "women's work" almost always requires multitasking. Most men today, in fact, won't even mind if told to do any one discrete task related to "women's work." A man can change a diaper, cook a casserole, or wash the dishes. It's the general tasks, those that require doing many things at once, like caring for the children, cooking a meal, or cleaning up, that truly challenge the typical man's inability to multitask. It's not that men can't do these things, but the fact that it's not quite natural to men makes these more general tasks cumbersome (For more detail about the differences between men and women, please see the article "Women and Men").

In fact, men will often do the general tasks, those that require multitasking, much differently than their female counterparts. Men will often be less intimately involved, and will often perform these tasks in, what seems to be, a much less considerate way than women will. Men will clean up later or more slowly, will make a very simple meal, or will let the children do what they want with relatively little supervision. Men often rationalize that these less involved forms of completing certain tasks are more efficient.

For women, however, it is often "the thought that counts," and women know that people feel cared for more when chores are accomplished with consideration as the primary objective rather than easiness. So men complain about multitasking chores, or don't do them, or they change those chores to be more like typical male tasks (fit them into a routine so they become one chore).

Girls and women, unfortunately, can't manage the expectations of society quite so easily because so much more is expected from them. They might change some tasks to more feminine versions of the same, but since they will most likely be judged based on how quickly the task was completed, or whether their directives were readily understood, they had better be aware that they are competing in a "man's world." In fact, everywhere you look, females are given competing expectations that require amazing balance.

Girls are, of course, expected to produce every bit as much as their male counterparts, but they are also expected to be nice and caring, and sometimes to look pretty, while they produce that same amount (I can hear some guys grousing that their appearance and grooming matter just as much as does that of the women on their job, but I know few men who spend more than an hour getting ready for work while I know few women who spend less than an hour doing the same).

The fact of the matter is, women generally keep their feminine instincts on the job and in society, while also competing with men in the areas where men feel more natural. Production of things, getting tasks done, working on one thing and then moving to the next, is all very natural to men. Women are also extremely efficient at getting things done, but they experience a need to approach those tasks with care for the well-being or comfort of others. That is where men and women differ greatly within the work place. Clearly, however, getting things done while simultaneously caring for others creates a far more complicated process than managing either goal alone. Nevertheless, because output, regardless of anyone's comfort, is so often the sole measure of a job well done, women have to compete with men, and sometimes must be cold and uncaring, to be given respect.

The work world has been so dominated by male thinking, in fact, most of the time there is an assumption by both men and women that the best way to get things done is by being cold and indifferent to the needs of people. In fact, when a man behaves in an indifferent fashion while getting things done he's considered very direct. On the other hand, the same actions from a woman, even if they lead to the same outcome, make her a b—, right? Truly, the balance expected from women in these kinds of jobs is amazing, and when someone sees a woman managing that balance it is also truly impressive. The woman who successfully masters the incredible feat of balancing care with authority is often a marvel in production and efficiency, as her workers respect her, get things done, and yet feel that their needs have been considered. The fact is, most workers will respond best to a caring management style as long as they also remain aware that there will definitely be consequences for inadequate work.

It is also quite obvious that in an increasing number of jobs today, being cold and indifferent is not generally the best course of action in supervision because the treatment of the customer is so directly related to how workers are treated by their boss. As our culture becomes increasingly service oriented, it is actually the care and comfort of others that is the most important aspect of production. In a restaurant many people will have no problem waiting for their food if they are treated in a polite and kind manner. The appearance of their surroundings, and often even the presentation of the food served, will be every bit as important as the taste of the food. When picking up one's dry cleaning or if dealing with a realtor, it is often the attitude and attention to peoples' feelings that will bring the customer back, not the cleanliness of the clothes or the kind of properties available. Where workers need to handle customers, how they feel on the job is intimately involved with how the customer will feel. So to an ever-increasing degree, the natural skills of women in being considerate to others is becoming the most important aspect of success.

Nevertheless, even though some typically feminine characteristics are beginning to garner appreciation in the work world, the mixed messages we give women from the time they are little girls continue to be severely confusing. One might think it's difficult for boys to be told they will have to support a family when they get older. It causes so much pressure. But when you think about the fact that everything we get done, and get done well, seems to happen because we know it will have to get done, then really, compared to girls, boys are given a far clearer path to follow. Boys are told "you will have to work hard to support a family some day, so you'd better be good in school, find a career, work hard, and take care of business." Girls, on the other hand, want to be mommies, are encouraged to fantasize about knights in shining armor, and often picture themselves raising children while their husband will make a living and support the family. At the same time, however, girls are also expected to be at least as motivated as boys to perform in school and to find a career path of their own.

Amazingly enough, girls do take school seriously and, at least in the early years, often outperform boys. Again, a feminine characteristic helps to explain this phenomenon. It is the girls' desire to take care of feelings that makes them better students because they desire to please their parents or show others that they are "good." The boys' need for a linear understanding of the meaning of tasks, and their more self-centered nature, often makes them falter academically until they find a path to success that feels a good and sensible fit. Boys often do not start to perform academically until they truly see how their studies are connected to the achievements they, themselves, desire. Somehow, and amazingly so, girls manage to perform even though, really, at least from a male perspective, there really should not be much motivation for them to do so.

When women do recognize the dilemma posed in achieving for pleasing others instead of themselves, a realization which often does not occur until they have already reached the career they were so sure would be right for them, their motivation really does often disintegrate. At this point, in fact, men often cannot understand why women need their work to be fulfilling since boys have been taught to simply plug along as though fulfillment is unimportant. The difference is, however, obvious. The girl has been told she would please others by being a good student and by having a great career. She then finds a career that is either fulfilling, or that has impressed others, or both. But now, somehow, she has to manage balancing that career against what is likely a biological imperative. The issue of family, husband, and children, perhaps now reconnecting to those domestic fantasies of childhood, comes back into play just as the career path seems to be preeminent. That is, just as a woman has reached the career she has so diligently trained to pursue, now she's experiencing an intense, but competing, urge to follow the child-rearing path as she comes to notice that the "biological clock is ticking."

If a woman does decide she'd better heed that biological clock and have children, the work world is none too pleased. Even before she has children, just the possibility that she might have children will often result in a woman being treated like she's less valuable than a man. And how she'll feel once she decides to forego the career she's been diligently working toward is often not so pleasant either. When a woman decides to stay home with her children, a decision she will be told is completely valid and important, she will quickly find that it feels almost completely unappreciated. Since children are born and not built, in fact, there can be little glory or recognition for a mom outside of the baby's cuteness. Because the woman loves her baby, that recognition feels good, but it does not replace a need for recognition of one's achievements. Even worse, the woman now finds herself accountable for endless arduous tasks, and if her child does not behave as others' deem appropriate, she's now open to scorn and ridicule. The little girl's desire to please, as it lives on in the grown woman, is thus completely thwarted as whatever career achievements she attained seem a thing of the past, and her current achievements in child-rearing are only recognized to the extent that the children are pleasing to others.

Men, on the other hand, have been told all along that the primary meaning of their career would be how well they'd be able to care for their family. Thus, the boy is perfectly comfortable with the idea that their goal will be to bring in money. The man may be better off enjoying his career, but it is not absolutely necessary because the goal of bringing in money is paramount. Of course, women want to be big earners too, but earning power is generally not their biggest concern. While the man can see his earning power as an end in itself, most women look for the lifestyle the money can buy as being far more important than the money. Essentially, the lifestyle bought with earning power takes the place of pleasing others. Others can be impressed with lifestyle, including how one adorns oneself with clothing, jewelry, homes, and cars, but also, for many women lifestyle fits well with caring for others. Providing a nice lifestyle is a caring activity, and often the stay-at-home mom is considered very lucky to have the opportunity to stay home and nurture her family. In that way, the women who decides that child-rearing is an important endeavor in itself, can feel good about how well they do take care of their children, which shows through the lifestyle they develop for the whole family. Unfortunately, however, in many circumstances, even the most lavishly feathered nest leads to a complete lack of fulfillment for a woman. If a woman attempts to define her own importance by her husband's status and the quality of her home, rather than what she accomplishes in that home, a complete disconnect ensues for her. If she is spending her time being a good mother, she is really accomplishing something wonderful and important. But if she attempts to act important because of who her husband is or because of the size of her home or the lifestyle she enjoys, there is absolutely no real satisfaction since there is truly and absolutely no accomplishment in being the spouse of someone else.

The woman who chooses her career over having children can also experience problems in feeling fulfilled. If she was like most (but not all) girls, someone who had badly wanted children, she cheats herself out of one of the most meaningful and legitimizing experiences a woman could know. Procreation is the primary biological imperative of all animals (clearly many couples do not desire children, but almost everyone has a desire to couple, which has no more obvious nascent purpose than procreation). Of course there are many ways for life to be fulfilling without having children, but if having children had ever been part of a woman's dream, choosing to forego child-rearing in pursuit of a career will often lead to a lack of fulfillment as the lifestyle earned from the career eventually pales in comparison to the meaning of life experienced within the connection between child and parent. If there is any truly fulfilling and meaningful experience in life, it is almost always related to connection with others in some way, and there is no more connected and bonded experience than the attachment between mother and child.

So this article ends essentially where it began. It must be really hard to be a girl. Girls and women are tasked with the impossible in our society from the very beginning. Their natural ability to handle many things at once is probably their saving grace. But satisfaction comes hard where expectations are so overwhelming. Women are expected to please others, pursue competitive aspirations, and then give up their own independent strivings and the plaudits that come with independent achievements, to pursue the fantasy of the perfect and loving family. Or they can continue in their strivings and have a family too, but that requires the most complicated and singular balance (which is, nevertheless, relatively common). In their work, women will be expected to get things done like men, but they better not be too direct in their directives or they'll be considered to be a "b—." On the other hand, perhaps their sensitivity will be valuable and acknowledged as such, but only if they're also able to garner the necessary respect required to make others work. If you can only imagine the balance it would take to work with care and sensitivity while also commanding appropriate respect, then just imagine the balance it takes in returning home from that job to make the dinner, clean the house, be sensitive to one's children and husband and, essentially, to hold the whole family together. The expectations we now hold on girls and women are truly incredible. Any woman who can handle all these expectations with any kind of grace, is truly an incredible person.

So, men, and you kids too, please make sure you have the proper respect. Please, please, fully partner with your wife, and/or help your mother. Most likely, whether she's chosen to be a dedicated wife and mother, or to be great in her career without pouring herself into a family of her own, and especially if she's trying to do it all, your wife or mother is probably managing an unbelievable number of tasks at one time. In fact, when you give it serious consideration, you should really think of your wife or mother as an amazing talent. She does so much. Your respect should be mandatory. Women certainly have my respect. All I know is this, and I believe this fact to be undeniable, it is obviously and truly, really hard to be a girl.

Section 11

Using Discipline

Tools for Supporting the Parenting Function within the Family Machine

Parents in a family are the governing system for the Family Machine. Their role is to monitor and adjust the family's functioning. Good discipline practices are the tools parents use to make those adjustments and keep the family on track. Good discipline is necessary for smooth operation and maneuvering within the larger Great Life Machine that is the community and the world beyond. Providing good discipline can, however, be difficult. As a governing system, parents often need help. The following articles are the necessary tools for managing slight adjustments, changing out parts, or performing a complete discipline overhaul. These articles can help diagnose a problem in discipline and they detail very specific practices for keeping kids in line. "Leaks in Discipline" discusses all the aspects of consistency that are necessary to create clear leadership from parents. Making sure that kids really understand their parents' expectations is the focus of "The Satisfaction Meter." "It's So Hard To Be Bad" aims at full comprehension of the motivation behind bad behavior. General discipline practices are outlined in "Good Discipline for Acting-Out Kids." Last, but not least, a "Sample Reward System" is presented that can be adjusted to fit the needs of any family or any situation.

CHAPTER 41

❧

Leaks in Discipline

"Unity is strength . . . when there is teamwork and
collaboration, wonderful things can be achieved."

—Mattie Stepanek

If you really think about it, there are only two reasons why our
children do not behave in accordance with our standards. These two
reasons are 1. inconsistency and 2. undermining. Really, undermining
is just a subset of inconsistency. If parents are consistent and do not
undermine one another, children will have to do whatever their parents
expect of them (as long as it's possible). If parents are kindhearted and
fair-minded people (who generally want to do as much as they can for
their children) their children truly should meet their expectations. In
fact, if the parents are, indeed, kind-hearted and fair-minded people,
meeting their expectations will lead to the greatest possible success
for their children.

Consistency

The fact is, most parents provide everything children want, limited
only by their own resources. Parents provide shelter. More often than
not that shelter is far better than the minimum required by law, right?

293

Parents also provide food, and more often than not they provide foods kids love, which goes well beyond what is necessary for nutritional standards or sustenance. Isn't that true? If their children are to have any fun that requires transportation or money, parents have to take part in planning that fun, don't they? Even the toys kids already have around the house, regardless of where they came from, require some kind of parental involvement since so many of those toys run on the electricity the parents pay for monthly. When you stop to think about it, kids can't have anything they want without their parents' involvement.

So if kids depend on their parents' good will for everything they want, how does it happen that so many parents have trouble with disciplining their children? Simply put, parents are inconsistent. We give warnings and make threats, but often we do not follow through. Due to that lack of follow through, our kids come to understand that we don't really mean it when we warn or threaten. Most of us have experienced what happens when our kids do know we're serious. Suddenly we find our previously stubborn child doing what they're supposed to do. If our kids really find that they lose a prized privilege when they fail to do what we ask, most of them tend to learn their lessons quite quickly.

While it is difficult to be consistent, the need for consistency can be stated and understood quite clearly. So why is it so difficult to carry out our desire to be consistent? Simply put, *love* gets in the way. Most reasonable parents of adequate resources want so badly for their children to know they're loved that they can't stand it when their kids have to go without. It's as if we think going without television or snacks is sheer torture for our children. When we stand by a consequence, it's too easy to feel as though we are responsible for depriving them. Of course, we know the truth. Our children are responsible for their behavior, and thus they must suffer the consequences of their misdeeds.

In fact, not only are we *not* responsible for their feeling deprived, we are 100% absolutely responsible for making sure they understand the importance of being well-behaved. Until they connect our dissatisfaction with their behavior to the reason for their consequences, they will not change. If they don't get real consequences, it's as if we are expecting them to grow up on their own, independent of parenting. If we don't discipline them, when will they learn to be civilized? How will they act when they're out on their own? The truth of the matter is that our interest in their future should be by far the most significant motivation for us toward making sure they do behave. We are desperate to ensure they have a good future, aren't we? The way we connect our interest in their future to their bad behavior is by making sure that they have consequences for their actions.

Undermining

Consistency and its relation to consequences is relatively easy to understand, but a particular kind of inconsistency, known as "undermining," is a far more complicated human process. When parents do not agree and the kids know it, especially when parents contradict one another directly in front of their children, it isn't even reasonable to expect kids to listen. It would be like having two ostensibly equal bosses on one job each who wanted completely different tasks completed, but you only had enough time to please one of them. It would be impossible. The boss you fail to please would surely fire you, unless the other boss saves you, which leads to a whole different level of undermining. When parents do not agree with one another, kids have no idea what to do. We don't fire our kids, but we sure can frustrate the heck out of them. Because we don't fire them, we inevitably do something worse. We actually make them take sides. It's as if the parent whose directions have been followed has saved the child from the other parent. Thus, the parent who is perceived to be the savior becomes the one to whom the child will listen in the future.

So with undermining occurring between parents, how would we expect children to act? Typically, kids follow the instructions of the parent they perceive to be more powerful. That makes the other parent feel crazy. In most cases, it even makes the two parents become more polarized in their parenting styles. One parent sees the other act strictly, and they become especially lenient. One parent sees the other discipline too leniently, and that parent becomes especially strict. In most cases, kids can even tolerate two completely different styles of parenting as long as only one parent is present at any given time, and as long as neither parent comments negatively on how the kids should react to the other parent when they're not around. When the two parents are together, however, the direction of the less dominant parent will be generally discounted if the views of the two parents seem contradictory. Alternately, often kids will simply behave in a confused manner, and sometimes they'll act almost as if they're paralyzed with an inability to take appropriate action.

The fact that undermining is such a problem does not mean that parents have to completely agree on discipline practices. What it does mean, however, is that they must aim to never contradict one another in front of the children (with the one exception being if one parent perceives the other one to be abusing a child). Each parent must have enough self-control to put their own directions on hold if those directions contradict the directions the other parent has already given. Of course, if parents disagree on how things should be done, it does necessitate a discussion on the topic between the parents when the children are not around. Parents do have to come to some consensus about how things should be handled the next time or they will be destined to repeating the same unresolved feelings into eternity. If people do work things out this way, of course most disagreements slowly dissipate and parents start acting much more consistently. There are only so many different kinds of situations with kids, and most will fall into patterns where the parents know they have already agreed on how to handle that particular kind of situation. But so many people seem to continuously lack agreement on how to handle situations, regardless of the amount of work that's gone into finding consensus. Why might that happen?

Although love can get in the way of a parent reining in their desire to undermine another parent (for example, "Oh, honey, let's just let him do it this one time"), competition for control is the primary factor underlying the act of undermining our parenting partners. Time and time again parents will undermine, even if they know it's wrong to do so, just because it is so uncomfortable for them to see the other parent parenting in a way that they feel is "wrong." Undermining will occur even after one has learned that undermining is far more damaging to children than the actual parenting technique they see being used, so it is clearly not their concern for the child that is uppermost in their thoughts (even though they sometimes think it is). In fact, quite often a parent can be observed to completely contradict their own stated preference for how something should be done just because the other parent is now using that same "preferred" technique. The repeated act of undermining can only be explained in this context by the need to be *the* parent in control.

To accomplish controlling the desire to undermine, parents need to see that their children's perception of them as being a team is far more important than either parent being "right" about how to discipline. Parents become far too wrapped up in the "right" way to parent, not realizing that disagreement between them is more destructive than any possible positive that could come from either parent using the "right" method. If parents can prevent their own desire to be in control, if they can manage to control their impulse to undermine or correct the other parent, if they can have the discipline to discuss their different methods when the children are not present, then their agreement on how to discipline, and a generally consistent pattern of parenting overall, will develop naturally within the family. If a generally consistent pattern does develop, children will have a chance to accomplish the very best future imagined by their parents. Without such a pattern, the parental team communicates a confused message about right and wrong, and how people get along, which puts children at a distinct disadvantage in dealing with the world and their future.

The answer to the riddle of why kids don't behave seems to be simple, but clearly it is not. Given how often kids misbehave, the answer to the riddle of why, is clearly quite complicated. The answer not only involves parents being consistent and not undermining each other, but also must include an understanding of why that is so hard to accomplish. To be consistent, parents need to put their children's future first and their children's immediate gratification must be put on hold. Parents need to put their own egos in check when deciding the "right" way to discipline, and they need to recognize that consensus and consistency between them is far more correct than any one approach to parenting. If parents are loving, caring, individuals, who want nothing more than to do for their children, then focusing on their children's discipline in the most consistent way possible is the most loving and caring way to do as much as they possibly can.

CHAPTER 42

❧

The Satisfaction Meter:
A Reward System for Regular People

"In all our contacts it is probably the sense of being really
needed and wanted which gives us the greatest satisfaction
and creates the most lasting bond."

—Eleanor Roosevelt

Having trouble with your kids, but you think it's bogus to create
a system where you give them rewards for good behavior? You have
no idea how many times I've heard that in my office. Typically, I
suppose, I don't actually hear it as much as I see it in people's eyes.
You might be happy to know, however, that there is an alternative. It
may sound silly, but it comes straight from the heart. If you use "The
Satisfaction Meter," you need only monitor your level of satisfaction
within your heart. If you are not satisfied, you merely say "I'm not
satisfied" and your children immediately experience the consequences
of your dissatisfaction. "The Satisfaction Meter" exists within each of
us and simply indicates whether or not we feel satisfied with our kids'
behavior. I know I'm making it sound real simple when sometimes
it's really not, but don't worry, I know it's going to take a bit of work.
The important and problematic part is that a parent must develop the

ability to look inside him or herself and honestly appraise whether or not they are satisfied with their child's behavior. If you can do that well, then you already know it's an extremely effective method. In fact, "The Satisfaction Meter" is truly the method people are using when they're parenting is going well.

Let's start with the basics. Your kids have one main job. If they adequately perform the duties necessitated by that job, us parents will typically give them all they could possibly want. That job is to SATISFY their parents. The only problem is that kids don't know that's their job. Us parents are so busy considering a wide variety of factors, that we don't make this job clear to our kids. In fact, most kids think it's their parents' job to satisfy the kids because our love makes us cater to their every whim. Once it is clear to kids that a kid's job is to satisfy their parents, it is so easy and straightforward for kids to earn their privileges, it's a joke. Parents really want to be satisfied and thus, most of us are, if anything, too easy on our kids.

Being too easily satisfied is just one of many reasons that kids don't know that their job is to satisfy us. Many other considerations also get in the way of acting upon the level of satisfaction we feel about our kids' behavior. We want to be fair. We want to be consistent. We want to be in agreement with our spouse or the other parents involved. We don't want to make a scene. We want to look like we are respected. We don't want to be judged by others. We're tired. We want to partake in the reward our children would get if they were good. The possibilities are endless. But none of that has anything to do with whether you actually feel satisfied. Those other considerations have everything to do with giving in and lacking consistency.

Once you get used to the idea of really basing privileges on how satisfied you are with your child's behavior, there are certain aspects of "The Satisfaction Meter" that must be discussed. Let's just talk about the essentials. Possibly the most important thing to understand is that you provide everything for your children. You also have the right to take it all away. Kids love to make the argument, "Grandma gave me the computer, so it's mine and you can't take it away." But Grandma doesn't pay for the electricity. Right? No matter what argument your future attorney might contrive, the fact will remain that they've got nothing without you. You can say and must believe the following: "the law requires I provide adequate food for nourishment, adequate shelter and clothing, and that I do something about it if you refuse to go to school, but that's about it." Everything else is a privilege if I deem it to be a privilege. If you are willing to follow that philosophy, you are well on your way to making good use of "The Satisfaction Meter."

Now you need to know the rules. "The Satisfaction Meter" is an all or nothing reward system. That is, if you are satisfied with your kids' behavior, they get all their privileges within the normal bounds of your usual family life. When you are not satisfied, your children lose all their privileges within the normal bounds. "Within normal bounds" means your kids still can't stay up till 2:00 AM on a school night even when they have satisfied you and have earned all their privileges. If in your family it's a privilege to have an ounce of cheese once a day, then your kids don't get cheese when you are not satisfied. You have to also realize here that some things can be a given. Maybe you don't think of an after school snack as a privilege, but a necessity. If it's not a privilege, it does not have to be something that is taken away. The things that are considered privileges will be different in every family. You should be careful, however, to put everything that is a privilege in the privilege category. For example, it is clearly a privilege to have a fun snack after school, but perhaps carrot sticks could be the nonprivilege item if you think your children are truly hungry (my guess is that many won't eat the carrot sticks, so they're probably not too hungry). Computer use for school could also be a problem, but you could have them do their homework at the kitchen table so they won't so easily enjoy the computer. As you can see, you might have to use some creative thinking on the specifics.

The next rule is that no one gets to interfere with the ruling of satisfaction by whichever parent has made the ruling. If Dad is not satisfied, all privileges are lost until Dad is satisfied. If Mom thinks Dad is wrong, she needs to keep it to herself. If she does want to talk to Dad in private, that's fine. Perhaps she can talk to him and he will become more satisfied. Nevertheless, if Dad said he was not satisfied, he has to become satisfied before privileges are restored. Just because one spouse argues in favor of the child does not mean the other spouse is now satisfied. In fact, if there is a solution, it usually requires some repair. Perhaps an apology is in order. Maybe an extra chore to make up for the transgression will help satisfy Dad. No matter what it is, it must result in satisfaction from the parent who was dissatisfied before privileges are restored—**no matter what!**

Something to realize about "The Satisfaction Meter" is that sometimes privileges are taken away for very short periods of time. It is essential that kids understand this part of the system since they will otherwise likely feel it is way too harsh. But think about how easily most parents would be satisfied if their children knew their primary job was to satisfy their parents. What if Mom walks in the door and her boy doesn't say a proper hello? Not that big of a deal. Right? She might nevertheless say, "I'm not satisfied." However, if her boy immediately says, "hi Mom," in an enthusiastic tone, she will likely be satisfied immediately. Although technically the kid has lost all privileges in this example the very moment Mom said she wasn't satisfied, he will really never feel the loss because he regains his privileges before he could possibly even realize he's lost them. On the other hand, if Mom gets really dissatisfied due to her girl coming in hours after dark, the extreme worry she experienced will likely result in dissatisfaction for several days. Clearly, if one is truly consulting their inner Satisfaction Meter, sometimes they will be quickly satisfied and sometimes satisfaction will require some time and some effort from the kids.

If you think about it, "The Satisfaction Meter" is really just a very clear communication tool. Our kids should be able to see what satisfies us and what doesn't. If we are their best guide for proper behavior and attitude, they really need to know what we think. Because we provide everything for them, even if we're not their best guide for proper behavior and attitude, they really ought to recognize that we need to be satisfied for them to get what they want. But all the other considerations in life have a tendency to get in the way. "The Satisfaction Meter" is merely a way of getting kids in touch with what we are feeling as their parents. In fact, if kids play it smart, they will quickly learn that many of their current behavioral habits, such as avoiding us or arguing, are exactly the wrong way to respond if they want to get the privileges they prize so dearly. If they are going to play it smart, and you are using "The Satisfaction Meter" well, when you say you're not satisfied, they will do whatever they possibly can to satisfy you as quickly as possible. While that might simply require an apology in some circumstances, if at other times it entails getting you a glass of water and cleaning up the living room, then that will be the smartest thing for them to do. Clearly avoiding you and arguing with you are merely going to make you less satisfied and thus prolong your dissatisfaction. If you're using "The Satisfaction Meter" making you even less satisfied is not smart.

One final caveat must be mentioned before "The Satisfaction Meter" can be put to good use. It has to be clear that no one should expect their children to make them happy. Your children are not responsible for your happiness, which is much different than your satisfaction. In fact they cannot even satisfy you if you are not satisfied with yourself and your own life. Your children only need to make you satisfied with their behavior. You have to try very hard to make sure that you are being as objective as possible in your satisfaction with your child. You must ask yourself, "is it my child's behavior that is making me dissatisfied, or am I going to be dissatisfied regardless of their behavior?" If you believe it is their behavior that is not satisfactory, then you need to state that you are not satisfied. If you feel you likely will not be satisfied no matter what they do, you will likely need to do something new in your own life to help you be more happy and satisfied without your kids' help.

Simply put, if your child's behavior is not satisfactory, he does not deserve privileges. Most parents are willing to let their kids have just about anything if their children are behaving in a satisfactory manner. The biggest road blocks to "The Satisfaction Meter" are the many considerations that tempt you to give up your consistency and ability to remain firm. Disagreement with your spouse is a second important factor. But if you are capable of looking inside yourself and really figuring out whether or not you are satisfied, and whether or not you should be satisfied, then using "The Satisfaction Meter" will quickly result in predominantly satisfactory behavior from your children. "The Satisfaction Meter" is the connection between who we really are and how our children really should behave. "The Satisfaction Meter" is truly the tool used by us all when we are at our most consistent and effective in our parenting.

CHAPTER 43

❧

It's So Hard To Be Bad:
So for Heaven's Sake, Just Be Good!

"When I do good, I feel good. When I do bad, I feel bad. That's my religion."

—Abraham Lincoln

When I see all the trouble encountered by kids who don't want to follow rules, kids who just never seem to do the right thing—when I see kids blow up in anger because they don't get their way, or take things they think they need because they just can't wait—when kids can't tell the truth or take responsibility—when they feel entitled, but don't like hard work—when it seems clear to me that a kid just won't get a grip on where they're going to end up if they keep going this way, I can't help but think the same thing every time: Why on God's green Earth would someone keep being bad when it's so much easier to be good?

Of course the answer is complicated! It must be. It can't feel good to have people angry at you all the time, or to have them be disappointed. As if the wrath of parents and teachers isn't bad enough, when the consequences are meted out, it must stink to lose privileges or be forced to do extra work. Even worse, it must feel devastating to go to court and/or Juvenile Detention. From the point of view of most ordinary people, it seems daunting enough just to have to associate with other people who also can't be trusted, or worse, people who might literally stab you in the back. Worst of all, however, is that being bad gets a person nowhere.

When someone is frequently bad, others will not trust them. If they can't be trusted, a person who is acting badly will not only lose privileges, but they will also lose their freedom. As children, only those who can earn their parents' trust are actually given freedom. If their parents trust too easily, or if their parents just don't care enough, of course, those kids end up in lock up. But in most cases where parents do care, we see the child slowly lose the ability to do anything that requires trust, even when no privilege has been taken. If a kid can't be trusted to go outside or have friends over, then even when the child's not in trouble, some fear within the parent will make them say no or find an excuse to avoid granting a privilege. If the parents care and they are afraid, they have to say no in order to keep their child safe. Sometimes parents even say no to the child being with the parent. If a parent believes their child is likely to get on their nerves when they go somewhere, that parent is likely to abstain from bringing the child just because it would be more trouble than it's worth. When it comes time for really big freedoms, like learning to drive, a caring parent would have to be crazy to allow a child who isn't trustworthy to get behind the wheel.

When you think of the long term, the outcomes are even worse. People who continue to do the wrong thing into their adult years rarely, if ever, truly succeed. No matter how you define success, it is unlikely one can become successful by doing bad things. Bad acting people come to bad ends. How many times do you hear about a criminal success story? No matter how many years they might successfully stockpile cash, criminals end up in prison or get killed. It is the very rare criminal who becomes a great success story.

Even those who make a living cheating others for long periods, or who treat people badly while they go about their business, rarely come to good ends. It is so frequent for these disrespectful and self-centered types to feel quite successful until, as they approach their senior years, they realize just how alone they are and how meaningless their life has been. The more you think about it, the more it's obviously true, it's really hard to be bad.

Clearly then, there must be something very compelling about being bad if so many people feel the need to be bad. In fact, there are three primary reasons that bad behaviors persist even when parents are trying their very best to quell them. First and foremost, children who engage in bad behavior appear to have very significant problems with the delay of gratification. Second, many kids with bad behaviors have an extreme need to be in control or dominant. Third, the insatiable need and desire for the approval of one's peers can be almost completely irresistible. Understanding why people act badly requires closer inspection. Perhaps a better understanding of why people do bad things will help lead to better ways of helping them get on track.

With respect to the inability to delay gratification, some children experience the desire for what they want so powerfully it's as if they're inexorably impelled to take immediate action. A child can feel that way about small things or big, a candy bar or a brand new bike. When a child is either told no or is made to wait, sometimes they feel controlling themselves is just beyond their abilities. Some children have such a powerful need within them that they will find almost any way to get the thing they want. They will steal if they can. They will beg and plead with their parents, or attempt a million kinds of manipulation, till their parents either acquiesce from enervation or become completely infuriated. Regardless of how many times this happens, such children never seem to learn.

When it comes to the need for dominance, it is unfortunately the case that many children feel like everything is chaotic and out of control unless they themselves are in control. Sometimes there is a need for dominance related to genetic insecurity, but the need for dominance can also be the result of experiencing trauma. When these children find themselves in new or frightening situations, they often have a need to be feared so they won't feel scared. All feelings associated with fear make these children feel an intolerable level of vulnerability. Because this vulnerability cannot be endured, such a child becomes dominant, controlling or aggressive before they are even aware of their fear. Once a person has used dominance and aggression to avoid their fear, they also experience a significant level of power as others back off and give in. That power can feel quite addictive and thus lead to more aggressive and dominant conduct in a cycle of behavior that may lead to some level of success, but never leads to satisfactory relationships (please see article "The Power and Control Addiction"). Unfortunately, trying to be dominant with authority figures outside the home is no more a good way to get along than attempting to dominate one's parents. In fact, even with one's peers, trying to be dominant has a tendency to result in frequent fighting or antagonism.

Peer pressure, along with the desire for approval from one's peers, also cannot be denied as a third factor in bad behavior. Some kids find it intoxicating to hear their peers laugh, and thus become class clowns. Some kids want their peers to think they're cool, or attractive, or wealthy, or unafraid. Because they want their peers to think those things, they'll behave in the ways others want them to behave, whether it be to use substances, to dress in a provocative fashion, to pilfer emblems of material success, or to behave in a challenging manner. It can be so ridiculously compelling to create a certain impression of oneself that some children will stop at nothing to make sure they feel accepted by their peers. There is good reason, however, that children should look to their elders in deciding how best to behave. Worry about what one's peers are thinking is so intrinsic to childhood, and children are so easily swayed by what is thought to be cool or funny, that only the leadership of one's respected elders, those who have already successfully traversed the tumultuous and murky rivers of childhood, can have any hope of keeping the desire for peer approval in check. Of course, these easily influenced kids have an extremely hard time becoming aware of that fact.

Thus parental leadership and discipline go hand in hand as the essential elements for combating bad behavior. Good parents are able to combine being firm and being consistent, while also maintaining kindness and affection toward their children (please see article "The Essentials of Parenting"). Their children become accustomed to being treated fairly, but good parents do not surrender their principles due merely to a showing of childish desperation. Good parents maintain a hierarchy in the household whereby children know their place and feel confident enough in their parents' affection that they do not need to fight their parents for control. Although children are always susceptible to peer pressure, if they learn to respect their elders, they will have adequate fear of transgressing their parents' admonishments. Good parents combat bad behavior, not only with discipline, but with love. They teach their children a path to success through hard work and taking responsibility. Their children learn to balance pride with humility, and desire with gratitude (please see article "From Materialism to Integrity").

In short, if a child can learn that they're special and unique and loved in this world, and if they can learn to strive for their goals in a way that does not cheat others or rob others of their chances at success, then they become capable of overcoming the inability to delay gratification, the need to dominate, and the perils of peer pressure. Good parenting leads to integrity and confidence. Fully developed integrity and confidence preclude bad behavior because they allow one to know without doubt that doing things right will lead to the kind of success that lasts. Fully developed integrity and confidence allow one to feel like they already have the things they need, that they are plenty strong, and that they are plenty likable, even if they want more, are striving to be stronger, and wish they had more friends.

But what, you may ask, happens when such good parenting is not available? That is a great question with no easy answer. Nevertheless, it remains the same, being bad is really, really, really hard. Given what's known about what will happen when one frequently does the wrong thing, how can anyone choose being bad as an acceptable alternative to being good. Being good is easy in comparison. Once you know the only way to any kind of success is doing things right—that is, working hard, taking responsibility, and being fair to others—even if you haven't developed integrity and confidence, then there is only one direction to go. The only reason not to go in that direction is if one just doesn't care enough about one's self to work hard, take responsibility, and be fair to others. Only if one just doesn't care about themselves does it make any sense that one would refuse to force themselves to delay gratification, contain the desire to dominate, and overcome pressure from peers. Give me hard work and the freedom earned from trust any day. I'll remain forever diligent, grateful, honest, loyal and fair anytime and every day over the alternative of going to prison or ending up alone. If there's a chance any kid out there might want my advice, well, here it is: it's really just so hard to be bad—so for heaven's sake, go easy on yourself, and just be good!

CHAPTER 44

⊂ℬ

Good Discipline for Acting-Out Kids

"Children should be led into the right paths, not by
severity, but by persuasion."

—Terence

Below you will find general instructions for good discipline practices that, while not comprehensive, can be very helpful in creating peace and harmony in your home. Please understand that these are general guidelines and that everything stated below has exceptions, or must be modified to some extent, for your specific situation. Nevertheless, it can be helpful to understand just a few key elements of discipline.

Consistency

1. Probably the single most important aspect of parenting an acting out kid is consistency. There are two main difficulties with being consistent.

    a. Some parents love their kids too much to see them "suffer" or go without. That is, they do not like it when their children cry or throw a tantrum. These parents will do anything to make it stop. Of course, that leads to the child thinking that he can get anything he wants just by acting upset. Kids learn to use their emotions at an extremely early age. If you know it's not hurting your child to go without TV (or dessert, etc.), then acting like the tantrum is ridiculous is exactly what you should do.

b. Some parents have a hard time agreeing on consequences and thus each undermines the authority of the other. If the father is strict and the mother is not (or vice versa), then of course the children are going to seek out the help of the nonstrict parent when they are told no by the strict parent. Sometimes parents are simply struggling to be the one in control, in which case both might vary their styles (too strict or too lenient) based on what the other parent is doing. Such wrangling leads to utter chaos with children.

c. Sometimes the problem is a combination of the two above. A loving parent sees her partner as too strict and thus undermines him. Unfortunately, this circumstance leads to even more strict behavior from him, which then leads to even more lenient behavior from her, and so on and so on and so on.

d. In general, kids do better if they feel their environment is predictable. They like to know what to expect from their parents and they will always respond to what they predict will be their parents' reactions. Your children are better off when t hey know what makes you mad, sad, and pleased. They can only know what makes you mad, sad, or pleased if you act consistently mad, sad, and pleased by the same behaviors.

Consequences

1. Appropriate consequences are a must for adequate discipline.

a. Consequences should always be as short as possible. Taking things away for a long time results in the consequence losing all meaning. With younger kids (one to five), it can be adequate to take things away for ten minutes. With older kids (five to nine), typically one day is enough to make your point. With pre-adolescents and teenagers (anywhere from nine to seventeen) usually one week is enough.

b. The chance to win back what has been lost should be made clear. When kids really miss something and then are given an opportunity to win it back, they tend to be highly motivated. The good behavior that is reinforced by getting back what was taken away, should also get reinforced by your praise of what they've done to get it back. Just because your child was motivated to get back a privilege, doesn't mean the effort at good behavior is meaningless. If you want that behavior to keep occurring after privileges have been restored, then reinforcing the behavior with praise is crucial.

c. Give praise as often as you can. If your child has had problems that you're trying to correct, praise them as often as possible when they are NOT engaging in undesirable behavior as well as when they ARE engaging in desirable behavior. In other words, even if you expect good behavior, praise it if you want it to continue.

d. You need to follow through. If you are giving a consequence and then giving in when you can't stand your child going without, then your child is learning that consequences are not real. If you give your kids three warnings, then you are teaching your children that they get three warnings. That is really not a problem—stating things only once and expecting compliance is considered too harsh by most parents to be too harsh. As long as you accept that you will always have to give three warnings because that's what your kids expect, then you shouldn't be at all upset until you have to tell them a fourth time.

e. Whenever possible, a consequence should be specifically related to the thing that the child did wrong. If a child doesn't clean his room, the consequence could be as simple as daily checking of the room. If a child goes outside without permission, he could be prevented from going outside for an hour. If a child doesn't go to bed on time, the consequence could be reporting to her bedroom half hour earlier the next night.

f. Whenever possible, do not use a consequence that is outside your control or one that you cannot observe. Just making room for cheating can often bring about such cheating. Some parents will tell their children that they are not allowed TV, but then expect the child to govern that behavior themselves while at home alone. Making the TV inoperable, or making no attempt to enforce that consequence while you're not home, are both perfectly good ways to handle that dilemma. It is the very rare child, however, who will monitor their consequences themselves.

g. Let consequences, not your mood or attitude, be the reason your child wants to improve. If you are going to let your mood be involved, let the emotions be sadness or being hurt, rather than anger and frustration. Kids feel demeaned, worthless, or angered when parents act frustrated or angry. In contrast, if you are sad, worried, or hurt, kids are more likely to take responsibility for what they've done (please see article "Communication from the Heart").

Corporal Punishment Is Unnecessary

3. My view on physical discipline is that it does not work.

a. If your child is responsive to physical discipline, it is because she fears your anger or knows you really mean business when you hit. As stated above, anger is not a good discipline practice. If you can be consistent with your approach and with consequences, you won't need to hit to be taken seriously.

b. If your child needs you to hit to know that you are serious, then you are not following through on consequences.

c. If the only thing your children needed to worry about was the pain you inflict, then spanking would be, by far, the most preferred discipline. Any physical discipline, short of abuse, lasts only a few minutes and then the pain is gone. What lingers in the child's mind is the fear of either your wrath or your disappointment.

d. If it is your mood that is the consequence, then find other ways to let your mood be known—as stated above, sadness and hurt, and even frustration, are much preferable to anger.

Time Out

4. The "time out" is one of the most popular consequences used these days. The idea behind a time out is to take a child away from rewarding feedback for long enough to get them to realize they have done something wrong.

   a. Time outs cannot be spent with an adult or anyone else because that is rewarding to the child (even, or perhaps especially, if the child is crying).
   b. Time outs do not need to be long. With young children (two to three, I do not recommend time outs with children under one and a half years of age) a time out needs to last only thirty seconds. If that doesn't work, probably time out is not the best approach.
   c. Even with children who are four to six, a time out only needs to last two to three minutes.
   d. Don't worry too much about getting the child to see what they've done wrong. Perhaps a short statement from the parent about what the child did wrong is helpful, but trying to get them to see what they have done wrong is almost useless. What a child understands while in a time out is that it would be more fun to get back into a fun situation. This creates pressure on the child to say whatever Is necessary to get out of the time out. Once the child gets out of the time out, you cannot be sure that the child has learned anything except to say the right thing.
   e. Until children are capable of much more complicated thoughts your chances of getting them to be "truly sorry" do not increase with longer periods of time. At that point (age seven and above) time out may well become sending the child to a room where the time out is actually more of a punishment with possible positive side effects rather

than an actual time out that is meant to take the child away from rewards.

e. If your child simply cannot do a time out of any length, don't worry about completely taking them away from positive feedback. But do make the positive feedback noninterpersonal. For example, you can have the child in a time out where they must stay in front of the television for three minutes. Although not ideal, such a time out helps some children be successful in meeting your expectations when being completely unoccupied is almost impossible for them. Remember, success needs to be easy. Any action that contributes to your child's frustration in meeting your expectations takes you one step backward in meeting your goal of creating a responsible child with good self-esteem.

Positive Feedback

5. One other key to good discipline is positive feedback.

a. With children who have had many troubles, it is necessary to try to tell them they're doing well every time they are not making trouble. Catch them being good and tell them then just how much you appreciate it.

b. Even with good kids, the more often they hear praise, the more likely it is they'll feel good about themselves.

Reward Systems

6. Reward Systems are the big hitter.

a. When things are really out of hand, quite often it can be helpful to introduce more specific consistency. One way of doing that is to create a reward system. I will discuss a basic structure that can be modified to fit your particular situation (please see articles, "Sample Reward System" and "The Satisfaction Meter").

b. Picking a good reward. Examples include money, stars, and check marks (with small children coins of any kind, meaning pennies, can be as rewarding as the worth of the coins. With older kids it is important to realize that the buying power of the rewards is very important.

c. When using money with small children, it can be a good idea to go with them to the piggy bank to let them drop the money in. One of the reasons stars are as good as money with young children is that it's the process or getting recognition, not the buying power of the rewards, that younger children find rewarding.

d. Charting. Once you have determined what is rewarding to your children, decide what they will need to do to earn the reward and how often the reward will be given. Chart the whole thing on a reusable paper (sometimes people use a Xerox sheet, so it can be reproduced, and sometimes people laminate the chart and use dry erase markers).

e. Once the chart has been produced, make sure your children are the ones keeping track (for kids seven and above, keeping track is typically possible, but if your child seems to have difficulty with keeping track, this is a minor issue). In order for motivation to develop within your children, they have to seek out the reward for themselves. When they have finished what they will be rewarded for, they need to come to you to report that the job is done and ask you to check it and give the reward (this sometimes takes a little training with younger children—those between seven and nine). Again, it is very important to recognize how much the process of doing the reward system helps to solidify the child's behavior. If they child doesn't have to have anything to do with the chart, the child will always think of the chart as yours. If the chart's accuracy becomes important to them, however (and no matter what age), then they will be very interested in maintaining *their* chart.

f. It can be helpful to break the day up into parts and allow each part to represent one reward period. A typical number of parts is three for school-age kids (morning, school time, and evening) or four for younger kids (morning to lunch, lunch to 3:00 PM, 3:00 PM to dinner, dinner to sleep). Kids often have a hard time maintaining a whole day. If they can have success one part of the day, then they won't feel like failures for the whole day.

g. Typically each part of the day will have particular expectations, including some activities that need to be completed. If you're using stars, it works well to use small stars for each of the smaller expectations and a big star for the whole period.

h. In general, the more activities that can be rewarded, the better (thus a star or check system works well).

i. It's also important to mention that success should be easy at first and slowly become more difficult. That is, at first the reward should be given for half (or maybe even less) of the things on the chart being done.

j. It's also important to mention that you cannot use "attitude" as something that is rewarded. You can, however, use "said 'please' and 'thank you' when communicating," "rolled eyes at others less than three times," etc.

k. Finally, it's important to start fresh after each period. If your children did not get the reward for the last period, that should have no bearing on whether or not they get a reward for the next period. They should be made acutely aware of this fact as well. That is, you should tell them at the end of a period (even if they have not sought you ought for the reward since they know they didn't make it), that they can get the next reward if they do what's on the chart.

l. If the school day is covered by the reward system, don't hesitate to get the school on board. Teachers and school administrators are typically eager to help out.

CHAPTER 45

❧

Sample Reward System

"Happiness seems to require a modicum of external prosperity."

—Aristotle

There are many different kinds of reward systems. The simplest possible way to structure a reward system is to give kids privileges when you feel satisfied with them and take away all their privileges when you're not satisfied with them (please see article "The Satisfaction Meter"). Some people just want a few specific activities to go right, or want the kids to complete their chores. If that's all that's needed, a simple chart on the refrigerator will do. The Sample Reward System presented here is relatively comprehensive. It is meant for people who want to really get things on track, and who are willing to work pretty hard at it. Please read the points beneath carefully to fully understand how the thing works. The items of focus within each part of the day can be changed to suit any child. The items chosen here were designed for a twelve-year-old boy. Younger children, of course, need very simple target goals.

Morning	*Daytime* weekend 10-4	*Evening*
Arguing/attitude*	Good Day at School	Arguing/attitude*
Do what you're told the first time	Arguing/attitude*	Do What you're told the first time
Get Self Up	Do What you're told the first time*	Homework*
Get in shower		Chores (Thursday night special cleaning)
Be ready on time in morning*		Get to bed on time—9:00 PM, lights out at 9:30 PM

1. The purpose of a reward system is to motivate children without frustrating parents. Kids do better when their behavior is not associated with being "bad" children, but is associated with success and getting what they want.
2. Four out of five things done to earn a chip. Items with asterisks (*) must be done.
3. If the ability to earn a reward is lost during one period, start the next period immediately so all time will be covered by the system.
4. With behaviors (arguing, talking back, doing what your told the first time), two warnings.
5. Parents are the judge and jury.
6. Create full list of what can be earned: screen time, trip to movies, desserts, time with one parent or the other, phone, etc.
7. Privileges are given at parents' convenience.
8. Chips are given at specific time. You might want the kids to be responsible for coming to you for the chips. You don't want to be in the position of remembering whether or not chips were earned several days after the fact.

9. Everything will depend upon the rewards being rewarding enough without being too rewarding. Some kids will save chips and then not care about earning them because they have so many. Some kids won't think what they can earn is worth the effort. So as their parents, you have to know what they will find rewarding. Like money, the reward must keep them working. Also, like money, becoming rich will likely result in laziness.

10. Encourage spending of chips so that not too many will be saved up and result in your kids feeling like chips are not worth earning.

11. Only give privileges for free if you are really doing it for yourself. If you want to go to the movies, you can go and take the kids. But if they want to go, they need to have some chips.

12. Consequences are still necessary when bad behavior is out of hand. For example, screens can be taken away for a week and thus become one reward that cannot be earned through the system.

13. Make laminated chart and get dry erase so kids can keep track themselves.

14. Sometimes it works well to give kids an added bonus for earning a certain number of chips during a week. For example, you can give a gift of any amount you think is appropriate for earning 14 of 21 chips in a week.

PART IV

DIAGNOSIS AND ITS
INTERPERSONAL COMPONENTS

Troubleshooting Individual
Parts of the Machine

Within the Great Life Machine, individual parts—individual people—are built and then break down in very specific ways. The particular fit of any one individual within the Great Life Machine, their genetics combined with their family dynamics and family circumstances, determines how they were built and how they break down. Correct diagnosis, that is the ability to identify how individual parts have broken and how they were built, is extremely helpful in getting them working again. It is frequently the case that simply getting a better understanding of how individual parts were built and how they break down initiates the repair of those parts, even with very little mechanical help (psycho-therapeutic intervention or medicine). Typically, when a person or a family comes to a therapist, the first thing the therapist attempts to do, and the very first thing the client(s) wants to know, is: "what is wrong?" In "Diagnoses and Their Interpersonal Components," the "what is wrong?" aspect of treatment will be addressed.

In the first subsection, "Major Diagnoses," how and why people break down will be discussed. Individuals tend to break down in ways that are familiar to us all, such as depression, anxiety, bipolar disorder, and post-traumatic stress disorder. Each of these diagnoses has a specific cause within the individual system of emotions that is common to us all (see article "From Id to Family System"). The causes of these major diagnoses will be discussed in each article, and solutions or guidelines for intervention will be offered.

The second subsection, "Personality Diagnoses," involves the unique way in which each of us is built, given our circumstances and experiences. Personality develops from a core of basic human characteristics into specific and detailed traits. The purpose of these traits, or personality attributes, is to balance intense and threatening emotions by maintaining a certain bearing or a certain type of role-relation to others. Through the developmental process in our families, we become a very particular type of person based on our particular family. Unfortunately, many individuals get stuck with the style they have developed when balancing within their own family, even though the world at large offers endless possibilities for interaction. These personality types are outlined within this section, and to the extent that each is maladaptive given the limitless possibilities of the world, directions toward new and better functioning will be shown.

The final subsection, "Addictions," focuses on the extreme behavior that develops when people seek to artificially balance emotions through a relationship with a substance. Codependency, or the way certain people seem to balance themselves by being with someone who is addicted, will also be covered. These two articles present a basic outline for understanding the addictive process and why it is so difficult to change.

Section 12

Major Diagnoses

Major psychiatric diagnoses are those psychological problems that everyone knows. The word "major" may seem to indicate something horrible, but as it is used to describe diagnoses, it simply denotes how common the diagnosis is, not how big a problem it causes. These problems can be devastating, but can also be mild. They can be long-lasting or short (chronic or acute, in psychology terms). Major diagnoses describe how a person can break down, even after long periods of normal functioning. They also include those illnesses for which it's thought there is a specific medical intervention that can be used to correct the problem. We have all had some experience, whether in ourselves or in someone we know, with depression or anxiety, some kind of trauma or extreme moodiness, difficulties with concentration or even a feeling of losing touch with reality. The articles in this section aim to clarify the psychological mechanisms behind the most common and well-known psychiatric categories.

CHAPTER 46

❧

Depression

"It is hardly possible to build anything if frustration, bitterness and a mood of helplessness prevail."

—Lech Walesa

Depression touches us all at one time or another. When a person is depressed, they typically experience several of the following symptoms: poor sleep (including too much), poor appetite (including too big), decreased interest in life or activities, worry and/or guilt, low energy, poor concentration, and thoughts about death or even suicide. The experience of these symptoms is often associated with anxiety and tension as well, although such symptoms can lead to a completely separate diagnosis of anxiety disorder if they are relatively disabling.

All kinds of depression have similar symptoms, and all kinds have similar dynamics, but there are two basic causes of depression. These two separate causes can often occur simultaneously. Depression can come from a basic lack of internalized love and/or it can come from feelings of helplessness, hopelessness, or loss in the face of bad circumstances.

By "lack of internalized love" I mean that some people have never experienced enough consistently positive feedback and affection to become confident about positive feedback or affection continuing into the future. Such people devise various personality strategies aimed at securing love which are typically controlling, manipulative, or desperate but can seem powerful, self-assured, and seductive. When such people do not get what they want, at first they might become more aggressive in their style. If that does not work, however, they become depressed, with relentless feelings of emptiness and dread as well as the typical feelings of helplessness, hopelessness or loss that are commonly experienced during depression.

These feelings of helplessness, hopelessness, or loss, on the other hand, can be a primary cause of depression in themselves, even when they occur in the life of someone who is relatively healthy. When a person has experienced consistent love in their upbringing, circumstances that cause feelings of helplessness, hopelessness or loss bring about depression in spite of the substantial emotional resources such a person's good experiences have helped them develop.

Mentally healthy people feel responsible for those close to them, and struggle to balance that responsibility with taking good care of themselves. When something horrible happens to such people, whether that horrible thing involves a traumatic experience in the life of a loved one or to themselves, they can become depressed as they struggle with feelings of guilt or wonder about how they could deserve such experience. Such people feel the need to care for those they love, and when others are suffering or when others leave, they can feel at fault and they often associate the cause to their own selfishness which then can lead to guilt. It's also often the case that when bad things happen, relatively healthy people often feel like they have been cheated or betrayed. Because relatively healthy people often think of themselves as deserving happiness in return for the good they have done for others, and because they have tried as hard as possible to be good, many relatively healthy people simply cannot understand how they could deserve heartbreaking and agonizing circumstances.

Regardless of the cause of depression, the dynamics and symptoms are typically quite similar in all cases. The depressed person undergoes a transformation from a state of relative emotional freedom and ability to withstand the daily pressures of life, to a state in which all of their energy goes into squashing emotions as though all emotions are "bad." A person afflicted with depression wallows in feelings of inferiority, weakness, and guilt, but they try to control the expression of these feelings for fear of hurting others or burdening others. They often feel that the world is caving in on them, that responsibilities are overwhelming, and that if anyone knew how they were truly feeling, they would lose all positive affection and love from others. Thus, depressed people tend to feel extremely lonely and isolated since they feel no one is connected with them or in touch with how they feel.

Paradoxically, depressed people typically do the opposite of what is necessary for them to recover. Since depression is so related to being accepted by others (even in cases of loss), an afflicted person needs to share feelings and be active in exposing their experience to others. Unfortunately, and most typically, depressed people isolate their feelings and themselves, and quite often their activity level decreases due to how hard it is to tolerate the vulnerability of feeling exposed. However, if the depressed person does expose their true feelings to loved ones with whom they can feel safe, they typically start to feel better relatively quickly.

This process allows their assumptions about how unacceptable their feelings are to be contradicted both in the real world and in their minds. The need for reassurance and a nonjudgmental attitude from those who could be close to the depressed person is therefore crucial. All too often, depressed behavior results in rejection from others who are afraid of being "brought down" or who feel vulnerable themselves when they don't know what to do. However, if the depressed person can see that they are still acceptable and loved, even when they have terrible feelings, a big part of their depression lifts since such a big part of depression is the feeling of being unacceptable, unlovable, and worthless. Activity itself can help create greater exposure. If a person is active, doing things, and getting things done, feelings of worthlessness are contradicted by that activity. Thus activity results in exposure and likely a feeling that one is acceptable even when the depressed person is not revealing their true feelings.

Psychotherapy works in a similar way. Although most patients do not feel that their therapist is a "loved one" as mentioned above, they do hopefully feel that the therapist is a relatively nonjudgmental and open-minded person who is not directly involved in their lives, and who is professional. When emotions are exposed within the context of psychotherapy, the same kind of process occurs as was discussed above. When the depressed person exposes their true feelings to the therapist, and the therapist does an adequate job of making them feel that their feelings are acceptable, the depressed person can generalize that feeling to their experience outside of therapy. They can start to feel that their emotions are okay, and they can start to regain some semblance of spontaneity in their lives.

The question of chemistry is also important. No one really knows whether or not depression is caused by chemical changes in the brain or whether the brain's chemistry changes when someone becomes depressed. Really, that question should not be very important to the depressed person who, typically, is simply desperate to feel better. The fact of the matter is that brain chemistry does change with depression, regardless of whether the changed chemistry or the depression occurs first. The dynamics and precursors of depression as outlined above are also a matter of fact, whether or not chemistry is involved. The human emotional system works by certain rules that make the depressed person react and think as has been discussed above. The truth of the matter is probably that some people are more prone to depression at the chemical/physiological level, and thus are more likely to see the world in the ways outlined.

Finally, there are two things I always recommend to depressed clients. The first is, be really, really good to yourself (please see article "Be Your Own Best Friend"). The second is, tell that nasty, nagging, critical voice inside your head to "SHUT THE HECK UP!" Most people say things to themselves that exacerbate their depression. They tell themselves they are not strong enough, that other people will think horrible things about them, that they are not worthy, or that they are worthless. Being kind to yourself, however, means to treat yourself like you think a kind and loving mother should treat a small child who is hurt or scared. Would you scream at, or criticize, a poor vulnerable child? I don't think so! So don't scream at or criticize yourself. Tell that voice to SHUT UP! Defend yourself against it fiercely. At the same time, tell yourself it is okay to be hurt, give yourself an emotional hug, and do anything you can to comfort yourself.

If you are feeling depressed, open up to loved ones, get active, be kind to yourself and, if you are having trouble beating it on your own, go see a psychotherapist. Research indicates that you will benefit most from a combination of antidepressant medication and psychotherapy. Understanding the patterns that get you thinking in negative and self-defeating ways is important, but do not underestimate the importance of simply feeling better, even if you need to alter your brain chemistry to do it. Sometimes, feeling better in itself, regardless of how you do it, is necessary in getting you growing in new and healthy ways. No matter how you view it, however, you cannot recover from depression unless you see that you are an important and worthwhile person who, it should be quite obvious, deserves to be loved. In fact, if you fully recover from your depression, you will probably see that you are more than deserving of love. If you start to see things accurately, in fact, you might even see, not only are you loved, but you are truly, truly great (please see article, "You Need to Know You're Great").

CHAPTER 47

❧

Anxiety

"People wish to be settled: only as far as they are unsettled is there any hope for them."

—Ralph Waldo Emerson

Feeling uptight or kind of shaky? Do you have muscle aches, heartburn, or stomach problems? Do you suddenly lose energy after feeling alright? Is the stress in your life taking you to the breaking point? Does it seem like no one does things right, or that you are just too irritable? Are you worrying a lot? Are you having trouble sleeping? Are you feeling restless, or does it seem like you can't sit still? Do you feel just plain nervous? Do your hands or feet get cold and clammy or start to tingle without cause? Do you get lightheaded and you don't know why? Do you find yourself avoiding certain situations, or sometimes find yourself so stressed in certain situations, that you think you might actually die from the pain in your chest or from dizziness or from the pounding of your heart? If you are experiencing some, many, or all of these symptoms, there is a good chance you are dealing with anxiety.

Although it is very important to be careful about many of these symptoms because they have causes other than anxiety, or because they can be dangerous even when they do involve anxiety, when these symptoms **are** caused by anxiety, understanding how anxiety works can be quite helpful. Anxiety actually has a purpose in human beings that is akin to its purpose in animals. In animals, there is a fight, flight or freeze pattern that occurs whenever there is something threatening in the environment. While the animal prepares to either fight, flee, or freeze to manage a threat, the animal's body makes certain changes. The blood flows to major muscle areas and away from the extremities and the gut, thus causing cold or tingly hands and butterflies in the belly. Adrenaline makes the heart pump and puts energy into the muscles, which become tense, causing headaches or pain in other muscle areas like the neck, shoulders, or back. Breathing becomes shallow so the animal can avoid detection, or so it can get ready for an anticipated blow.

These changes ready the body for danger, but when *human beings* experience this reaction, most of the time there is no imminent danger in the environment. Humans tend to be sensitive to the environment, and react to it rapidly, even when the dangers to which we are reacting pose no physical threat. Rather, we react to emotional threat, even when it is rather subtle. Getting ready to speak in front of a group can cause extreme anxiety and really there's no physical danger there. But even much more subtle circumstances can cause significant anxiety. When there is a chance that someone will be mad at us, or when we think we need to get our work done more quickly, or when we think we need to rush to get somewhere on time, or for many people, when we're merely listening intently to what others are saying . . . etc., our bodies will react with the fight, flight or freeze syndrome. We ready ourselves for aggression, like a mountain lion protecting its cub, or we start with a frenzy like a gazelle fearing we might be that lion's next meal, or we freeze up with tension like a raccoon stiffly staring back into headlights hoping it will not be seen.

Luckily, we are not animals. Equal to the fight, flight or freeze syndrome (also known as the sympathetic nervous system response) is the relaxation response (known as the parasympathetic nervous system response). While the fight, flight or freeze syndrome tends to begin without our knowledge or control, we can if we wish, initiate its opposite, the relaxation response, on our own. When we are relaxed, blood flows throughout our entire body distributing oxygen as homogeneously as possible. The heart slows down and the muscles lengthen and loosen. Blood flows to the stomach so it can do its job of digesting the food there. Breathing deepens and we feel at peace. Sometimes we begin to get sleepy.

We can begin the relaxation response simply by forcing ourselves to breathe deeply for a few minutes (please see article "Breathe!"). Most people who try breathing to recover from anxiety stop their breathing after a few breaths and then give up because they still feel tense. The trick is to keep breathing deeply for several minutes (if you become lightheaded you need to be less dramatic in your deep breathing, or make sure your breaths are truly deep), while trying to experience a sensation of floating as you inhale and sinking as you exhale. I have not yet met a person for whom this technique or process, when taken seriously, does not work.

Several other relaxation techniques include 1. scanning your body for tension through every muscle group and then loosening your muscles (eventually learning to pay more attention to your body and loosen the muscles as soon as they become tense); 2. imagining yourself in a pleasant, relaxing place, while noticing everything you experience there through all five senses; and 3. rocking yourself with eyes closed while finding your natural rhythm. The relaxation response of the whole body occurs automatically when you do these things and, because the relaxation response is diametrically opposed to the fight, flight or freeze response, the tension in your body cannot continue while you are relaxed. In fact, because the body and mind are part of one big system, making the body relax also helps the mind relax, and one's thoughts will typically calm as relaxation continues.

Knowing how to handle the anxiety one already has is helpful, but knowing how to prevent anxiety could be even better. The prevention of anxiety requires that its causes be understood. There are really two main causes. There is some overlap between these two causes, but in their essence they are very different.

The first of these causes is that some people have truly experienced many threats in their environment and now interpret the world as a threatening place. When a person has experienced abuse, unfair treatment, or trauma, they use their way of experiencing to help keep them safe in the future. Thus, they (we will call them "traumatized" people, for lack of a clearer way to put it) interpret many different circumstances as threatening and will become anxious in many different circumstances as well. When you think about it, if a person's past experiences are extremely traumatic, it would be foolish for them to respond differently. It seems they have learned that the world is a dangerous place and that they must be ready for more danger.

However, most of the time that natural response is incorrect. Traumatic experiences of the past are not truly predictive of ongoing experience, except that behaving as though danger is always lurking has a tendency to cause more traumatic experience as a traumatized person tends to place themselves in the familiar, but dangerous, surroundings to which they have become accustomed. Thus, because a traumatized person predicts danger, their anxiety is exaggerated. Yet simultaneously, such a person is truly more likely to experience trauma later, not because their surroundings must be dangerous, but because often only dangerous surroundings and circumstances seem normal to them (please see article "Post-Traumatic Stress Disorder").

The second primary reason for anxiety is that some people have developed so much feeling of responsibility for loved one's that they become stressed with tension any time any nonloving feelings are evoked within them. They perceive these feelings to be dangerous to those they love (please see article "Obsessive-Compulsive Personality" and attend to the "responsibility fragmented individual" within that article). Guilt can grow for such a person from having any self-centered thoughts. Feelings of anger are especially difficult to tolerate for these "responsible" people (we will refer to them as "responsible" people for lack of a clearer way to differentiate them). Any hint in their thinking that the responsible person may have feelings that might damage others makes them become anxious and worried. They become especially tense if they fear their potentially hurtful selfishness or anger might become so powerful that it could leak out and be detected by others. This process often leads to panic (or panic disorder) as the feeling that one's "bad" feelings might come out leads to very sudden feelings of being overwhelmed, and then a feeling that everything is completely out of control or that something as bad as death could be imminent.

With respect to the traumatized person, the anxiety that derives from trauma in one's past bubbles up when such a person's environment is not in their absolute control, or when others will not conform to their way of doing things. Thus, the traumatized person also can experience panic. For the traumatized person, panic is typically mixed with a fair amount of anger, and these people can become emotionally aggressive when life becomes stressful, whether panic is involved or not. The guilty, nonaggressive, responsible type, in contrast, typically tries to be kind and good all the time. However, because no one is always kind and good, whenever their unkind and not completely good thoughts threaten to become conscious, they feel shame and worry about rejection. This responsible "good person" group often worries about others, and they frequently come to realize that their greatest fear is loss (loss that occurs because they are "bad" or loss that occurs because others are free to leave or make mistakes). Thus, where the traumatized individual is truly concerned with danger, whether it's realistically perceived or not, the responsible individual is more concerned with guilt and fear of loss, whether that's realistically perceived or not. Both groups can suffer from panic, but the traumatized individual is more likely to be repressing anger about very real problems from the past, while the responsible individual is more likely to be repressing all sorts of feelings (including anger) that they fear will damage their relations with others. In other words, panic always involves feelings of being overwhelmed, but for the traumatized individual there is often real fear of their own aggressiveness in response to past trauma, while for the responsible type panic is much more likely to be related to feelings of being unworthy and thus rejected.

For anyone experiencing significant anxiety, when something terrible happens that is beyond one's control, the reaction is often depression, and anxiety is exacerbated. They have been trying so hard to maintain things, or to be as good as they possibly could be, that it simply does not make sense to them that something bad could happen to them. Thus, for everyone experiencing anxiety it is important to recognize how little control one really has and to understand that to be human, at least partially, means to be selfish, needy, aggressive, hurt, and sometimes fearful. We can only do what we can do. We can try to be our best and to help those that we love. But we cannot be perfect. We cannot always do everything right. We cannot control how others do things. We have to maintain humility about our frailty and our imperfection and we have to realize that we are merely small cogs in the giant machinery of life. When we maintain a balanced view of our place in the scheme of things, and let others share in our imperfect humanity, we are much less likely to become overwhelmed with anxiety.

It is also important to discuss the chemical components of anxiety. No one really knows the extent to which anxiety is caused by chemical changes in the brain or whether the brain's chemistry changes when someone becomes chronically anxious. If one can find some relief from disabling anxiety, it doesn't really matter if its cause is chemical or psychological. No matter how you view it, it is a fact that there are brain chemistry changes concomitant with the experience of anxiety. The psychodynamics behind anxiety are also a matter of fact, whether or not chemistry is involved. The human emotional system works by certain mechanisms that make people react with anxiety to a history of traumatic interpersonal experience or responsibility taking beyond one's control. There are certainly people who are more prone to anxiety at the chemical level, and they are more likely to respond with fear, an inability to trust, or a need to hide all selfishness or anger to avoid overwhelming levels of guilt.

If you are experiencing anxiety, please breathe and try to relax. Share your feelings with others whom you trust. Let yourself be vulnerable with those you trust. Try to recognize that you are just an infinitesimal being in a huge interpersonal world. With effort, you might be able to get things to go your way, you might even be able to stay somewhat safe, but you can't truly expect to have any real control over anything or anyone but yourself. You may care very deeply about others, and you may actually know what's best for them, but you will never be able to prevent them from making mistakes. You should also realize, however, that most of the time, those mistakes won't cause horrendous disasters. You must also realize that you are human and that we humans have selfish thoughts, even mean and angry thoughts, but only our actions can truly hurt others. You don't have to be perfect in any way, not in hiding your imperfections and not in doing it all. It's as simple as this, although it might not seem to be so, you need only be able to give and receive love and everything will be okay. But that's not always so easy to do. If you just don't think you can beat anxiety, there's no shame in seeking help. If you need to talk, there's no shame in seeking a psychotherapist. If medicine might help, why hesitate? The truth is, you need to feel good to be the loving person you need to be. There is also another truth when it comes to anxiety. Everybody gets it sometimes. Reach out and you will undoubtedly find, as isolated and alienated as you might feel, you are definitely not alone.

CHAPTER 48

❧

Bipolar Disorder

"Happiness is not a matter of intensity but of balance, order, rhythm and harmony."

—Thomas Merton

It's a matter of intensity! It's really as simple as that. Bipolar disorder has many faces, and gets involved in so many other mental health issues, that it often seems quite complicated. Individuals with personality disorders are frequently very intense, and they often end up being given the bipolar diagnosis. Individuals who become psychotic (which means they lose touch with reality) often do so partially because of their intensity. Sometimes it's hard to tell the difference between the impulsiveness involved in hyperactivity, autism or post-traumatic stress disorder, or even mental retardation, and the impulsiveness related to bipolar disorder. The fact is that moodiness and intensity are so often a part of other diagnoses that understanding bipolar disorder, and understanding how bipolar disorder can be a part of other diagnoses, is necessary in understanding psychopathology itself.

A person's intensity affects how they react to everything they experience. The stronger a person's feelings are, the harder it is for that person to modulate those feelings. The bipolar can feel intensely depressed, intensely nervous, intensely excited, or intensely angry. Sadness becomes overwhelming rumination, anxiety becomes panic, and anger becomes rage. Feeling good becomes a flood of intricate, but often loosely connected, brilliant ideas, or a desire to save the world, or the feeling that one can fly.

The best way to think about the intensity of the bipolar individual is to understand that the reptilian part of their brain is far too powerful. Neuroscience suggests that the lower parts of the human brain appear to be just like those of lower animals. That part of the brain handles automatic functioning and is largely based on the animal's need to stay protected and find sustenance. When a reptile fears a predator it has to ready itself for fleeing, fighting or freezing. When a reptile feels hunger it has to find something to eat. The higher brain, or cortex, modulates the lower parts of the brain. We use our understanding of things to mitigate the strength of the lower brain. However, the reptilian brain can have such intensity that it overwhelms the cortex. Or conversely, the cortex can be underdeveloped in some ways, limiting the extent to which it sufficiently modulates the intensity of the lower brain. In bipolar disorder, the intensity of the lower brain is not adequately modulated which makes the bipolar behave at times like a T-Rex, vicious and starving, and at other times like a frightened little rabbit, jittery and afraid. If one can express an experience in terms of hunger and satiation on one hand, or fear and self-protection on the other, then it's an experience that will express itself intensely, behaviorally speaking, in the actions of the bipolar.

Individuals with bipolar disorder are known to buy impulsively, as if their hunger for material possessions can't be sated. Similarly they often desire sexual activity and find themselves unable to control their passions regardless of the consequences. Anyone with bipolar disorder has had problems in controlling what they want. They react to what they want as though they need it desperately. They often want it right now, and they have a hard time really differentiating wants from needs. With respect to their hunger for things, or affection, or control, or any other kind of desire, the bipolar behaves as if they have been starved for years and will perish immediately unless sustenance can be found (please see article "The Power and Control Addiction").

Likewise, the bipolar reacts to threats of any kind in extremely exaggerated ways. If they're cut off on the road, the bipolar may go into a "road rage." Alternatively, they might develop a phobia to driving or to the area on the road where they were cut off. When it comes to interpersonal threats, the bipolar reacts with venom and aggression or with desperate fear. Where your average person might get miffed at a friend and decide to say nothing in spite of holding back some rankling emotions, the bipolar likely tries to cut the friend down to size and may just end up cutting off the friendship altogether. When in a dating situation, your average person might react to the ogling of one's partner with anger and an admonishment that it should never happen again, holding off judgment as to whether it might be a real problem. The bipolar is likely to slap or punch or verbally bash their date and/or the person who was ogled, thus requiring some kind of outside intervention, even if it's the first time it has happened. People with bipolar disorder often have problems in controlling the extent to which they feel threatened, and thus the extent to which they react to such threats. With respect to their need to protect themselves from competition with others, people bossing them around, the feeling that someone might be insulting them or might be trying to get one over on them, the bipolar behaves as if their very existence hangs in the balance. And if they do not bolt off or violently attack, they appear to feel like they might just be viciously torn limb from limb at any moment.

Dominance and submission often become the theme where bipolar disorder is concerned. Even where most people would understand that everyone determines their own fate and that no one controls anyone else, someone with bipolar disorder is quite likely to behave as though they must end up on top or they might lose their very life. They are extremely sensitive to criticism, control, attitude, slights, being ignored, etc . . . all of which make them feel downed, and all of which are likely to result in aggression or severe anxiety or sadness, since the bipolar will likely feel they need to get back on top or risk being dominated by others. Even when someone with bipolar disorder experiences temptation or is having fun, they might move to dominate a situation with aggression so they can have what they want or prevent it from being controlled. If they can't have what they want or are prevented from their fun, the person with bipolar disorder can feel as though they might as well die since there is nothing left for which to live.

Thus we see how some of the more serious personality disorders get confused with bipolar disorder. That is, these issues of intensity seem to affect those who have not developed the ability to soothe their own emotions, an ability which can only develop within a consistently loving and safe feeling family atmosphere. A person can have both a serious personality disorder and bipolar disorder since it is so common for bipolar parents to be untreated, and then provide inconsistently loving, dangerous feeling environments for their children. Of course, such children can also inherit bipolar disorder at a genetic level.

When a person with bipolar disorder does not have a personality disorder, the two can be easily differentiated by the bipolar individual's tendency to take responsibility, and the regret they experience after impulsive acting out behavior occurs. These individuals can also be differentiated based on their description of their upbringing. If a person appears to describe a relatively consistent and regular home life from their childhood, but nevertheless exhibits extremely intense emotionality, they are most likely suffering from bipolar disorder as opposed to personality disorder. Overall, such individuals appear to be extremely intense in their reactions, but are also quite empathic and compassionate, which is not found in the more serious personality disorders.

The psychological concept of "repression" is key here. When people are brought up in a relatively trusting and caring environment, they develop a sense of responsibility and depth of caring. Those attributes make a person deny the impulses they experience that are deemed to be threatening to their relationships. Threatening impulses, like aggressive, sexual, or even loving feelings, that would seem to be wrong or damaging to others in some way, are pushed downward and held inside. In the bipolar individual, these feelings become too intense and overcome repression. If the individual does not have a significant personality disorder, the tremendous guilt they experience after these behaviors have been exhibited is clearly palpable and often results in extreme depression. With serious personality disorders, guilt is only fleeting and serious depressions are more centrally located in a deflation of self-esteem, or hating one's self, than in guilt about what's been done.

Repression and intensity are also involved in psychotic disorders. When repression is an especially powerful force, its failure in containing intensity is extremely dramatic, thus causing hallucinations (hearing and/or seeing things that are not there) and/or delusions (strong beliefs about what is happening that defy reasonable judgment), and the psychotic disorder will be thought of as more in the realm of Schizophrenia (a psychotic disorder in which hallucinations, delusions, and/or disorganized confusion occur without significant mood swings). When intensity is the primary issue, but repression fails because it has only developed to normal levels, the psychotic disorder is more in the realm of bipolar disorder. As many will observe, there is great overlap in the medicines used to treat each of these disorders. The overlap between these two disorders is significant because they both involve raw animal emotions filtered through, and morphed by, the desire to protect one's relationships. That is, repression aims to force down feelings, but sometimes those feelings are so powerful that they must be expressed. In order to make them less scary or damaging, repression changes these raw emotions into symbolic beliefs—hallucinations or delusions—that somehow represent the feelings pushing for expression. In psychotic disorders, both repression and intensity are powerful forces. But intensity is primary in the bipolar, while psychosis and the failure of overburdening repression are primary in the Schizophrenic.

It can also be difficult to differentiate impulsiveness related to attention and concentration issues (attention deficit hyperactivity disorder—ADHD) from impulsiveness related to bipolar disorder. Again, one must be able to sense whether the problem is related to intensity, as would be the case with bipolar disorder, or if it is due to a need for stimulation, as is the case in ADHD. Unfortunately, the two overlap, just as they seem to in so many other disorders. People with bipolar disorder are often very sensation seeking because they experience powerful needs. Individuals with ADHD, however, are not filling a void, but rather are just trying to avoid boredom. The best way to tell the difference between the two is in the bipolar's ability to focus very intently on the things that interest them. In those with ADHD it is difficult to focus on anything for much time even if it's fascinating (unless it is also consistently stimulating, like television or video games).

Post-traumatic stress disorder (PTSD) also has significant overlap with bipolar disorder. In the pure case of PTSD a person who has been otherwise quite mentally healthy experiences a traumatic event. That event brings their safety into question and thus stirs up all the most severe emotions related to self-protection. Because those feelings become so intense, people with PTSD can become very aggressive and angry as well as withdrawn and avoidant. The intensity of those feelings becomes overwhelming to someone with PTSD and defies repression, similar to how it does in psychotic disorders. However, because the trauma is very real and the feelings associated are not merely a part of a person's unacceptable self (that is, their rawest emotions), hallucinations and delusions are not a typical part of the picture. That is, the very real emotions of trauma are not thought of as unacceptable aspects of the self because they derive from very real experience that was not within one's control. With PTSD, truly intense feelings are created, but the psychological problem that develops originates in the need to avoid the pain of the experience, which is quite difficult because the memories are extremely powerful and threatening. Avoidance of pain is primary with PTSD as opposed to the expression of intensity as in bipolar disorder.

Even developmental delays involving mental retardation or autism can frequently be mixed with bipolar disorder. Individuals with developmental delays often experience, as part of their disorder, extreme sensitivities or irritability. They frequently become even more susceptible to their own impulses because they do not have the intellectual capacity and/or interpersonal confidence to mitigate the effect of their environment with thought or understanding of their past experiences. Although it is often obvious that the primary issue for such an individual is the developmental delay, the aspect of their disorder that makes them too intense, similar to all the other diagnoses mentioned above, will often be diagnosed as a "dual diagnosis" of bipolar disorder.

Essentially bipolar disorder is a disorder of intensity. Because of that fact, bipolar disorder is often diagnosed within the same person as many other diagnoses. It can also be noticed that the same medications used to treat bipolar disorder are frequently prescribed when the primary diagnosis is in a different area, including personality disorder, schizophrenia, post-traumatic stress disorder, and even in developmental delays. The intensity of bipolar disorder can be likened to that of a reptile that knows only urgent fleeing from predators, fighting for life, and voraciously searching for food. To the bipolar, almost every experience can be interpreted in those terms. Thus, sensitivity to slights, or possible threats, or desires for all sorts of things, often lead to exaggerated intense reactions from the bipolar individual. There is, however, some good news! In helping people manage their intensity it can actually be helpful to liken their intensity to the emotional functioning of a reptile, just as described above in discussing the reptilian brain. Once any individual afflicted with inordinate intensity comes to understand that their reactivity is not reasonable or realistic, they can be motivated by their desire to be caring for loved ones to prevent their extreme reactions. They can learn to talk themselves down, excuse themselves from situations before they get too angry, assign friends or family to signal to them when they're showing signs of upset (please see article "Key Signals"), take a medicine, or learn to breathe more deeply and rhythmically. Once one knows, and is willing to accept, that they have a hidden reptile inside them, and as soon as they are willing to accept that it can abruptly transform them into a T-Rex with little provocation, in the case of the true bipolar who genuinely cares deeply about loved ones, it is frequently the case that they will do whatever it takes to tame the primitive beast within.

CHAPTER 49

ೞ

Psychotic Disorders

"Doubt is to certainty as neurosis is to psychosis. The neurotic is in doubt and has fears about persons and things; the psychotic has convictions and makes claims about them. In short, the neurotic has problems, the psychotic has solutions."

—Thomas Szasz

When your average person says the word "psychotic," they're typically referring to someone "weird" or "wacky" or "wild." The word "psychotic" actually means that a person has lost touch with reality. At the time of a psychotic break, a person with a psychotic disorder is not seeing things in a way that is consistent with generally recognized facts, or is finding it difficult to communicate or find common ground with anyone else. There is more than one way to lose touch with reality. A person can have hallucinations and believe they hear voices or other noises that don't exist, or they can actually see things. A psychotic person can also start to feel confused, disoriented and jumbled. Yet a third kind of psychosis is to become delusional and believe things are happening that are not, or that one is part of a grand scheme or is being plotted against in some kind of grand conspiracy.

People can have some of the symptoms related to psychotic disorder for other reasons. Substances and other chemicals can lead to some of these symptoms, either when ingested or absorbed (substance, chemical or hallucinogen intoxication), or when the body has become accustomed to those substances or chemicals and then develops withdrawal (delirium). Sometimes when the brain malfunctions in various ways that are not related to psychosis, such as when someone develops dementia, confusion can develop that is not completely dissimilar to psychosis. But psychosis develops for very different reasons than substance abuse, delirium or dementia, and thus the character of psychotic symptoms differs quite significantly from those experienced due to chemicals or deterioration of the brain.

In psychosis, confused symptoms, hallucinations, and/or the experience of special importance within strange and twisted conspiracies occurs due to the experience of extremely intense and seemingly destructive emotions quaking and churning within a person who is desperate to deny such emotions. Psychotic symptoms can arise due to either the intensity of the emotions, or the rigidity of the need to deny the emotions, or both. The more intense the emotions, the less rigid one's denial and repression must be for psychosis to develop. The more rigid one's denial and repression, the less intense the emotions need to be for psychosis to develop. Psychotic symptoms are most typically a part of two particular diagnoses, bipolar disorder and schizophrenia.

When psychotic symptoms occur in the bipolar patient, the primary cause is the intensity of emotions. Human emotions are animalistic in nature. That is, human emotions are a more developed version of the survival instincts of the lowest creatures, whether those creatures are more the vicious type or the timid type. Thus, the intensity of human emotions at the extremes can often and easily develop into murderous thoughts or a desire to rip and shred and split. On the other hand, one might become so frightened of violence and aggression in the everyday workings of common day to day experience that one develops a desire to vanish completely or disappear. It's also a common human experience to feel as though one's swallowed up by the chaos of the world and is out of control, or that one's importance is so ubiquitous that one is the controller of life itself or that life itself is the story of that person. In the bipolar person who becomes psychotic, it is primarily the intensity of the emotions that makes it difficult to contain those emotions. The feelings themselves simply have too much potential for destruction to oneself or to loved one's. The intensity itself is not, however, the entire problem. Without some need to deny or repress these intense impulses because they are so destructive, there would be no need for the impulses to be twisted into psychotic symptoms.

In the schizophrenic patient, psychotic symptoms often arise primarily due to rigidity of thought and defense against harmful emotions. The same kinds of emotions described above are often at the core of the problem, but they need not be so intense to cause psychotic symptoms because the schizophrenic has a need to twist and distort the feelings merely because they believe so strongly that these feelings are horrible and unforgivable. The schizophrenic typically has an extremely powerful belief in right and wrong that can be either genetic or trained into them from experience. The schizophrenic often sees any thoughts even remotely close to those described above as extremely damaging, inappropriate, bad, and deserving of punishment. Beliefs about right and wrong in the schizophrenic are so powerful, in fact, that normal feelings of anger, desire, embarrassment, fear, guilt or shame, can lead to psychotic symptoms even though such feelings are so common and not typically thought to be particularly dangerous or harmful to others.

The psychotic need to create symptoms that make little sense, or that do not fit with what others perceive to be reality, or the need to lose touch with what others view as safe and reasonable, often comes from getting too close to the feelings described above because those feelings are potentially so damaging to oneself and to others. In the bipolar patient, psychosis will often occur due primarily to the intensity of the emotions, but also because those emotions could be dangerous if allowed to dominate one's mind unabated. In the schizophrenic patient, psychosis will often occur due primarily to the feeling that even small amounts of these extreme emotions are completely unacceptable. But in identical fashion to the bipolar patient, with the schizophrenic it is the dangerousness of the emotions that remains the central problem.

If one is extremely threatened by the aggressiveness or chaos of the world, it might make sense to withdraw into oneself rather than to perish or disappear. When the mind is convinced that the only other option is psychological death, psychosis can appear to be a far preferable alternative. If a person is having murderous or suicidal impulses and they have been taught to be "good," it can make sense for them to start hearing voices or start seeing things that express those feelings rather than to ascribe those feelings to oneself and being "bad." Within the mind, it is a far better alternative to hear a voice telling one to kill others or oneself than to think of oneself as a killer or as suicidal. Likewise it is a far better alternative to see images related to death than to actually make those images occur in real life. When a person is feeling like they are the ruler of the world, or that their importance is magnificent to the extreme, it can make sense for them to build up a grandiose scheme of their own instrumental importance for the existence of the world. A paranoid plot becomes the clear choice when the only alternatives appear to be accepting one's lack of importance or soberly facing disdain from others who will not tolerate solipsistic grandiose beliefs.

The psychotic process involves a conflict within the mind between horrible, life threatening and relationship damaging emotions on one hand, and the fear of what will happen if those thoughts are directly expressed on the other. Interestingly, it is the expression of the psychosis that results in the ultimate alienation of the individual with psychotic symptoms. Psychotics are generally shunned due to their odd and nonsensical behavior. Nevertheless, those symptoms present a far better alternative, and much less destruction to the world or oneself, than the direct expression of the intense emotions the psychotic fears within themselves. Those emotions, if unleashed, would lead to the most unabashedly aggressive and violent and suicidal impulses imaginable.

Given the circumstances of the particular individual afflicted with psychotic disorder, its symptoms can arise due to extreme intensity or extreme rigidity or both. Intensity can be innate or developed. Rigidity can also be innate or developed. But no matter the particular reason the psychotic symptoms arise, the fact that psychotic symptoms do arise, as opposed to unadulterated animalistic instincts, is far preferable to the extremity of emotional behavior that would occur without the psychosis. In an odd way, psychotic symptoms are actually an expression of an individual's desire to control their animalistic instincts so that they and others are not severely damaged.

In that way one can come to understand why there always appears to be some real sense of humanity in those who become psychotic.

With very few exceptions, individual's who become psychotic have been taught to care about others very deeply, or have an inborn and tenacious connection with others. Even if most of the people in their lives have been abusive or manipulative, for some reason the psychotic individual has typically made some significant connection with others that prevents them from being able to act upon extreme emotions.

Some individuals with bipolar disorder or with severe personality disorders act out on extreme emotions with little or no compunction. The intensity of their rage, grandiosity, intimidation, depravity, paranoia or isolation manifests within their relationships often creating terrible trauma and immeasurable pain. Psychosis, as terrible as it is, especially for the individual plagued by its confusion and interpersonal alienation, is from a social perspective, a far safer alternative than the wild, self-centered, manipulative, vitriolic, and often aggressive behavior observed in the unbridled and tumultuous behavior of the most degenerate personality disorders or bipolars. Although psychosis is often thought to be the very worst kind of mental health problem a person can experience, it is somewhat contradictory that psychosis generally indicates some level of the one trait that truly differentiates relatively healthy personalities from relatively unhealthy personalities. A person with psychosis almost always feels some level of responsibility for his fellow man.

The treatment of psychosis has most recently become much simpler than it had ever been before. Medicines for psychosis are almost always effective in helping bipolars and schizophrenics to avert psychotic symptoms. Although at one point in time, psychotherapists believed it was possible to treat psychosis with interpersonal therapy alone, powerful medicines are almost always a part of successful treatment today. A mixture of antipsychotics, mood stabilizers, and antidepressants are typically prescribed. These medicines both calm one's intensity and relieve some level of rigidity. Psychotherapy does continue to be useful on a variety of fronts. Individuals with psychotic symptoms can learn to calm their own emotions and become less judgmental of themselves. Since they often have experienced trauma, discussion of traumatic events is often necessary. In addition, individuals with psychotic symptoms have often been traumatized by their own experience of becoming psychotic, both because they have completely lost control, and due to the interpersonal alienation experienced during a psychotic break.

Psychosis is the clinical term for losing touch with reality and really doesn't mean that the afflicted person is wild, flipped out, or wacky in the way most people seem to think. There are a variety of ways that psychosis takes form, including complete and utter confusion, the experience of hallucinations, and the belief in intricate delusions related to one's importance. Psychotic symptoms are caused by a combination of extremely intense emotions and a brittle rigidity of thinking about one's intense emotions. Bipolars who experience psychotic symptoms do so because their emotions are immoderately intense. In contrast, schizophrenics generally experience their rigidity as their primary difficulty. In both types, it is the perception that the expression of intense emotions could lead to interpersonal destruction that leads to the twisting of these feelings into psychotic symptoms. From an interpersonal perspective it is far better to withdraw into confusion, create elaborate plots or schemes regarding one's importance, or to hallucinate in symbolic ways, than to psychologically eviscerate others or oneself. Strangely, the experience of psychotic symptoms indicates some level of humanity within the person with such symptoms, as opposed to how the most antisocial of the personality disorders seem to directly express intense emotions regardless of how damaging to others that might be. Although individuals who develop psychotic symptoms suffer horribly, and may even be a burden at times, the purpose of their symptoms is to protect themselves and others from the licentious and savage violence their emotions are enacting within them. Thankfully, a mixture of medicine and psychotherapy can help those plagued by psychotic symptoms to regain a sense of normalcy.

With the right help, in fact, those with psychotic symptoms often return to lives of extraordinary and singular vision, of exquisite interests, and of intricacy of thought. With the right help, those afflicted with perhaps the most alienating of all illnesses, psychosis, make use of their most important attribute in regaining their lives. With treatment the relatedness and humanity within the psychotic, the same tendency that led to the urgent and severe sense of responsibility and need to protect others from the seemingly terrible eventuality of exposing others to the psychotics unbridled animalistic nature, begins to grow in a natural and organic fashion within themselves and helps to nurture lively, loving, and fulfilling interpersonal relationships.

CHAPTER 50

❧

Post-Traumatic Stress Disorder

"Conflicts may be the sources of defeat, lost life and a
limitation of our potentiality but they may also lead to greater
depth of living and the birth of more far-reaching unities,
which flourish in the tensions that engender them."

—Karl Jaspers

Psychologists are always talking about "inner conflicts." Why
is that? Well, certainly "inner conflicts" can't have anything to do
with a disorder that arises due to trauma. Right? . . . NO, WRONG!
Post-traumatic stress disorder (also known as PTSD) is, believe it or
not, also caused by an inner conflict. The inner conflict of PTSD,
however, is not borne from a troubled past or conflicted feelings about
right and wrong. Those kinds of issues can exacerbate PTSD, sure,
but they are not what causes it. PTSD is actually caused by a conflict
between two essential biological imperatives. These imperatives are
at the core of health and development. The first is the avoidance of
pain. The second is the integration of experience.

It should come as no surprise that we avoid pain. It is obvious that
we humans, just like all animals, survive largely because we do avoid
pain. Most organisms move away from physical pain instinctively. The
instinctual first cry of birth is an impulse to have some kind of tension

or discomfort soothed, whether it be the actual pain of being born, the first pangs of hunger, or the first experience of terror. We then move on to cry for comfort of all kinds, which is not just avoiding pain, but is also deeply involved in connecting to others. And of course, from the earliest ages, although we might reach out to touch the glowing embers of the fire or the red hot burner on the stove, our first burn teaches us a clear respect for anything with a yellow, red, or orange glow.

Trauma is, by definition, out of the ordinary, extremely painful, experience. Sometimes severe physical pain is involved, but often the most horrendously damaging aspects of a traumatic experience involve the impact it has on others whom we love or for whom we feel responsible, or our feeling that we might be to blame for the trauma. Emotional pain is somewhat different than physical pain. Nevertheless, the impact of emotional pain is every bit as powerful as physical pain in traumatic experiences. Just like any other kinds of pain, it is natural that we avoid all the different kinds of pain involved in trauma, including both the physical and the emotional aspects. Avoiding emotional pain is at the core of PTSD.

The second primary factor involved in PTSD, the integration of our ongoing experience, is just as essential for living as the avoidance of pain. Life has little meaning without the ability to remember what we've been through, or who we know, or where we've been. Our earliest experiences, perhaps by design, are especially difficult to integrate. Maybe that is one of the reasons that being born is not especially traumatic (from the viewpoint that it is not recalled repeatedly with horror). At that point we have not yet integrated any of our experiences. As we develop, however, our ability to recognize our closest caregivers, to know how best to get their attention, and to steer clear of physically painful objects grows in importance. Soon, our understanding of everything we perceive gets organized for the specific purpose of helping us manage our ongoing functioning in the most efficient manner possible.

Trauma is especially chaotic experience that defies logical understanding and thus is especially difficult to integrate. Although we typically expect to be able to avoid disasters, traumatic experience brings into question our ability to avoid accidents or painful experience. Thus, we don't want to integrate traumatic experience because doing so requires us to admit that we might be in danger that is unavoidable.

Not only are many accidents unavoidable, but we also would like to remain in denial about how true it is that we are taking chances on a daily basis. Our desire to deny the possibility of danger, even when it might be avoidable, makes it difficult to integrate trauma in that doing so requires us to realize how dangerous things are. When we're making ourselves vulnerable in some way, we're typically in denial of the danger we're in. For example, we operate motor vehicles so frequently that we forget how ludicrous it is to believe that it's safe to hurtle ourselves at 60 mph in a metal box on wheels, and to expect our vehicle will never malfunction, and to expect that we ourselves will never malfunction, and to expect that all the other drivers will follow all the rules.

In spite of how safe we'd like to think we can make ourselves, when something does go wrong, the results can be horrifying. We likely blame many circumstances and perhaps we blame others we don't know. We can blame ourselves as if our ability to avoid disasters should be flawless. Any loss of material possessions, a loss of the feeling of safety, or God forbid, loss of life or limb, can seem utterly incomprehensible. Although traumatic events should be integrated into our understanding of life, maybe even more than other experiences since they could help us learn better what to avoid, these events defy logic, seem to make little sense, and hurt us so deeply and personally, that such events are often not remembered at all (even when head injury is not involved). Our desire to avoid the pain of trauma often actually makes us forget the incident entirely.

More than anything else, really, it's the severity of the emotional terror that makes it impossible to integrate a trauma into our ongoing experience. Our emotions go into turmoil over the trauma, and the pain is so bad that we just can't bring ourselves to think about it. Yet we can't help it. Our minds do want to make sense of the event. Flashes of the event thus push themselves into our consciousness, begging for recognition. Although we do not want to think about the trauma, the trauma will not leave us alone because it must be integrated. We do need to understand what went wrong and how similar disasters might be avoided. If we cannot get such an understanding, we're likely to feel we're damned to experiencing the same trauma again and again. That is the essence of PTSD. *The traumatic experience is both impossible to remember or integrate, and impossible to forget or avoid.*

So we avoid the pain by avoiding memories and thoughts about the trauma. We attempt to avoid anything that reminds us of the trauma. Yet reminders are everywhere. Colors, sounds, smells, and all sorts of familiar everyday occurrences make us think and feel about the trauma. Anything that could remind us of the trauma brings back a flood of thoughts and memories. We busy ourselves so our mind can't possibly let thoughts or feelings related to the trauma bother us. But as soon as our defenses are down, when we're not so busy, thoughts push their way into our minds. Our defenses are always down when we sleep, and nightmares related to the trauma begin to plague us.

When we're supposed to be at our most relaxed, instead we find ourselves in hyper-vigilant states, watching out for anything that might hurt us. In fact, quite often, because we have not properly integrated our trauma into our understanding of life, we start to generalize our traumatized state to areas that are completely unrelated to the initial trauma. We start to be on edge all the time. We can become hyper-vigilant to the point that we become paranoid. Now, because we have not integrated our traumatic experience, the trauma sneaks into our way of being in the world. We are avoiding all sorts of things. We're irritable, tense, often paranoid and angry. Now, because we have generalized our emotional state to all our experiences, the trauma in effect, has us avoiding relationships altogether.

In spite of how much we love our loved ones, it's often our relationships that suffer more than any other area of our lives. Those closest to us are typically those who see us at our worst. Unfortunately, the anger we feel about how unfair things are, or the anger that simply derives from feeling so tense, is often aimed the most at those at home. Suspicion leads to lack of trust. Simultaneously, the confusion of someone with PTSD often leads to their need for immediate gratification. Family members rarely understand the need of the afflicted family member to have some sense of control which might permit them to feel things are not in complete chaos. In short, trauma creates a complete mess, not just for the individual who develops PTSD but also for his entire family.

It is also typical that a person with PTSD gets no treatment whatsoever. Because they are paranoid and avoiding the pain of the trauma, someone with PTSD often has no desire to visit a complete stranger for the purpose of confronting their problems. It is far more likely that they will become increasingly withdrawn and find various ways to escape even from themselves. Substances or behaviors that help numb the pain of the trauma are sought and often result in addictions. Anything is better than experiencing the feelings and recalling the events of a serious trauma. When the victim of PTSD does not seek help, their problems often fester within their hearts and minds and dissolve their relationships, and all too often, the trauma ruins their life.

There is hope, however. Treatment for trauma generally focuses on helping people integrate the traumatic response in spite of the pain involved. Talk therapies, hypnosis and EMDR (Eye Movement Desensitization Reprocessing) help individuals combine the meanings they have derived from the trauma, with their memories, emotions, and body feelings. It is remarkable how often traumatized individuals have taken the trauma to mean they are responsible for the pain of others, or have no one who cares about them, or that they just have bad luck. Others will think the trauma happened for a reason. If the trauma occurred at the hands of a loved one, they'll think the trauma was related to their behavior or that it showed them who they really are, or who they will always be. Treatments for PTSD help people see how memory involving the trauma is associated with body sensations as well as painful, but irrational, feelings.

In the absence of, or in addition to, interpersonal psychotherapy, writing can provide huge relief (please see article "The Writing Cure"). Strangely, this simple tool can help a person get feelings, thoughts, and body sensations out of one's mind and onto paper. The desire for integration in the mind pushes thoughts and memories into consciousness almost as if there's fear that the thoughts and memories will be forgotten. In fact, in the case of PTSD, the mind is trying to forget that which must be remembered. But when things are written down, the mind can start to work through the complications of the trauma. An individual should specifically attempt to remember every detail—everything said, all the colors and movement, shading, textures, times of day, sensations, smells, tensions, stresses, tastes, emotions. One can also try to remember the beliefs these feelings and sensations bring them to and how the feelings make them view their role in the world. When it seems there may not be any more to write, any other thought evoked should also be written down. Writing makes the mind know that what must be integrated has been acknowledged. As long as the information is all written down, the mind often finds much less need to repeat the experiences, almost as if the mind believes the trauma has been integrated simply because it is written down.

Although trauma can be psychologically devastating, and can lead to a short-circuit in normal functioning as painful memories are avoided and integration of experience is prevented, it need not always be a completely life-changing event. Treatments for trauma are very effective and are often relatively accessible. In the absence of treatment, some individuals can treat themselves with focused writing, or can find that expressing their feelings to friends is not as unacceptable as they might have thought. There is great hope for those with PTSD even though a lack of treatment can lead to a lifetime of avoidance and withdrawal. With proper help, the splintered life of the trauma victim can be rebuilt so that pain is no longer considered impossible to face, and integration of experience can lead to a newly integrated life. In recovery from trauma, the victim of PTSD puts life back in perspective, opens up to new possibilities, and begins to develop new relationships. With recovery, the traumatic experience is integrated and the pain it inflicted, although remembered, is no longer overwhelming. Often, then, the traumatic experience can be utilized in helping one relate to others who have also experienced trauma, and can actually thus make a person a more connected individual than ever. With treatment, once traumatic memories are successfully integrated, what was once horrifically traumatizing is reduced in intensity to a powerful learning experience, and that age-old adage is often true, "what doesn't kill you, can make you stronger."

CHAPTER 51

❦

Attention Deficit (Hyperactivity) Disorder

"Concentrate all your thoughts upon the work at hand. The sun's rays do not burn until brought to a focus."

—Alexander Graham Bell

The diagnosis, Attention Deficit (Hyperactivity) Disorder, or Attention Deficit Disorder with Hyperactivity (generally referred to as ADHD) is everywhere these days. In some communities it seems almost everyone supposedly has it. The stimulant medications used to treat ADHD are about as commonly prescribed for children as antidepressants are prescribed for adults. Some people think that's all plumb crazy. Some think it's an indication of a runaway rat-race culture where kids need to be stimulated to compete while adults get depressed because competition has replaced connection with others. Without a doubt, there is significant interest in knowing what ADHD really is. It is also extremely common to wonder if you have ADHD or if your children have ADHD.

So what is ADHD? This disorder, and its variants, involves a consistent deficit, over many settings, in one's ability to focus or pay attention and/or in one's ability to control their activity level. The person who is afflicted seems unable to concentrate, is often fidgety, or seems to have a need to be fully engaged in activity at all times.

It is very important when diagnosing ADHD to be sure the problem occurs in many settings. When doctors see patients who have these behaviors at home, but not at school or at work, or when the problem seems to occur at school or work but not at home, most likely the problem is not ADHD.

One common misunderstanding in the diagnosis of ADHD is that people notice their children focusing in certain ways, even though they cannot focus in almost any other way. Although the diagnosis of ADHD must be a problem in many settings to be diagnosed, there are certain activities that are so stimulating that a person's ability to focus on them does not preclude the diagnosis. Specifically, any activity that involves a screen, such as television, video games, or any kind of computer activity, typically does not pose a problem for a person who has ADHD. People afflicted with ADHD also often have no problem with especially active pastimes, such as sports. Stimulation is the central ingredient for any activity that will not be a problem for the person with ADHD.

In fact, stimulation is really the key to understanding ADHD. ADHD that does exist over many settings is caused by a feeling that the environment is not stimulating enough. That is the simplest way of understanding why stimulant medication seems to help in the treatment of ADHD. As part of a need for stimulation, the person afflicted with ADHD gets lost in the thoughts of their own mind or within the excitement in their environment. The person seeking stimulation within their own mind seems spacey and seemingly cannot focus on either the simplest instructions or on more detailed information such as a teacher's instructions in the classroom. The person seeking stimulation in the environment behaves in a hyper-kinetic fashion, almost as though there is a need to stir things up just to make things interesting. In seeking stimulation within the environment, staying on any one task simply isn't enough to keep the ADHD individual's interest.

The primary treatments for ADHD are stimulants, and some of the antidepressants can also be helpful. When a person needs stimulation, these medicines provide that stimulation so the person can focus. There can be, however, reasons unrelated to ADHD that cause chronic under-stimulation. An observed lack of focus and/ or hyperactivity may actually be caused by an overfocus on what others are thinking or doing (especially in inattention without hyperactivity) which can indicate anxiety. Lack of focus can also indicate a need to withdraw from the emotional and social constraints of normal interpersonal communication (when inattention takes place accompanied by hyperactivity) which can involve other kinds of mood disorder. Inattentive and hyperactive behaviors occur in these cases for emotional and personality-based reasons, and do not necessarily indicate ADHD. Yet stimulants and antidepressants do, at times, seem to help even when ADHD is not the problem. The fact is that stimulants increase focus in most people as they find their environment more stimulating, regardless of the reason for the lack of focus. On the other hand, if the problem is emotional, the reason an antidepressant would be helpful is obvious.

Although stimulant medications will sometimes help even when ADHD is not the correct diagnosis, there are also significantly negative side effects about which people need to be aware. Children who are unfocused because they are anxious will often feel much more anxious when prescribed a stimulant. Some will even start feeling panicky. When prescribed a stimulant, children who are unfocused and also have anger problems can become extremely emotional and tearful without provocation or, alternately, can spin up into a rage. Many children will feel numbed and lose their spark when taking a stimulant medication. Although that can be a normal reaction for a few days, if the spark never returns, that particular stimulant is likely the incorrect match for that child.

Incorrectly diagnosing and treating ADHD can cause other difficulties as well related to the impact of being labeled "ADHD" when the problem is really something emotional. Once the problem is given the name ADHD and the child believes the problem exists, ADHD can become a way of being for that child all of the time, instead of just in uncomfortable situations. If the problem is actually related to emotional factors, treatment with the wrong medicines can even preclude or delay the discovery of the real cause of the behavior. One of the worst outcomes from an incorrect diagnosis is that a child can come to believe that a pill is necessary to treat the problem, thus making them unlikely to develop the skills necessary to overcome the problem without medicine when that would actually be possible. When a child is diagnosed with ADHD, they often stop trying to concentrate. In some ways it's almost as if they're encouraged not to focus.

Because of these dangers of incorrect diagnosis, there are several ways to address issues of focus and hyperactivity that should be tried before medicine is considered. These same interventions should be used as an adjunct to treatment with medication even when the diagnosis of ADHD is certain. In people who have difficulty focusing, but who are not hyperactive, there is often extreme sensitivity to what others are doing or feeling. Because sensitivity to others is such a strong factor, studying or doing homework in a quiet, solitary setting can enhance focus. Such people also benefit from taking more time to complete tasks and from being in close proximity, with eye to eye contact, when listening. Activities that bolster confidence, and interpersonal support that reflects a true belief in the child's abilities, are also essential. In cases where the lack of focus is not due to ADHD, if the unfocused person can begin to believe in himself, often his difficulty with focusing resolves as he worries less and less about the judgments of others. Even when the problem does truly involve ADHD, confidence acts as a buffer to the disorder and helps the child focus in spite of the attention deficit.

Cases of inattention with hyperactivity also benefit from the interventions indicated above, but the hyperactive behavior leads to more complications. These complications are primarily addressed by consistency. In childhood cases of hyperactivity, it often helps to initiate behavioral programs that allow the afflicted boy or girl to experience consistency from the environment and from authorities. Such children often have difficulty understanding when their behavior is upsetting others because they are not intentionally bothering anyone. When a person regularly experiences negative feedback from others for acting in a way that is natural to them, they soon develop a negative attitude toward others simply because they feel others think their true self and natural way of being is "bad." They also sometimes develop a need to get attention through negative behavior because of the feeling that getting positive attention is hopeless. The consistency of reward programs helps to overcome all this negativity as a child develops confidence that doing what is right and attempting to control one's behavior leads to positive outcomes. With a behavioral program, the child learns to behave in ways that are positive and constructive because they receive affection and privileges when they are getting closer and closer to meeting specific positive goals. Behavioral programs help parents to be consistent, and help children to understand how to earn loving attention for positive behavior (please see articles, "The Satisfaction Meter and Sample Reward System").

If you are concerned about the possibility of ADHD in yourself or your child, contact a mental health clinician. Whether medication is required or not, you might benefit from learning new ways to cope with these difficulties. There are currently a great number of diagnosed cases of this disorder, but many people, clinicians as well as school officials and parents, typically believe it is diagnosed too frequently. Because diagnosing ADHD when it is not really there can have a very negative impact, really knowing whether one has ADHD is extremely important. Although the medications themselves can have a negative impact, these medications actually tend to help many people concentrate better, even when ADHD is not the central problem. But mistakenly treating a patient for ADHD when the problem is actually emotional or interpersonal can have serious negative effects that must be avoided for the sake of the child's or adult's general well-being. If you are, and always have been, inattentive, unfocused, or hyperactive in a large variety of settings, there is a good chance you have some form of ADHD. ADHD can cause people very significant problems in getting along with others or doing good work. If correctly diagnosed, stimulant medications can be a god-send for those suffering from ADHD. Perhaps ADHD is too frequently diagnosed. Maybe its prolific diagnosis does indicate something about the exaggerated desire for success in our children. But when diagnosed correctly, treatment of ADHD isn't crazy at all—it's a necessity.

Section 13

Personality Diagnoses

Personality is that part of the individual human system that is primarily built from one's experiences. Although genetics and environmental circumstances play a role, it is the relationships with those closest to a person that really form one's personality. The earliest years are most crucial in the formation of the personality because those are the years a person is most dependent and vulnerable. The personality forms as a way of making sure that emotional needs are met and the vulnerability of the self is protected. A person's personality can be dominant to ensure that others won't be able to hurt them. A person's personality can also be submissive for the purpose of always pleasing those who seem dangerous. Essentially, personality develops for the purpose of balancing and modulating extreme emotions, which have been variously churned up or soothed within widely disparate circumstances in our families. Once personality is formed, it is almost as if the personality is a very specific type of cog in the Great Life Machine. Each personality fits in a very specific way with other personalities. These diagnoses are central to understanding interpersonal dynamics. Many readers will want to find others in their lives within these pages. Some will want to find themselves. Either way, the articles here will help shed light on the dynamics one experiences due to being part of a greater machine, which itself has many other parts that are the many other personalities that surround us.

CHAPTER 52

ᘓ

Histrionic Personality

"The drama is make-believe. It does not deal with truth but with effect."

—W. Somerset Maugham

Drama! That's what most people think of when they hear the word "histrionic." In fact, that's exactly what it means with respect to personality. Histrionic Personality is the term used to describe a person who engages in drama as the primary way of defending against the vulnerabilities they fear most. Typical traits of the Histrionic Personality include exaggerated responding, a need to be the center of attention, a seductive nature, extreme femininity in feminine histrionics and extreme masculinity in masculine histrionics, as well as a tendency to be easily influenced. Other less obvious traits include the inability to take responsibility and the inability to feel special. Although histrionic behavior is utilized frequently when a person does not actually have Histrionic Personality (for example, individuals with Borderline Personality frequently behave histrionically), for the individual who truly manifests this personality, it is the need to feel special and the inability to take responsibility that is truly at the core of Histrionic difficulties.

Typically the development of the Histrionic Personality begins very early in life. Two factors—(1) the natural, self-centered nature of the infant and (2) extreme interpersonal conflict in the infant's environment—combine to create a torturous level of responsibility and a complete lack of specialness. It may sound strange, but the natural tendency of the baby, the tendency to feel that they exist at the center of the universe, gives life to the core of the problem. New-born babies have a completely chaotic experience that is structured by the parenting they receive. The baby cries and then waits for the parents to respond. From the perspective of the adult, it would seem like such an experience would lead the child to feel that nothing is in their control. To the ever-learning baby, however, the experience is more like everything is about them. They poop or pee and the foul mess is whisked away with a pleasant wipe wipe, googly bubbly noises, and a reassuring smile. They feel hungry, whimper or cry, and they're offered sweet milk from a breast or a bottle, while they bask in glorious repose with a warm pleasant body. Out of disorganized chaos of unmet needs and instincts emerges a sort of magical sense of power over the world. Unfortunately, in the world of the child who will develop histrionic personality, the magic does not last as long as necessary for healthy development.

Although the history of the Histrionic person typically involves a loving mother, and sometimes a loving father, as the child develops, there also tends to be dramatic conflict between their caretakers. Frequent, and vociferous arguing, with lack of resolve, dominates the experience of the child. Even worse, the actual conflict is often about the child because each parent feels the other should be doing more, or because the child's behavior is out of control (like that of the parents) and each adult argues about how to handle that behavior. Because the child feels that they are at the center of the universe and that everything happens because of them, the child starts to feel that the conflict is their fault. In fact, the child often feels as though each of the parents can only be comforted by the child. When it is the opposite sex parent that needs most of the comforting, it is quite typical for the child's behavior to become sexually charged.

The sense of responsibility for the conflict and heightened chaos, along with the feeling of being the go-to person of one of the parents during conflicts, leads to tremendous guilt. In fact, the possibility that the tearing apart of one's parents could possibly be the child's fault, in turn leads to extreme discomfort with any kind of responsibility. This is the hallmark of the Histrionic. Histrionics eschew even the most mundane kinds of responsibility as though any kind of responsibility reminds them of the trauma they experienced when their caretakers could not stand each other. In severe Histrionics, there can be almost wholesale avoidance of responsibility, while in less severe cases only social/relational responsibilities pique the pathological vulnerability.

Drama becomes a part of the picture for complex reasons. Initially, the child simply finds that the behavior they see in their parents can be used by the child to stop the parents' fighting and to get attention for themselves. On one hand, parents tend to stop fighting when kids act really badly so that they can attend to the child's behavior. On the other hand, and as indicated above, often the child's behavior leads to more fighting. Thus, while bad behavior may secure attention for the child in the short run, in the long run that attention is lost when the parents return to conflict over how to handle the child's behavior. One way or the other, the child quickly learns that only the most exaggerated behaviors get any attention at all. In the child who comforts one of the parents, very specific kinds of exaggerated responding can start to be shaped, including ways of making that parent feel special such as sexual seductiveness. It is unfortunately all too common for those cases in which a child takes to comforting the opposite sex parent that the hurt parent turns to the child for the kind of closeness that is meant to remain between adults.

The effect of the dramatic behavior engendered in the child is very difficult to repair. The child becomes dramatic to get attention instead of just acting like a regular child. Thus the specialness of the child, that unique spirit that can come only from an individual who is comfortable enough to be true to their nature, is banished. The child learns to be dramatic to get special attention. But the drama is exaggeration. It is not the real child. Thus, the child, and the Histrionic adult the child becomes, can never feel truly recognized as special. In fact, if anything, their histrionic behaviors worsen over time as they continue to attempt to get a feeling of being special with behaviors that are not true to their own spirit and thus can never lead to a true feeling of specialness.

The inability to take responsibility also precludes the possibility that the Histrionic will get any feeling of specialness. In general, as people become adults, it is their hard work that distinguishes them from others. In order to achieve, it is necessary to take responsibility. This is true in work or education, of course, but it is also true in relationships. Our teachers, our supervisors, and our loved one's all need to be able to count on us and trust us in order to work with or stay with us. In school, assignments must be done. At work we are not promoted unless the boss thinks she can trust us. When we disappoint a potential mate repeatedly we're not likely to get more intimate with them. Thus, the Histrionic, unable to take responsibility, consistently disappoints or irritates others with whom they relate. Thus, they cannot get a feeling of special recognition through achievements, nor can they develop any special feeling within their relationships.

Yet the relationships of the Histrionic are constantly affected by their desperate desire to be treated as special. Typically, the intimate involvements of a Histrionic begin in extreme excitement. People in need of drama find the Histrionic irresistible. Very few people, however, can tolerate an ongoing relationship with them. When their behavior is not treated as special, the Histrionic becomes extremely upset. But they do not allow special intimacy. Thus they are expecting their drama to gain them this special recognition, but when their partner no longer thinks of the drama as special, since really only one's true vulnerabilities really make them special, it becomes very difficult to continue treating the drama as special. To make matters worse, when the Histrionic is confronted, they will not, of course, take responsibility. The suggestion that they are responsible results in extreme anger, denial, and blame. The Histrionic tries to do anything they can to put the responsibility back on their accuser (or someone else if possible). Meanwhile, they continue to try to get special attention in the same way they always have. If they can't get that attention from their partner, they will look elsewhere. They will also not take any responsibility for that behavior, even though it is tremendously hurtful and clearly violates the bond they expect to have with their partner.

With all that said, it may seem that there is practically no way to solve the dilemma of the Histrionic personality. They are locked in to looking for attention in a way that will never truly make them feel special because their drama is not connected to their authentic nature. They will never even feel recognized or important because the inability to take responsibility precludes true accomplishments. While it may be difficult to see at first, it is the taking of responsibility, however, that can actually lead to a cure. Unfortunately, because the Histrionic is so averse to responsibility, finding a way to get the Histrionic to be responsible is very difficult.

There is really only one way to directly effect change in the Histrionic. When the Histrionic's behavior has been hurtful, the hurt must be stated in such a way that the Histrionic is unable to deny the effect of their actions. Of course, the Histrionic will do everything possible to avoid such responsibility. They will intensify their own reaction to make the other person back off. They will blame the other person so it won't be their own fault. They will ridicule the other person to shame them and weaken them. All of these maneuvers will be tried, and tried in the most intense fashion, for one main reason. The Histrionic cannot stand the idea that they have caused pain in someone else. That one factor has led to the creation of their whole personality. It is their own pain they are avoiding, and actually holding onto the idea that they are creating pain makes them go haywire. They do not want any pain that has been caused to be their fault because it brings them back to the original and damning vulnerability that they themselves are the cause of the pain that created conflict between their parents. So if someone who they feel is dear to them will not remit in stating that they feel hurt because of something the Histrionic has done, the Histrionic will break their own facade. They will take responsibility and apologize. When this is done, they get one minute step closer to becoming a person who can take responsibility.

While this process is clearly quite slow, it does nevertheless, lead the Histrionic to becoming more responsible and thus to becoming a fully integrated person. The feeling that they are unacceptable as a person because they are at fault for causing huge pain, slowly erodes as they see the other forgive them for what they thought was so unacceptable. Their own pain, caused by loss of security in their family when their loved ones were at war, heretofore hidden because it too was tied up with feelings of being unacceptable, gets freed up as they see for themselves that they did what they had to do to protect themselves as youngsters. They see that what they did, how they felt, and how they continue to behave, are all connected and that the true, vulnerable self beneath the surface that they had always hidden, needs attention, understanding and love. In a word, they finally see that they are truly special. They see that what makes them special is the unique softness within and how it expresses need and desire as well as strength and integrity. Once they see their own specialness, their ability to be responsible leads to ever greater connectedness with their intimates whom they now prize and nurture. Because they see themselves as special and deserving, they also now expect others to prize and nurture them for their real self and not for their drama. What was once dramatic flair, only indirectly related to true self expression, becomes authentic spontaneity. Others can see the authentic spontaneity in its full flower and are drawn to it where they had once been merely entertained by, but not connected to, the Histrionic's flamboyance.

This process of taking responsibility is very rare and only a small minority of individuals suffering from Histrionic personality will ever recover. Recovery takes a commitment that can only come from a feeling that life never seems to work out and that there has to be some reason to explain it. The Histrionic must come to some initial realization that they are responsible before they can begin the journey of becoming more and more responsible. If the Histrionic can endure the pain of accepting responsibility, however, they can learn to accept themselves. When they do, when they finally see that they are deserving of the special love they have always craved, when they can see their own ability to care for the specialness in others, and to operate in their families and in their world in a way that demonstrates their integrity as a caring and connected individual, all that the world has to offer is made available, and the Histrionic they once were becomes a full and healthy, spontaneous and authentic partner within their community and within the universe as a whole.

CHAPTER 53

❧

Passive-Aggressive Personality

"Hatred is active, and envy passive dislike; there is but one step from envy to hate."

—Johann Wolfgang von Goethe

"That is soooooo passive aggressive!" I don't know about you, but I have heard that so many times. Often people merely mean to say that a person's actions may seem nice or cooperative on the surface, but those actions truly make others feel like crap. Sometimes people call someone passive aggressive just because they are angry about someone being nice when they themselves think the situation is not really so nice. To psychologists, however, the term means quite a bit more. In fact, there is a whole personality designation, or diagnosis, that goes along with the term.

Behaviors indicative of passive-aggressive personality at a clinical level include being argumentative yet avoiding confrontation, having difficulty with authority, having difficulty finishing things, being lazy, and fearing the judgment of others. At the core of being passive aggressive is a conflict between feeling good about oneself (and sometimes exaggeratedly great), while simultaneously feeling as though it is a must to please others. Because the Passive Aggressive feels the need to please others, they also perceive themselves to be constantly doing for others and rarely getting anything in return. They perceive others as controlling them because they feel they have to do what is asked of them. The life of the Passive-Aggressive Personality is constantly filled with depleting disappointment as they perceive the world to be unfair and unjust.

The typical Passive Aggressive appears to be very pleasant and mild-mannered, but is generally filled with resentment. They lack assertiveness, not because they don't think they are deserving but because they are mortally fearful of others' disappointment or anger. Although they love to take the devil's advocate position in debates and often hone their arguments fastidiously, they can't stand competition of any kind if they think anyone's feelings might get hurt. They are perceived as lazy largely because, in trying to please, they agree to do things but rarely follow through because they don't like being told what to do. They are especially sensitive to judgment in others, not just because they feel it is wrong, but because their lack of assertiveness leads to constant misunderstandings and misjudgments. In short, the Passive Aggressive very rarely gets what they want because they are afraid of hurting or disappointing others if they say what they want. Although they want to succeed and achieve, their inability to compete and their inability to respect authority combine to make success, or any kind of finishing, impossible. The Passive Aggressive feels cheated by life, but because of their self-perception, and the behavior associated with that self-perception, they actually cheat themselves. Because they rarely get what they want and fail to achieve, the Passive Aggressive is typically either depressed or headed for inevitable depression.

The development of the Passive-Aggressive Personality can be delineated through a few common factors. The Passive Aggressive's response to their environment, in fact, often makes perfect sense given what they have experienced as children. In the family that will spawn the Passive Aggressive, there is typically a great deal of drama and judgmental behavior. As a young child, the Passive Aggressive quickly learns that, although they are loved, at least one of their parents, and possibly others in the family, are quick to anger or disappointment when independent thoughts are expressed or when independent action is taken. In fact, at least one of the parents is extremely difficult to please and often wants all the attention the family has to offer. A parent of the Passive Aggressive does not like to be challenged and needs others to find them fascinating and exciting. Thus, the Passive Aggressive learns that their feelings are unimportant, or at the least, must be put on hold till the needs of others are addressed. It is interesting, however, that the Passive Aggressive does seem to feel loved.

If it were not for the fact that the Passive Aggressive is confident that they are loved and loveable, their personality functioning would be far worse. In the same type of family from which the Passive Aggressive comes, some individuals will seemingly choose to compete with the drama of the parent(s) and become uncontrollable and irresponsible. However, such competition will prevent that person from experiencing a feeling of specialness because their drama will preclude the possibility of anyone appreciating who they really are (please see article "Histrionic Personality"). In families where there is too little love and/or abuse, personalities that develop are almost devoid of all compassion due to overwhelming storms of emotion within those personalities related to exquisite vulnerability, vengeful rage, complete deprivation, and a voracious need to control. Knowledge that the Passive Aggressive is loved, and the hope that they can be loved, are at the core of the Passive Aggressive's functioning. They use their well-developed ability to read the needs of others, an ability honed out of trying to please others much of the time, to remain connected. The pleasing of others, although resented by the Passive Aggressive, is the life line for the Passive Aggressive and can be harnessed to help them find a cure to their painful functioning.

When things seem to get worse for the Passive Aggressive, it typically has occurred because their personality characteristics have led them to relationships with others who need someone to constantly care for their needs. Such a person feels familiar to the Passive Aggressive who has experienced such people in their family of origin. Because the Passive Aggressive is so good at pleasing during the initial phases of a relationship, the person who needs so much attention will feel especially loved by the Passive Aggressive. Unfortunately, over time, the Passive Aggressive, who was hoping that all their care would lead to the final undoing of their unrequited existence, finds that the other is so used to being on the taking end of the relationship that they are unwilling or unable to give up the deal. They have been having everything their way and they think that's the way things should be. To them it doesn't even make sense to give back. The Passive Aggressive, thus is confirmed in their belief that others are unfair and that they will never get what they want.

Quite often, it is not necessary that the people they meet be at all selfish. Just the fact that the Passive Aggressive seems to have few needs leads most people to take what they want first. Most people assume a person who says they have no preference for things actually has no preference. So they get what they want because they know they have a preference. When such a situation devolves into the Passive Aggressive becoming increasingly negative, the other person typically feels like they have been misled by the Passive Aggressive. They resent that they are being resented when the Passive Aggressive did not even do anything to suggest their needs weren't being met until they are suddenly completely upset and acting cheated.

The typical person will respond appropriately, however, if the Passive Aggressive can manage to develop the behavior that will help cure them of their difficulties. Assertiveness is the cure. In their relationships, and upon entering relationships or any new situation, the Passive Aggressive must be assertive. Being assertive is completely alien to the Passive Aggressive, so it must be learned (please see article "Assertiveness: The 30% Solution"). Essentially, being assertive means expecting, and asking for, your needs to be met, while simultaneously understanding the needs of others and the context of the whole situation. Assertive people tend to get what they want enough of the time to feel happy. When they enter new situations or new relationships, others know who they are and what they want, but they also know the assertive person will be fair most of the time in understanding the needs of others. Thus, relationships are much more likely to move forward in healthy directions and no one is likely to feel cheated. Two parts of assertiveness actually come quite easily to the Passive Aggressive. Because they have spent their lives trying to please others, they are exceptionally good at understanding the needs of others and the context of situations. To be assertive, the Passive Aggressive really only needs to figure out how to say what they want.

It is typically quite difficult for the Passive Aggressive to change while in a relationship with someone who is already used to them being so pleasing. In those cases where the other is relatively healthy, however, even though it is difficult, two main tools can be used to bolster assertiveness and help the Passive Aggressive figure out what they want. In the Passive Aggressive's striving for assertiveness, they will need to amplify their preferences and view their own needs as completely legitimate. In the process of pleasing others, the Passive Aggressive has learned to fool themselves into truly believing their preferences are not very important (they often tell themselves they are strong enough not to have needs). In that process, they are actually acting as though their own needs are less legitimate than the needs of others. If they amplify their preferences and treat themselves as legitimate, the Passive Aggressive can, simply stated, put themselves at the same level as others. By seeing their own feelings as legitimate and amplifying their preferences, the Passive Aggressive can get used to figuring out what they want and how to say it.

Assertiveness leads the Passive Aggressive to normal functioning. As they start to get their needs met, the idea that their needs will never be met starts to crumble. Others start to understand them because they are no longer so indirect. The feeling that they get what they want when they try, leads to ever increasing efforts and hard work. Their need to argue about impersonal topics, borne from feelings of powerlessness, diminishes and is replaced by a legitimate desire to push for what is important to them. Carping at authority figures merely due to resentment about control is replaced by cooperation with authority (when authority is congruent with one's own interests) with the confident knowledge that everyone, including them, makes their own choices. Successful efforts in being assertive leads to the complete turnaround in functioning. Where once depression was the only possible outcome for the Passive Aggressive, after assertiveness is learned, growth becomes inevitable and life can then be fully embraced.

CHAPTER 54

❧

Narcissistic Personality

"The most vulnerable and yet most unconquerable of things is human vanity; nay, through being wounded its strength increases and can grow to giant proportions."

—Nietzsche

The narcissist is the ultimate man! He's confident and self-assured. He's tough. He's competitive. He's often gorgeous, and if not, he is definitely likely to dress in some kind of style. He's hardworking and successful. He's got it all. He's a master of the universe. He also has to have his way. He's in a world of his own. He rarely maintains any kind of real relationship, and when he does maintain a relationship, it's hard to tell he cares. He has to be right. He has to be the best. He pursues the finest of everything and he feels he's entitled to it. But nobody knows the narcissist, and essentially he's alone. In fact, the narcissist doesn't even know himself. The problem is, in fact, that there's no *self* there to know. At least there's no self there that reflects his humanity or any sense of vulnerability, and no self that seems to hold him together with integrity of his own.

Narcissism, strangely, is exactly the opposite of what it seems. While the narcissist behaves selfishly and confident in almost every situation, it is his lack of self that makes him act that way. The narcissist grows up in an environment in which vulnerability is unacceptable. Any sign of weakness in this environment is met with disdain and disgust. On the other hand, independent activity is necessary and significant achievements are glorified. Thus, the narcissist develops his personality for the specific and express purpose of achieving recognition and being treated as special. When all goes well, the narcissist is quite successful in this pursuit. Unfortunately, the narcissist can never achieve the one pursuit that is truly worthwhile for him. That is, he can never find his true self.

The true self resides in those feelings that are most core to life itself. Life with one's fellow man is created through the balance of these core feelings, but the particular balance maintained by the narcissist limits any development in the feelings that involve connection to others. Vulnerability, weakness, need of any kind, things being out of control, all those experiences that must be calmed and soothed by love, and thus those feelings that form the connection with others, have been abandoned in the narcissist. The one connection the narcissist attains is the sense of recognition he experiences when his achievements reflect well upon his parental figures. At those times, the narcissist feels special and important. Unfortunately, because these achievements are essentially accomplished for the impact they make on others, the narcissist never experiences true satisfaction. That is, he is achieving what makes his parents feel like they are achieving, or what impresses others most, and he never even knows what he would like to achieve.

Thus, the pursuit of success, achievements, fine things, good looks, and power becomes his unitary focus. He is desperate for the recognition of his achievements, and achieve he does. But the true desire beneath his facade, that is any desire to develop a true self that the narcissist does have, and any desire to be recognized for who he is, can only come from unconditional love and acceptance of his true nature. Although he does not always know it, he is desperate for love of his true nature in spite of his weakness or foolishness, and in spite of his truly selfish nature which is common to all in infancy. And the more the narcissist surrounds himself with the trappings of success, the less likely it will be that he will achieve true recognition of his character. Others will glory in his facade, which in turn, will help him continue to believe it to be a valid pursuit. At the same time, he will demean weakness and vulnerability in others and do anything he can to avoid it within himself. Thus, although he will be aware of a lack of meaning in his life, accompanied by an inability to attain satisfaction, and a lack of consistent closeness with others, the narcissist will generally find it impossible to understand how it could even be possible that his problems are problems.

When the narcissist does experience problems, it is typically because a particular kind of depression takes its grip on him. The lack of meaning, satisfaction and closeness in his life combine to create a kind of fragmentation of feelings. Because there is no self, no feeling that there are particular aspects of who the narcissist is as a person separate from what others see, nothing really holds together. It is as though the glue that makes all the parts of a person stick together is missing. For relatively healthy people, everything sticks together into a meaningful view of who they are. The love they have for others, their interests, their morals, what they find important, and even the things they dislike or despise, make them who they are. They carry that conglomeration of what it means to be a person with them throughout their day, their week, and their entire existence so that they can be close with others, sense meaning and attain satisfaction. What for most people can be a troubling difficulty in balancing their many roles, for the narcissist becomes complete fragmentation and a breakdown into profound depression. Only newly found specialness in the recognition of greatness from an esteemed or coveted other can forestall such fragmentation.

Even as the narcissist manages to survive and appear to thrive above his vulnerabilities, he remains quite delicately and precariously connected to his vulnerabilities in an odd way. His consistent disdain for particular weaknesses in others is, in a way, his connection to his own vulnerabilities. The connection is most clearly evinced when the narcissist believes there is a suggestion that one of those weaknesses may apply to him. At that point, the most likely reaction from the narcissist is narcissistic rage. The narcissist defends so heartily against even a possibility that he might have such weakness that he becomes completely lost in his venomous and malignant anger and spews it upon anyone who might chance upon such possibility. He cannot see the weakness, and he won't allow himself to see the weakness, and thus his best option is to completely and utterly prove that only others could have such weakness. This occurs so automatically within the narcissist that it never enters their awareness. The narcissist reacts like a cornered, feral beast, and reacts by clawing, scratching, biting and smashing until there can be no doubt that he is victorious, dominant, and superior.

Thus, the narcissist has two avenues for remaining afloat above what he believes to be despicable vulnerability. He searches for, and cultivates, recognition and specialness so his grandiosity will make sense. He also rages vociferously at any suggestion or hint of his own humanity. Unfortunately, the narcissist's grandiosity and rage preclude the possibility of finding himself and true happiness. Strangely, the only hope of finding fulfillment for the narcissist is in his fragmentation. When the narcissist fragments there is some small chance that he will seek help in others. In seeking that help, the narcissist has a chance, although relatively slim, at allowing his weaknesses to be seen and appreciated. Before that can happen, however, the typical and practiced defenses must be overcome.

Once he has sought help, the most common occurrence is for the narcissist to go back to his defense of being the "best" and being "special." He will likely try to get those to whom he has turned to see just how great he truly is. He will do so in a way that is extremely likely to achieve his aim of gaining great recognition since he has developed the ability to be the kind of "great" that others need. He also has a tendency to seek out those who are very likely to find his particular skills especially impressive. If these others agree that the narcissist is great, and if they are deemed worthwhile judges, he will return to his grandiose state and feel good again. If they do not seem to agree that he is great, most likely they will be deemed unworthy (often with an expression of narcissistic rage), and the relationship will end. If either of these two ways of defending occur, of course, the narcissist will have no possibility of recovering. However, the occurrence of fragmentation, and even the behaviors that help the narcissist get back to grandiosity, including rage, offer an opportunity for recovery.

On the offhand chance that people will respond correctly, either due to their training or because they are especially healthy people (which would also require that they have a very good reason to work things out with the narcissist since healthy people only commune with people to whom they connect, and do not tolerate disrespectful behavior unless there is a good reason to do so), the fragmentation of the narcissist offers an opportunity for things to be different this time. Only when the narcissist shows vulnerability is it possible for anyone to connect with him. In those moments, if someone can see the vulnerability and understand just how painful it is to the narcissist, while simultaneously demonstrating that it is acceptable, and perhaps even that it has a special kind of poignancy within the narcissist, the narcissist can begin to see his true self.

By seeing his true self, no matter how painful, the narcissist can slowly begin to love his true self. In order for the narcissist to love himself, in spite of his exquisite pain, the narcissist's vulnerability must be viewed and shown to be acceptable in the reactions of another. But if the narcissist can begin to accept and love his true self, he can slowly learn to give up the grandiosity and superiority he requires in proving himself invulnerable. His vulnerability can then make it possible to more easily connect with others, which thus makes it possible for him to connect to his true specialness. His acceptance and love of himself allows him to see how his vulnerability is what makes him truly fascinating. His focus turns away from what others will think is great, and turns toward what he himself thinks is great. Because he now cares about himself, he develops the ability to care about others, not for how they reflect upon him, but for what is special and fascinating about them.

An interesting path toward growth and development thus opens up. In fact, while narcissists improve, they are often seen to become more focused on their pursuits than ever before. However, there is also a completely different quality to their new pursuits. They do not seek to be seen as superior, but instead begin to develop their own true interests. They might work hard to be the best at what they do, but now it is because they are following their own dreams as opposed to showing off. The quality of their interactions in their pursuits changes as well. Instead of communicating with others to show off their greatness, they start to truly connect with others and learn from them in meaningful ways. In a way, when the narcissist feels that his vulnerability is acceptable, and maybe even wonderful, he experiences a reawakening. When at long last the narcissist finds his true self for the first time, he finally starts to live, and he experiences exponential growth and glorious, abundant transformation he could have never before imagined.

CHAPTER 55

☙

Borderline Personality

"Desperation is sometimes as powerful an inspirer as genius."

—Benjamin Disraeli

Have you ever been in a chaotic relationship and had your friend say "maybe she's/he's a borderline"? Unfortunately, topsy-turvy beginnings are very common in relationships. When people are trying to meet that special someone, they often have all their feelings on the line. That level of vulnerability can bring out both the best and the worst in people. Emotions run hot in these circumstances . . . and sometimes frigidly cold. We want to impress, but we don't want to seem desperate. We want to be attractive, but not too sexy. Many people start to look for future potential long before they even know the other person. And looking for such potential makes one treacherously vulnerable indeed (please see article "The Dating Fantasy"). Vulnerability involving intense or poignant desires and fantasy about the future can lead to tension, conflict and exaggerated behaviors, but elucidating the workings of the borderline personality goes well beyond these often normal experiences.

Borderline personality has now commonly come to be the description given for a person who is exceedingly unstable in relationships, seems to switch from clingy to vindictive behavior with immoderate fluidity, and who, when all else fails in recapturing the affections of their desired lover, foists responsibility on their desired lover for their own instability (most notoriously by becoming suicidal). Individuals with borderline personality become attached to new lovers almost immediately as if they know them deeply and intimately. Due to their perception of a deep relationship, the borderline individual is then hyper-vigilant with respect to any slight indication that their love for their desired partner is unrequited. Unrequited love, or any possible indication thereof, will lead to "talionic" rage or its opposite, increased clinging, or both, as the borderline attempts to bring their desired lover back into the fantasy of true, deep, and magical love. The borderline imagines this elaborate fantasy to be necessary for their very life sustenance.

To complicate matters, since their desired lover is typically quite aware that the relationship is not yet deep, many of the desired lover's behaviors really do indicate that the desired level of response is not going to occur. In a way, the fact that the desired lover does not act like they're all the way into the fantasy romance world of the borderline is good, since a lot of very chaotic behavior in the beginning of a relationship should result in its breakup. If the messy relationship with the borderline is short lived, it will cause only very temporary, though sometimes quite significant, pain and suffering.

It is the endeavor of figuring out what's going on, or trying to be nice, or attempting to somehow salve the problem so the relationship can continue, that really causes more long term suffering for the desired lover. When the borderline becomes angry, some people might be sorry, in spite of the fact that they have done nothing wrong. When the borderline becomes too clingy, some people will avoid a conflict with the borderline and then allow the borderline to carry on in the fantasy that both parties desire everlasting togetherness, instead of asking for some normal level of space. When borderline behavior is accommodated, the borderline fantasy of perfect merger is allowed to continue. Thus, the consequent rage or clinging of the borderline, which occurs when independent action of the desired lover inevitably becomes necessary, is only delayed by such accommodation. The borderline's anger, or their need to withdraw, or their even more desperate clinging is also likely to be even more intense when accommodated since the borderline is allowed to become even more intensely consumed by the merger fantasy.

It is the concept of independence, also known as individuation, and its opposite, dependence, that is at the core of the borderline's difficulties. The borderline has experienced an ongoing abandonment of their own independence. As a child, the borderline experiences the feeling that they should never become independent as a direct result of most of their independent behavior being ignored, denied, or ridiculed. In contrast, the healthy response of parental figures is to celebrate safe independence, and to curb such independence only where it conflicts with the feelings of others, or societal norms. In the case of the borderline, however, it is the family situation or the needs of a parent that necessitate a denial of independence. Sometimes the problem is merely significant family illness that makes a parent unable to appropriately notice a child. More typically, however, significant psychopathology in a parent makes it impossible for that parent to tolerate any independent thinking or behavior of the child. Either way, the normal independent striving of the prospective borderline individual are thwarted, leaving the borderline with a particular sensitivity to their own needs and independent proclivities. In fact, because appropriate independence is not allowed, and because any sign of normal independence results in abandonment, the borderline behaves very much like they are starved for affection to such an extent that they desperately cling. On the other hand, while clinging, in answer to their feeling of starvation, the borderline seemingly stuffs themselves with the other to the point that they feel as though the other is undifferentiated from themselves, which scares them to death.

Because they've been abandoned, the borderline desires closeness to the point of merger with another, where it is normal to desire companionship. On the other hand, merging threatens and distresses them and makes them feel vulnerable to domination or control where, perhaps, its normal to feel like one's going too fast in a relationship or maybe even simply wanting too much. The desire for merger makes the borderline behave in a clingy manner, but only till the desired lover appears to desire merger as well. Once the desired lover seems to want to merge, the fear of domination or control makes the borderline desperate for independence, even to the extent that the aforementioned desired lover will be found to be despicable, weak, or disgusting. Further efforts by the lover which might seem like a desire to merge (which could merely be an effort to please the borderline, since the desired lover has no clue about this "merging") or that might seem like control (which could merely be trying to help the borderline with advice or some kind of favor), can lead to extreme rage as the borderline, who had once wanted merger, now appears desperate and fiercely motivated to prove their separation.

Essentially, what develops from the desire to merge, countered by the fear of such merger, is the borderline's need to be the one in control at all times. If the borderline is sure that they determine just how close or distant they stay within a relationship, they do not have to fear merger or abandonment because the other person does not have the power to accomplish either state with them. Unfortunately, being the one who is always in control precludes the possibility of finding real love since the borderline desires love and recognition of their true independence which has no worth if granted from someone who has no control over giving such love. If a person is literally starving, but has food, they can tell someone to give them their food, but they cannot truly feel like the one who gave them that food actually gave it because it was already theirs. Thus the borderline's controlling behavior also fails to give them any sense of sustenance even if it keeps them from complete starvation. The borderline must be vulnerable if there is to be any chance at true recognition of their independence. However, because they must try to be in control, any vulnerability they experience will most likely lead to more clinging, withdrawing, or rage.

It is interesting to note what is most likely to occur when the borderline becomes a parent. Typically, a borderline adult gets exactly what they feel they have always needed when they have a baby. That is, while it has proven almost impossible to merge with another adult, while simultaneously maintaining control over the relationship, with a baby that is exactly what the borderline achieves. The situation is, at first, tantalizingly perfect. The borderline wants perfect recognition of their own independence and that is what they perceive within their merger with the infant. As long as they respond to the child's biological needs in the first few months, the child is very likely to seem to be giving perfect recognition of the borderline's independence. To the borderline, the fact that they are now a parent, seems like individuation. To the baby, the soothing the borderline can accomplish makes them gaze contentedly into the glow of the borderline's eyes, thus giving recognition of the borderline's independence.

Predictably, however, as soon as the baby has independent striving, the borderline parent experiences abandonment at the hands of their very own child. Such abandonment or individuation is impossible for the borderline to tolerate and thus they react to their own child with distaste, anger, ignoring behavior, and they use any other means necessary to thwart their child's independence. The child learns that independence and individuation is horrifying to the parent, on whom the child absolutely depends for everything. The child then adapts to the parent's needs by maintaining some level of merger with the parent, and denying their own need for recognition of their true nature and/or independence. The behavior developed by the child is only the behavior that is pleasing to the parent, and thus does not reflect what is specifically special in the child.

The cycle continues in this way. The child now desires true recognition of their independent striving which has been abandoned. They desire merger and cling to others, but fear others taking over and controlling them, just as their parent did. Sometimes they rely on rage to help prove their separation from, and control over, others. They attempt to be in control over their merging or withdrawing from others. They are left, in this way, unable to maintain any real lasting relationships in which they are capable of getting their true needs met. They constantly look for true recognition but cannot achieve it because they are unable to tolerate the vulnerability of truly acknowledging the extent to which they feel starved for real love. When someone appears to have enough control to bestow true recognition on this new borderline, the borderline's reaction remains defensive withdrawal, clinging, and rage, often with suicidal tendency and clear blame toward the desired other, all in the attempt to regain the sense that they are indeed the one in control of the relationship.

It must also be mentioned that some of the characteristics of other personality types are often taken on by the borderline to the extent that they help in modulating the intense emotions involving individuation, merger, and abandonment. Many borderlines take on narcissistic traits which help them maintain distance from others, and thus a sense of control. It is also extremely common for borderlines to behave much like histrionics since they can use dramatic and flamboyant behavior to gain some sense of recognition while also avoiding responsibility (responsibility leads back to a feeling of worthlessness and abandonment when independent striving is expressed and the borderline feels that their independence makes them responsible for the pain of those who would depend on them). Borderlines can also mimic passive-aggressive personality when they are of the type that mostly withdraws to prevent merger, but then also become angry about being withdrawn (and thus not getting any recognition of independence) and must passive aggressively blame others for their position.

It is important in looking at any personality type to uncover the central issue. If the issue is abandonment of independence, the person is suffering from borderline tendencies, while issues of specialness and responsibility are central to the histrionic and passive aggressive personalities, and issues related to abandonment of one's vulnerability are central to the narcissist. In any case, deciphering the central issue leads to the method that must be employed in helping that particular personality type, even if such methods might be quite difficult to manage.

The borderline individual's chance at recovery from their desolate and chaotic state, unfortunately, only occurs in extraordinary circumstances. Recovery requires frequent contact with a person who can simultaneously demonstrate, with unwavering certainty, that they care very deeply for the borderline and that they will not tolerate interference with their own boundaries. Such a person must possess supreme confidence in their own personality. They must be able to manage every kind of attack or manipulation with kindness and understanding, and yet never give in. Giving in to the borderline's merger fantasy, or accepting their withdrawal, rage, or blame, results in the borderline believing they are in control. True recognition of the borderline's independence cannot thus occur and the borderline can never achieve a feeling that they are truly independent. In the end, only the recognition of their true self, given from a truly independent yet loving other, can permit the borderline to build within themselves the confidence they need to truly be independent. In the end, only the recognition that no one has control in relationships, and that everyone must control themselves, a recognition that is made possible only by becoming truly independent, can save the borderline from never-ending sorrow within relationships, and can finally make the borderline feel whole by themselves and capable of living full and integrated lives within relationships and among others.

CHAPTER 56

❧

Obsessive-Compulsive Personality

"It is only imperfection that complains of what is imperfect. The more perfect we are, the more gentle and quiet we become toward the defects of others."

—Francois de Fenelon

Perfectionism, the desire to do everything perfectly, or the desire to be perfect, is at the core of the obsessive-compulsive personality. But there's no such thing as perfect. Right? That is the dilemma that plagues the obsessive compulsive. Most individuals with obsessive-compulsive personality (as opposed to obsessive-compulsive disorder*) have developed within relatively healthy circumstances, except for one thing. For some reason they have developed the impression that they could easily lose the love of their parents if they did not do things "right." In an alternate variant of obsessive-compulsive personality (which is equally, if not even more prevalent), some people develop the idea that they must always be "good" to earn parental love. Through some mixture of genetic sensitivities and parental authority, the obsessive compulsive learns to do it "right" or to "be good" or face significant disapproval. Guilt is thus always connected to obsessive-compulsive patterns as the obsessive compulsive determines that they are, of course, to blame for parental disapproval. Although they typically feel cared for at the most elemental levels, this last but essential element, the feeling that one is loved unconditionally, is not quite complete for the obsessive compulsive.

Now this might not sound especially important at first. And perhaps my description of the problem, as the potential loss of love, may sound a bit overly dramatic. But for the obsessive compulsive these ideas rule their life. To make matters worse, the whole dilemma is largely unconscious—that is, the obsessive compulsive doesn't even know that the potential loss of love is ruling their life. Part of thinking one is doing things "right" or is "being good" is the thought that it is simply the "right" or "best" thing to do. If it's just the "right" or "best" thing to do, certainly there can be nothing wrong with it. In fact, most of the time things go so right for someone who is obsessive compulsive that there really doesn't appear to be much wrong.

Doing things "right" and being "good" leads to hard work and a job well done. People who are obsessive compulsive are appreciated by others for what they do. Their work often leads to financial success. They take care of their things and their homes, and typically they also dress well. They're also helpful in most circumstances and, generally speaking, they can be relied upon. They do not miss work. They are neat and clean and organized. Obsessive compulsives are the people who, on job applications, make the statement true: "My biggest weakness is I try to do things too perfectly."

Although many things go "right" for the person with obsessive-compulsive personality, some very significant problems do, nevertheless, arise. The inability to feel one's own innate worth as a human being is at the core of the problem. When other problems arise, such as how obsessive-compulsive traits affect relationships or the depth of desperation that overtakes the obsessive compulsive when something does go wrong, all other issues come back to this basic inability to love oneself. Obsessive compulsives lack the automatic thought that they are worthwhile and important because they feel the love they have received is conditional. As indicated above, they feel that they had to do things "right" or to "be good" or they would lose the love of their parents. This inability to experience an innate sense of self-worth makes the obsessive fend off disaster by proving their worth repeatedly. When problems arise, their self-worth is left perilously dangling over an abyss of self-doubt, and at those junctures obsessive compulsives often plunge into desperate, guilt filled, depression.

The obsessive compulsive may not realize it, but they are constantly trying to prove themselves worthy of love. They don't realize it, however, because, oddly, their experience of trying to prove their love doesn't feel that way at all. Most of the time, in fact, the obsessive compulsive perceives themselves as being the one to whom others must prove themselves. And strangely, that is also true. In fact, the obsessive compulsive expends so much effort at being beyond reproof, that they are often almost unassailable. The obsessive compulsive attempts to see every possibility and take care of every eventuality before anyone else possibly could. Even in psychotherapy, the obsessive compulsive experiences such pain and shame over someone else seeing their tendencies before they see them for themselves that they often rush to beat the therapist to the punch when it comes to insights. Most of the time self-analysis is positive in psychotherapy in that therapists usually find it most useful if a client finds their own truths, but in the case of the obsessive-compulsive insight is less important than relationship.

The very fact that the obsessive compulsive has to prove their worth clearly demonstrates that they are not convinced of their own self-worth. The obsessive compulsive, however, does not truly rely on love from others for their self-esteem, as it may at first seem. Unlike other personality disorders in which there was no love for the individual's true self as a child—that is, their weaknesses, desires, need for independence, their natural-born assertiveness or aggressiveness—the obsessive-compulsive personality knows that those things have been accepted within them. As opposed to feeling those things should not exist within them, the obsessive compulsive instead feels those things should never be allowed to harm their relationships. They have observed disdain and rigidity with respect to those aspects of themselves and have thus deemed those aspects harmful. The obsessive compulsive thus aims to control these harmful emotions by doing things "right" or by "being good."

The control obsessive compulsives maintain over their very human attributes does not require wholesale denial as it does in other personality types, but the rigidity that was once experienced as disapproval is now co-opted within the obsessive compulsive to ensure those traits are not expressed. The obsessive compulsive does not need love for those attributes. They do know they can be loved in spite of them. But because they are deemed to be harmful, the obsessive compulsive works diligently so these potentially harmful feelings will not be seen. In that process, they become their own harshest critics. Instead of proving themselves to others, the obsessive compulsive aims to continually prove themselves to themselves. If they can be perfect enough, they believe, perhaps they will be beyond criticism. In the psyche of the obsessive compulsive, to be beyond criticism is to be worthy of unconditional love.

Again, it's important to mention that the obsessive compulsive often does not realize they are trying to prove themselves. If they are good at doing things perfectly, they often have themselves quite well convinced that they are worthwhile. Because their perfectionism is so appreciated, their worth is reflected back to them constantly. Others love their work ethic, their knowledge, their ability to get things done. Likewise, although guilt is a huge motivator for the obsessive compulsive because they feel they have failed their parents which has resulted in the loss of their parents' love, they typically experience very little guilt. Of course that sounds very strange, doesn't it? How could it be possible that avoiding guilt is a primary motivator if it's rarely experienced? The fact is, however, as long as the obsessive compulsive's perfectionism is working adequately, they need not feel guilty, and do successfully avoid guilt, because they are doing everything so "right" or are being so "good." Thus, the obsessive really has no reason in the present, while all is going well, to doubt their own confidence, rightness or goodness.

Unfortunately, things can begin to unravel. The rigidity the obsessive compulsive has developed may help them deny their feelings of being not quite good enough by making things too perfect to go wrong, but because that rigidity prevents closeness with others, it also causes others to be conditional in their affections for the obsessive compulsive. People feel close to one another when they experience one another as human—that is, imperfect. In the obsessive compulsive, the inability to have others see their imperfections prevents healthy connection with them. The relationships obsessive compulsives develop are often predicated on the function each person has within the relationship. Because their relationships are functional, they aren't intimate. Their relationships remain conditional because others are always depending upon them for very particular responses. Others feel the obsessive compulsive gets certain things done and is hardly affected by what's going on around them. Thus, there is little reason to be concerned about them having sensitivities that must be taken into account. If their sensitivities need not be considered, there is unlikely to be any real connection. In this "perfect" way, obsessive compulsives actually prevent themselves from gaining love from others.

Even worse, while the obsessive compulsive does not appear to have any particular sensitivities, they are sticklers for detail, either about how things are done or about how to do the right thing for others. Others around them are not concerned about hurting them in any way, but they are very concerned about disappointing the obsessive compulsive. The obsessive compulsive is generally very critical. They hold everyone to very high standards. When their rigid standards are not met, they can become extremely upset, condescending and judgmental. They are also perceived to be controlling because they act as though they know the "right" way for things to be done and everything must be done that particular "right" way. Of course, this behavior in the obsessive compulsive prevents closeness as well. It is so typical for an obsessive compulsive to create obsessive-compulsive children because, even though they care very deeply about their children, their children experience the love they're given to be conditional. Instead of paying attention to their children's sensitivities, the obsessive compulsive focuses on whether or not their children do things "right" or whether their children are "good" people. The cycle thus continues with the children lacking that particular kind of closeness with their parent that would give them the ultimate confidence in their innate worth.

It is important also to mention some specifics related to the second type of obsessive compulsive. As stated above, the classic type of obsessive compulsive is perfectionistic about how things are done. Their aim is to avoid things falling apart (what I call "responsibility fragmentation") and the guilt associated with things falling apart, so all their effort is focused on control and their typical pattern of life gives the appearance that everything is completely fine. The subtype, and there is tremendous overlap between the two, are those obsessive compulsives who are particularly perfectionistic about being "good" people. Although this second type also wants to maintain control and prevent disaster, their most important aim is avoiding blame for others being hurt and the guilt associated with others getting hurt, not avoiding responsibility fragmentation. The most horrifying eventuality for the second type is the possibility of being isolated due to the potential loss of love from loved ones. If they don't take "perfect" care of others, and then something difficult occurs in the life of some other, the "good" obsessive will typically assume they could have helped prevent that problem or could have somehow influenced the other to do something differently that might have prevented that problem. The second type of obsessive compulsive attempts to avoid guilt at all times, but will feel tremendously guilty when they fail to prevent any kind of disaster or if anyone ever perceives them as putting their own needs first.

This second type of obsessive compulsive often can't say no. They so often think of what others need that they really think they are hardly doing anything for themselves. In fact, they feel as though they are never thinking of themselves and they typically act as though they have no preferences of any kind. For that reason, this second type of obsessive compulsive often appears to be quite responsibility fragmented in their lives as their obligations take them in so many directions simultaneously that they often literally feel as though they're being pulled apart. They often feel as though each person they encounter takes a chunk of them and, in the end, they feel like they have nothing left for themselves. In fact, where the classic type of obsessive avoids responsibility fragmentation but often feels alone, only to experience responsibility fragmentation and guilt when they fail to do everything "right," the second type avoids blame for hurt but often feels fragmented, only to experience extreme feelings of isolation and guilt when they fail to be as "good" as they possibly could be.

This "responsibility fragmented" type of obsessive compulsive holds extreme standards for themselves and for others mostly in the areas of *doing* the "right" thing and being moral, and they are not so concerned with how more mechanical types of things are accomplished. While being obsessive compulsive involves behaviors that prevent closeness with others and, with respect to child rearing in particular, results in the perception that there is no unconditional love, the "responsibility fragmented" obsessive spends every effort at being loving and caring. Thus, they end up especially frustrated that others feel they are selfish. They simply cannot believe it, in fact, since they are putting so much effort into being as "good" as they possibly can be for others. In some cases the "responsibility fragmented" type of obsessive is also relatively unassertive because they always put others first. When these obsessives find themselves being called selfish, they are especially frustrated. Not only do they do everything they can for others, but others also treat them badly since they are so unlikely to defend themselves or strongly state their own wishes. Nevertheless, because others can feel their disappointment when they have not met this obsessive's standards for "goodness" or have not done things in the "right" way as this obsessive sees things, even this most unassertive and indirect type of "responsibility fragmented" obsessive personality is typically thought of by others as being very controlling.

Even if a person's true aim is to care for others, if others must do everything the "right" way according to that person's standards, others will never feel like they are truly cared for. Others only experience the feeling that they're not doing things well enough or the "right" way. Where doing things "right" is concerned, others will mostly perceive themselves as valued by the classic type of obsessive compulsive to the extent that they do things "right." This remains true with the "responsibility fragmented" type of obsessive compulsive. Where being a "good person" is concerned, others will mostly perceive themselves as valued by the "fragmented" obsessive to the extent that they maintain moral standards similar to those of the obsessive. Although this type of obsessive compulsive feels they are anything but controlling, others feel controlled by them, just as they do by the more rigid, classic type of obsessive compulsive, but they feel more controlled by the standards held by the "responsibility fragmented" obsessive compulsive as opposed to by being told exactly what to do.

All of the personality characteristics and interpersonal dynamics discussed above develop around the fact that the obsessive compulsive never experiences unconditional love and that they do experience the lack of unconditional love as the potential loss of love. There is also a particular thought pattern the obsessive compulsive develops in order to further prevent the experience of possible loss. For the obsessive compulsive, part of the need to prove themselves to themselves is a defense against possible loss of others in that they believe that by making themselves perfect, those they love will love them, and that those they love will be protected since the obsessive compulsive takes care of everything as perfectly as possible. In a way, the obsessive compulsive makes a very specific deal with life. The deal is this: If I do everything "right," and always try my best, then nothing will go wrong. The problem with that deal should be clear. While most problems can be prevented, a few, like natural disasters, all kinds of accidents, and many illnesses, cannot. The obsessive compulsive's gambit really does not become a problem until some kind of disaster occurs.

The most prevalent kind of disaster that wreaks havoc to the defense of perfectionism is when a loved one leaves or rejects the obsessive compulsive. Because they are often critical, condescending and controlling, although the obsessive compulsive typically really does mean the best, their loved one's often experience a need to escape or to otherwise reject the obsessive compulsive. Children grow up and leave, and sometimes don't want to remain in contact. That is especially true when they feel they have not met the obsessive compulsive's standards. They experience their obsessive compulsive parent to be smothering and difficult. If, on the other hand, they are developing their own obsessive-compulsive characteristics, then they often experience their parent's criticism as undermining, unsupportive and competitive, even as they are trying their best to be perfect as well. Their parent's behavior becomes a reminder that love has been conditional. Spouses also find a need to leave for similar reasons. They feel unable to gain the love of the obsessive compulsive, they feel put down and never good enough, and eventually they feel they can't take it anymore.

Any other kind of disaster also causes extreme emotional hardship for the obsessive compulsive. Auto accidents, loss of loved ones to medical problems, loss of jobs, natural disasters, etc., all make no sense to a person who has thought that everything would go well if they just did everything as "right" as possible. Because the defense of perfectionism is supposed to protect the obsessive compulsive from all that may harm them or their loved ones, the obsessive compulsive can quickly begin to think the sky is falling. They become racked with anxiety to the point of panic and depressed to the point of feeling life has lost all meaning. They believe they have been proven worthy of love, and they have convinced themselves that they are immune to disaster because they so diligently attempt to anticipate every possible danger. So how is it possible that disaster still comes? They feel that they had a deal. When the disaster comes, they immediately perceive themselves to be unworthy of love. And they perceive themselves to be defenseless in the face of a chaotic dangerous world. The deal has been broken and they feel cheated and angry. They have always thought the world was being fair to them because they had tried so hard. Now it becomes clear, in the most intolerable way, that the world is truly unfair in some regards. Bad things really do happen to good people. There is no ultimate control. There is no absolute safety. Just as in the case of losing those they love due to their critical and/or exacting nature, the obsessive compulsive experiences a great loss with any kind of disaster since they lose the ability to believe they are immune to such problems.

As is the case with many personality problems, strangely, disaster brings with it the opportunity for change. It is unfortunately all too common for the disaster to simply embitter the obsessive compulsive while they continue to use the defense of perfectionism, and possibly even become more critical and condescending toward others, and sometimes even more fragmented with responsibility. However, when the obsessive compulsive begins to recover from the disaster that has befallen them, they can also start to love themselves more unconditionally. They become able to see that there is no "perfect" and that, even though life can be managed relatively well with great effort, it is not possible for them, or anyone else, to prevent every problem. In that way the obsessive compulsive becomes more grateful for every moment and more accepting of others. Others start to feel more comfortable with them then, and where they once lost others over competition for who is right, or because others wanted to feel accepted in spite of their differences, now others more freely appreciate the recovering obsessive compulsive. Because they are more appreciative of others differences and the vagaries of a chaotic world, the recovering obsessive compulsive becomes more immune to disaster than they had ever been before. Although they continue to be careful, they recover from the idea that they have a deal in which nothing should go wrong. They benefit then from the care they take, without being so vulnerable to being blindsided by that which is out of their grasp or control.

More than any other disorder, the obsessive compulsive makes tremendous strides in their recovery. Although their obsessive compulsive issues have led to the very loss they had always hoped to prevent, those very same tendencies have often led to great accomplishments. The obsessive-compulsive personality is really only one step away from true mental health. With the recovery that comes from accepting disaster, whether that disaster be interpersonal or natural, comes a new understanding of the world around them, including their relationships. With this final step of beginning to treat themselves and others with unconditional positive regard, the recovering obsessive compulsive begins to also receive unconditional positive regard from others. Part of recovery involves becoming more assertive. The more classic type of obsessive compulsive continues to care about what he wants, but becomes much less aggressive in pursuing it since he now cares what others want as well. The "responsibility fragmented" type now realizes that she cares about what she herself wants, but unlike before she now starts to be direct in asserting those desires while continuing to be sensitive to the needs of others as she has always been.

The obsessive compulsive also benefits tremendously from the fact that they have always worked so hard to do things well. Because they have already built up so many accomplishments with their obsessive compulsive tendencies, the obsessive compulsive in recovery now stands ready to take pleasure in all they have built. With their new found ability to accept themselves and others with compassion and without critique, in recovery the erstwhile obsessive compulsive initiates a new, positive, growth in the fertile soil they have already so "perfectly" tilled and sowed. In their recovery, the obsessive compulsive takes in a bountiful harvest for which they are truly grateful. They finally develop the ability to offer unconditional love to those they hold most dear. But most importantly, in their recovery the obsessive compulsive discovers unconditional love for their self right there where it really should have been all along—within their very own heart.

(*There are two similar and overlapping psychological problems known as obsessive-compulsive personality and obsessive compulsive disorder. Because they tend to overlap quite a bit, they are often confused with one another. In this article, I discussed aspects of obsessive compulsive disorder to the extent that they are involved in the obsessive-compulsive personality. That is, ritualistic cleaning or hand washing, counting, obsessing on particular thoughts, locking and re-locking doors, checking all sorts of things, buttoning and re-buttoning, etc., are all symptoms of obsessive compulsive disorder, but not necessarily related to obsessive-compulsive personality. Differentiating thee two issues is important because much of obsessive compulsive disorder is genetic, while obsessive-compulsive personality may be related to genetic issues, but is more specifically related to a particular orientation to life. Obsessive-compulsive personality, and especially mere traits of obsessive-compulsive personality, can have very little relation to genetics at all.)

CHAPTER 57

❦

The Other Personalities

"People seem not to see that their opinion of the world is also a confession of their character."

—Ralph Waldo Emerson

Every aspect of our communication with others involves personality. That's why categorizing personalities is so important. By specifying the inner workings and motivations involved in each major type of personality, we can understand those with whom we come into contact, and thus communicate with them in more constructive ways. In several other articles I have delineated those personality types that are most commonly seen in my psychotherapy office. In everyday life, however, the other major personality types are equally common. Certain individuals are, for better or worse, less likely to show up in the psychotherapists office. Below you will find each of the other major personality styles, described in their most elemental forms. For each, the central conflict driving the personality style will be outlined. For each, the path toward growth through that conflict, or the necessary path for others in dealing with that personality style, will be illuminated.

Dependent Personality

Individuals with dependent personality are typically observed staying in relationships where they are treated in relatively abusive ways. They often appear to have a complete inability to stand up for themselves, even when they know they really should. On the other hand, they often don't feel they have a right to anything, and thus they are always giving in to the wants and needs of others. It is very typical for individuals with dependent personality to come from homes where a parent was significantly abusive and/or undermining of their independence. They have experienced interpersonal aggressiveness, even if they have never been physically abused (although they often have been). That is, by powerful influence of someone with whom the dependent was unable to confront, the dependent has been convinced that they are worthless. The dependent is often not especially fearful of others, but is, rather, fearful of being independent. At the same time, the dependent disdains any sign of anger within themselves. They have felt how anger and intimidation work, and they never want to hurt anyone like they themselves have been hurt. They maintain a clinging, needy, and fearful orientation to life as a defense against the possibility that their own angry and controlling tendencies, about which they successfully remain unconscious, could surface. In effect, they behave in opposite fashion to the feelings within themselves that they fear most. Dependent personalities only recover from their own self-destructive paths when they allow themselves enough anger and self-righteousness to act assertively. Assertiveness is clearly not aggressive, but to the dependent personality even assertiveness seems to be aggressive. To overcome their dependence on aggressive, controlling others, the dependent personality must see that some anger within them is acceptable and normal, and they must stand up for their rights.

Antisocial Personality

Antisocial personality is exactly the opposite of dependent personality. However, quite often these two disparately oriented individuals can come from very similar backgrounds. When the antisocial experiences intimidation and abuse, however, instead of becoming weak and needy like the dependent, they long for a time when they will be the masters of intimidation, aggression and manipulation. Typically the antisocial will not take on the dominant parent in the family until their size permits them to do so, but in the meantime they will find ways to intimidate and dominate others outside the family. They become the bully at school and take on authority figures who will not physically punish them. The antisocial develops a sense that accomplishment is something to be taken rather than earned. They do not care enough about others to develop any true feeling of responsibility for others. They have no sense of what is right or wrong. They want what they want, and they will do whatever they can to get what they want immediately. Antisocial personality generally cannot be rehabilitated because recovery requires caring. That is, if someone is going to have an influence on another person, that person must care enough to start taking responsibility for their reciprocal influence on others. There is, however, hope for antisocials. Although the antisocial will not develop healthy relationships, they can become productive members of society. Once the antisocial realizes that the only way to truly succeed in life, without going to jail or getting killed, is to play by society's rules enough to get along with others and maintain gainful employment, the antisocial can do so. In fact, many antisocials become extremely financially successful as they move ahead in life knowing the rules better than anyone else, and then using the rules to their advantage.

Avoidant Personality

Individuals with avoidant personality feel extremely uncomfortable around other people. Like the dependent personality, the avoidant has typically come from a home in which there was some level of interpersonal aggressiveness. However, the avoidant is much less likely to have actually been physically abused. The avoidant has developed within relationships at home that make them feel judged to the extreme. In their homes they have been both controlled and undermined. They have often been overprotected to an extreme level as well. They start to see themselves as interpersonally inadequate even as they experience some of their personal characteristics as worthwhile. Where the dependent believes they have no rights and no worth and thus must stay with someone who is powerful and strong even though angry and hurtful, the avoidant holds no hope that others will ever notice their worth and believes that others will repeatedly hurt them with judgment, ridicule, and lack of recognition. Like the dependent, recovery for the avoidant can develop from assertiveness. In one way assertiveness is easier for the avoidant since they already believe themselves to be worthwhile. However, in the avoidant, recovery requires them to discount the importance of others. Avoidants give others too much power by thinking that the opinions of others matter much more than they actually do. Interestingly, the avoidant's self-critical nature, which they have developed for the purpose of controlling the level to which criticism by others can hurt them, is actually far harsher than the criticism anyone else feels. If the avoidant can learn to care less about judgments of others, and more about their own judgments, which must become far less harsh, they can become more interpersonally comfortable, and thus develop full and healthy relationships.

Schizoid Personality

Schizoids have extremely little interpersonal involvement. Unlike the avoidant, however, who is a person who cares a great deal about others, the schizoid has little interpersonal involvement because they simply don't care. The schizoid typically comes from a home in which they were controlled by a parent to such an extreme level that their needs never counted for anything. They had to do like the parent, and think like the parent. In essence, they were merely the instrument of the parent. Experiencing those feelings in childhood leads to a complete lack of feeling since our feelings involve communicating our needs to others. If one's needs seem to have no importance whatsoever, they are pushed deep within where others can have no effect. Schizoids are sometimes seen in relationships because they are attractive to others who need to be with someone who has no needs. Although the schizoid has no need for relationship, they do desire sexual release, and thus they do seek out interpersonal contact. It is very difficult for someone with schizoid personality to change. They are literally locked into having no emotion, and that remains to be a useful orientation to life since anyone with whom they come into contact is viewed as another person to whom they must submit.

In couples counseling schizoids do sometimes change because the level at which they are completely controlled by their spouse becomes so intolerable that even the schizoid starts to notice how bad they feel. At times, the schizoid can start to crack in such circumstances. Although the most likely scenario is an explosive outburst followed by a return to emotionless robotic compliance with expectations, occasionally the breakdown leads to a flood of feelings which can develop into a rebuilding of emotional life one step at a time. Such rebuilding requires, unfortunately, extreme changes in the spouse as well, who must relinquish significant control simultaneously to the schizoid learning to pay attention to their feelings.

Paranoid Personality

We all become paranoid at times. A person with paranoid personality, however, is suspicious of everything. Most frequently a person with paranoid personality grew up feeling ridiculed and put down, and also often abused, within a family where everything had to be kept secret. The more aggressive or powerful such ridicule was, and the closer to the paranoid the perpetrators of that ridicule, the more likely it is that the paranoid's current perspective will include feelings of persecution as opposed to mere ridicule. Feeling persecuted for the paranoid can lead to violently aggressive emotions. Because there is such a powerful need to hide that aggression for fear of what others might do in response, however, some paranoid personalities can become psychotic in their paranoia as their aggression turns to violent fantasy. As a child, the paranoid typically felt like everything they did was watched, analyzed and judged. It is common that the paranoid was unfavorably compared with others in the family as well. Frequently, they felt as though they might have traits that would make them successful, but even achievement could not prove them to be worthwhile human beings to those from whom they desired recognition. Meanwhile, it is often the case that others in the family were treated as though clearly worthwhile. Quite often the reason the paranoid was watched and analyzed so regularly was that his or her parents themselves were also paranoid. They suspected bad intentions from the paranoid in spite of some talents or possibly some usefulness. They would not trust him no matter what, and thus he felt untrustworthy as well as ridiculed. In turn he became the person who would not trust others so that he would no longer have to feel his own lack of trustworthiness. That is, instead of feeling untrustworthy, the paranoid chooses to see others as untrustworthy. Unfortunately, the paranoid's sensitivity to secrets, and his feeling that everyone is against him, results in others keeping secrets from him to keep him from getting upset. Thus, his fears become reality and prove him correct in his view that others cannot be trusted. In spite of the clear connection between his inability to trust and the fact that others behave in an untrustworthy manner, the paranoid never becomes aware of his own influence in making others keep secrets from him or talk behind his back. The paranoid rarely becomes close to anyone and thus it is quite difficult to disprove their view of an untrustworthy world. At times they do become close to others from whom they believe they might actually gain the approval they have always needed but have given up seeking. However, those individuals often remind them of family members and thus are likely to be somewhat conspiratorial in their own behavior. The conspiratorial nature of these few with whom they become close can lead to more proof that the world is untrustworthy. The paranoid, for obvious reasons, rarely shows up in a therapist's office. They do not want anyone to see their true feelings for fear that the other will take advantage, or worse, that the other will see that the paranoid is truly worthless. Nevertheless, if the paranoid does show up in therapy, perhaps as a child brought by a parent or by a spouse who has managed to be the one to whom the paranoid looks for possible acknowledgment, it is absolutely necessary to bolster an understanding of the paranoid as a legitimate, important, person, and to encourage openness. The paranoid must come to believe that he is worthy of love and affection, and that others will recognize that worth. Essentially, the cure for the paranoid is the discovery that openness does not necessarily lead to ridicule and that he is not elementally "bad." This cure can only take place if the primary relationships within his life transform from suspicious to trusting.

Personality disorders are extremely common. Although the personality disorders described above are not seen in therapy as much as narcissistic, borderline, passive aggressive, histrionic and obsessive-compulsive-personality disorders, they are likely equally common. Thus, many individuals seeking help for these problems, or seeking understanding of them due to how their own relationships are affected by others with these disorders, are perhaps in need of information about them that they are unlikely to find anywhere but in a book. Although these small vignettes of personality could prove insufficient, for anyone looking to find information about these disorders, it is hoped that these descriptive snippets offer a beginning in the search for better understanding.

Section 14

Addictions

All addictions, those involving substances, of course, but also those involving food, shopping, or any other compulsive behavior, involve an unmet emotional hunger or need, and a desire to have some kind of control over that need—without relying on others. People who are prone to addiction often use the addiction to either fill themselves up or to calm themselves down (which can be excitement or relaxation or euphoric feelings). A feeling of unmet need, or difficulty in calming down, typically involves incomplete development stemming from unmet needs in childhood, but is also genetic—that is, one can be born with greater intensity, more anger, more emotional hunger, and/or more anxiety. The power of unmet needs combines with the immediacy of, or control over, gratification, a factor that is always involved in addictions, to make addictions irresistibly compelling. Because gratification is relatively instant, the addict internalizes the illusion that they can control gratification of unmet needs without involved human relationships. That is, the addict has the power to secure and use the addictive substance or activity, and solve their unmet human needs, without other people. It is this illusion that makes addiction so difficult to overcome. The unmet needs that are meant to be solved within relationships are solved by the addict without involving the unpredictable nature of other people. If other people could be trusted to be perfectly responsive and always positive, then addictions would hold no sway whatsoever. However, no person can possibly be as predictable as the object of addiction in the addict's own hands. The addict's illusion, unfortunately, always gives way to the reality that people and real relationships are necessary, as the object of addiction inevitably consumes the addict's life.

CHAPTER 58

Cଔ

Addictions: A Relationship to Remember

"All sins tend to be addictive, and the terminal point of addiction is damnation."

—W.H. Auden

It's the addict's most important relationship—their relationship with the bottle, the pipe, the pills, or the needle, and often their relationship with food or sexual activity. Remember what it feels like to fall in love? There's that crazy chemical attraction. You can't think of anything else but seeing your lover. You feel like you'd do anything for your love. You feel like you can't sleep or eat without thinking of them. You let everything else go. Your work suffers. Studying hardly matters. You spend more time out. Your friends and family have far less influence than usual. Even those who have always been there for you, or those who you know count on you for everything, can sometimes take a back seat to a great love. The addict's relationship with their drug, whether it's beer, cocaine, heroin, pharmaceuticals, food or sex, exactly mimics a crazy love affair.

Sometimes people develop this love for their drug slowly. At first, they don't quite trust the relationship. They know it feels good, but they know they'd better be careful. They've heard that drugs can be a devilish mistress. On the other hand, your drug could be just the thing that lets you relax enough to deal with your day. It just takes the edge off or gives you that little boost. But slowly you need it a little more and you start to trust. It's not a big deal just having a little more. You deserve it, just like you deserve to be with someone who makes you feel calm or strong or smart or fun or attractive. How could it harm you to have a bit more? Who cares what it costs? If others don't like it, they don't even have to know. Or the hell with them, you can be with anyone—that is, you *can do* anything—you want!

Soon, you trust your drug more than you trust anything else. After all, you know it well. You know what to expect from it, and you know how it makes you feel. You feel you have control over it. You use it when you want. When you need it again, you know where to get it. Unlike a human being, it's reactions seem perfectly predictable. There's no reason to miss your drug, or to feel like it might let you down. It's not like a lover who might turn to someone else or who might not answer the phone when you call. You always know where to find it—that is, as long as you have access to it. If it's hard to get, though, you still know there are things you can do to get it, even if those schemes could be uncomfortable or slimy or perhaps even illegal.

Some people experience love at first sight, or sip, or puff, or snort, or draw. It's as though the addict and the drug were made for each other—a match made in heaven (and ready to burn). The addict can look at their drug and say "*you* . . . complete *me!*" With this kind of addiction, you see the happy couple together everywhere, although you don't always know the drug is there. When they're together the addict is happy and confident and maybe even excited or, on the other hand, calm and at peace. That the addict is coupled is much more obvious when they're fighting with their drug. Then, the addict is petty, ugly, mean, and/or pathetic. But they're less likely to be seen when they're at odds with their drug because the addict withdraws and won't be seen by anyone but close family members (if even them).

The addict sees the relationship with the drug as just the way to escape the pressures of everyday life and society. With the drug the addict can be wild or just let it all go. "No one's going to control me," the addict says to the drug (now a buddy) . . . and the addict and the drug are perfect rebels together. They sneak off to be together when they're expected to be nearby. Yes, together they're bad, but in a way the addict thinks is "cool." When they're together, an addict and his drug can accomplish anything and can act any way they want. No one can stop them, and they'd better not try.

In the relationship between an addict and a drug, the sex is out of this world . . . if only it weren't just a bit like masturbation. The addict feels as though in control of the whole situation, and the orgasm comes off impeccably every time. The addict knows every nuance of his drug—just the right way to romance it, the perfect caress, all the right spots, all the right moves. The addict fondles his drug and cuddles and coos. It's so sweet it almost makes you sick. Sometimes the addict likes the romance and the anticipation of making love. Sometimes it's just a quickie—the perfect release. Either way, the sex is great. There's the love, the desire, the intermingling of souls. There's also make-up sex after a dire row. Even though you can count on your drug kicking you like it doesn't care if you're crap, almost as though it's delivering the most perfect affront that only your most intimate companion could know, you can count on achieving that mind-blowing rapprochement within the inevitable reconciliation. In fact, the make-up with one's drug is just that much better, much like make-up sex, because the addict has been kicked like crap. After the big fight, there's the struggle over what to do, and then a kiss to make up . . . and then wild make-up sex, the pattern repeating every day like clockwork, perhaps making it just that much more compelling than a real relationship.

With all that fighting, however, after a while there can be regret. Things start to feel a mess. Life seems to be falling apart. Just like in a chaotic love affair, the drug gets blamed for the behavior of the addict. "I'm not happy because of you," the addict says, blaming the drug because it takes up too much of the addict's time or because it entices the addict to be lazy or mean, or because it spends too much of the addict's money. Maybe the regret begins in the disdain felt from others or because the addict's family seems to be hurting. Regret might even include some minimal level of taking responsibility, and could even appear to include true self-reflection, but typically the addict is far too fragile to tolerate maintaining a responsible view. Responsibility is interpreted by the addict as blame, and quickly turns the addict to blaming everyone else.

Nevertheless, because of the regret, the addict tries to leave the drug. The drug doesn't like it, and protests. It screams in the addicts ears and claws at the addict's intestines. Like a scorned lover, the drug alternately allures the addict and then, if the addict tries to resist, gets pissed and slashes the addict's tires or tries to break the windows out of the addict's home. The drug might actually appear to give up at times, but the addict, not fully understanding the vulnerability within, is lonely and an easy target for a return to the torrid love of the drug.

If only the drug somehow gets to see the addict somewhere unexpectedly. The drug doesn't want to be left, and feeling abandoned, will do anything to get the addict back. It can be tricky, and though the addict in recovery tries like hell to take things one day at a time, the drug slyly seeps through every crack in the addict's recovery armor. Every difficulty during the day, every memory of what's "cool," everyone to whom the addict is attracted, happy times, sad times, conflict and resolution, everything . . . absolutely everything leads the addict to the drug. And for some inexplicable reason, all memory of misery from the drug is so easily forgotten. Where recovery requires responsibility that the addict interprets as taking the blame, and thus other people are hard to face, the drug soothes and tells the addict that all is well. The addict is supremely vulnerable and desperately needs the perceived love of the drug. Most of the time, thus, the breakup between the addict and the drug is short, or at least not permanent, no matter how much regret the relationship might have previously generated.

So now I speak to you. Yes, you! You the addict, or you, the person who is in a relationship with the addict, yes, I am speaking to you. The relationship with the drug is the only relationship that really matters to the addict. You, the addict, you know this is true. You are thinking so much more about your drug than you are about your loved ones. You just can't wait till you meld with your lover (the drug) again. Is there any person about whom you feel like that? You, the person involved with the addict, you do not have a relationship—at least it should be clear that you have no relationship while the drug is still cheating with your lover. The addict is not there for you. The addict is there for the drug. If the addict is with you, then you have something to do with the drug, or are tolerated as a necessary sideshow. You, the addict, fess up, you're not even really there with your lover. You're wherever you need to be where you know you'll get your drug. If your lover will let you use the drug, or maybe even help you use it or acquire it, of course it's okay with you to have them around. But you, the person who thinks you have a relationship with the addict, what do you think will happen when you challenge your love's relationship with the drug. The addict may try to convince you to stay. The addict might tell you how desperate they are that you not abandon them. They might even betray the drug for the moment in seemingly heartfelt repentances. But most likely, the addict will leave you before they leave the drug.

To you, the addict, you must realize you can have only one true love. You should not expect your human lover to understand your relationship with your drug any more than you could expect them to understand if you were courting their best friend. To you, the human lover, please don't understand your addict's dalliance with the drug. Your understanding merely makes you a chump who is aiding your addict's infidelity. To you both, if you do truly want to be together, there is no room for this drug or any drug in your relationship. Where there's any addiction involved in relationships between people, every day into the future will remain in vigilance to overcome the drug's incessant seduction. To you both, please, please, if you are in a relationship where there has been a relationship with a drug, you must understand, addiction is the relationship to remember.

CHAPTER 59

☙

Codependency

"A simple and independent mind does not toil at the bidding of any prince."

—Henry David Thoreau

Codependency is the human complement to addiction. Where there is an addict, there tends to be at least one codependent to the addict. Codependents are sometimes thought to be weak by those who really don't understand the issue. How could someone not force the addict to quit? How could they put up with the addict's chaotic style of living? How could someone let someone else treat them that way? Most people who haven't dealt much with addictions do not understand how someone could love an addict. They also don't see how the codependent's behavior is an expression of the codependent's own needs, and how their relationship with the addict is instrumental in how they define themselves.

In essence, the codependent, although they might not realize it, understands their life's purpose in relation to the addict. Every codependent needs someone to need them. They sometimes want to be useful. Sometimes they want to be the catalyst for change. Sometimes they need someone to treat them like crap. Sometimes they need someone to look to them for strength. There are different kinds of addicts, but whichever addict the codependent chooses, that person will fulfill the needs of the codependent beautifully. Instrumental to the needs of the codependent, however, and unfortunately, is that the addict remain an addict. Even where the addict gets into recovery from the addiction, if the codependent does not get into their own recovery, continued relationship with the codependent will push the addict into addict behavior, if not a wholesale return to use of their drug.

Now this issue, the needs of the codependent, couldn't be any more complicated. There are codependents who actually take part in the creation of the addict's personality. These are usually the parents, but can be long time companions or spouses. And there are codependents who merely help to maintain the negative behaviors of the addict. Either way, by definition, if the codependent continues to be codependent, they are not helping the addict no matter how many helpful things they might do, and no matter how much they believe they are doing the right thing.

Some cases of codependency are easy to identify. The group is typically defined by the codependent who allows the addict to use their drug, makes excuses for the addict, and/or keeps understanding the addict and giving the addict breaks. There are, however, some people who are codependent in much more subtle ways. In all cases of addiction and codependency, the use of substances and/or the general behavior of the addict need to be confronted. Any communication with the addict that is not confrontational, even if in only very small ways, has relatively little use in disrupting the addictive process (except perhaps in forging trust with the addict so that confrontation will be more successful later). But I have seen numerous situations in which the codependent is apparently doing lots of confronting and criticizing, and yet they do not see that their behaviors are, nevertheless, codependent.

Whether a person is confronting or aiding the addict, it is the level at which they need the addict to continue behaving in their basic addict role, with or without their drug, that makes that person more or less codependent. The codependent can need the addict to remain "sick" where the codependent is "healthy," "mean" where the codependent is "nice," "weak" vs. "strong," "irresponsible" vs. "trustworthy," "smart" vs. "foolish" . . . etc. On the other hand, the codependent may well need the addict to be "tough" where they are "vulnerable," "confident" where they are "diffident," "witty" where they feel "dull," or "exciting" where they feel "boring." There are an endless number of combinations of these traits that can constitute the bond between the codependent and the addict. This relationship is often completely unconscious and the codependent truly believes they want the addict to get better. Nevertheless, if the addict getting better means the codependent will no longer be able to define themselves in distinct contrast to the addict's behaviors, the relationship between the addict and codependent can get quite dicey.

When the codependent expects the addict to stop using, but to continue to be the same person they have always known, it can prove practically impossible. Without the substance, the addict often cannot engender the trait that is needed by the codependent. Even worse, often the very traits the codependent has said are unforgivable, and must be changed, are the traits the codependent needs to see in order to continue defining themselves in the contrasting, positive way to which they have become accustomed. Without the addict being a "loser," they cannot feel like a "winner." If the addict starts to give them respect, they will have to explain why they so frequently criticize. When the addicted spouse is expected to loosen things up at a party, but now without their drug remains restrained, remote and shy, the other spouse will now feel embarrassed that the addict isn't active enough. In these situations, the codependent's behavior will induce pressure on the addict to use. The "winner" will compete with the addict until they win so the addict will feel like a using "loser." The addict being criticized will get depressed, give up, and turn to their drug to avoid the codependent's wrath, and for solace. The embarrassed spouse may well hand the addict a drink to douse their own embarrassment, still expecting the addict to have just one. The more diffident codependent may feel completely lost without the clearly dominant addict, who has always bolstered their confidence with the use of a substance. The codependent rarely sees the significance of their own needs or just how badly they need things to stay as they are. Nevertheless, when the addict stops using, to whatever extent the codependent really needs to see themselves in a particular way, they will be impelled to act in accordance with the old patterns that will likely once again bring about addict behavior in the addict.

So how, you might ask, does a person become a codependent? Again, there are more and less obvious paths to codependent behavior.

The most obvious paths are those in which the codependent has grown up in the home of an addicted parent (really these patterns develop quite similarly around major mood disorders, but it's amazing how often substances are related to such mood disorders, and it's amazing how often the drug involved takes on a separate and defining meaning from moods). In the home of addiction everyone develops patterns in relation to the addicted person. The literature on this topic is immense, so the details will not be described here, but the primary patterns involve helping the addict and avoiding the addict's or the codependent's wrath as well as figuring out where one is positioned with respect to dominance within the family hierarchy (please see article "The Power and Control Addiction," which can apply to either the addict or the codependent depending on the particular family).

While everyone must attempt to help the addict or avoid the addict's wrath in the family where a parent is addicted, they will choose very different paths with respect to dominance. Some members of the family will identify with what they perceive to be strength in the addict, and others will choose to identify with what they perceive to be strength in the codependent spouse. Sometimes the spouse of the addict is the dominant personality, in which case their wrath must be avoided, and other family members feel sorry for, and protect, the addicted spouse. Sometimes, although the addict has the dominant personality, the children perceive the helping of the spouse as the real strength in the family, since the codependent helper often keeps everything going in a positive direction. Often kids in a family will line up on the side of having behavior problems, possibly in imitation of the behaviorally dominant spouse, because the anger they experience within themselves, and the level to which they feel cheated by their situation, makes them especially sensitive to slights and makes them need to be dominant (in all situations that do not include the dominant parent). Often other kids within the family will line up on the side of the parent who is less dominant because they cannot tolerate how the dominant parent makes them feel, and they never want to engage in those behaviors themselves. These patterns can be intricately complex and confounding. For example, a child can be protected from the wrath of the dominant parent, but thus be allowed to get away with everything, which eventually results in a lack of responsible thinking, a need to be dominant due to vulnerable feelings that develop from accomplishing nothing, and very likely addictlike or codependent qualities.

Whether a child in the home of the addict identifies with dominance or not, they have an increased likelihood of becoming an addict or codependent merely from being exposed to the chaos that often develops around the use of substances. In many families, because there is so much potential for things getting out of control, or for getting one's feelings hurt when vulnerable, children of addicts cling desperately to the roles they have carved for themselves. Those roles have become so familiar to them that, truly, they only feel comfortable with other people who seem to have similar values. They think of those who feel familiar to them (as in, almost like family) as the "normal" people. These familiar people are those most likely to develop complementary roles to the roles chosen by the child from a home of addiction or compulsion. If a person has identified with the dominant parent, they quite likely will later be a substance abuser or a codependent who looks for someone over whom to be dominant, which thus helps soothe them and makes them feel less chaotic. On the other hand, if a person identifies with the nondominant parent, they could later be a substance abuser or codependent who looks for someone to dominate them and treat them like their pathetic.

There is also a subset of codependents that differ quite significantly from the rest in terms of their psychological health. When a person grows up in a positive and supportive family where very few problems have occurred, codependency can develop out of naiveté and guilt, even when there has been very little contact with addictive behaviors. Some people grow up without an accurate understanding of human behavior. Because they've been treated so well, they see the best in everyone and discount the negative behaviors of others as though those behaviors do not reflect the others' true spirit. If this were the only problem, these "positive home" codependents would soon grow out of their naïve ways as their experience with a recalcitrant addict would lead to ever-increasing upset, anger and disappointment. However, quite often these individuals also develop massive guilt over having been so lucky. They feel they have not truly deserved their good fortunes or that they must be especially kind and loving because they have been given so much. Thus, these individuals are particularly prone to a codependency in which they continuously put their own feelings off and see the best in the addict. They will maintain that view, and engage in codependent behaviors, even when there is little evidence of change, or even effort at change, in the addict, because they continue to feel guilty and do not want to confront the addict, or anyone else, for fear of being selfish.

These particular codependents do get something out of their relationship with the addict in that, because of their relationship with the addict, they are now able to feel like they are experiencing their fair share of problems. They are also the type of codependent who is most likely to recover from their codependency. This type of codependent sometimes manages to separate from the addict because they do truly possess adequate self-esteem, and they eventually feel that they have had enough. Unlike most codependents, this type does not generally enter a relationship with the addict based on their own past pathology, but rather simply due to being so naïve. When they do finally feel they have had enough, this type of codependent stops feeling sorry for the addict, and the addict must either change or truly face losing them completely.

Finally, it is important to say that, of course, no one starts out seeking a partner who abuses substances or aims to be a substance abuser. And no potential addict looks for someone to need them in a codependent way. However, it is so typical for a person to think substances are okay when they've been raised in a substance abusing family that behaviors that start out as "fun" can often end up involving substance dependence and the codependency that comes with it. People are quite responsive to the behaviors of others. If a person who was "fun" in spite of their partner's use of substances, starts to judge that person for their substance related behavior, abuse of the substance can actually get reinforced because the substance begins to become the only thing that makes the addict feel free of their partner's judgment. On the other hand, if a person acts wild and ugly when they use a substance, but only "fun" behavior had initially been associated with that person's use of substances, the partner may well feel they must judge the behavior because the substance now causes so many problems.

Codependency is such a complicated issue because it involves doing what comes naturally. The fact of the matter is, people are attracted to others who are familiar to them. Those are the people who treat them in a way that makes sense to them, given the fact that they have always been treated in similar ways within their own families. Codependents don't look for addicts. They look for familiar types with whom they can behave in familiar patterns. The same is true for addicts. They don't look for codependents. They look for those with whom they feel familiar, and those familiar people respond to their addict behavior in ways that are very similar to the actions seen and experienced in their families when they were growing up. The codependent wants to care for loved ones and feel good because they are caring. Unfortunately, their role can often slip into being controlling and perhaps superior, on one hand, or on the other hand, pathetic and abused. The essential and core issue in codependency is that regardless of the codependent's actions, whether they seem helpful or confrontational, somehow those actions lead to more and more bad behavior in the addict, without what should be the natural consequence for the addict—losing their relationship with the codependent. The cure to codependency is the addict's knowledge that the codependent will leave if the behavior continues. Leaving does not always cure the addict. However, if the codependent has healthy self-esteem, the addict's behavior will not be acceptable enough to continue in the relationship, no matter what the relationship was in the past. Even the parent of an addict will not put up with addict behavior unless the parent is a codependent. If a person leaves, they are no longer codependent in that relationship. Thus leaving does cure the codependent, at least temporarily, even if it does not cure the addict. True willingness and determination to leave if things remain the same, but not leaving, can also free a person from codependency. That is, when the addict really knows that abandonment will be faced if their behavior continues, they do sometimes change. Thus, fortunately, sometimes the mere willingness to really and truly leave does lead to recovery for the entire family. In the end, it is one's confidence to stand alone and be independent, if necessary, that can truly free them from codependency.

Author's Note

Psychology is everywhere. I can't help but see it in individuals, couples, families and in world affairs. It's in every motivation and thus in every interaction. Psychology is in each of us to our depths as it's been deposited there by genetics and cultivated by our circumstances. We breathe it in, forge it into, and bleed it into our loved ones and they, in turn, do so with and into theirs. But psychology is not always easy to understand and, in making personal changes, it's rarely easy to utilize the understanding one does achieve. In this book I present many articles on many disparate topics, but there is one very significant common attribute. In essence, these articles are me. Over time I have developed my own unique understanding of psychology, and these articles are an attempt to transfer my understanding to my readers. With these articles, I hope to bring clarity where once there had been confusion, and a possibility of change where once change had seemed too daunting.

My particular understanding of psychology developed over some struggling years of reaching for enlightenment. I had always been fascinated by the workings of the mind, and by the time my prolonged and personal epiphany occurred I had already embarked upon an in-depth study of the epistemologies known as "psychoanalysis," "object relations theory," "self-psychology," and many forms of "family systems theory." In the late 1990s, however, frustrated by what appeared to be a missing link in these psychological theories, I turned toward developing my own model of emotional bonds, attachments, and influence, specifically to account for the connection that fuses interpersonal (between people) to intrapsychic (within one person) psychological dynamics. Informed by "family systems theory," on one hand, and the various "psychoanalytic theories," on the other, I came to realize that this connection between intrapsychic and interpersonal was entirely seamless, as of course it has to be, even though the connection had been, up to that time, only very clumsily drawn by others. Whereas other theorists had discussed how the intrapsychic and interpersonal might fit, I felt a powerful need for a real unification theory. I then developed such a theory, which is "The Relational Systems Model." Although I will not get into the details here (the theory in its entirety is presented in layman's terms in an article in this book entitled, "From Id to Family System," and in much more complete detail in my first book, *The Therapist's Use of Self in Family Therapy,* Bochner, 2000), it is largely because of my unique theoretical understanding, and the desire to allow my clients more benefit of that understanding, that the articles in this book were written.

From my perspective, when working with clients it is often beneficial for them to read about the concepts that I am considering while listening. The articles within this volume represent an attempt to bolster therapy with insights that cannot always be transferred to the patient within the therapeutic process. Therapy is a process of relationship and insight, and often too much sharing by the therapist can get in the way of the client(s)' self-discovery. Nevertheless, referring clients to specific articles does not seem to interfere with the therapeutic process to the same degree as excessive talk from the therapist (largely because it does not interfere with face to face time between therapist and client). It seems to makes sense then, if it is possible to present a coherent and significant insight for any particular individual within just a few pages, it would be a shame to let such an opportunity pass. Thus, this book came together over time as sort of a "Dr. Bochner in a box" supplement to office work.

On the other hand, it has also occurred to me that there is great benefit for any potential student of the mind in having many of the concepts written about here presented in smaller chunks. Although, of course, the long term goal for training is always integration, chunking the concepts to be integrated makes them far more comprehensible. One of the reasons high-level psychotherapy requires so much training is that high-level concepts always seem to be presented in the most inscrutable ways. Thanks to the clarity of my own "Relational Systems Model," many of the articles here manage to boil down extreme complexity into the essentials. Thus many of the articles in this volume address very deep and complex constructs, yet do so in a way that the typical "common man" or "common woman" interested in psychology and/or psychotherapy can appreciate and assimilate.

It should also be noted that these articles are not specific to any one patient. Only those concepts that are so frequently encountered in therapy as to suggest they are frequently encountered by many people outside of therapy seemed to urge me into writing about them. You will notice that most of the articles are, in a sense, tools for gaining a better understanding of oneself or one's family. On the other hand, some of the articles are not merely tool-like, but are actual tools I use with my clients to help them in their lives. That is, most of the articles consist of information about relationships or concepts involved in relationships, but some actually teach a specific skill or help clients make a specific plan of action. Even those articles about relationships or concepts, however, will be found to offer some kind of solace or redemption to balance and soothe whatever kind of pain that might have drawn someone to read that particular article.

The Emotional Toolbox is, in the end, *a manual for mental health* compiled from the ins and outs of psychotherapy. It is a compendium of articles, each of which originated in my office for the express purpose of adding to what occurs in the office by offering information that is not always readily available. Therapy involves a relationship between therapist and client(s), insight, and often specific changes in thinking or action. The information contained within these articles will hopefully provide insight to help people identify or change the way they think and react. It is my hope that some readers who do not, or cannot, visit me will start to feel as though they have a relationship with me through my writing. For those clients I see in my office, I certainly think these articles add a dimension of aid. The themes these articles represent are extremely varied, from instruction about how to better oneself to discussion about how people develop mental illnesses, from themes as complex as the inner workings of interpersonal relationships to the more utilitarian themes such as parenting techniques. The articles come from my work with individuals, couples and whole families. It is my hope that my readers will find themselves using the book to understand themselves and their relationships better, but will also find the articles on parenting useful and the articles on diagnosis clarifying.

In a sense, it's my hope these articles will offer the keys to running one's life in a healthy manner. After these articles accumulated over time, I realized that their theme as a whole was the same theme as my office work in a very general sense. That is, I do whatever I possibly can to help people move themselves and their families in more positive and healthy directions. So in that way, the combination of articles in *The Emotional Toolbox* represents a relatively complete manual for life. In using this manual, it is my hope that all my readers, from the professional, to the student, to the person in need, will find themselves thinking and acting in healthier ways, both for themselves and for others, within their families and with their friends, and even within the greater world community.

Index

Note: Locators with the letter *f* refer to figures.

V

W